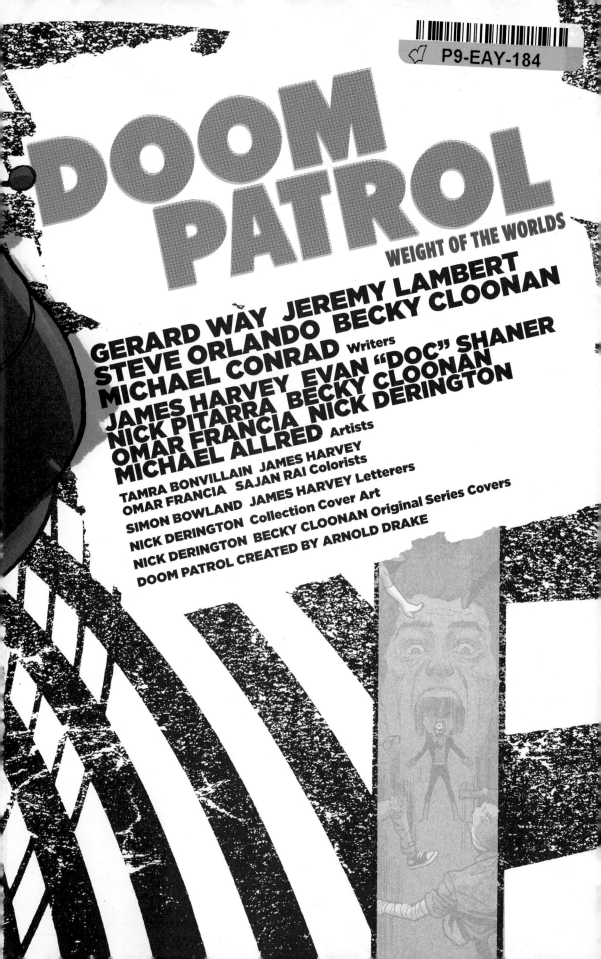

DOOM PATROL

WEIGHT OF THE WORLDS

GERARD WAY   JEREMY LAMBERT
STEVE ORLANDO   BECKY CLOONAN
MICHAEL CONRAD Writers

JAMES HARVEY   EVAN "DOC" SHANER
NICK PITARRA   BECKY CLOONAN
OMAR FRANCIA   NICK DERINGTON
MICHAEL ALLRED Artists

TAMRA BONVILLAIN   JAMES HARVEY
OMAR FRANCIA   SAJAN RAI Colorists

SIMON BOWLAND   JAMES HARVEY Letterers

NICK DERINGTON Collection Cover Art

NICK DERINGTON   BECKY CLOONAN Original Series Covers

DOOM PATROL CREATED BY ARNOLD DRAKE

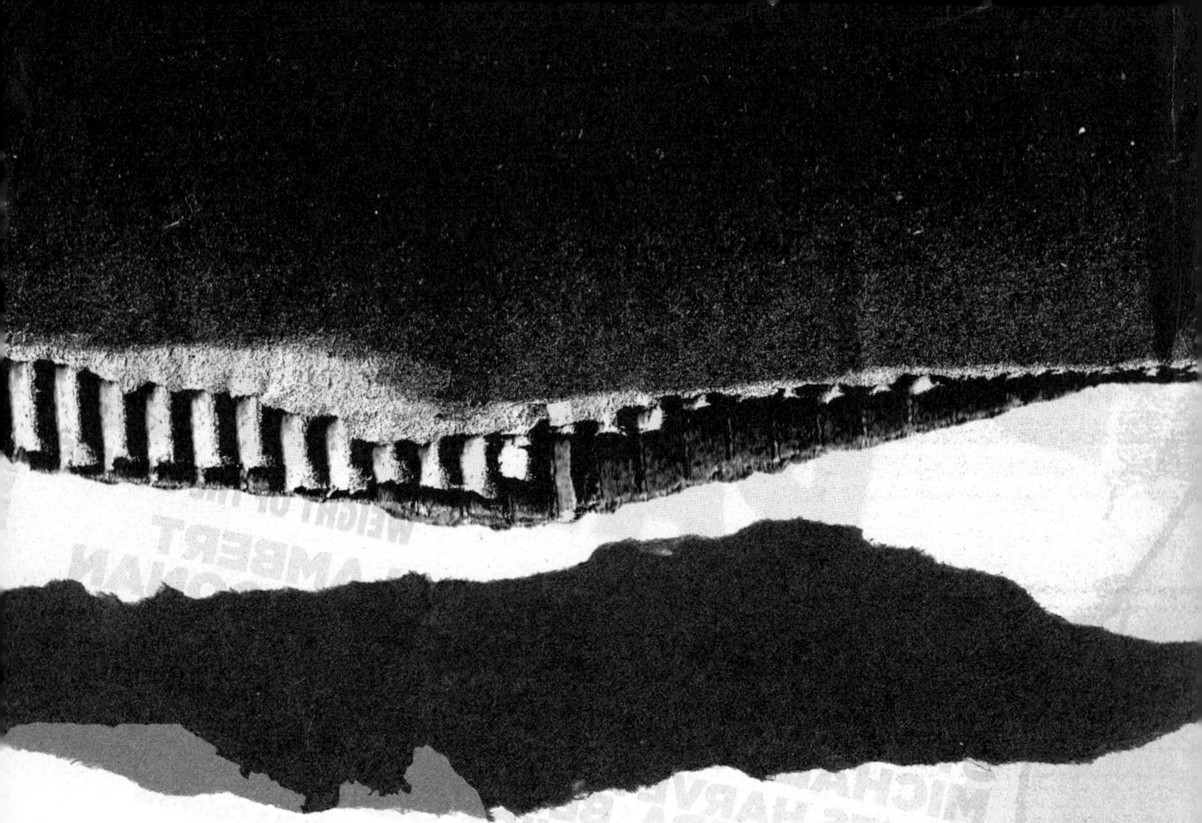

ANDY KHOURI MOLLY MAHAN Editors – Original Series
MAGGIE HOWELL Assistant Editor – Original Series
JEB WOODARD Group Editor – Collected Editions
SCOTT NYBAKKEN Editor – Collected Edition
STEVE COOK Design Director – Books
LOUIS PRANDI Publication Design
TOM VALENTE Publication Production

BOB HARRAS Senior VP – Editor-in-Chief, DC Comics
MARK DOYLE Executive Editor, DC Black Label

JIM LEE Publisher & Chief Creative Officer
BOBBIE CHASE VP – Global Publishing Initiatives & Digital Strategy
DON FALLETTI VP – Manufacturing Operations & Workflow Management
LAWRENCE GANEM VP – Talent Services
ALISON GILL Senior VP – Manufacturing & Operations
HANK KANALZ Senior VP – Publishing Strategy & Support Services
DAN MIRON VP – Publishing Operations
NICK J. NAPOLITANO VP – Manufacturing Administration & Design
NANCY SPEARS VP – Sales
JONAH WEILAND VP – Marketing & Creative Services
MICHELE R. WELLS VP & Executive Editor, Young Reader

DOOM PATROL: WEIGHT OF THE WORLDS

DC Comics
2900 West Alameda Avenue
Burbank, CA 91505
Printed by LSC Communications, Owensville, MO, USA. 8/14/20. First printing.
ISBN: 978-1-77950-078-6

Library of Congress Cataloging-in-Publication Data is available.

PEFC Certified
This product is from sustainably managed forests and controlled sources
PEFC
PEFC/29-31-337
www.pefc.org

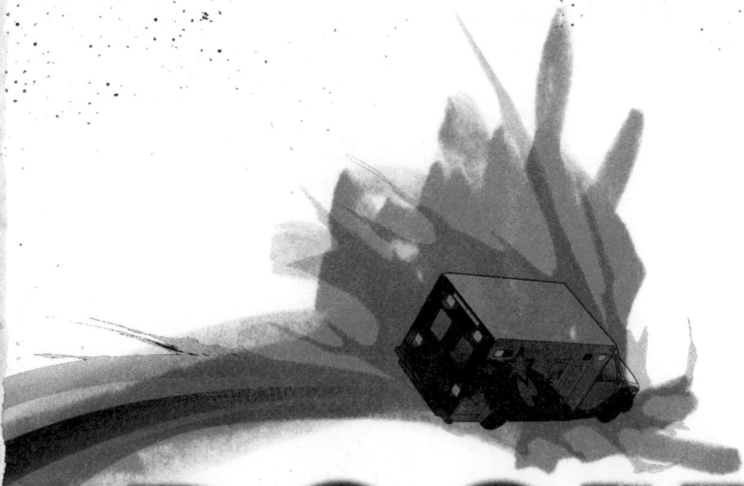

DOOM PATROL

WEIGHT OF THE WORLDS

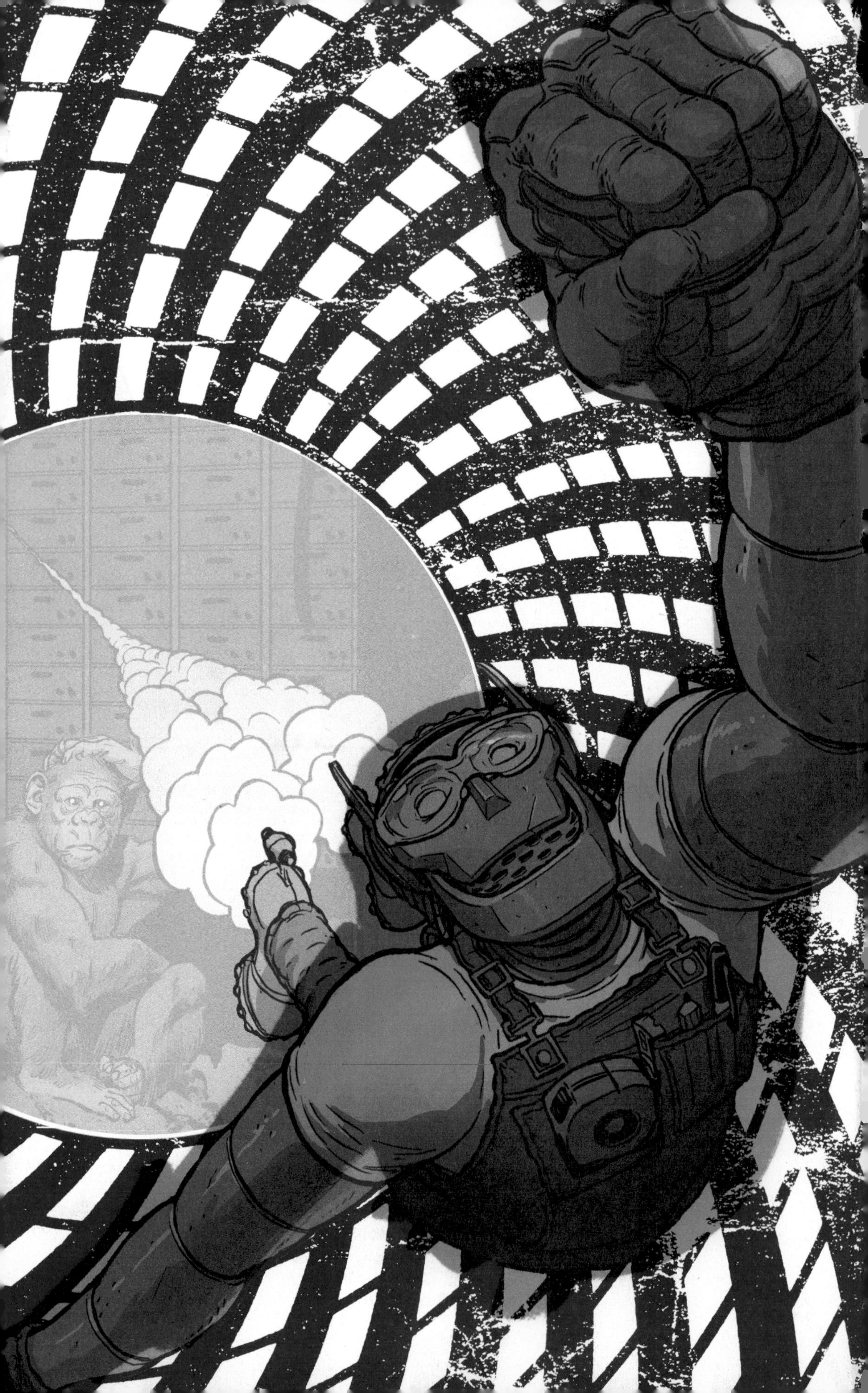

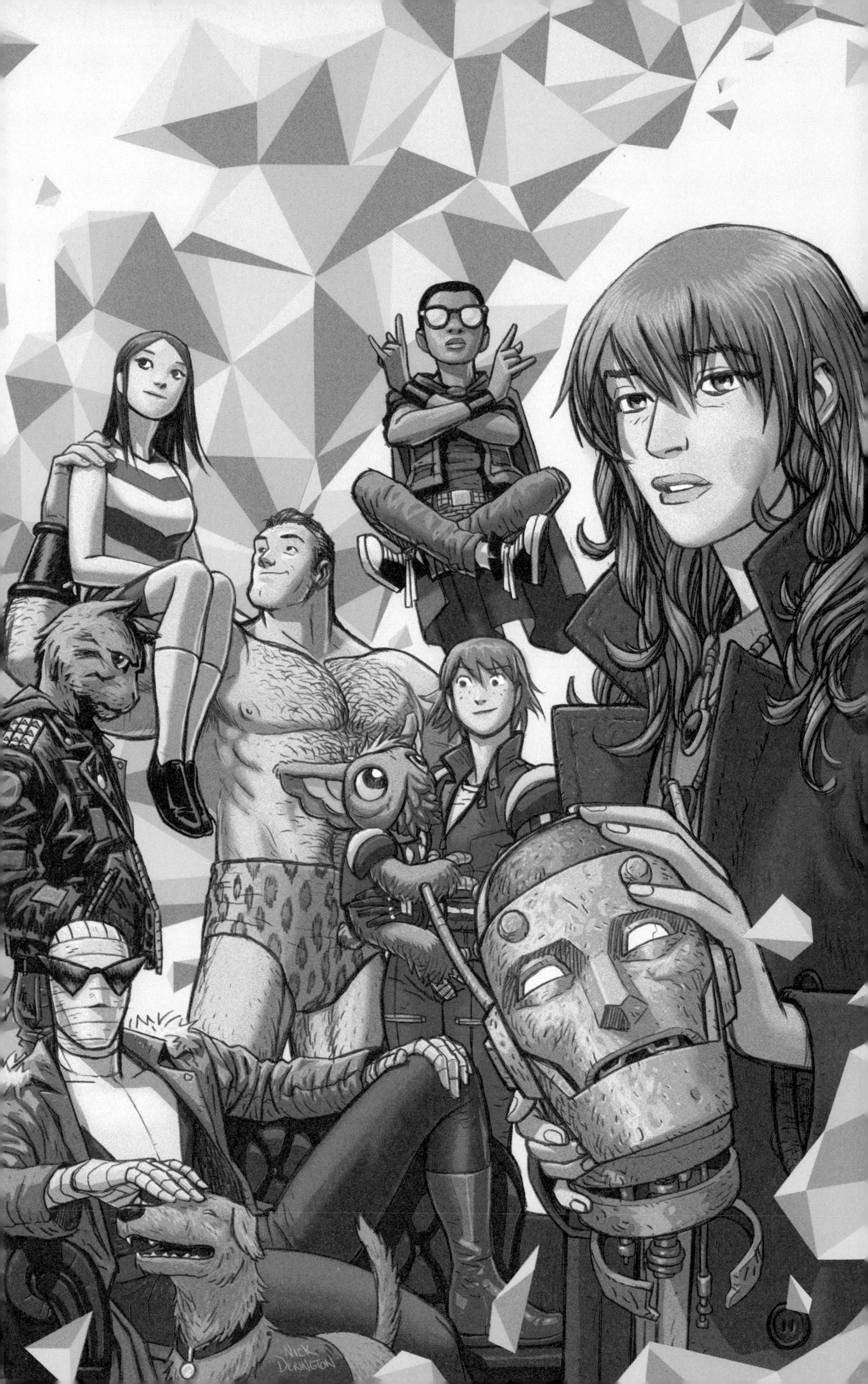
NICK DERINGTON

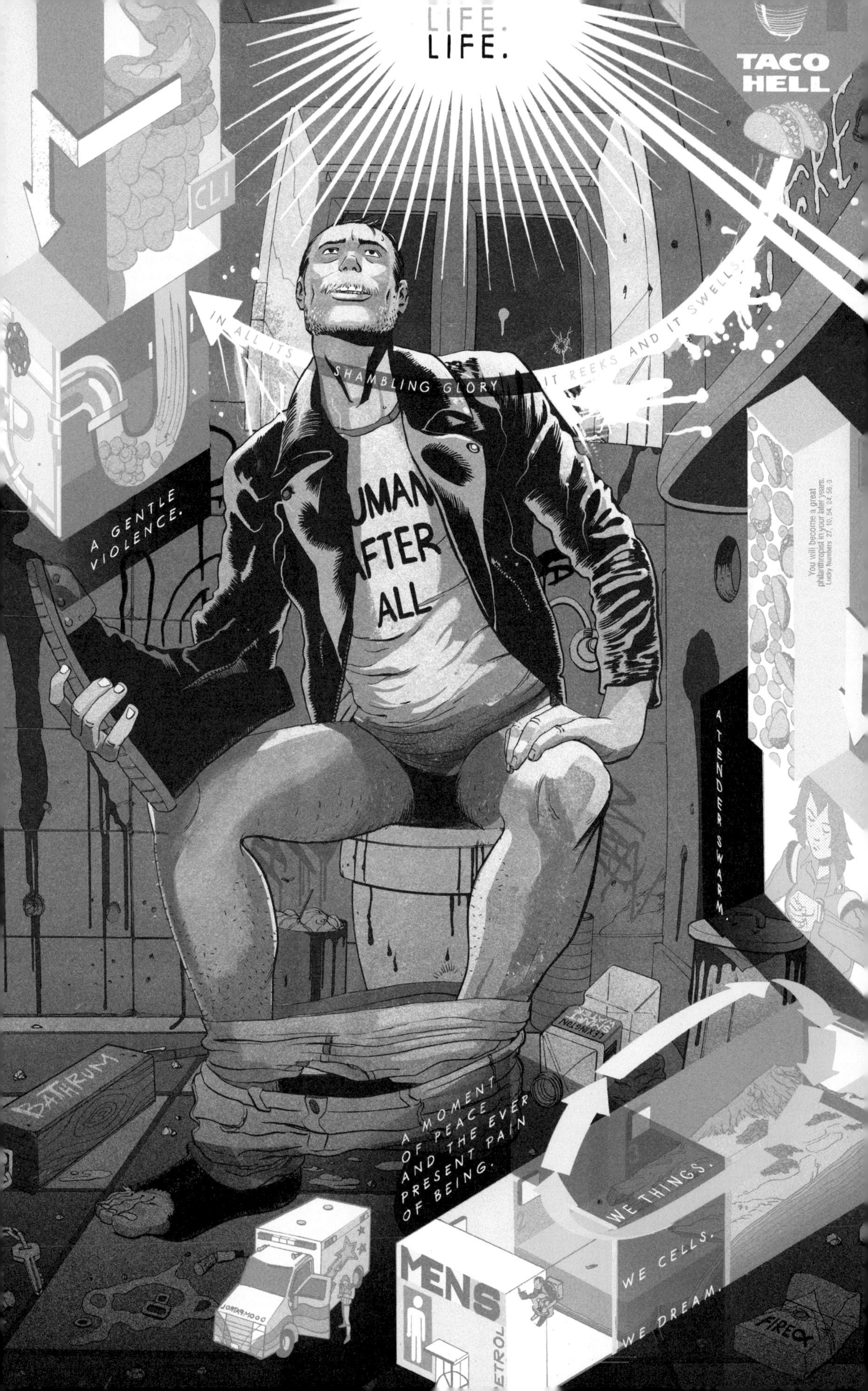
LIFE.
LIFE.
TACO HELL
CLI
IN ALL ITS SHAMBLING GLORY
IT REEKS AND IT SWELLS.
UMAN
FTER
ALL
You will become a great philanthropist in your later years.
Lucky Numbers 27, 10, 54, 24, 56, 3
A GENTLE VIOLENCE.
A TENDER SWARM.
BATHRUM
A MOMENT OF PEACE AND THE EVER PRESENT PAIN OF BEING.
WE THINGS.
WE CELLS.
WE DREAM.
MENS
PETROL

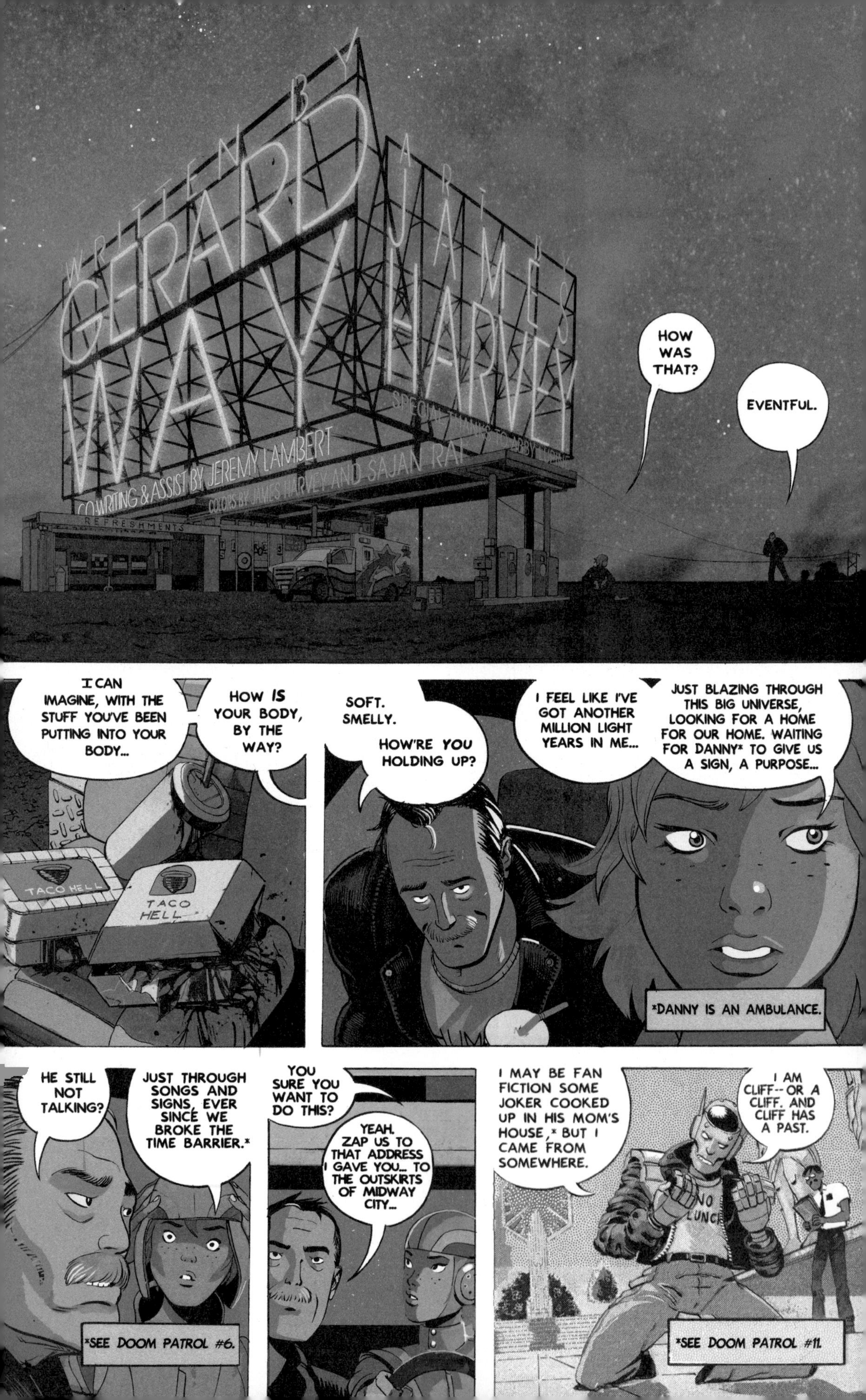

WRITTEN BY
GERARD WAY
ART BY
JAMES HARVEY
CO-WRITING & ASSIST BY JEREMY LAMBERT
COLORS BY JAMES HARVEY AND SAJAN RAI
REFRESHMENTS
HOW WAS THAT?
EVENTFUL.
I CAN IMAGINE, WITH THE STUFF YOU'VE BEEN PUTTING INTO YOUR BODY...
HOW IS YOUR BODY, BY THE WAY?
TACO HELL
TACO HELL
SOFT. SMELLY.
HOW'RE YOU HOLDING UP?
I FEEL LIKE I'VE GOT ANOTHER MILLION LIGHT YEARS IN ME...
JUST BLAZING THROUGH THIS BIG UNIVERSE, LOOKING FOR A HOME FOR OUR HOME. WAITING FOR DANNY* TO GIVE US A SIGN, A PURPOSE...
*DANNY IS AN AMBULANCE.
HE STILL NOT TALKING?
JUST THROUGH SONGS AND SIGNS, EVER SINCE WE BROKE THE TIME BARRIER.*
*SEE DOOM PATROL #6.
YOU SURE YOU WANT TO DO THIS?
YEAH. ZAP US TO THAT ADDRESS I GAVE YOU... TO THE OUTSKIRTS OF MIDWAY CITY...
I MAY BE FAN FICTION SOME JOKER COOKED UP IN HIS MOM'S HOUSE,* BUT I CAME FROM SOMEWHERE.
I AM CLIFF-- OR A CLIFF. AND CLIFF HAS A PAST.
*SEE DOOM PATROL #11.

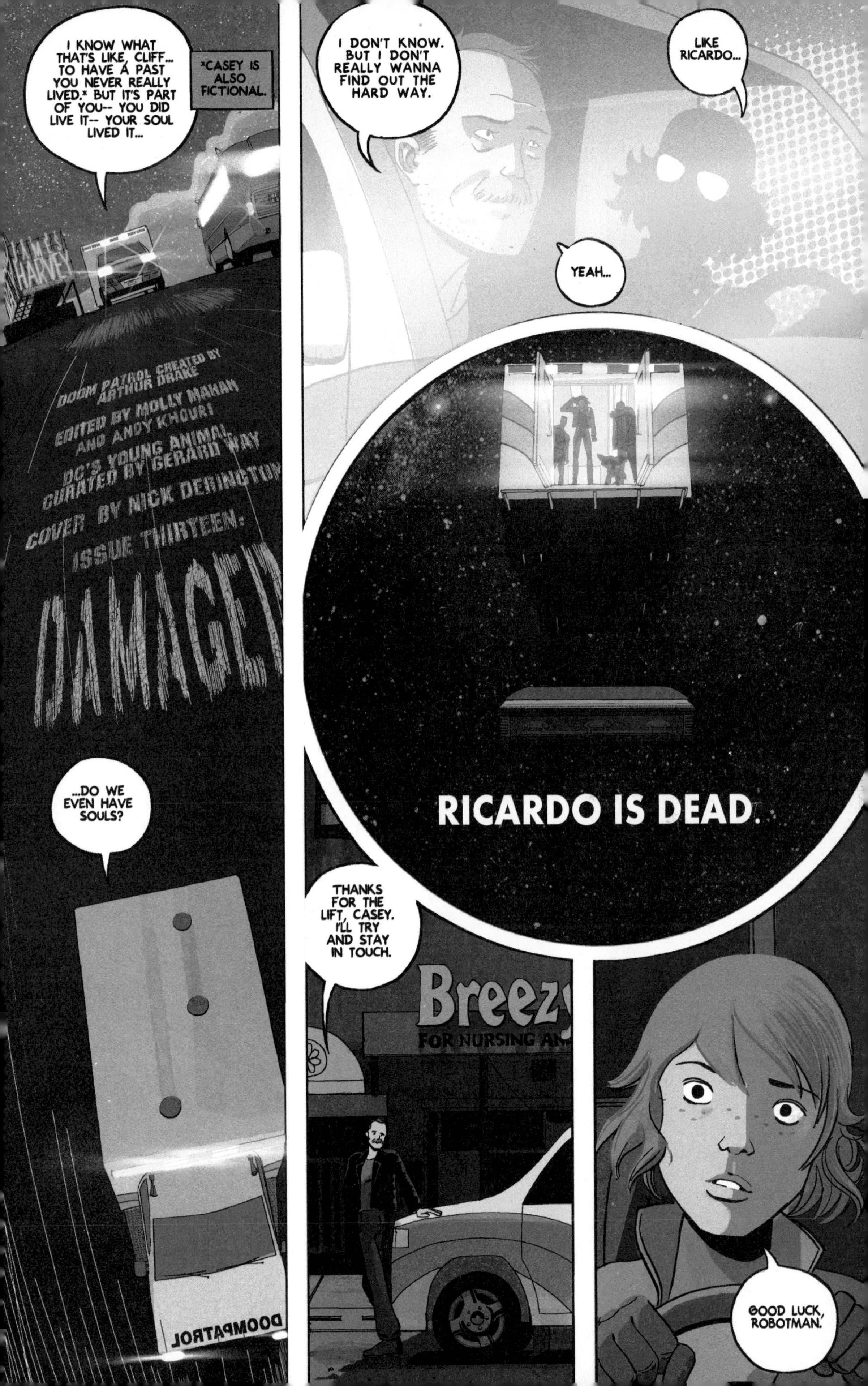
I KNOW WHAT THAT'S LIKE, CLIFF... TO HAVE A PAST YOU NEVER REALLY LIVED.* BUT IT'S PART OF YOU-- YOU DID LIVE IT-- YOUR SOUL LIVED IT...
*CASEY IS ALSO FICTIONAL.
DOOM PATROL CREATED BY ARTHUR DRAKE
EDITED BY MOLLY MAHAN AND ANDY KHOURI
DC'S YOUNG ANIMAL CURATED BY GERARD WAY
COVER BY NICK DERINGTON
ISSUE THIRTEEN:
DAMAGED
...DO WE EVEN HAVE SOULS?
DOOMPATROL
I DON'T KNOW. BUT I DON'T REALLY WANNA FIND OUT THE HARD WAY.
LIKE RICARDO...
YEAH...
RICARDO IS DEAD.
THANKS FOR THE LIFT, CASEY. I'LL TRY AND STAY IN TOUCH.
Breezy
FOR NURSING AN
GOOD LUCK, ROBOTMAN.

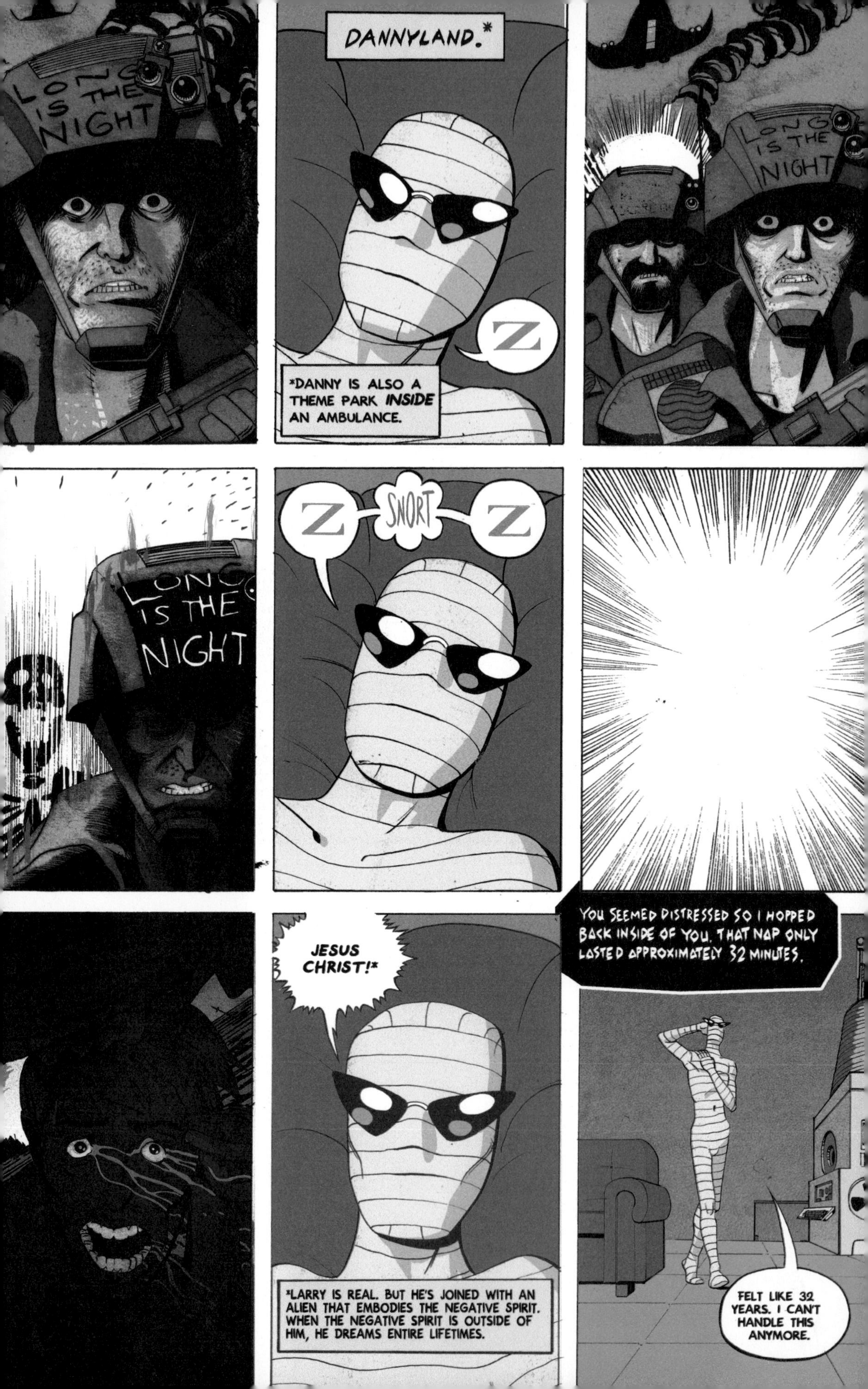
LONG IS THE NIGHT
DANNYLAND.*
Z
*DANNY IS ALSO A THEME PARK INSIDE AN AMBULANCE.
LONG IS THE NIGHT
LONG IS THE NIGHT
Z
SNORT
Z
JESUS CHRIST!*
*LARRY IS REAL. BUT HE'S JOINED WITH AN ALIEN THAT EMBODIES THE NEGATIVE SPIRIT. WHEN THE NEGATIVE SPIRIT IS OUTSIDE OF HIM, HE DREAMS ENTIRE LIFETIMES.
YOU SEEMED DISTRESSED SO I HOPPED BACK INSIDE OF YOU. THAT NAP ONLY LASTED APPROXIMATELY 32 MINUTES.
FELT LIKE 32 YEARS. I CAN'T HANDLE THIS ANYMORE.

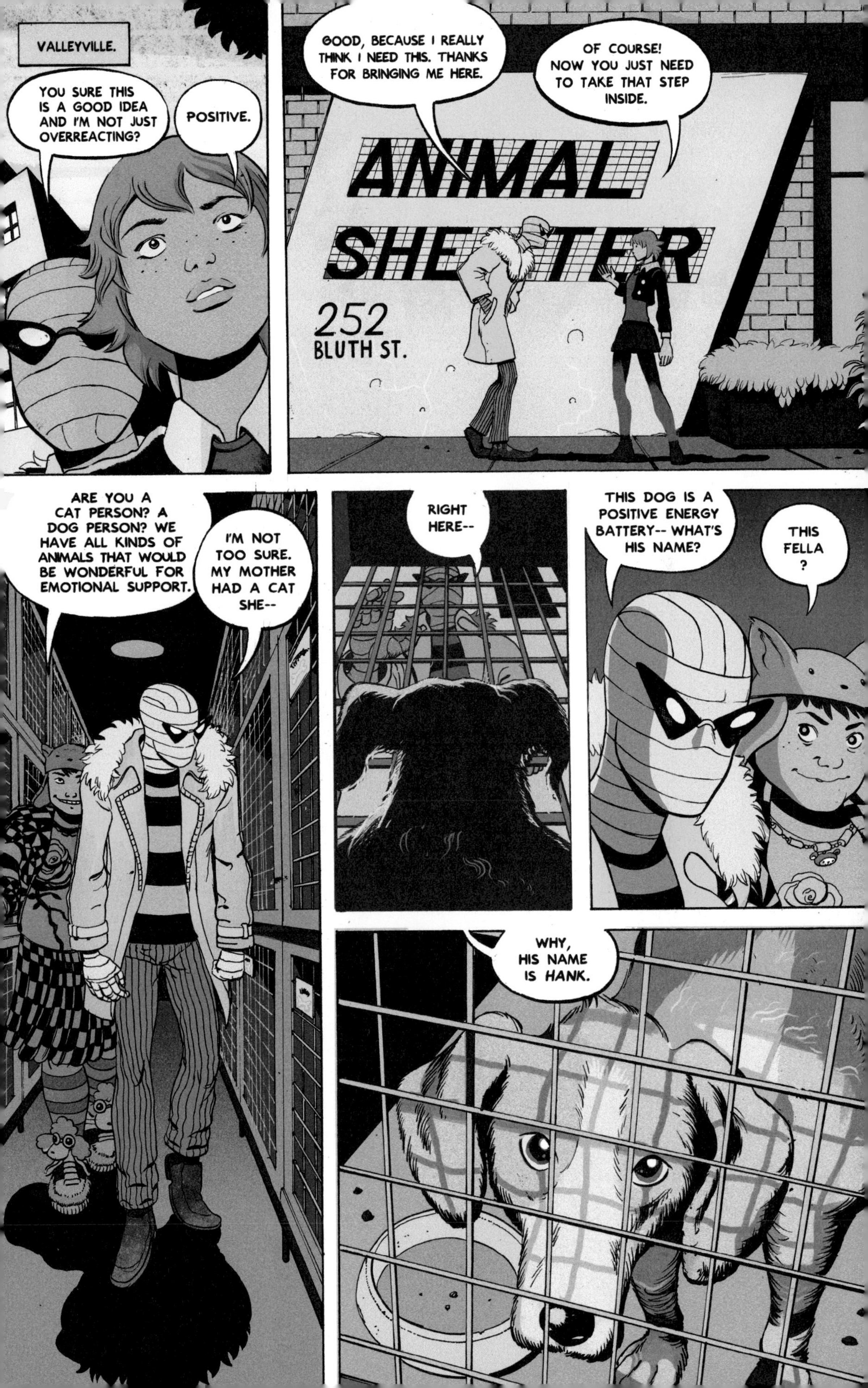
VALLEYVILLE.
YOU SURE THIS IS A GOOD IDEA AND I'M NOT JUST OVERREACTING?
POSITIVE.
GOOD, BECAUSE I REALLY THINK I NEED THIS. THANKS FOR BRINGING ME HERE.
OF COURSE! NOW YOU JUST NEED TO TAKE THAT STEP INSIDE.
ANIMAL SHE TER
252 BLUTH ST.
ARE YOU A CAT PERSON? A DOG PERSON? WE HAVE ALL KINDS OF ANIMALS THAT WOULD BE WONDERFUL FOR EMOTIONAL SUPPORT.
I'M NOT TOO SURE. MY MOTHER HAD A CAT SHE--
RIGHT HERE--
THIS DOG IS A POSITIVE ENERGY BATTERY-- WHAT'S HIS NAME?
THIS FELLA ?
WHY, HIS NAME IS HANK.

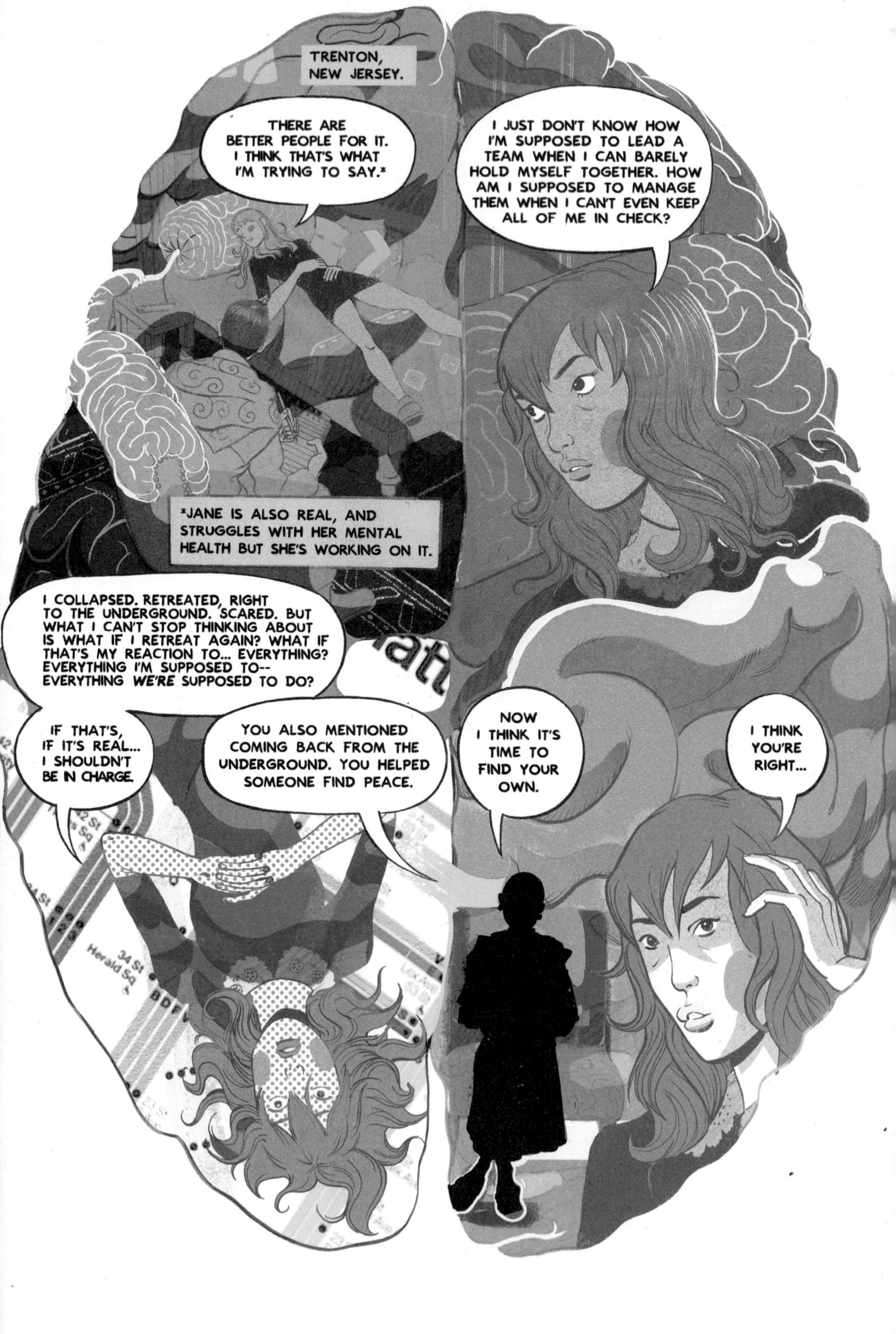
TRENTON, NEW JERSEY.
THERE ARE BETTER PEOPLE FOR IT. I THINK THAT'S WHAT I'M TRYING TO SAY.*
I JUST DON'T KNOW HOW I'M SUPPOSED TO LEAD A TEAM WHEN I CAN BARELY HOLD MYSELF TOGETHER. HOW AM I SUPPOSED TO MANAGE THEM WHEN I CAN'T EVEN KEEP ALL OF ME IN CHECK?
*JANE IS ALSO REAL, AND STRUGGLES WITH HER MENTAL HEALTH BUT SHE'S WORKING ON IT.
I COLLAPSED. RETREATED, RIGHT TO THE UNDERGROUND. SCARED. BUT WHAT I CAN'T STOP THINKING ABOUT IS WHAT IF I RETREAT AGAIN? WHAT IF THAT'S MY REACTION TO... EVERYTHING? EVERYTHING I'M SUPPOSED TO-- EVERYTHING *WE'RE* SUPPOSED TO DO?
IF THAT'S, IF IT'S REAL... I SHOULDN'T BE IN CHARGE.
YOU ALSO MENTIONED COMING BACK FROM THE UNDERGROUND. YOU HELPED SOMEONE FIND PEACE.
NOW I THINK IT'S TIME TO FIND YOUR OWN.
I THINK YOU'RE RIGHT...

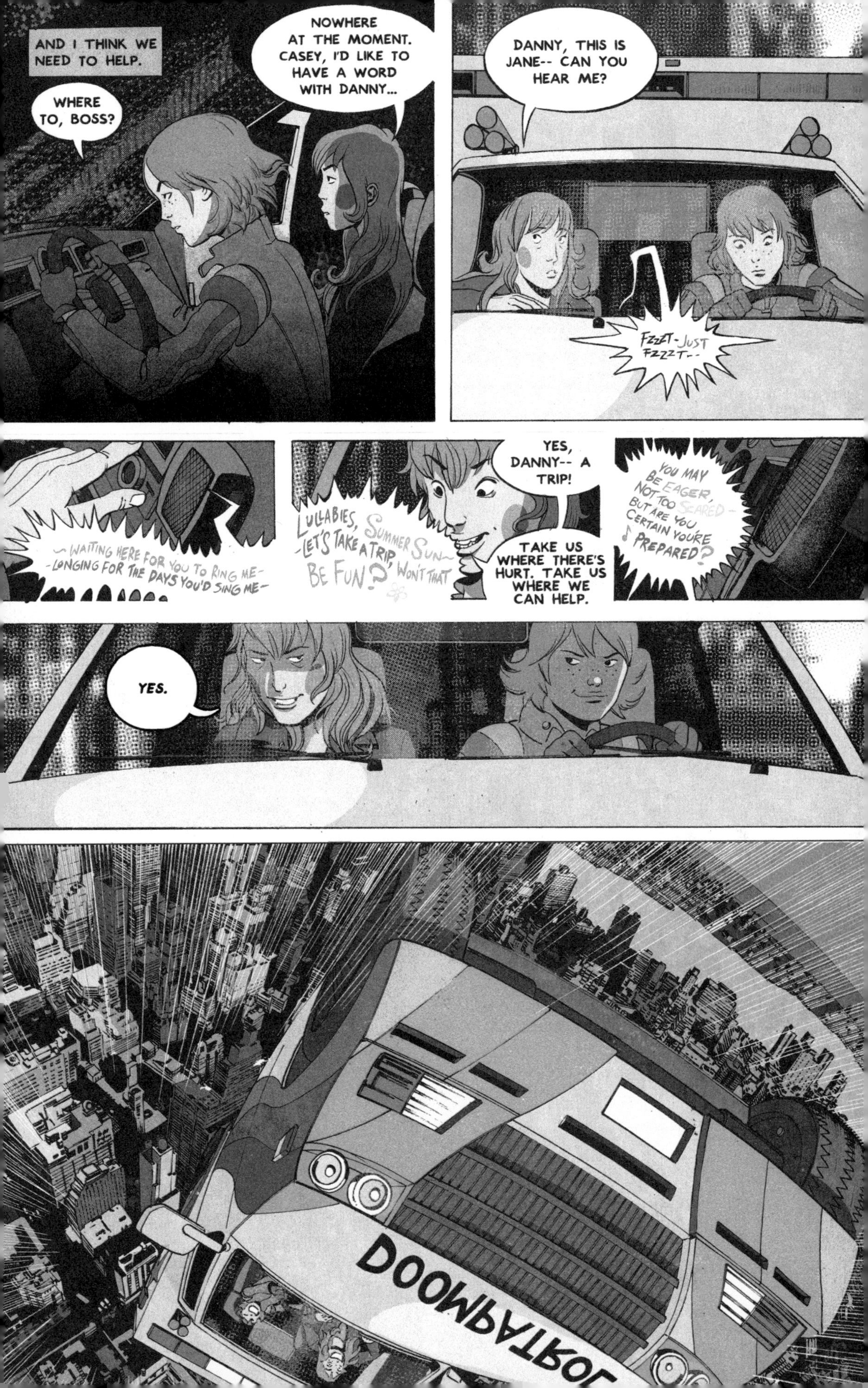
AND I THINK WE NEED TO HELP.
WHERE TO, BOSS?
NOWHERE AT THE MOMENT. CASEY, I'D LIKE TO HAVE A WORD WITH DANNY...
DANNY, THIS IS JANE-- CAN YOU HEAR ME?
FZZZT-JUST FZZZT--
~WAITING HERE FOR YOU TO RING ME-
-LONGING FOR THE DAYS YOU'D SING ME-
LULLABIES, SUMMER SUN~
-LET'S TAKE A TRIP, WON'T THAT BE FUN?
YES, DANNY-- A TRIP!
TAKE US WHERE THERE'S HURT. TAKE US WHERE WE CAN HELP.
YOU MAY BE EAGER, NOT TOO SCARED-
BUT ARE YOU CERTAIN YOU'RE PREPARED?
YES.
DOOMPATROL

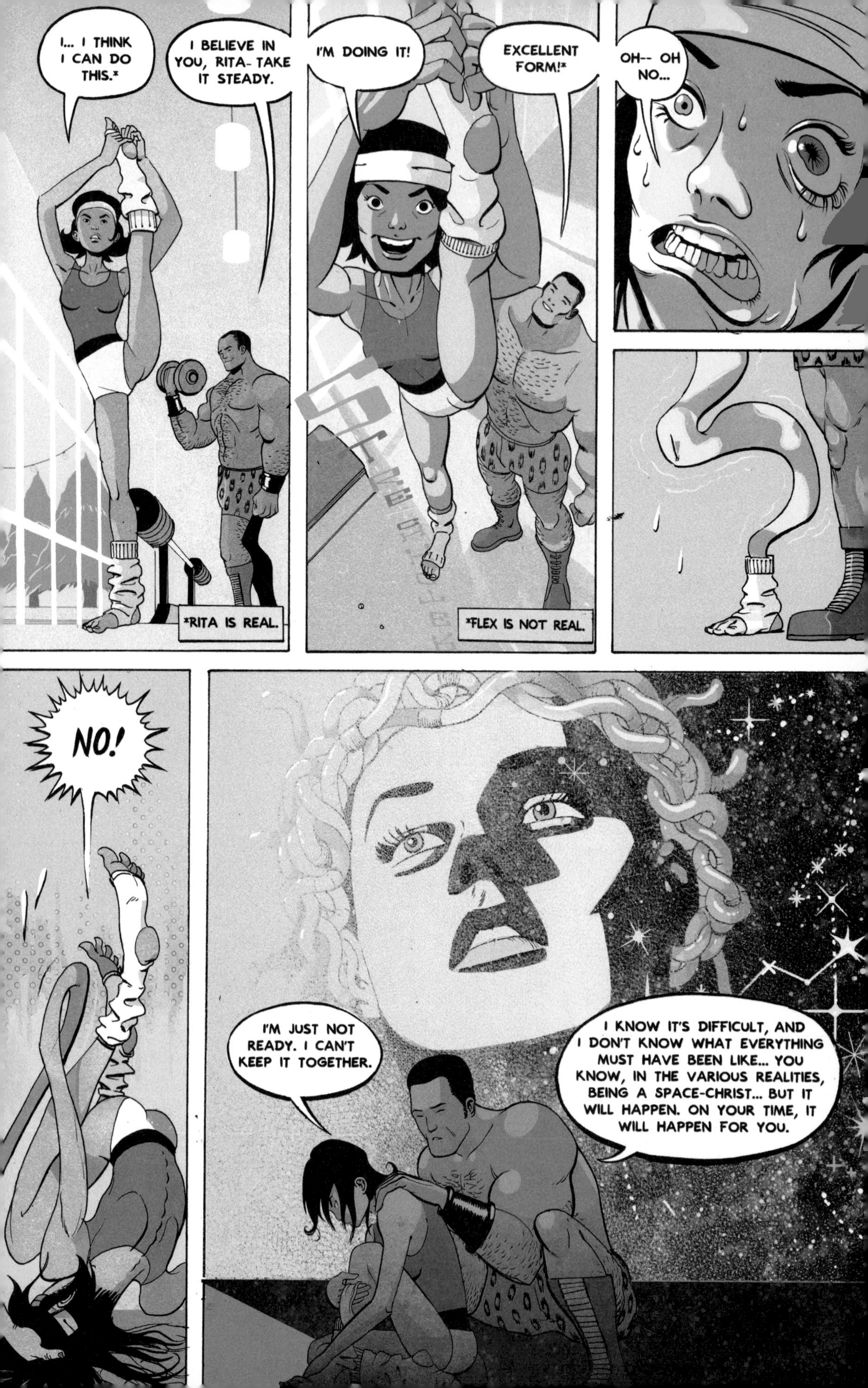
I... I THINK I CAN DO THIS.*
I BELIEVE IN YOU, RITA- TAKE IT STEADY.
*RITA IS REAL.
I'M DOING IT!
EXCELLENT FORM!*
*FLEX IS NOT REAL.
OH-- OH NO...
NO!
I'M JUST NOT READY. I CAN'T KEEP IT TOGETHER.
I KNOW IT'S DIFFICULT, AND I DON'T KNOW WHAT EVERYTHING MUST HAVE BEEN LIKE... YOU KNOW, IN THE VARIOUS REALITIES, BEING A SPACE-CHRIST... BUT IT WILL HAPPEN. ON YOUR TIME, IT WILL HAPPEN FOR YOU.

THANKS, FLEX... I WON'T GIVE UP.

SO YOU'RE REALLY GOING FOR IT, EH?

10,000 KG

I'VE BEEN WORKING TOWARD THIS GOAL FOR QUITE SOME TIME. MORE WEIGHT THAN I'VE EVER LIFTED BEFORE. AND NOW, I THINK...

HFFFF!!

WOW, I--

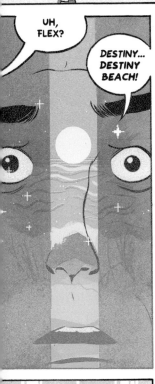

UH, FLEX?

DESTINY... DESTINY BEACH!

KLONK

WHAT?

DESTINY BEACH! A PLACE--! BURIED IN MY MEMORY ALL THOSE YEARS AGO BY DR. LEGS DURING THE HALCYON FIASCO...

I BARELY REMEMBER... BUT THOSE SANDS OF STRENGTH...

...THOSE WAVES OF WONDER...

SOUNDS AMAZING! BUT... WHERE IS IT?

OH, I KNOW WHERE TO FIND IT-- I JUST DON'T KNOW HOW I EVER FORGOT! WE MUST ANSWER THE CALL TO DESTINY BEACH!

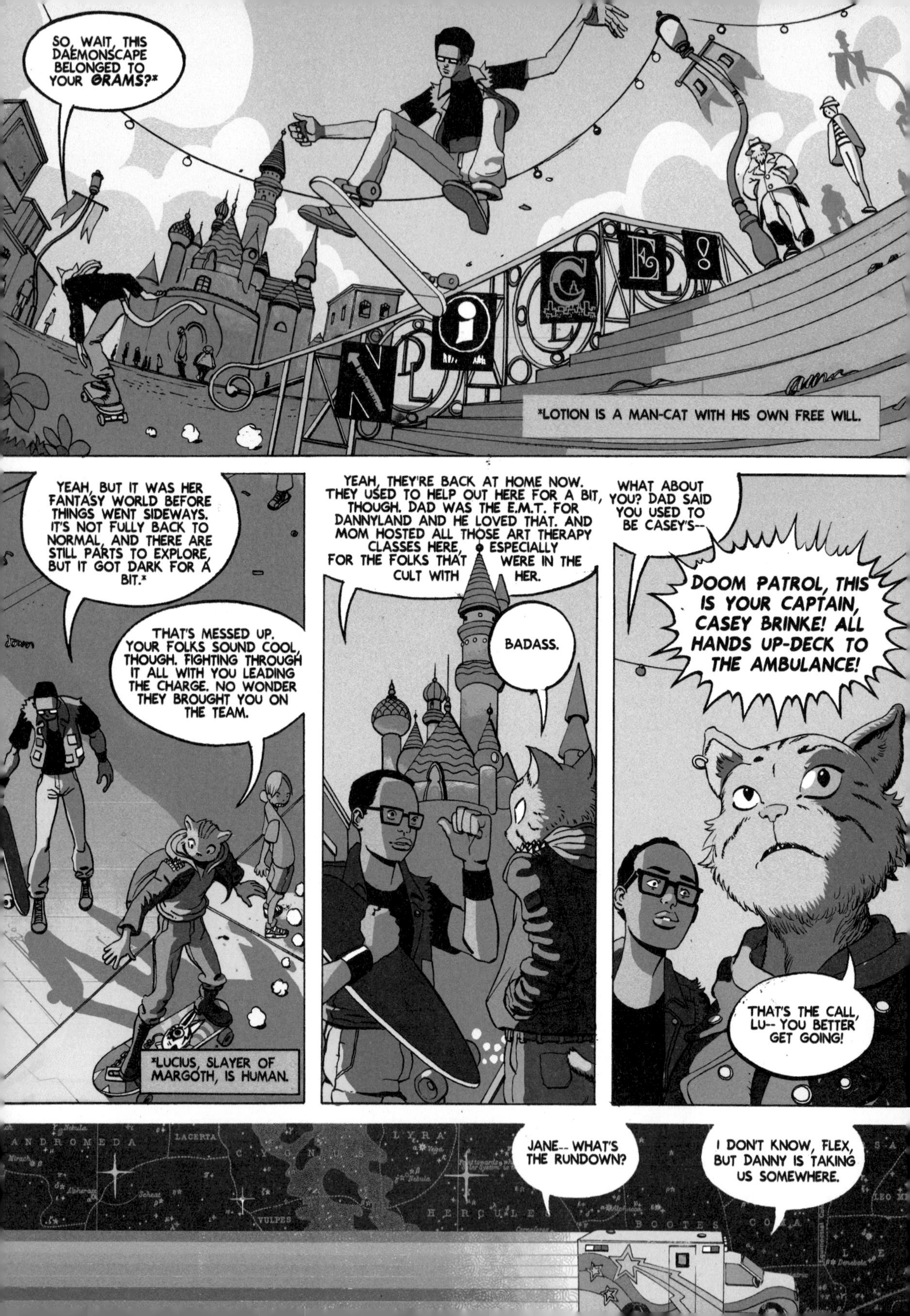
SO, WAIT, THIS DAEMONSCAPE BELONGED TO YOUR GRAMS?*
NICE!
*LOTION IS A MAN-CAT WITH HIS OWN FREE WILL.
YEAH, BUT IT WAS HER FANTASY WORLD BEFORE THINGS WENT SIDEWAYS. IT'S NOT FULLY BACK TO NORMAL, AND THERE ARE STILL PARTS TO EXPLORE, BUT IT GOT DARK FOR A BIT.*
THAT'S MESSED UP. YOUR FOLKS SOUND COOL, THOUGH. FIGHTING THROUGH IT ALL WITH YOU LEADING THE CHARGE. NO WONDER THEY BROUGHT YOU ON THE TEAM.
*LUCIUS, SLAYER OF MARGOTH, IS HUMAN.
YEAH, THEY'RE BACK AT HOME NOW. THEY USED TO HELP OUT HERE FOR A BIT, THOUGH. DAD WAS THE E.M.T. FOR DANNYLAND AND HE LOVED THAT. AND MOM HOSTED ALL THOSE ART THERAPY CLASSES HERE, ESPECIALLY FOR THE FOLKS THAT WERE IN THE CULT WITH HER.
BADASS.
WHAT ABOUT YOU? DAD SAID YOU USED TO BE CASEY'S--
DOOM PATROL, THIS IS YOUR CAPTAIN, CASEY BRINKE! ALL HANDS UP-DECK TO THE AMBULANCE!
THAT'S THE CALL, LU-- YOU BETTER GET GOING!
JANE-- WHAT'S THE RUNDOWN?
I DON'T KNOW, FLEX, BUT DANNY IS TAKING US SOMEWHERE.

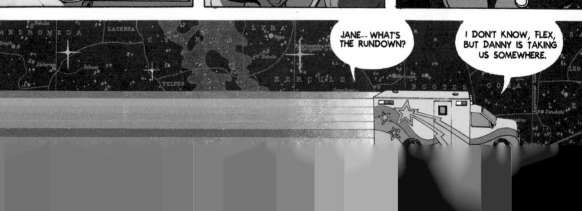

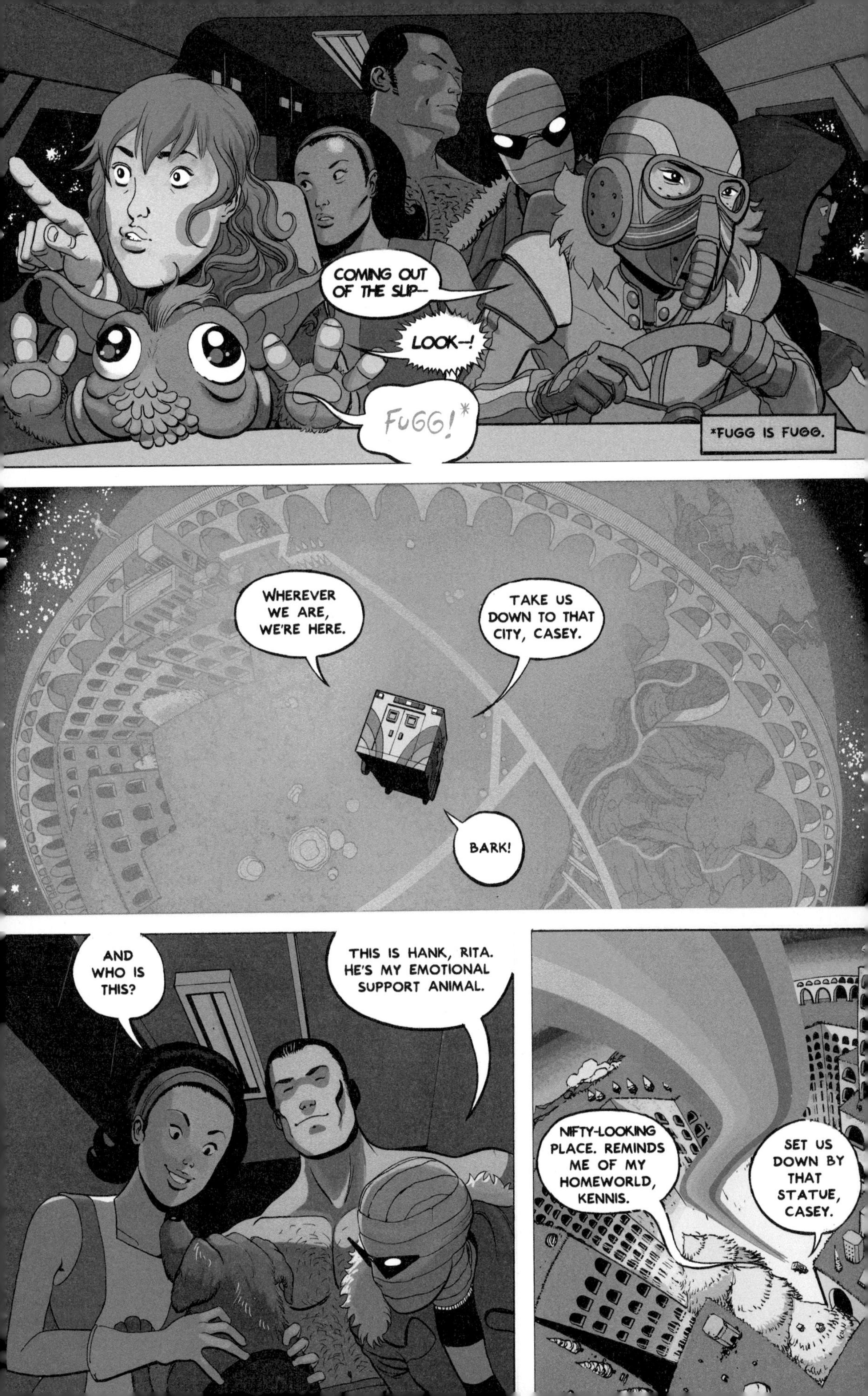
COMING OUT OF THE SLIP--
LOOK--!
FUGG!*
*FUGG IS FUGG.
WHEREVER WE ARE, WE'RE HERE.
TAKE US DOWN TO THAT CITY, CASEY.
BARK!
AND WHO IS THIS?
THIS IS HANK, RITA. HE'S MY EMOTIONAL SUPPORT ANIMAL.
NIFTY-LOOKING PLACE. REMINDS ME OF MY HOMEWORLD, KENNIS.
SET US DOWN BY THAT STATUE, CASEY.

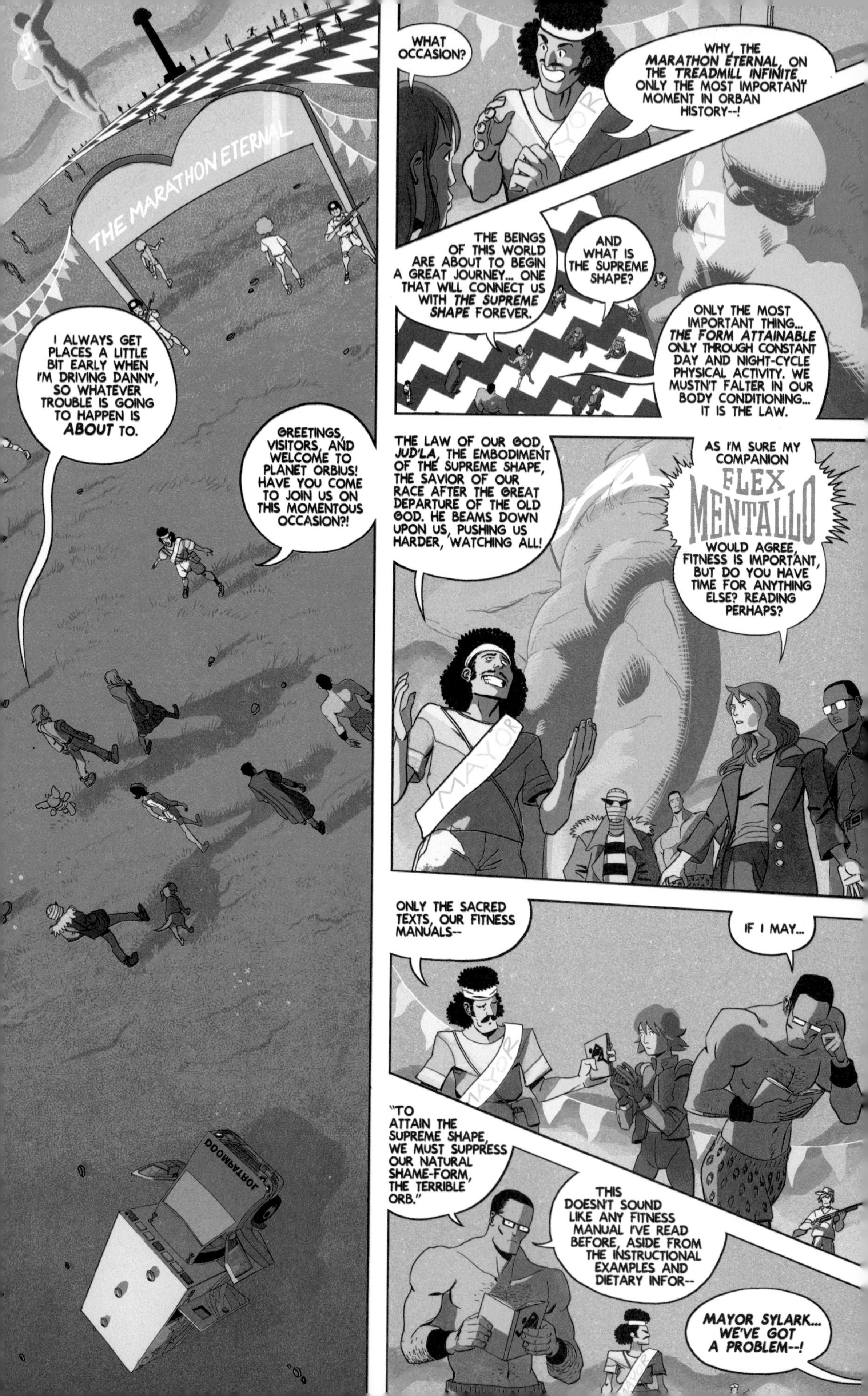
THE MARATHON ETERNAL
I ALWAYS GET PLACES A LITTLE BIT EARLY WHEN I'M DRIVING DANNY, SO WHATEVER TROUBLE IS GOING TO HAPPEN IS ABOUT TO.
GREETINGS, VISITORS, AND WELCOME TO PLANET ORBIUS! HAVE YOU COME TO JOIN US ON THIS MOMENTOUS OCCASION?!
DOOMPATROL
WHAT OCCASION?
WHY, THE MARATHON ETERNAL, ON THE TREADMILL INFINITE. ONLY THE MOST IMPORTANT MOMENT IN ORBAN HISTORY--!
MAYOR
THE BEINGS OF THIS WORLD ARE ABOUT TO BEGIN A GREAT JOURNEY... ONE THAT WILL CONNECT US WITH THE SUPREME SHAPE FOREVER.
AND WHAT IS THE SUPREME SHAPE?
ONLY THE MOST IMPORTANT THING... THE FORM ATTAINABLE ONLY THROUGH CONSTANT DAY AND NIGHT-CYCLE PHYSICAL ACTIVITY. WE MUSTN'T FALTER IN OUR BODY CONDITIONING... IT IS THE LAW.
THE LAW OF OUR GOD, JUD'LA, THE EMBODIMENT OF THE SUPREME SHAPE, THE SAVIOR OF OUR RACE AFTER THE GREAT DEPARTURE OF THE OLD GOD. HE BEAMS DOWN UPON US, PUSHING US HARDER, WATCHING ALL!
AS I'M SURE MY COMPANION FLEX MENTALLO WOULD AGREE, FITNESS IS IMPORTANT, BUT DO YOU HAVE TIME FOR ANYTHING ELSE? READING PERHAPS?
MAYOR
ONLY THE SACRED TEXTS, OUR FITNESS MANUALS--
IF I MAY...
MAYOR
"TO ATTAIN THE SUPREME SHAPE, WE MUST SUPPRESS OUR NATURAL SHAME-FORM, THE TERRIBLE ORB."
THIS DOESN'T SOUND LIKE ANY FITNESS MANUAL I'VE READ BEFORE, ASIDE FROM THE INSTRUCTIONAL EXAMPLES AND DIETARY INFOR--
MAYOR SYLARK... WE'VE GOT A PROBLEM--!

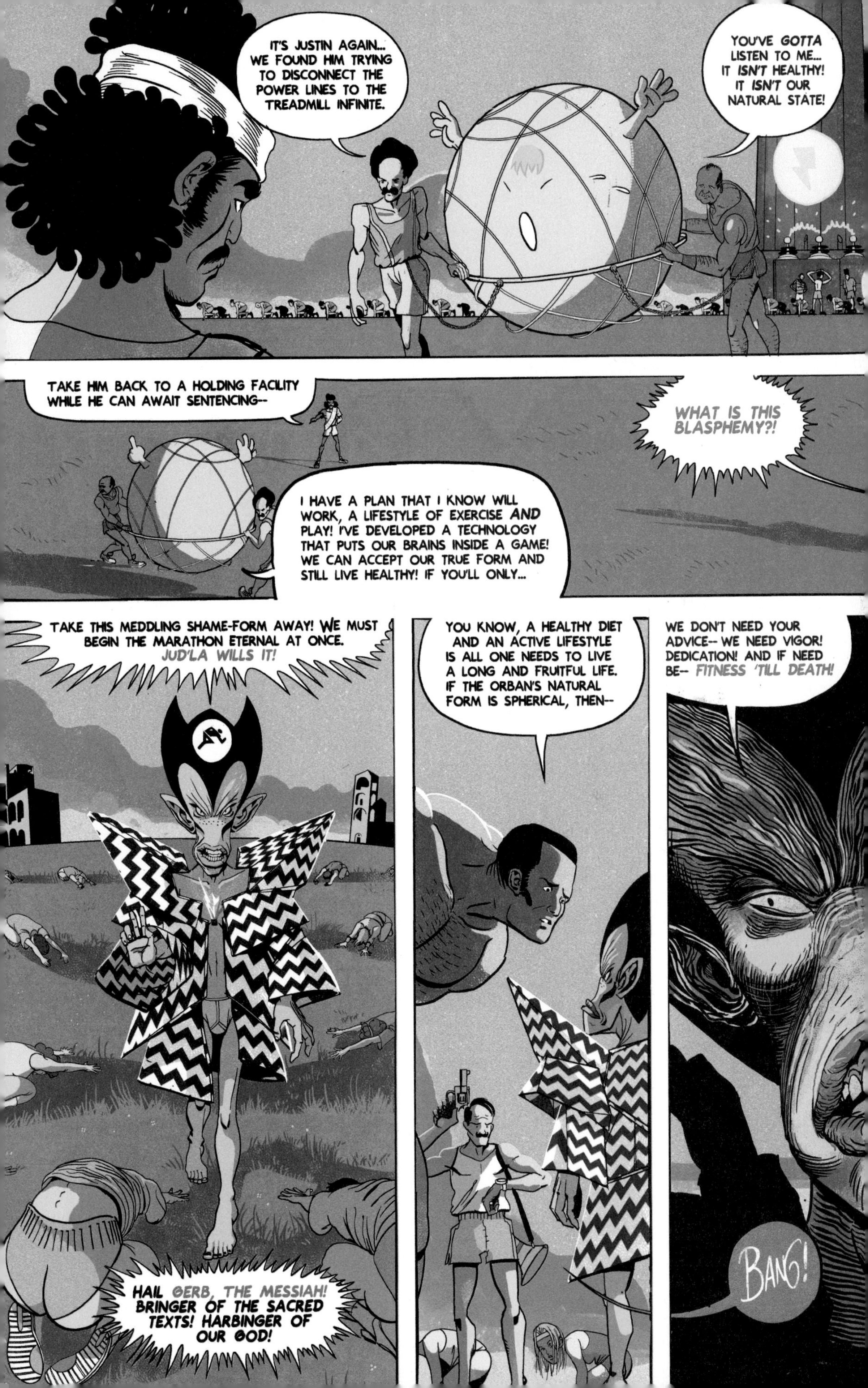
IT'S JUSTIN AGAIN... WE FOUND HIM TRYING TO DISCONNECT THE POWER LINES TO THE TREADMILL INFINITE.
YOU'VE GOTTA LISTEN TO ME... IT ISN'T HEALTHY! IT ISN'T OUR NATURAL STATE!
TAKE HIM BACK TO A HOLDING FACILITY WHILE HE CAN AWAIT SENTENCING--
WHAT IS THIS BLASPHEMY?!
I HAVE A PLAN THAT I KNOW WILL WORK, A LIFESTYLE OF EXERCISE AND PLAY! I'VE DEVELOPED A TECHNOLOGY THAT PUTS OUR BRAINS INSIDE A GAME! WE CAN ACCEPT OUR TRUE FORM AND STILL LIVE HEALTHY! IF YOU'LL ONLY...
TAKE THIS MEDDLING SHAME-FORM AWAY! WE MUST BEGIN THE MARATHON ETERNAL AT ONCE. JUD'LA WILLS IT!
HAIL GERB, THE MESSIAH! BRINGER OF THE SACRED TEXTS! HARBINGER OF OUR GOD!
YOU KNOW, A HEALTHY DIET AND AN ACTIVE LIFESTYLE IS ALL ONE NEEDS TO LIVE A LONG AND FRUITFUL LIFE. IF THE ORBAN'S NATURAL FORM IS SPHERICAL, THEN--
WE DON'T NEED YOUR ADVICE-- WE NEED VIGOR! DEDICATION! AND IF NEED BE-- FITNESS 'TILL DEATH!
BANG!

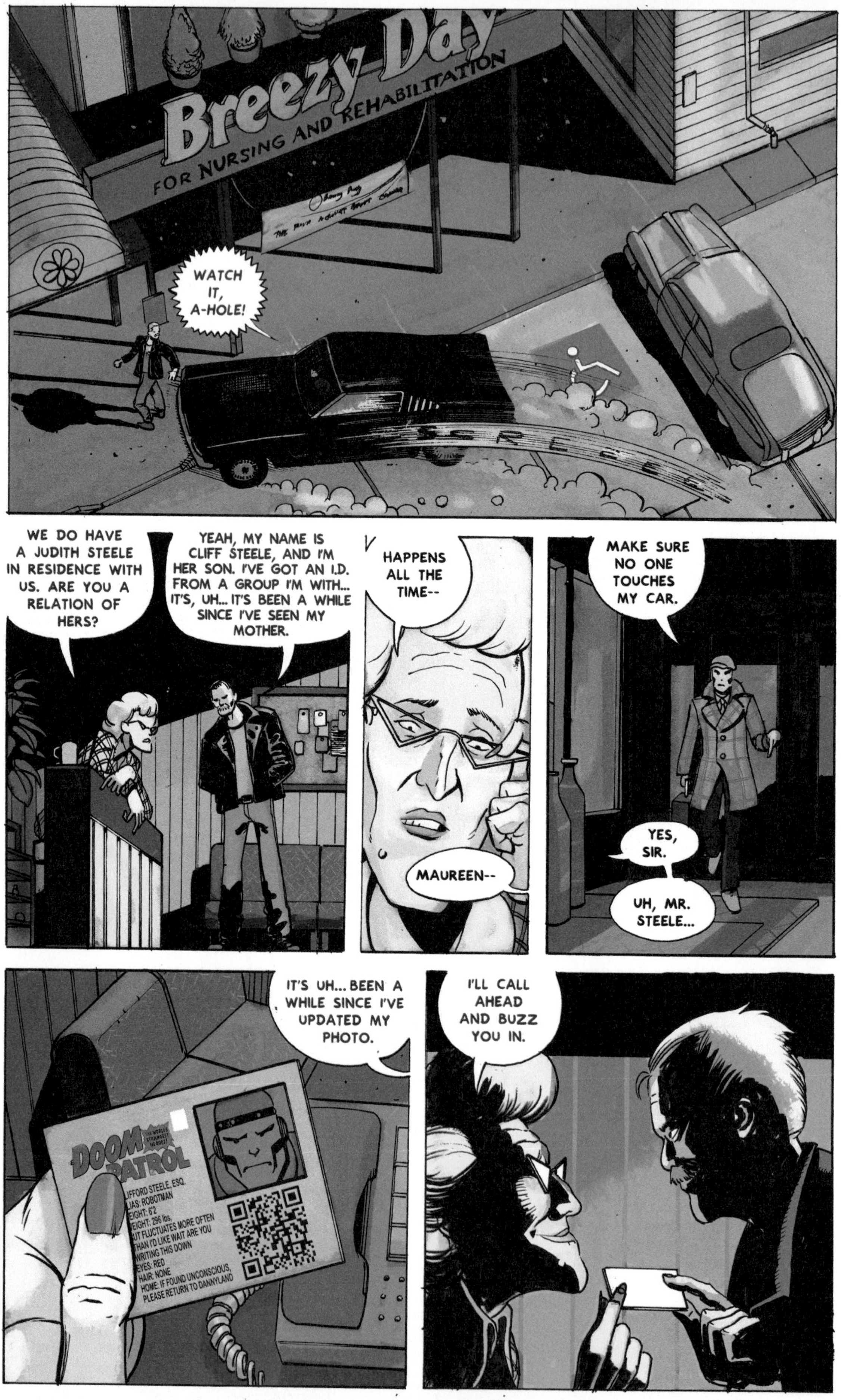
Breezy Day
FOR NURSING AND REHABILITATION
WATCH IT, A-HOLE!
SSREEEE
WE DO HAVE A JUDITH STEELE IN RESIDENCE WITH US. ARE YOU A RELATION OF HERS?
YEAH, MY NAME IS CLIFF STEELE, AND I'M HER SON. I'VE GOT AN I.D. FROM A GROUP I'M WITH... IT'S, UH... IT'S BEEN A WHILE SINCE I'VE SEEN MY MOTHER.
HAPPENS ALL THE TIME--
MAUREEN--
MAKE SURE NO ONE TOUCHES MY CAR.
YES, SIR.
UH, MR. STEELE...
DOOM PATROL
THE WORLD'S STRANGEST HEROES!
LIFFORD STEELE, ESQ.
LIAS: ROBOTMAN
EIGHT: 6'2
EIGHT: 296 lbs,
UT FLUCTUATES MORE OFTEN THAN I'D LIKE WAIT ARE YOU WRITING THIS DOWN
EYES: RED
HAIR: NONE
HOME: IF FOUND UNCONSCIOUS, PLEASE RETURN TO DANNYLAND
IT'S UH... BEEN A WHILE SINCE I'VE UPDATED MY PHOTO.
I'LL CALL AHEAD AND BUZZ YOU IN.

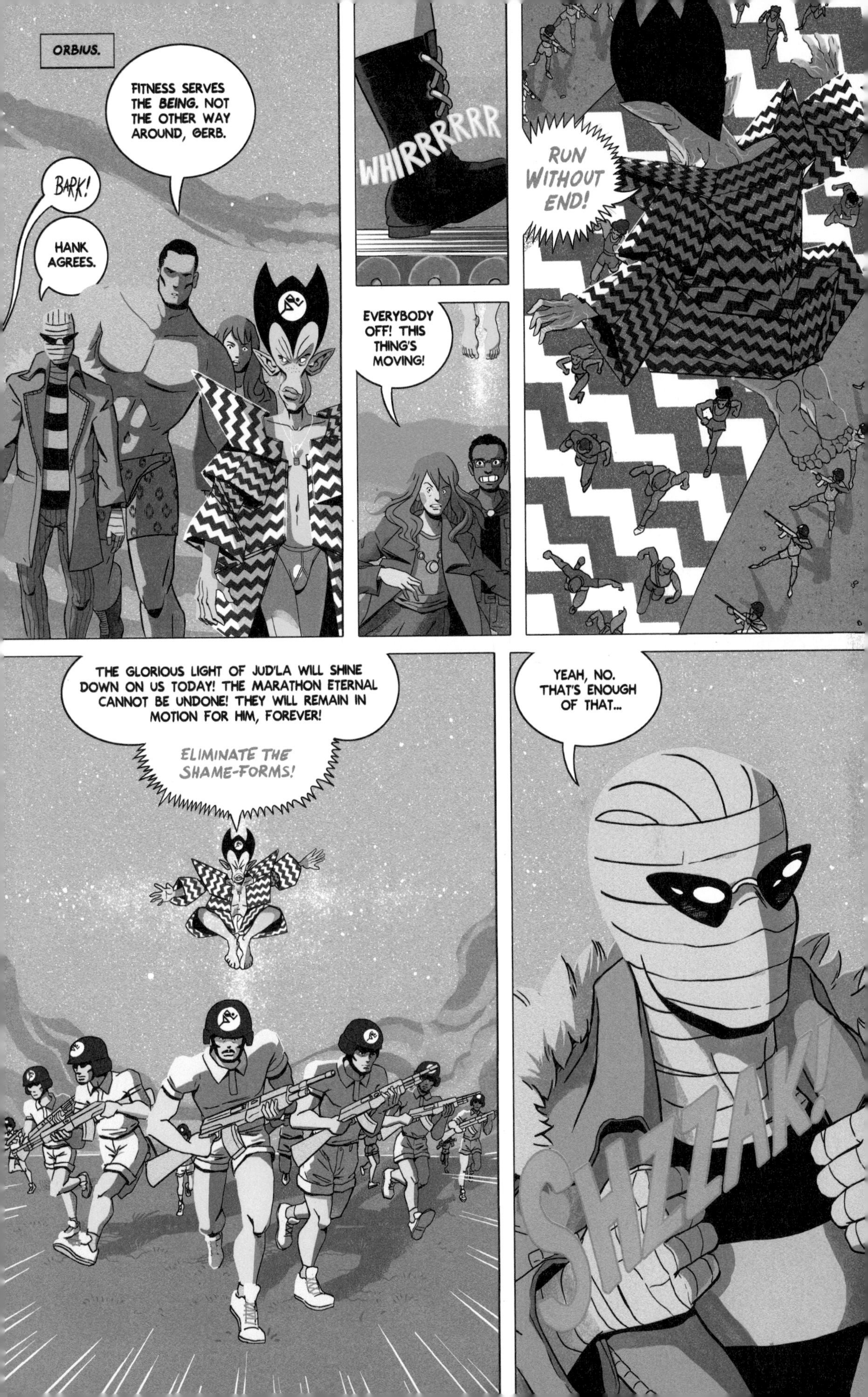
ORBIUS.
FITNESS SERVES THE BEING. NOT THE OTHER WAY AROUND, GERB.
BARK!
HANK AGREES.
WHIRRRRRR
RUN WITHOUT END!
EVERYBODY OFF! THIS THING'S MOVING!
THE GLORIOUS LIGHT OF JUD'LA WILL SHINE DOWN ON US TODAY! THE MARATHON ETERNAL CANNOT BE UNDONE! THEY WILL REMAIN IN MOTION FOR HIM, FOREVER!
ELIMINATE THE SHAME-FORMS!
YEAH, NO. THAT'S ENOUGH OF THAT...
SHZZAK!

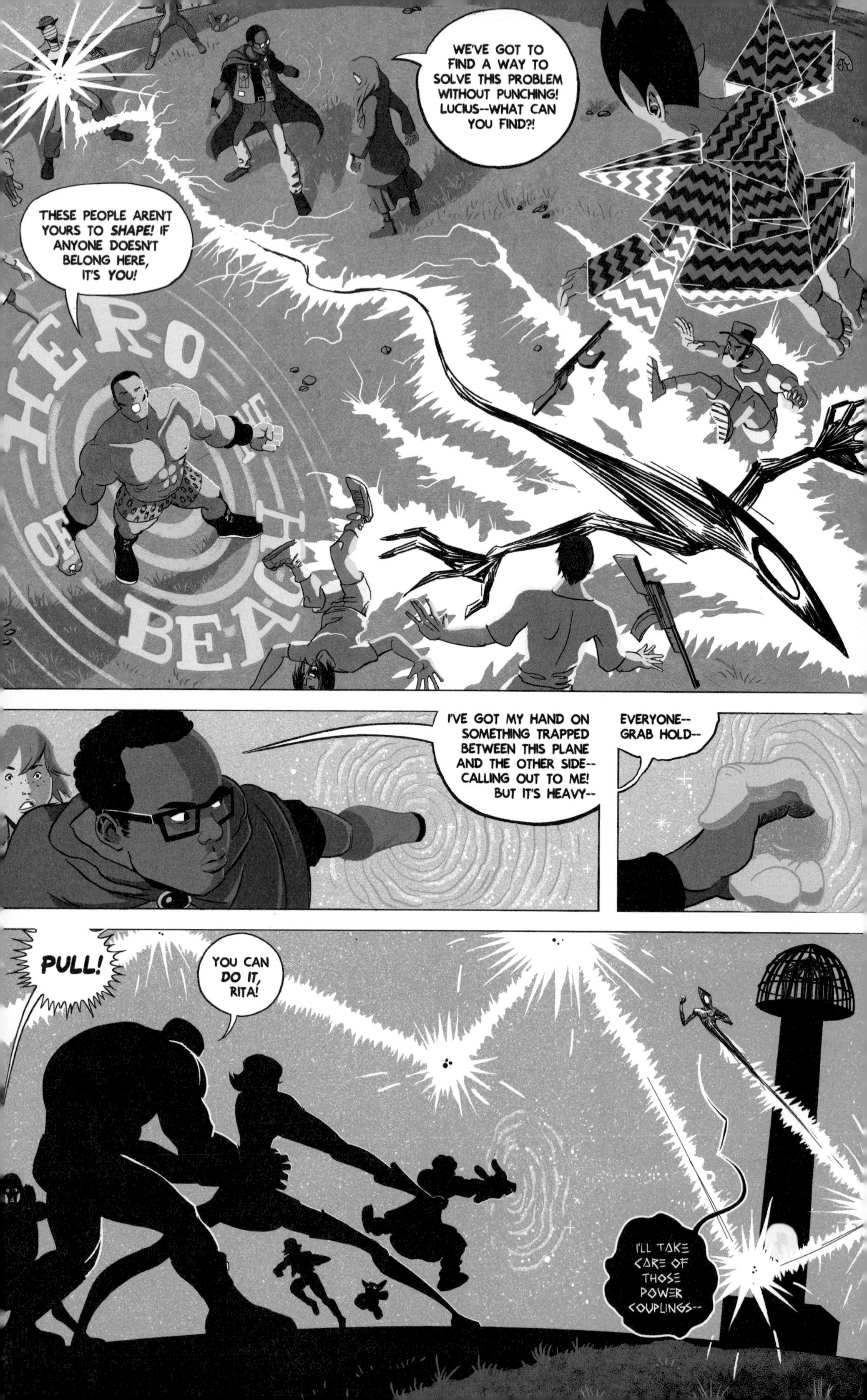
WE'VE GOT TO FIND A WAY TO SOLVE THIS PROBLEM WITHOUT PUNCHING! LUCIUS--WHAT CAN YOU FIND?!
THESE PEOPLE AREN'T YOURS TO *SHAPE!* IF ANYONE DOESN'T BELONG HERE, IT'S *YOU!*
I'VE GOT MY HAND ON SOMETHING TRAPPED BETWEEN THIS PLANE AND THE OTHER SIDE-- CALLING OUT TO ME! BUT IT'S HEAVY--
EVERYONE-- GRAB HOLD--
PULL!
YOU CAN *DO IT,* RITA!
I'LL TAKE CARE OF THOSE POWER COUPLINGS--

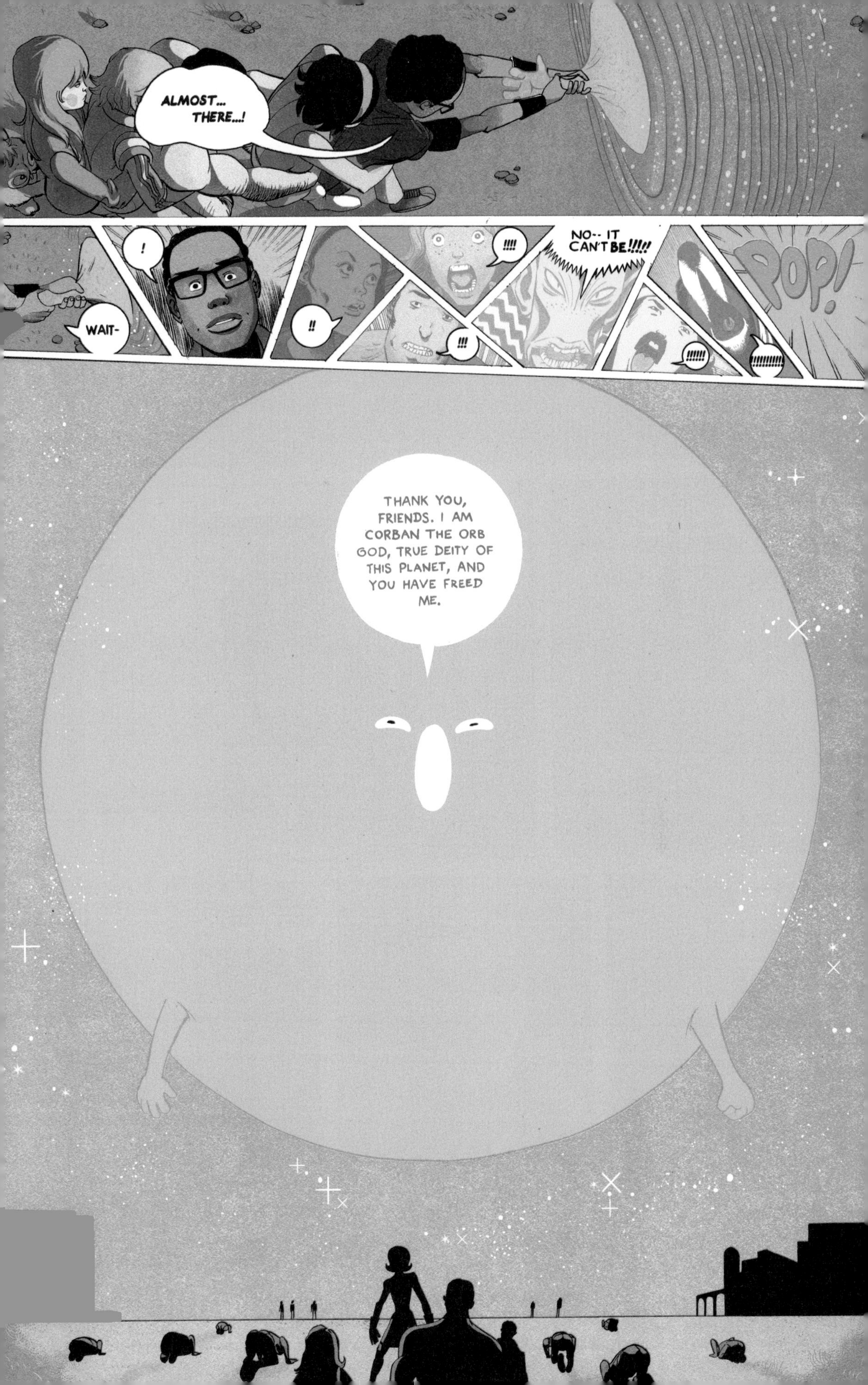
ALMOST... THERE...!
WAIT-
!
!!
!!!!
!!!
NO-- IT CAN'T BE!!!!!
!!!!!!
!!!!!!!!!
POP!
THANK YOU, FRIENDS. I AM CORBAN THE ORB GOD, TRUE DEITY OF THIS PLANET, AND YOU HAVE FREED ME.

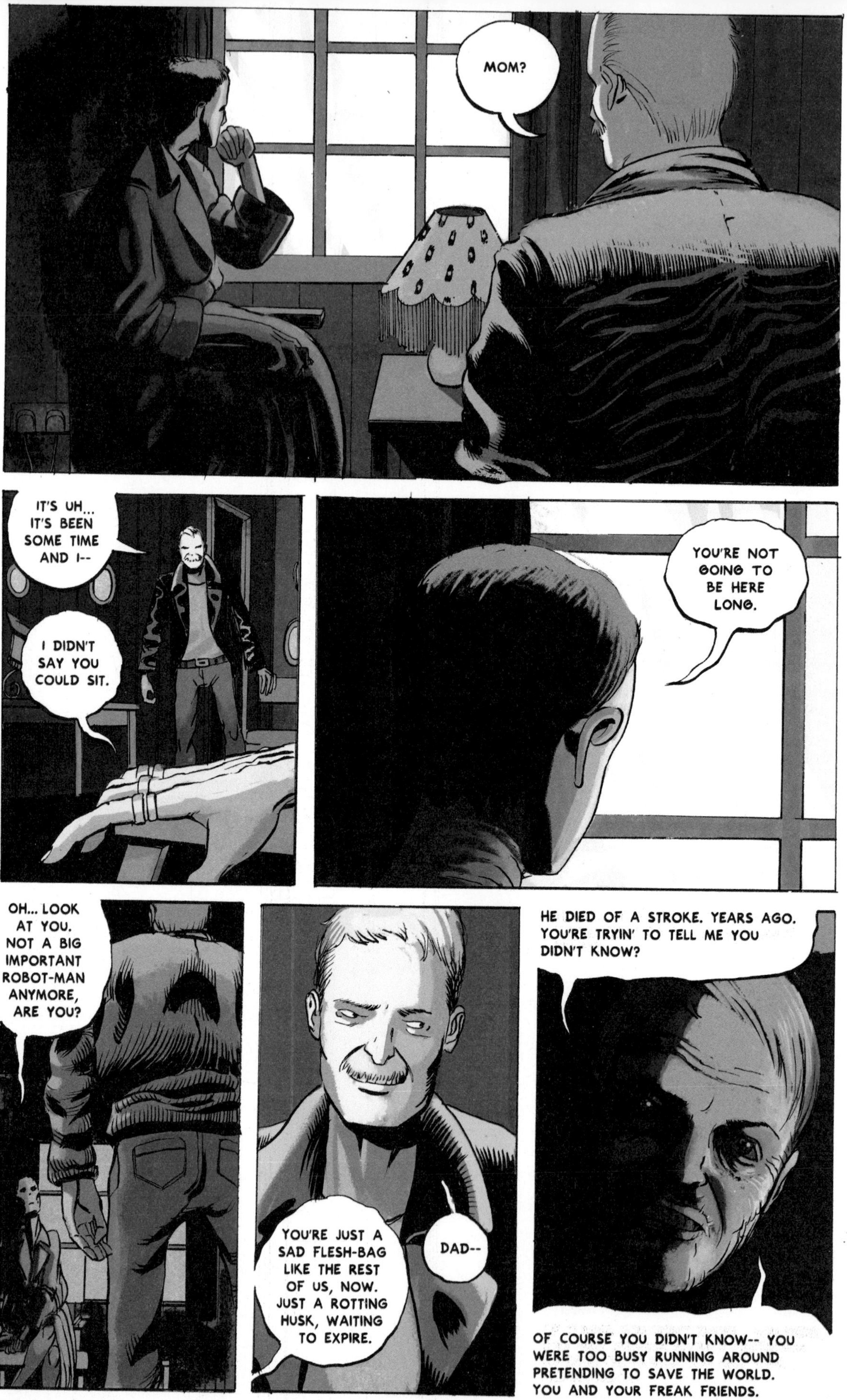
MOM?
IT'S UH... IT'S BEEN SOME TIME AND I--
I DIDN'T SAY YOU COULD SIT.
YOU'RE NOT GOING TO BE HERE LONG.
OH... LOOK AT YOU. NOT A BIG IMPORTANT ROBOT-MAN ANYMORE, ARE YOU?
YOU'RE JUST A SAD FLESH-BAG LIKE THE REST OF US, NOW. JUST A ROTTING HUSK, WAITING TO EXPIRE.
DAD--
HE DIED OF A STROKE. YEARS AGO. YOU'RE TRYIN' TO TELL ME YOU DIDN'T KNOW?
OF COURSE YOU DIDN'T KNOW-- YOU WERE TOO BUSY RUNNING AROUND PRETENDING TO SAVE THE WORLD. YOU AND YOUR FREAK FRIENDS.

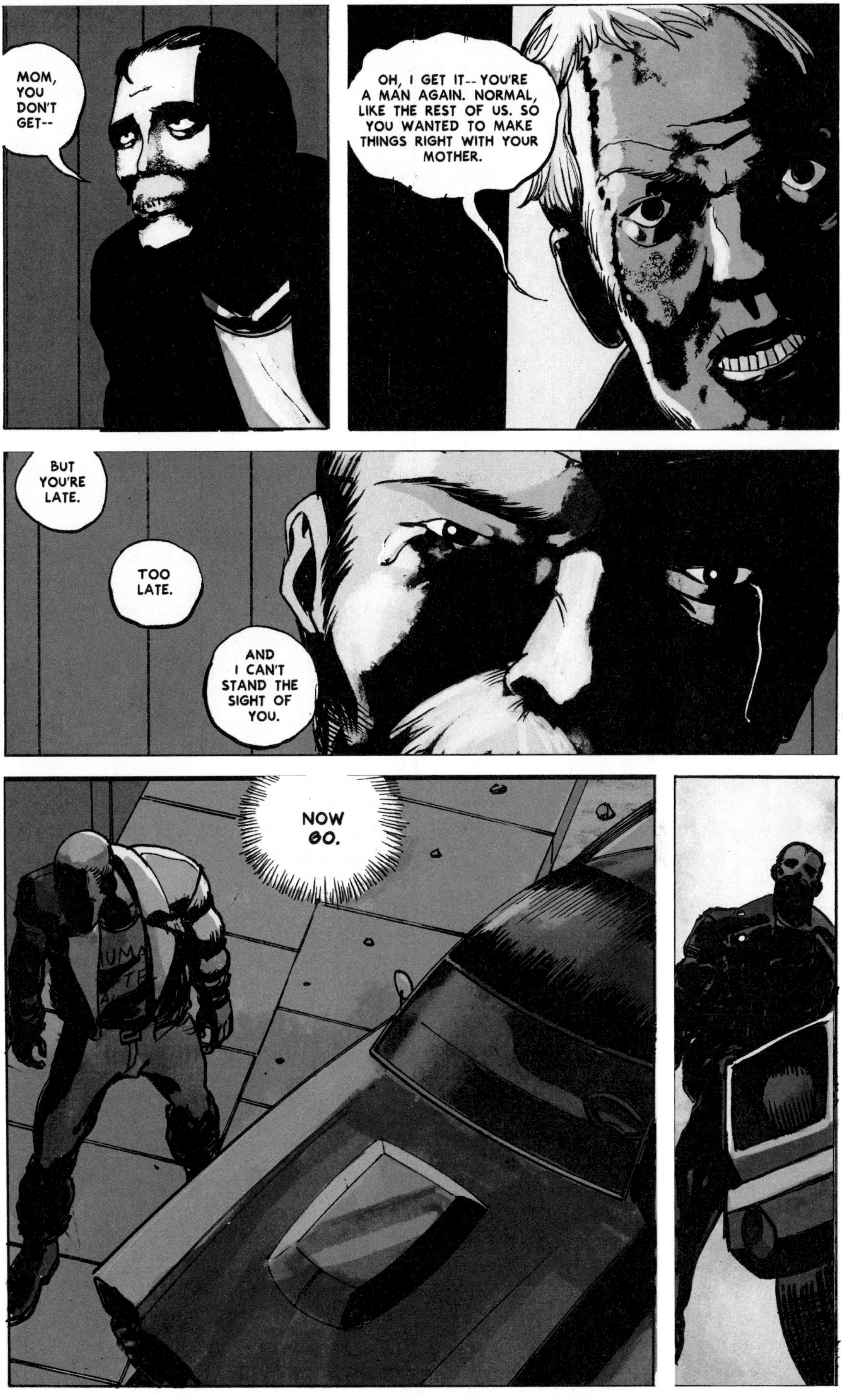
MOM, YOU DON'T GET--
OH, I GET IT-- YOU'RE A MAN AGAIN. NORMAL, LIKE THE REST OF US. SO YOU WANTED TO MAKE THINGS RIGHT WITH YOUR MOTHER.
BUT YOU'RE LATE.
TOO LATE.
AND I CAN'T STAND THE SIGHT OF YOU.
NOW GO.

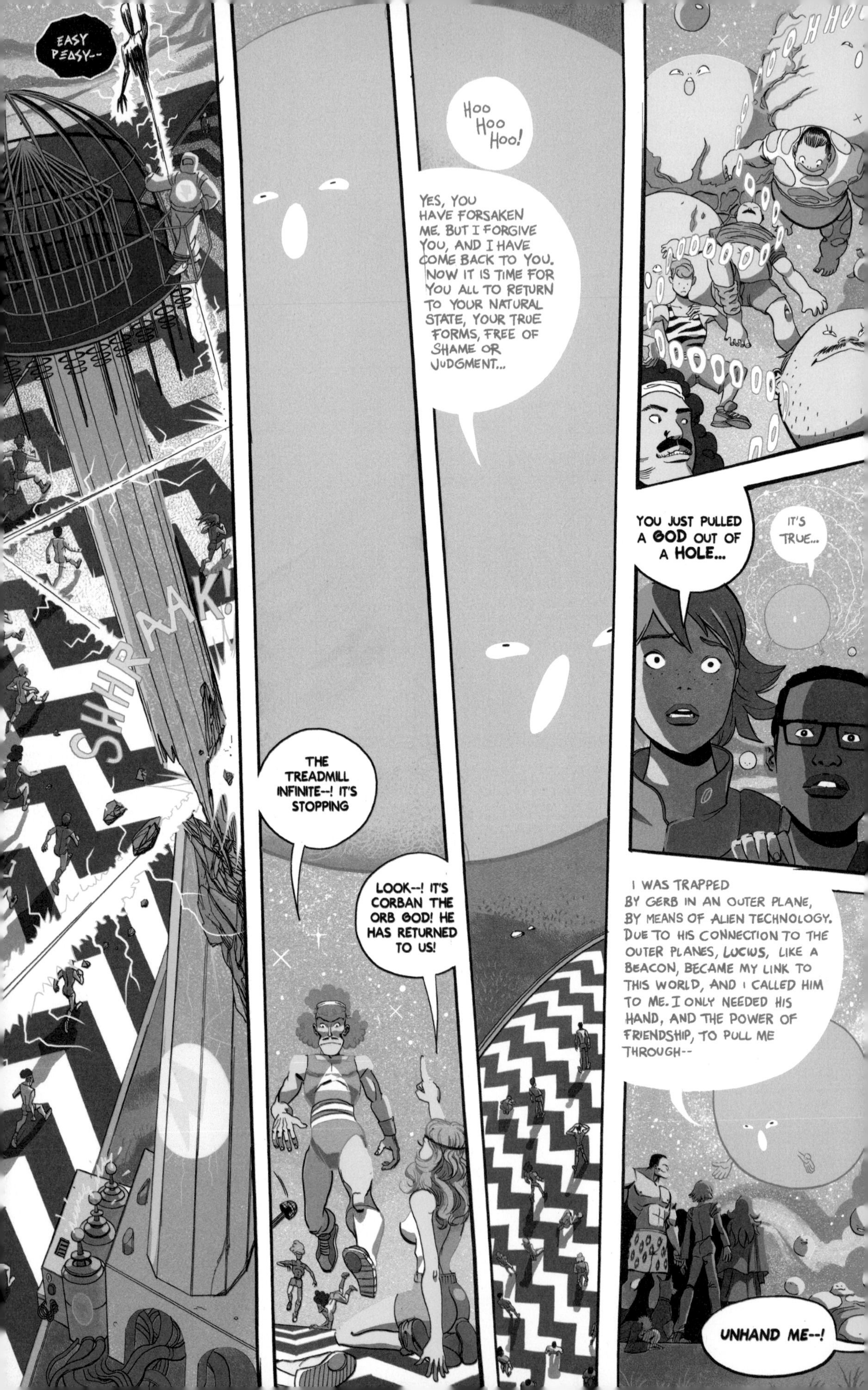
EASY PEASY--
SHHRAAK!
HOO HOO HOO!
YES, YOU HAVE FORSAKEN ME. BUT I FORGIVE YOU, AND I HAVE COME BACK TO YOU. NOW IT IS TIME FOR YOU ALL TO RETURN TO YOUR NATURAL STATE, YOUR TRUE FORMS, FREE OF SHAME OR JUDGMENT...
THE TREADMILL INFINITE--! IT'S STOPPING
LOOK--! IT'S CORBAN THE ORB GOD! HE HAS RETURNED TO US!
YOU JUST PULLED A GOD OUT OF A HOLE...
IT'S TRUE...
I WAS TRAPPED BY GERB IN AN OUTER PLANE, BY MEANS OF ALIEN TECHNOLOGY. DUE TO HIS CONNECTION TO THE OUTER PLANES, LUCIUS, LIKE A BEACON, BECAME MY LINK TO THIS WORLD, AND I CALLED HIM TO ME. I ONLY NEEDED HIS HAND, AND THE POWER OF FRIENDSHIP, TO PULL ME THROUGH--
UNHAND ME--!

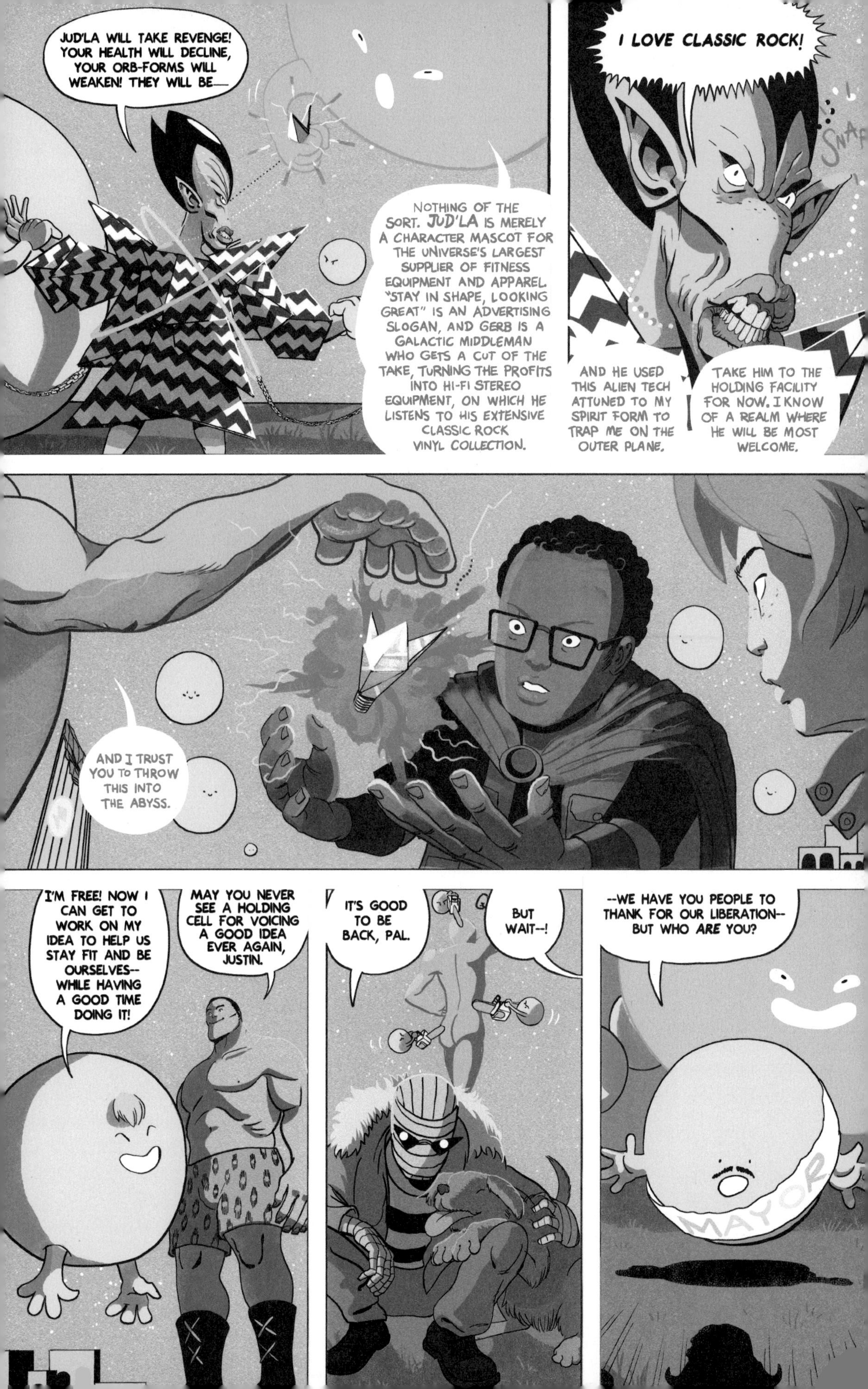
JUD'LA WILL TAKE REVENGE! YOUR HEALTH WILL DECLINE, YOUR ORB-FORMS WILL WEAKEN! THEY WILL BE—
NOTHING OF THE SORT. JUD'LA IS MERELY A CHARACTER MASCOT FOR THE UNIVERSE'S LARGEST SUPPLIER OF FITNESS EQUIPMENT AND APPAREL. "STAY IN SHAPE, LOOKING GREAT" IS AN ADVERTISING SLOGAN, AND GERB IS A GALACTIC MIDDLEMAN WHO GETS A CUT OF THE TAKE, TURNING THE PROFITS INTO HI-FI STEREO EQUIPMENT, ON WHICH HE LISTENS TO HIS EXTENSIVE CLASSIC ROCK VINYL COLLECTION.
I LOVE CLASSIC ROCK!
SNAP
AND HE USED THIS ALIEN TECH ATTUNED TO MY SPIRIT FORM TO TRAP ME ON THE OUTER PLANE.
TAKE HIM TO THE HOLDING FACILITY FOR NOW. I KNOW OF A REALM WHERE HE WILL BE MOST WELCOME.
AND I TRUST YOU TO THROW THIS INTO THE ABYSS.
I'M FREE! NOW I CAN GET TO WORK ON MY IDEA TO HELP US STAY FIT AND BE OURSELVES-- WHILE HAVING A GOOD TIME DOING IT!
MAY YOU NEVER SEE A HOLDING CELL FOR VOICING A GOOD IDEA EVER AGAIN, JUSTIN.
IT'S GOOD TO BE BACK, PAL.
BUT WAIT--!
--WE HAVE YOU PEOPLE TO THANK FOR OUR LIBERATION-- BUT WHO ARE YOU?
MAYOR

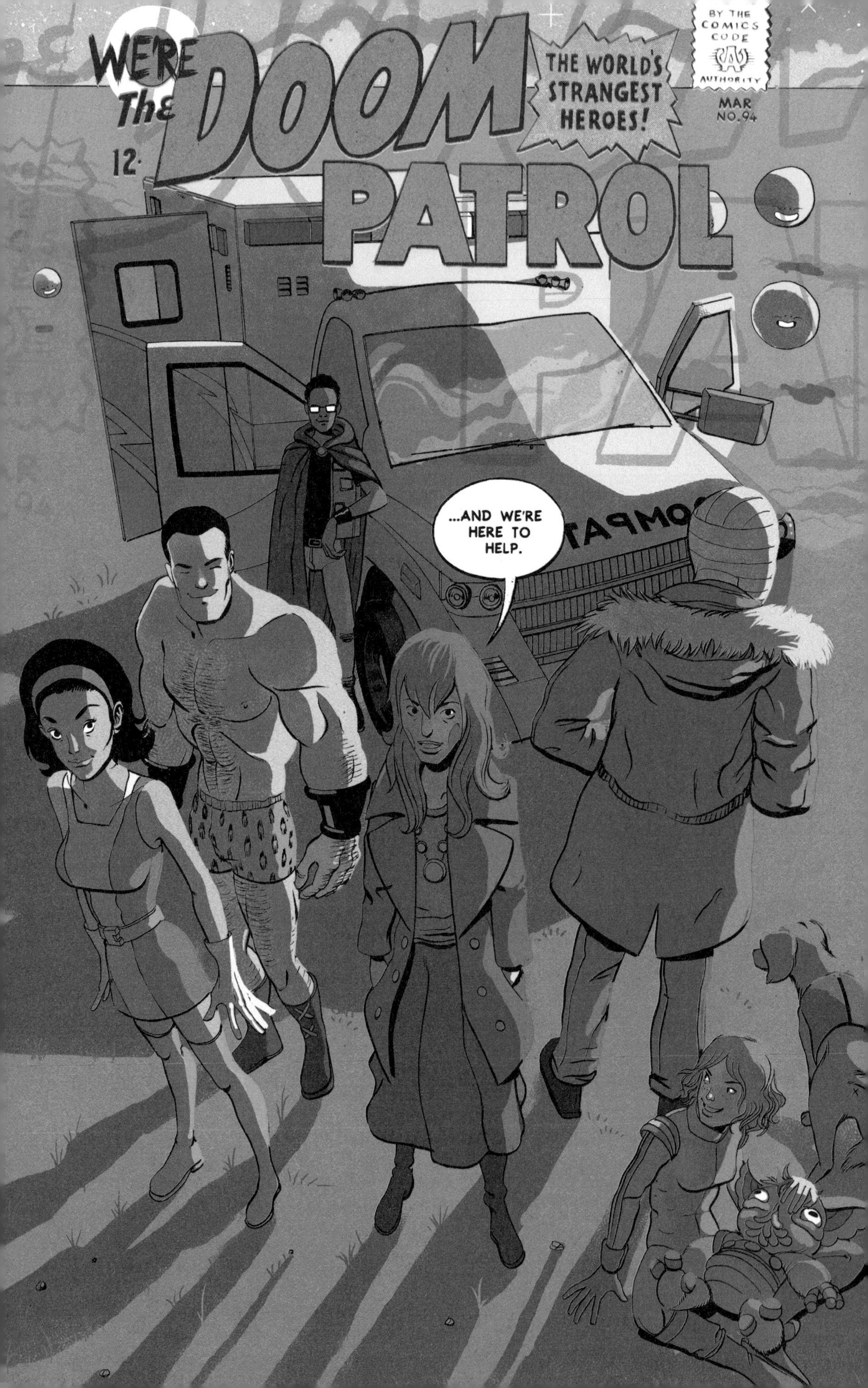
WE'RE The DOOM PATROL
THE WORLD'S STRANGEST HEROES!
12¢
BY THE COMICS CODE AUTHORITY
MAR NO.94
...AND WE'RE HERE TO HELP.

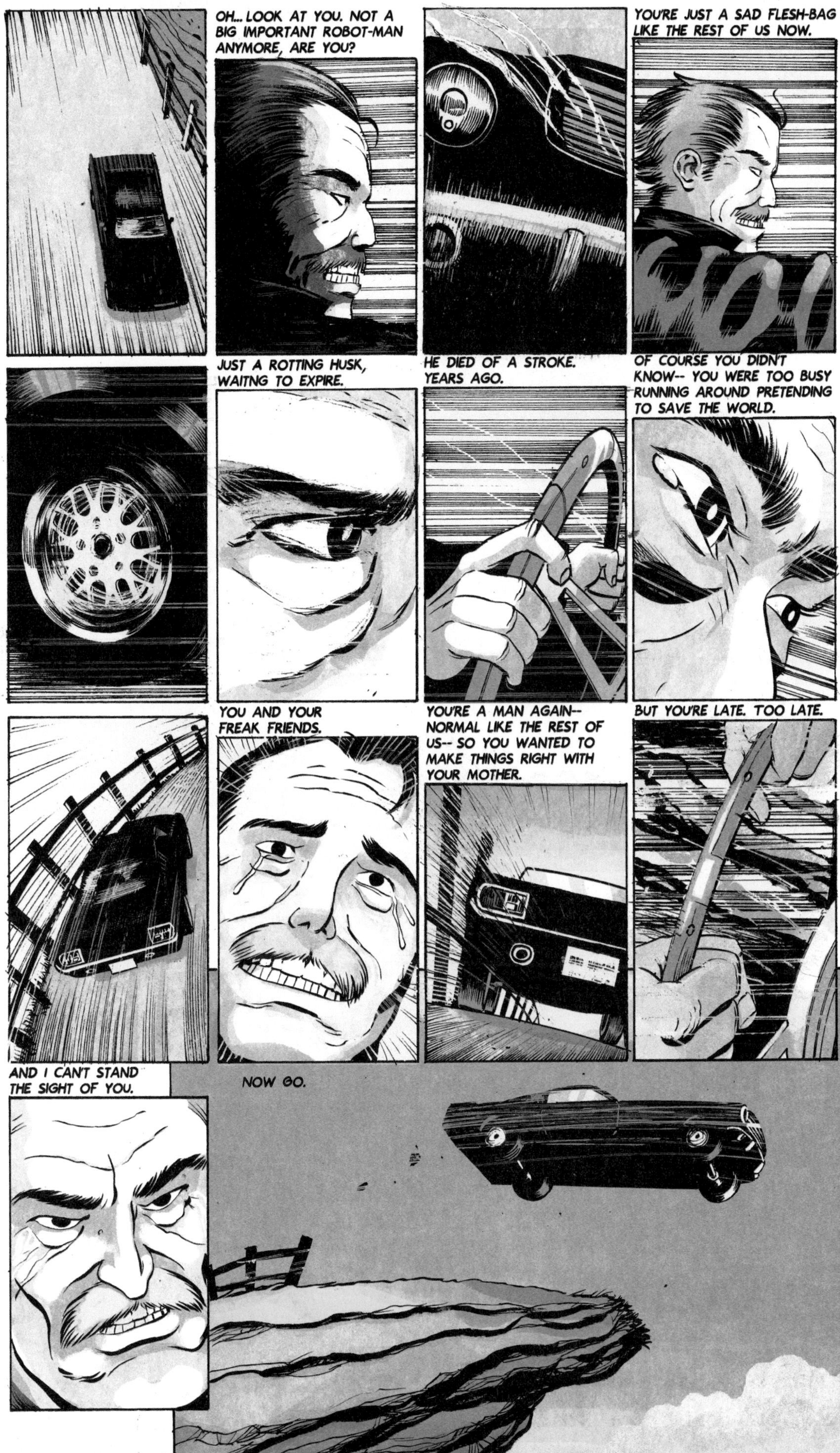
OH... LOOK AT YOU. NOT A BIG IMPORTANT ROBOT-MAN ANYMORE, ARE YOU?
YOU'RE JUST A SAD FLESH-BAG LIKE THE REST OF US NOW.
JUST A ROTTING HUSK, WAITNG TO EXPIRE.
HE DIED OF A STROKE. YEARS AGO.
OF COURSE YOU DIDN'T KNOW-- YOU WERE TOO BUSY RUNNING AROUND PRETENDING TO SAVE THE WORLD.
YOU AND YOUR FREAK FRIENDS.
YOU'RE A MAN AGAIN-- NORMAL LIKE THE REST OF US-- SO YOU WANTED TO MAKE THINGS RIGHT WITH YOUR MOTHER.
BUT YOU'RE LATE. TOO LATE.
AND I CAN'T STAND THE SIGHT OF YOU.
NOW GO.

NEXT:

HELLO METAL, MY OLD FRIEND

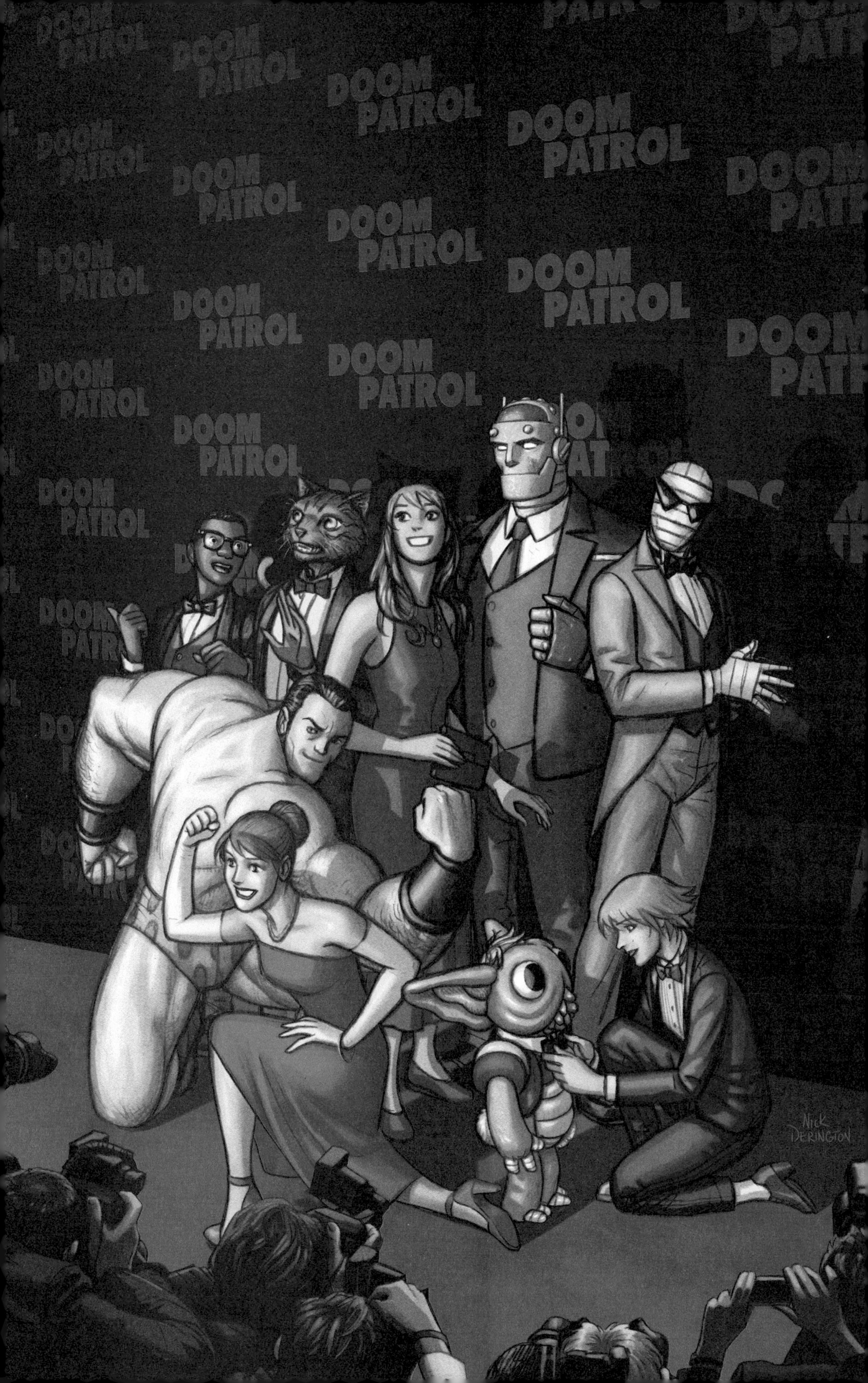
DOOM PATROL
NICK DERINGTON

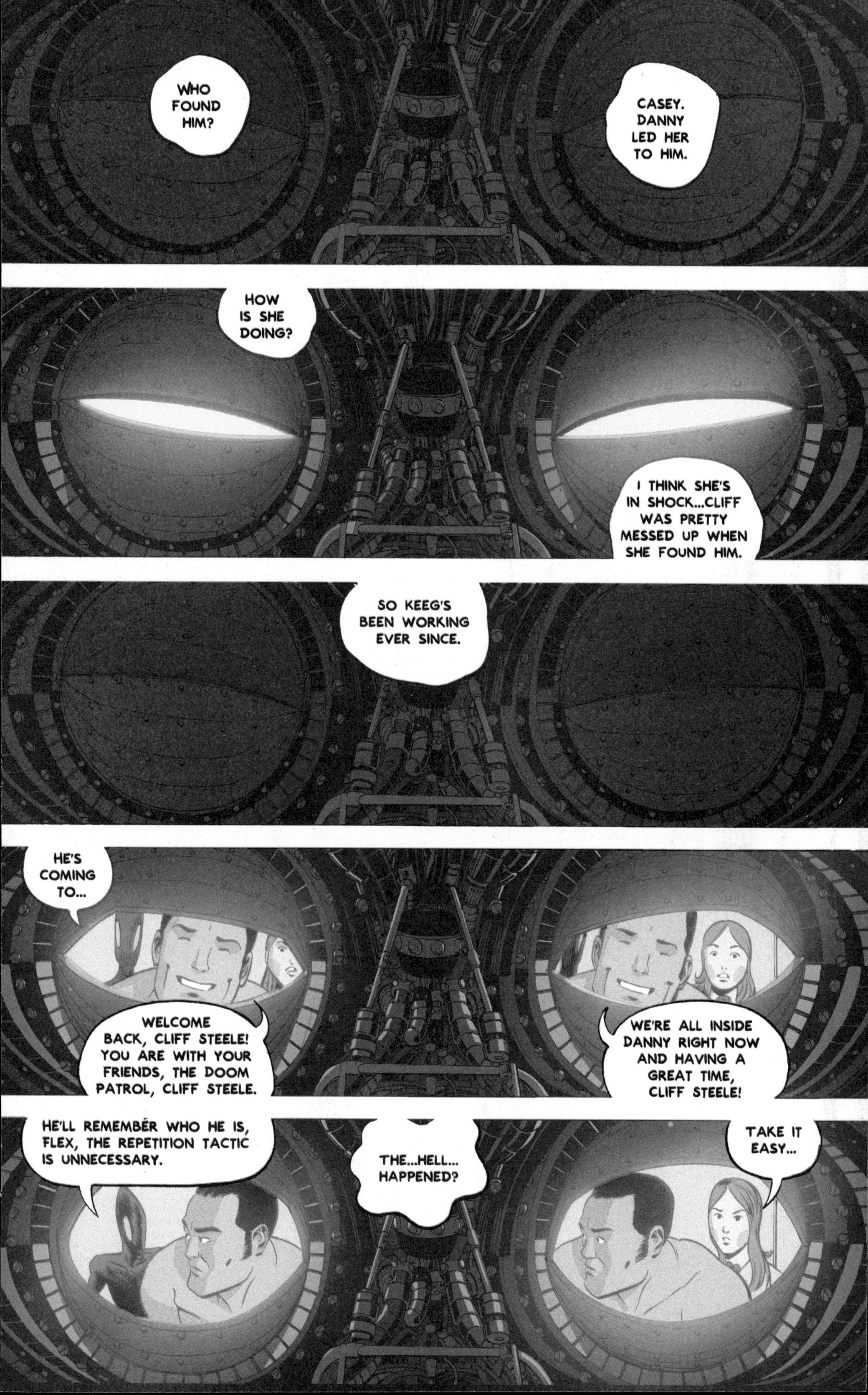
WHO FOUND HIM?
CASEY. DANNY LED HER TO HIM.
HOW IS SHE DOING?
I THINK SHE'S IN SHOCK...CLIFF WAS PRETTY MESSED UP WHEN SHE FOUND HIM.
SO KEEG'S BEEN WORKING EVER SINCE.
HE'S COMING TO...
WELCOME BACK, CLIFF STEELE! YOU ARE WITH YOUR FRIENDS, THE DOOM PATROL, CLIFF STEELE.
WE'RE ALL INSIDE DANNY RIGHT NOW AND HAVING A GREAT TIME, CLIFF STEELE!
HE'LL REMEMBER WHO HE IS, FLEX, THE REPETITION TACTIC IS UNNECESSARY.
THE...HELL... HAPPENED?
TAKE IT EASY...

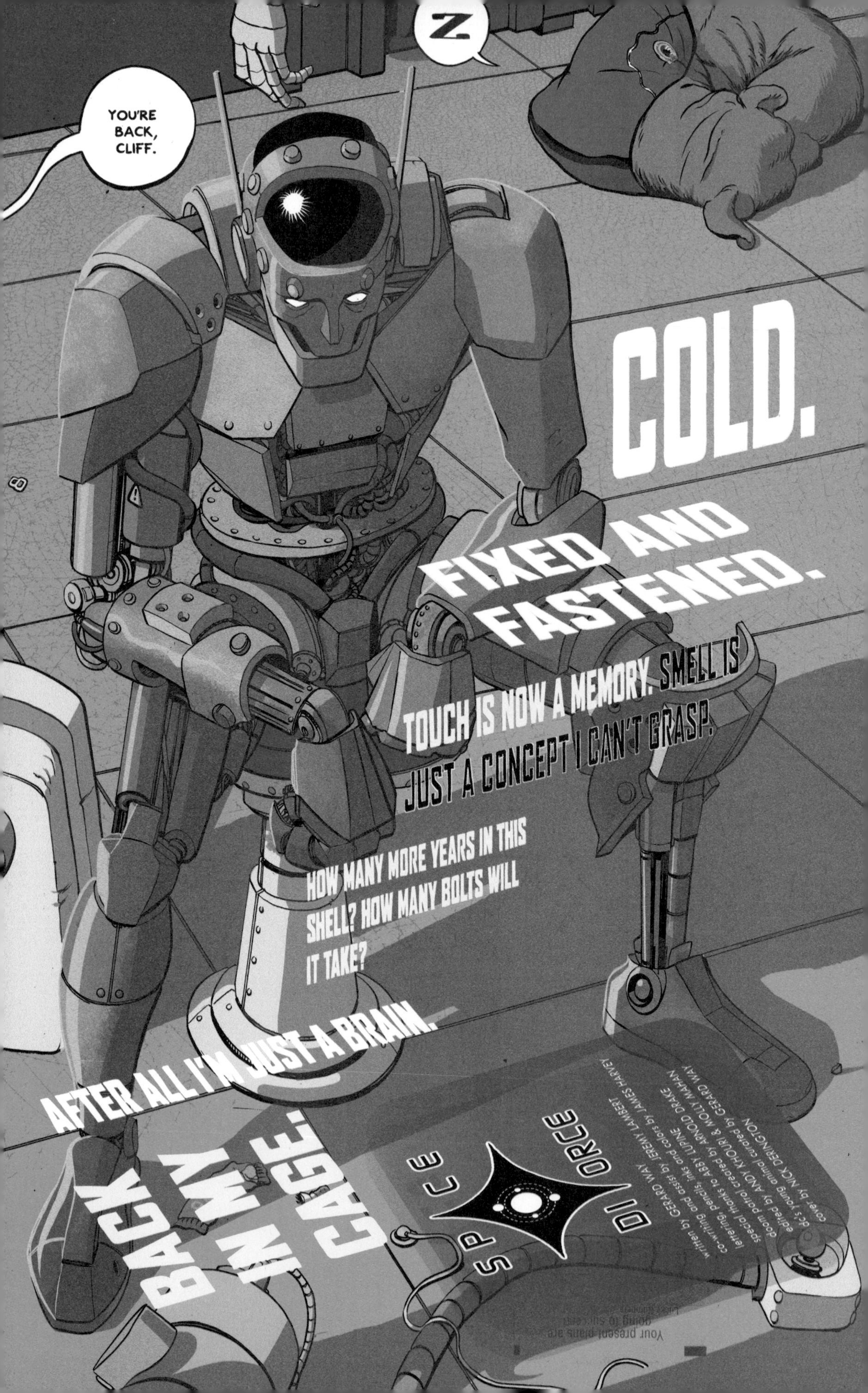
Z
YOU'RE BACK, CLIFF.
COLD.
FIXED AND FASTENED.
TOUCH IS NOW A MEMORY. SMELL IS JUST A CONCEPT I CAN'T GRASP.
HOW MANY MORE YEARS IN THIS SHELL? HOW MANY BOLTS WILL IT TAKE?
AFTER ALL I'M JUST A BRAIN.
BACK IN MY CAGE.

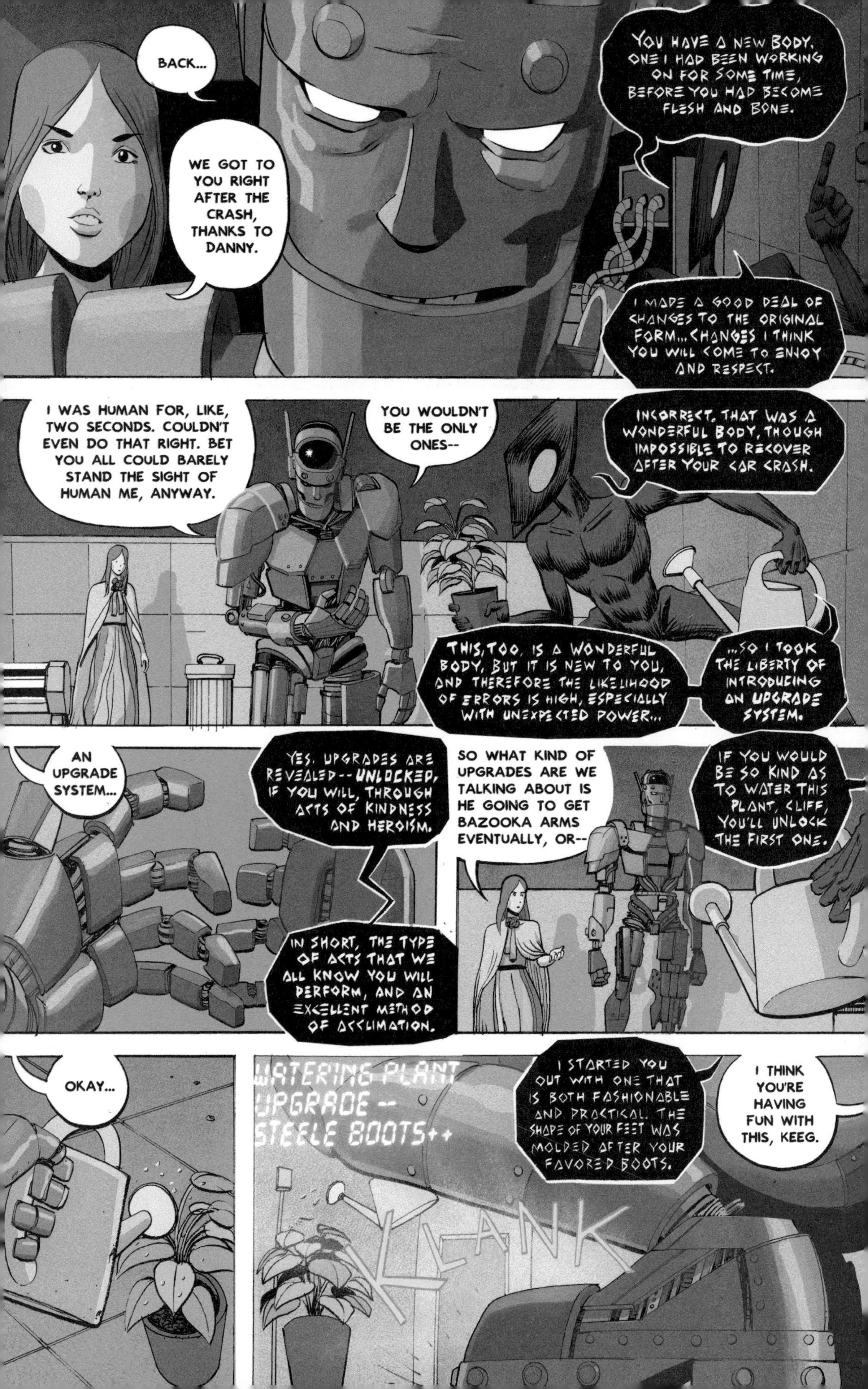
BACK...
WE GOT TO YOU RIGHT AFTER THE CRASH, THANKS TO DANNY.
YOU HAVE A NEW BODY. ONE I HAD BEEN WORKING ON FOR SOME TIME, BEFORE YOU HAD BECOME FLESH AND BONE.
I MADE A GOOD DEAL OF CHANGES TO THE ORIGINAL FORM... CHANGES I THINK YOU WILL COME TO ENJOY AND RESPECT.
I WAS HUMAN FOR, LIKE, TWO SECONDS. COULDN'T EVEN DO THAT RIGHT. BET YOU ALL COULD BARELY STAND THE SIGHT OF HUMAN ME, ANYWAY.
YOU WOULDN'T BE THE ONLY ONES--
INCORRECT. THAT WAS A WONDERFUL BODY, THOUGH IMPOSSIBLE TO RECOVER AFTER YOUR CAR CRASH.
THIS, TOO, IS A WONDERFUL BODY, BUT IT IS NEW TO YOU, AND THEREFORE THE LIKELIHOOD OF ERRORS IS HIGH, ESPECIALLY WITH UNEXPECTED POWER...
...SO I TOOK THE LIBERTY OF INTRODUCING AN UPGRADE SYSTEM.
AN UPGRADE SYSTEM...
YES. UPGRADES ARE REVEALED--UNLOCKED, IF YOU WILL, THROUGH ACTS OF KINDNESS AND HEROISM.
IN SHORT, THE TYPE OF ACTS THAT WE ALL KNOW YOU WILL PERFORM, AND AN EXCELLENT METHOD OF ACCLIMATION.
SO WHAT KIND OF UPGRADES ARE WE TALKING ABOUT IS HE GOING TO GET BAZOOKA ARMS EVENTUALLY, OR--
IF YOU WOULD BE SO KIND AS TO WATER THIS PLANT, CLIFF, YOU'LL UNLOCK THE FIRST ONE.
OKAY...
WATERING PLANT
UPGRADE--
STEELE BOOTS++
KLANK
I STARTED YOU OUT WITH ONE THAT IS BOTH FASHIONABLE AND PRACTICAL. THE SHAPE OF YOUR FEET WAS MOLDED AFTER YOUR FAVORED BOOTS.
I THINK YOU'RE HAVING FUN WITH THIS, KEEG.

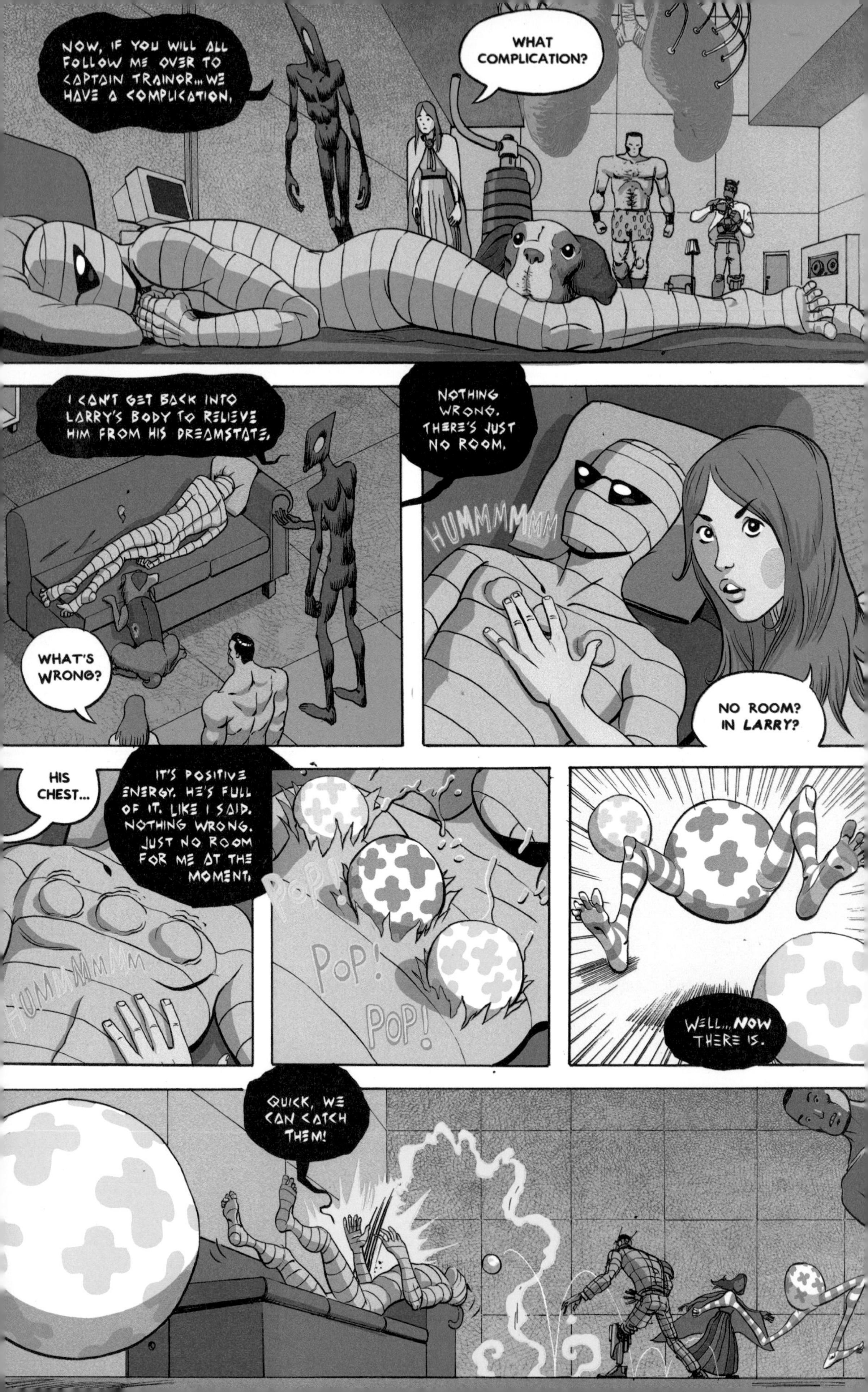
NOW, IF YOU WILL ALL FOLLOW ME OVER TO CAPTAIN TRAINOR... WE HAVE A COMPLICATION.
WHAT COMPLICATION?
I CAN'T GET BACK INTO LARRY'S BODY TO RELIEVE HIM FROM HIS DREAMSTATE.
WHAT'S WRONG?
NOTHING WRONG. THERE'S JUST NO ROOM.
HUMMMMMM
NO ROOM? IN LARRY?
HIS CHEST...
IT'S POSITIVE ENERGY. HE'S FULL OF IT. LIKE I SAID. NOTHING WRONG. JUST NO ROOM FOR ME AT THE MOMENT.
HUMMMMMM
POP!
POP!
POP!
WELL... NOW THERE IS.
QUICK, WE CAN CATCH THEM!

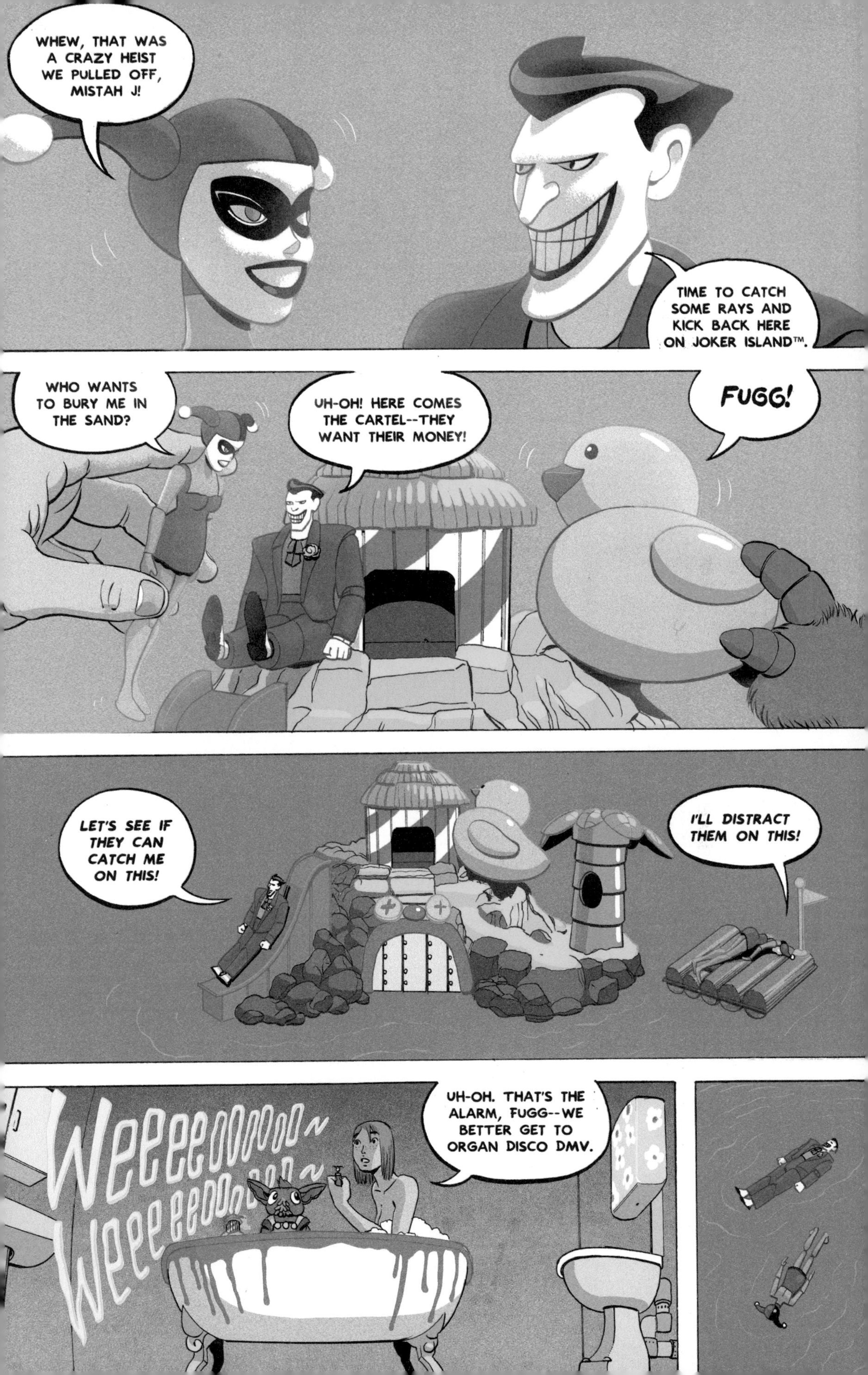
WHEW, THAT WAS A CRAZY HEIST WE PULLED OFF, MISTAH J!
TIME TO CATCH SOME RAYS AND KICK BACK HERE ON JOKER ISLAND™.
WHO WANTS TO BURY ME IN THE SAND?
UH-OH! HERE COMES THE CARTEL--THEY WANT THEIR MONEY!
FUGG!
LET'S SEE IF THEY CAN CATCH ME ON THIS!
I'LL DISTRACT THEM ON THIS!
WEEEEOOOOOO~
WEEEEEOOOOOOO~
UH-OH. THAT'S THE ALARM, FUGG--WE BETTER GET TO ORGAN DISCO DMV.

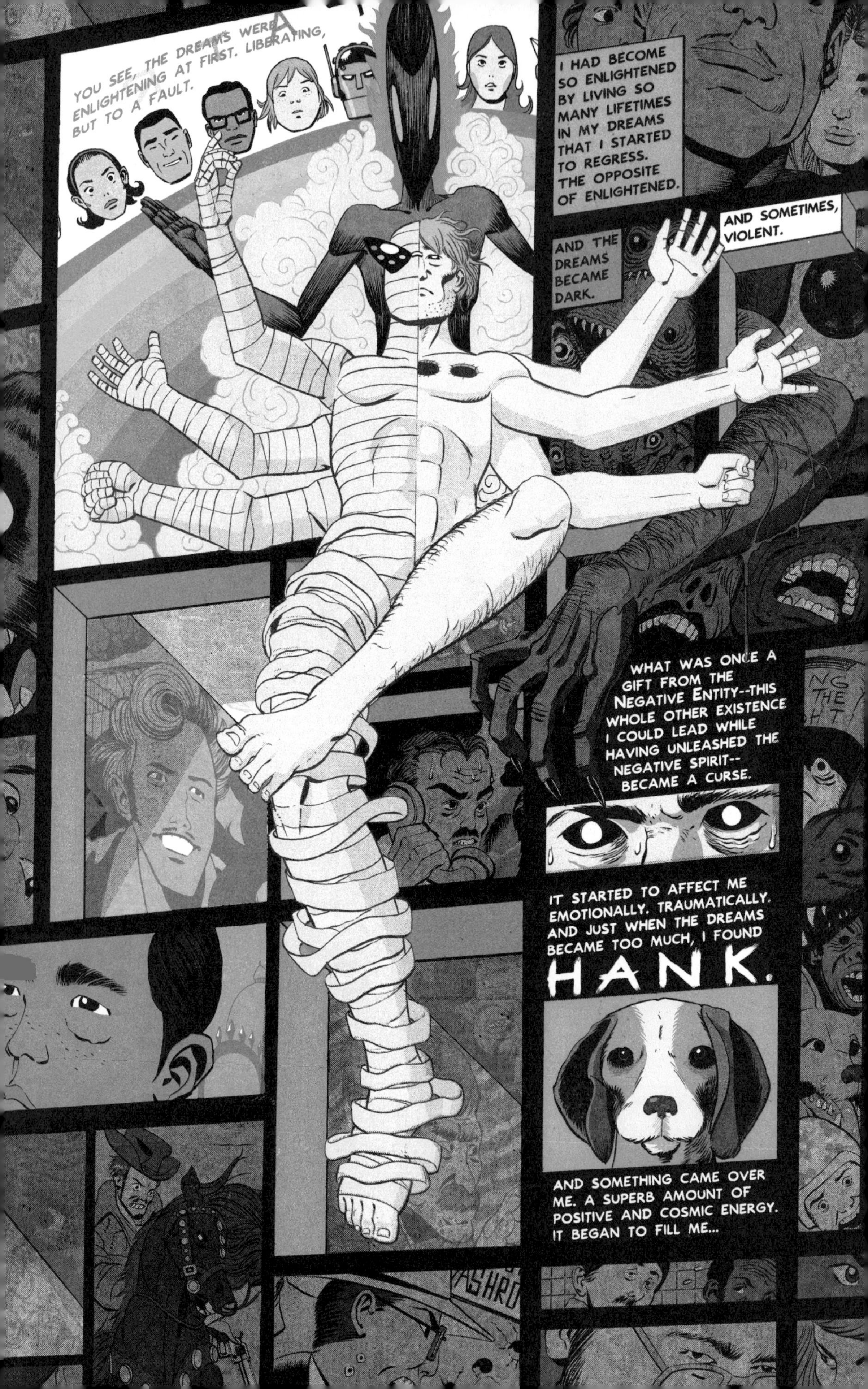
YOU SEE, THE DREAMS WERE A ENLIGHTENING AT FIRST. LIBERATING, BUT TO A FAULT.
I HAD BECOME SO ENLIGHTENED BY LIVING SO MANY LIFETIMES IN MY DREAMS THAT I STARTED TO REGRESS. THE OPPOSITE OF ENLIGHTENED.
AND THE DREAMS BECAME DARK.
AND SOMETIMES, VIOLENT.
WHAT WAS ONCE A GIFT FROM THE NEGATIVE ENTITY--THIS WHOLE OTHER EXISTENCE I COULD LEAD WHILE HAVING UNLEASHED THE NEGATIVE SPIRIT--BECAME A CURSE.
IT STARTED TO AFFECT ME EMOTIONALLY. TRAUMATICALLY. AND JUST WHEN THE DREAMS BECAME TOO MUCH, I FOUND
HANK.
AND SOMETHING CAME OVER ME. A SUPERB AMOUNT OF POSITIVE AND COSMIC ENERGY. IT BEGAN TO FILL ME...

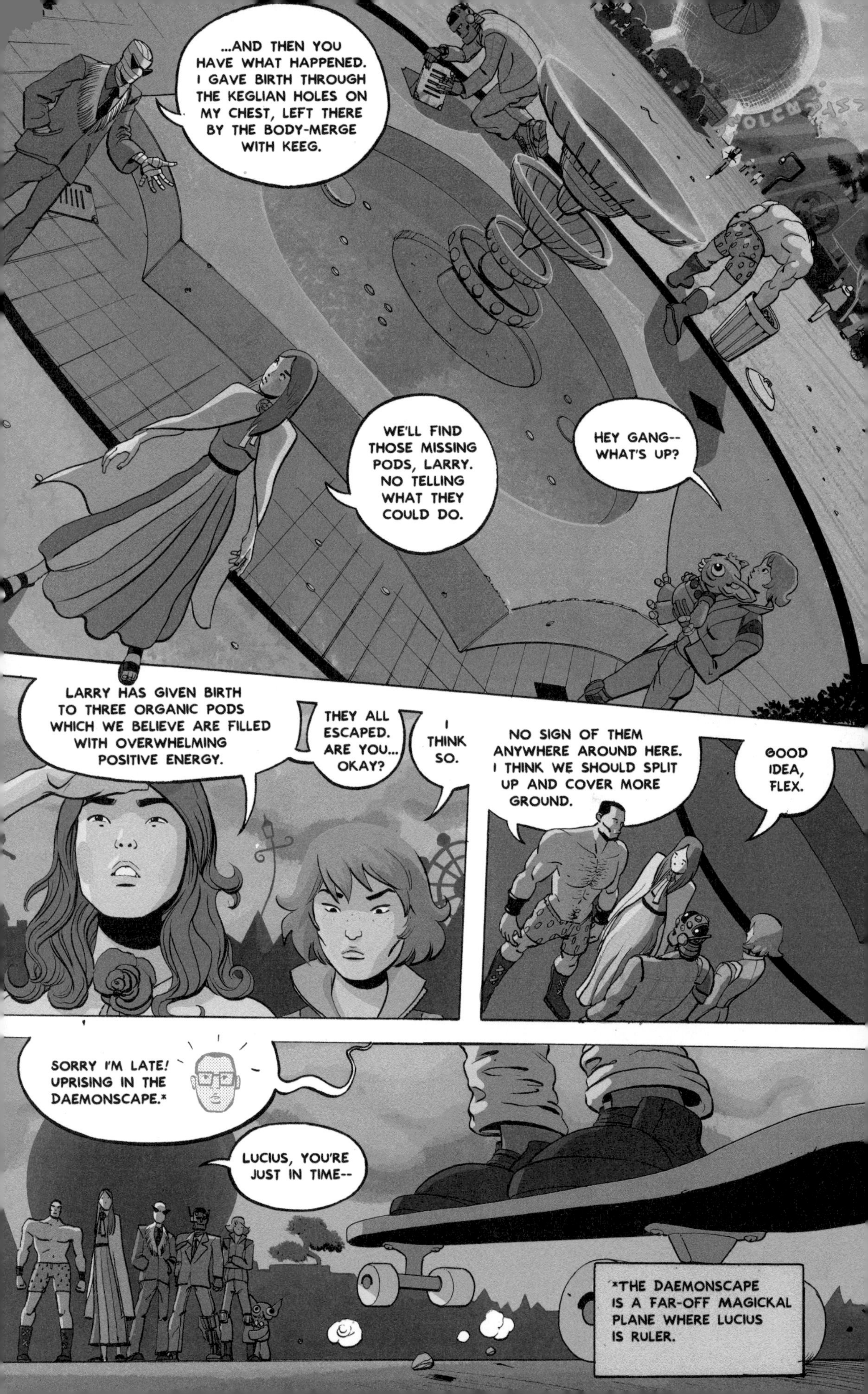
...AND THEN YOU HAVE WHAT HAPPENED. I GAVE BIRTH THROUGH THE KEGLIAN HOLES ON MY CHEST, LEFT THERE BY THE BODY-MERGE WITH KEEG.
WE'LL FIND THOSE MISSING PODS, LARRY. NO TELLING WHAT THEY COULD DO.
HEY GANG-- WHAT'S UP?
LARRY HAS GIVEN BIRTH TO THREE ORGANIC PODS WHICH WE BELIEVE ARE FILLED WITH OVERWHELMING POSITIVE ENERGY.
THEY ALL ESCAPED. ARE YOU... OKAY?
I THINK SO.
NO SIGN OF THEM ANYWHERE AROUND HERE. I THINK WE SHOULD SPLIT UP AND COVER MORE GROUND.
GOOD IDEA, FLEX.
SORRY I'M LATE! UPRISING IN THE DAEMONSCAPE.*
LUCIUS, YOU'RE JUST IN TIME--
*THE DAEMONSCAPE IS A FAR-OFF MAGICKAL PLANE WHERE LUCIUS IS RULER.

DOOM PATROL-- LET'S FIND THOSE PODS!!

A GUIDE TO

Danny Land

• FUGG PLANET

Fugg comes from this delightful, soft, pink and green planet. In order to preserve the planet, Casey had it miniaturized and stored in Dannyland. To get there, park patrons are miniaturized, too, in an attraction called *"Fugg, I Shrunk the Guests."* On the planet, we see that all Fuggs are different colors and they reproduce in a manner that's unprintable. A

• TRAIN OF THOUGHT

No grinding to a halt. No end of the line. Have a seat and forget where you're going. No frets here, it'll only stop when you've finished your think. B

• WANDERLAND

It's a vast desert where people can wander and find themselves. If you like, you can go into *"Fugg, I Shrunk the Guests"* and shrink yourself beforehand. The smaller you make yourself, the more vast the desert becomes! At the end of the desert is swingin' Cabana Island. It's pretty cool and all, but if you reach it as a tiny person, it becomes the enormous **CABANALAND.** What looked like a regular unattended Mai Tai is in fact a giant lake in a cocktail glass, and the pineapple slice in the middle is a far-out spot named "Acceptance Island." The plastic poolside rocks are now treacherous mountain peaks upon which you can have a spiritual experience, since there's a monastery on the top. Flex went there once, regular-sized, and nearly knocked the monastery over. Now they worship him as a god. Leopard print, everywhere.

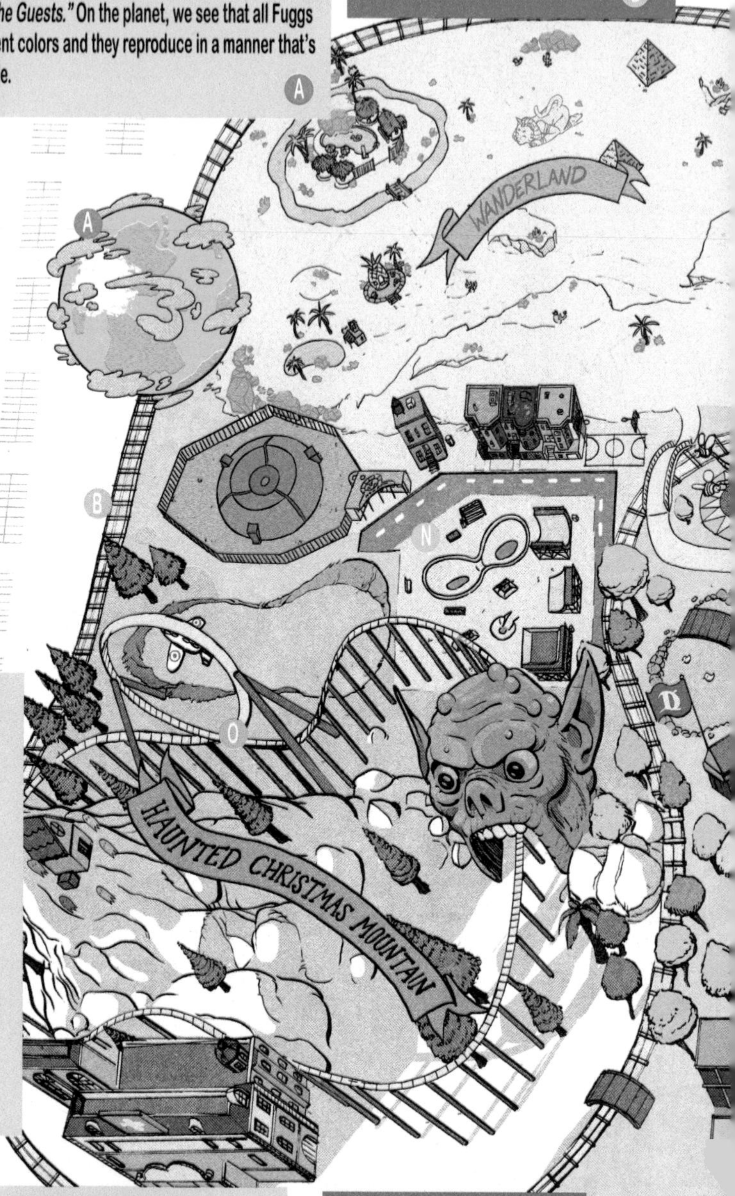

A
WANDERLAND
B
N
O
HAUNTED CHRISTMAS MOUNTAIN
D

• HAUNTED CHRISTMAS MOUNTAIN

Sure, Haunted Christmas Mountain has that charming, handmade, alpine aesthetic, but don't let it fool ya. In the universe of *St. Michael's Children's Hospital Jamboree Fighter Squadron**, the hospital is situated at the foot of this mountain, and the mountain is haunted by the ghosts of the kids they couldn't save. Cruelly, there's a gingerbread house at the top of the mountain which the ghost kids want to eat but can't, and they can't find their way back down the mountain, either. So they're stuck in this house surrounded by gingerbread they can't eat. Forever. Honestly, the comic goes to some pretty dark places and you shouldn't read it.

**See: Danny Comics #38 - #233.*

• KING OF THE BEES Q

Are YOU King of the Bees? No. You are not. Currently that's Lotion. But give it a go! Usurp the throne!

• ST. MICHAEL'S CHILDREN'S HOSPITAL JAMBOREE FIGHTER SQUADRON LOOP-DE-LOOP BARREL ROLL BONANZA O

You haven't had a roller coaster like this, no way no how! Hop in your fighter jet, it's time to take down Torminox!

•SKATE PARK

Perk up your Aunt Nells and blast your type of metal, it's more than welcome here. Lucius and Lotion run the place and welcome all to this wonderland of skate. N

P

• PARKING LOT OF INFINITE EMPTINESS

Where the spaces are wide and spots aplenty. There is no end to this lot. Really. It just keeps going, right off into the horizon. Don't try it, love. It really does go on forever. P

• DANNY THE MAIN STREET

Go back in time to late 20th Century small-town America! All your pappy's favorite stores just the way he remembered 'em, dressed in a way that, deep down, your pappy has never truly been okay with.

- Army Navy
- Bona Drag (formerly "Mike's")
- BURLESK (formerly "Steve's")
- Butch's Flowers
- CASH
- Corn Dog Emporium

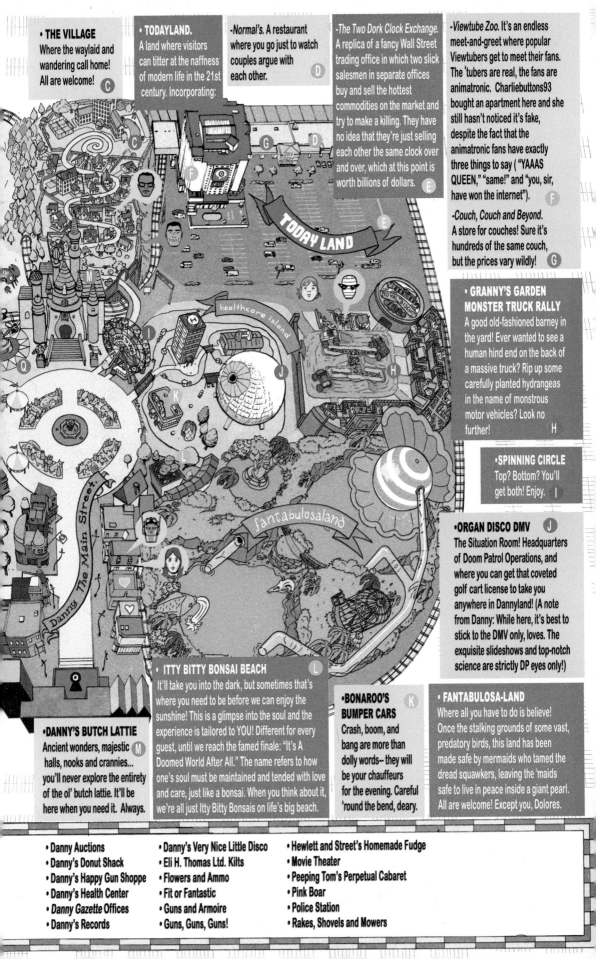

• THE VILLAGE
Where the waylaid and wandering call home! All are welcome! C

• TODAYLAND.
A land where visitors can titter at the naffness of modern life in the 21st century. Incorporating:

-*Normal's.* A restaurant where you go just to watch couples argue with each other. D

-*The Two Dork Clock Exchange.* A replica of a fancy Wall Street trading office in which two slick salesmen in separate offices buy and sell the hottest commodities on the market and try to make a killing. They have no idea that they're just selling each other the same clock over and over, which at this point is worth billions of dollars. E

-*Viewtube Zoo.* It's an endless meet-and-greet where popular Viewtubers get to meet their fans. The 'tubers are real, the fans are animatronic. Charliebuttons93 bought an apartment here and she still hasn't noticed it's fake, despite the fact that the animatronic fans have exactly three things to say ("YAAAS QUEEN," "same!" and "you, sir, have won the internet"). F

-*Couch, Couch and Beyond.* A store for couches! Sure it's hundreds of the same couch, but the prices vary wildly! G

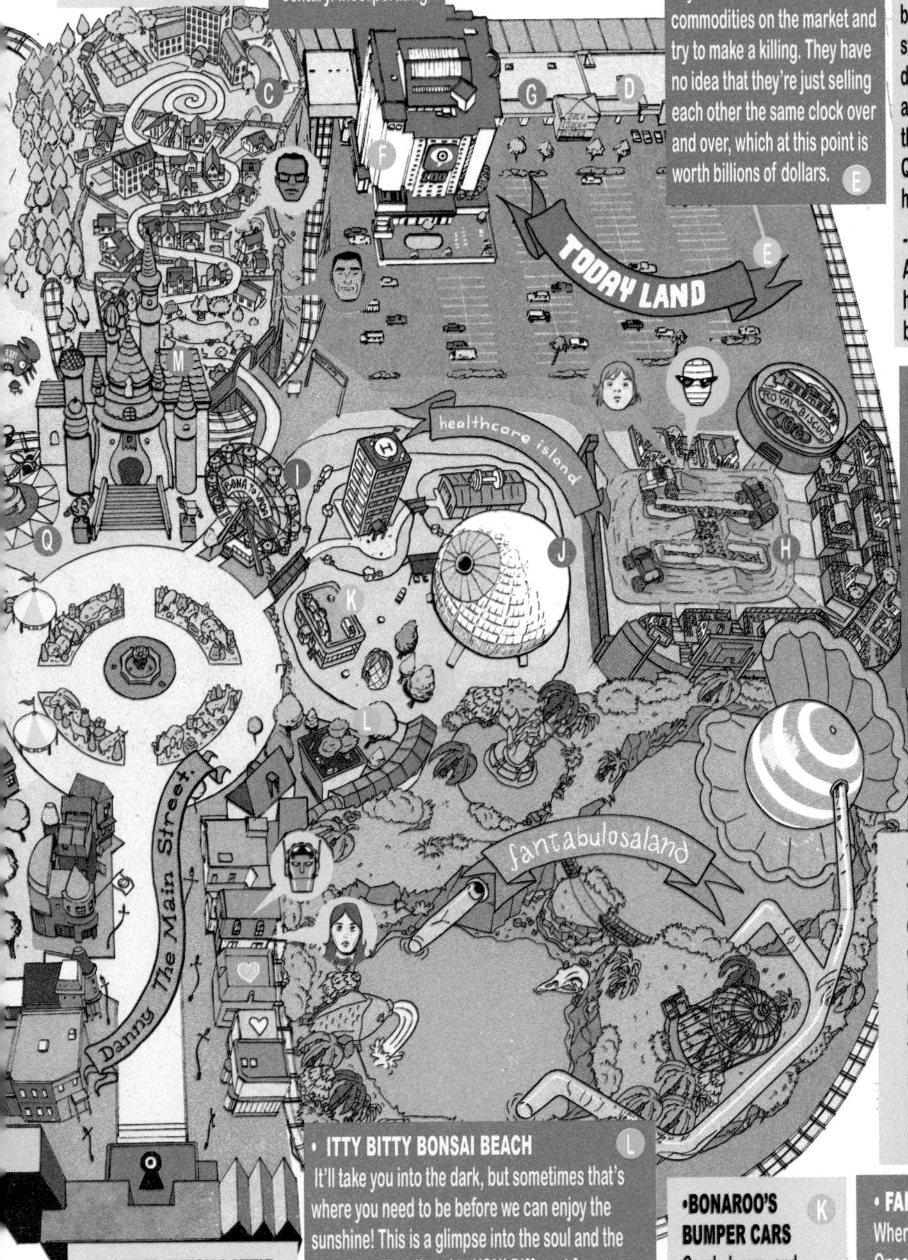
TODAY LAND
healthcare island
fantabulosaland
Danny The Main Street
ROYAL BISCUIT

• GRANNY'S GARDEN MONSTER TRUCK RALLY
A good old-fashioned barney in the yard! Ever wanted to see a human hind end on the back of a massive truck? Rip up some carefully planted hydrangeas in the name of monstrous motor vehicles? Look no further! H

•SPINNING CIRCLE
Top? Bottom? You'll get both! Enjoy. I

•ORGAN DISCO DMV J
The Situation Room! Headquarters of Doom Patrol Operations, and where you can get that coveted golf cart license to take you anywhere in Dannyland! (A note from Danny: While here, it's best to stick to the DMV only, loves. The exquisite slideshows and top-notch science are strictly DP eyes only!)

• ITTY BITTY BONSAI BEACH L
It'll take you into the dark, but sometimes that's where you need to be before we can enjoy the sunshine! This is a glimpse into the soul and the experience is tailored to YOU! Different for every guest, until we reach the famed finale: "It's A Doomed World After All." The name refers to how one's soul must be maintained and tended with love and care, just like a bonsai. When you think about it, we're all just Itty Bitty Bonsais on life's big beach.

•BONAROO'S BUMPER CARS K
Crash, boom, and bang are more than dolly words-- they will be your chauffeurs for the evening. Careful 'round the bend, deary.

• FANTABULOSA-LAND
Where all you have to do is believe! Once the stalking grounds of some vast, predatory birds, this land has been made safe by mermaids who tamed the dread squawkers, leaving the 'maids safe to live in peace inside a giant pearl. All are welcome! Except you, Dolores.

•DANNY'S BUTCH LATTIE M
Ancient wonders, majestic halls, nooks and crannies... you'll never explore the entirety of the ol' butch lattie. It'll be here when you need it. Always.

- Danny Auctions
- Danny's Donut Shack
- Danny's Happy Gun Shoppe
- Danny's Health Center
- *Danny Gazette* Offices
- Danny's Records
- Danny's Very Nice Little Disco
- Eli H. Thomas Ltd. Kilts
- Flowers and Ammo
- Fit or Fantastic
- Guns and Armoire
- Guns, Guns, Guns!
- Hewlett and Street's Homemade Fudge
- Movie Theater
- Peeping Tom's Perpetual Cabaret
- Pink Boar
- Police Station
- Rakes, Shovels and Mowers

CHIME CHIME CHIME

ATTENTION DOOM PATROL—RITA FARR HERE—

DANNY REQUESTS YOUR PRESENCE UP TOP IN THE AMBULANCE—

THERE IS AN EMERGENCY THAT REQUIRES OUR IMMEDIATE ATTENTION!

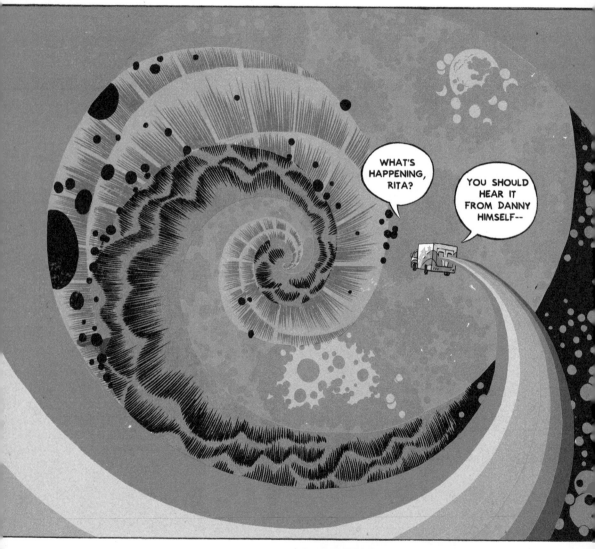

WHAT'S HAPPENING, RITA?

YOU SHOULD HEAR IT FROM DANNY HIMSELF—

ONE PLANET DREAMS FAR UP ABOVE~ THEN THERE WAS A RIFT A FIGHT AND A TIFF THE PLANETS ARE NOW OUT OF LOVE~

SPACE DIVORCE!

SPACE DIVORCE?

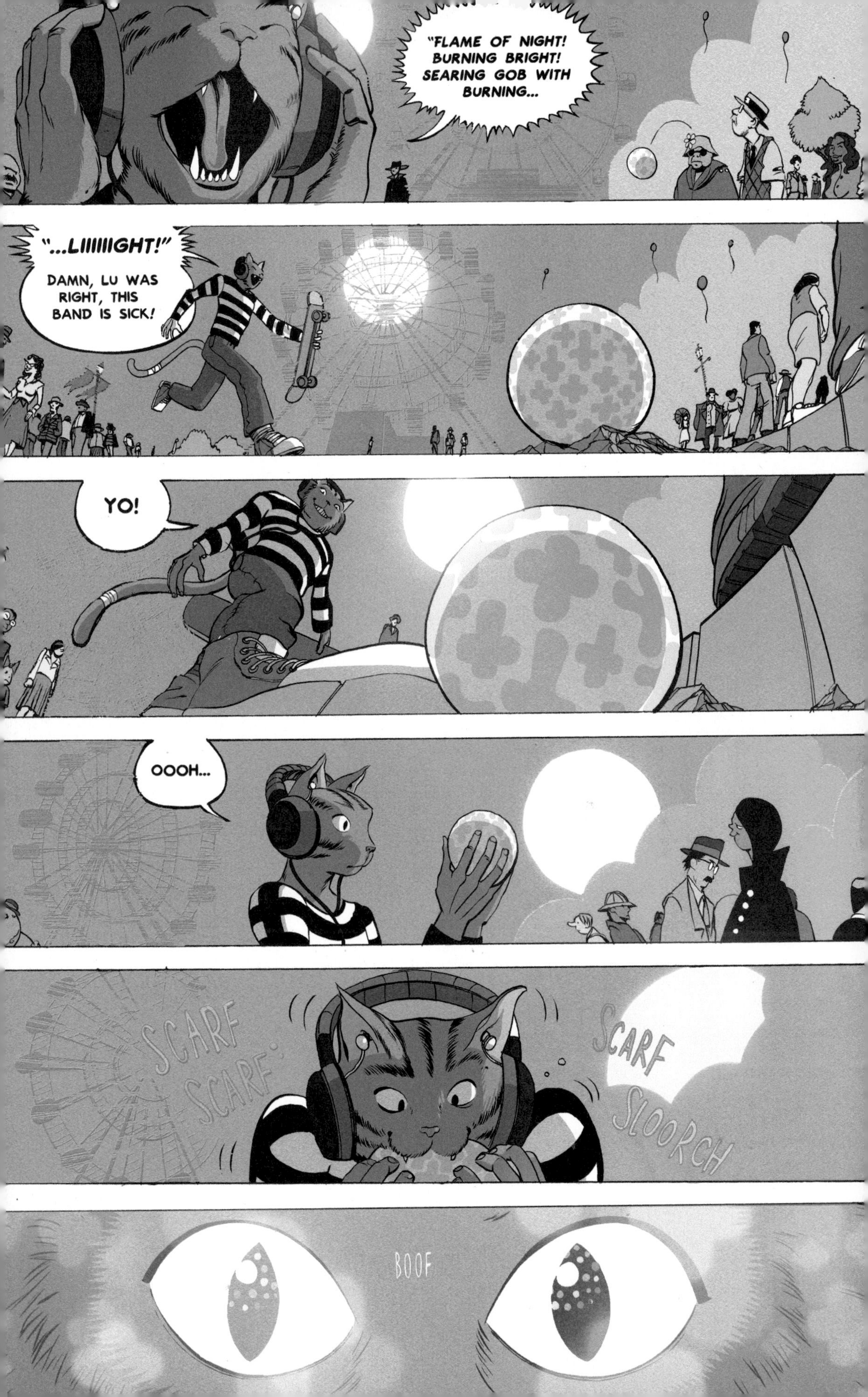
"FLAME OF NIGHT! BURNING BRIGHT! SEARING GOB WITH BURNING...
"...LIIIIIIGHT!"
DAMN, LU WAS RIGHT, THIS BAND IS SICK!
YO!
OOOH...
SCARF
SCARF
SCARF
SLOORCH
BOOF

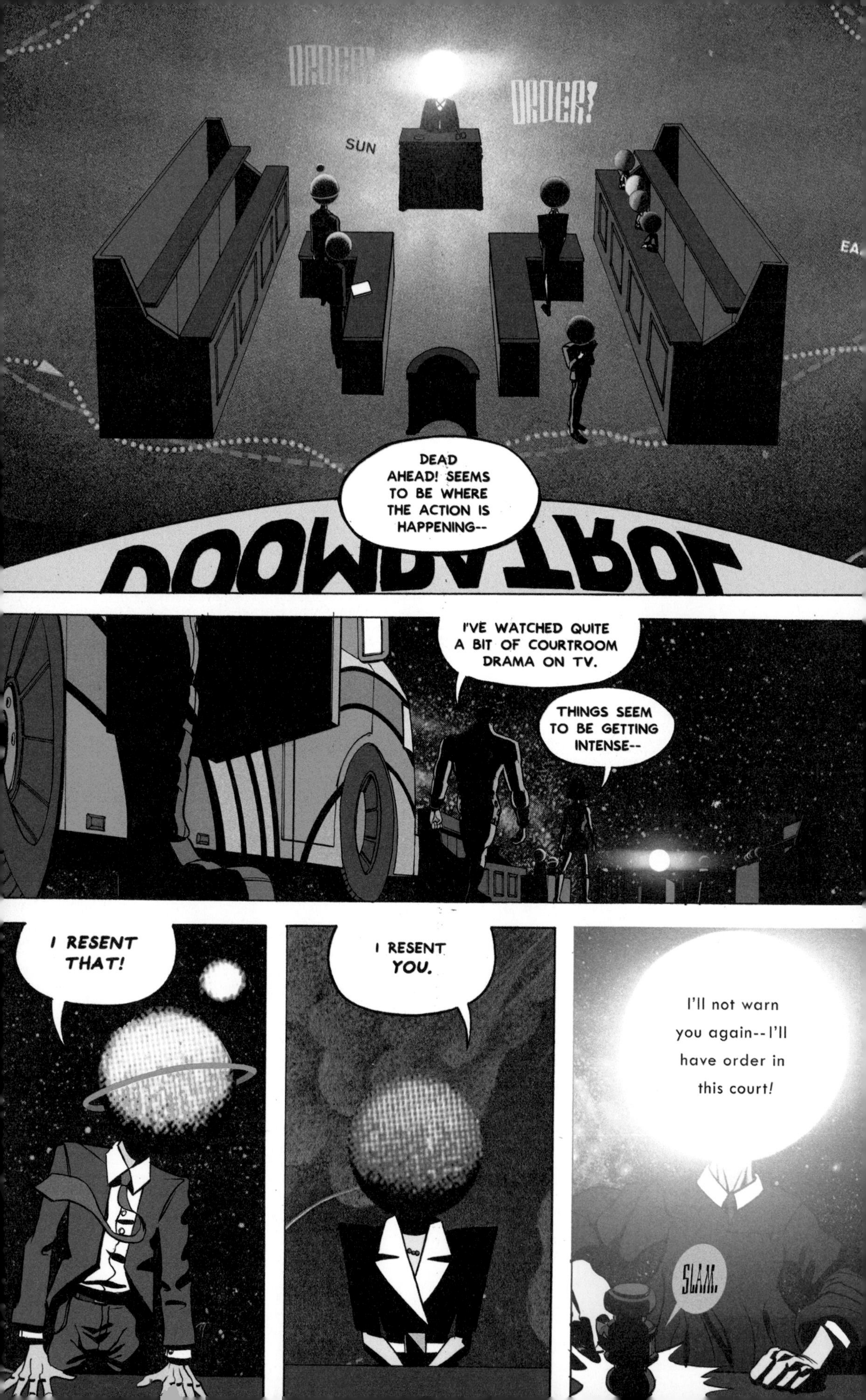
ORDER!
ORDER!
SUN
DEAD AHEAD! SEEMS TO BE WHERE THE ACTION IS HAPPENING--
I'VE WATCHED QUITE A BIT OF COURTROOM DRAMA ON TV.
THINGS SEEM TO BE GETTING INTENSE--
I RESENT THAT!
I RESENT YOU.
I'll not warn you again--I'll have order in this court!
SLAM.

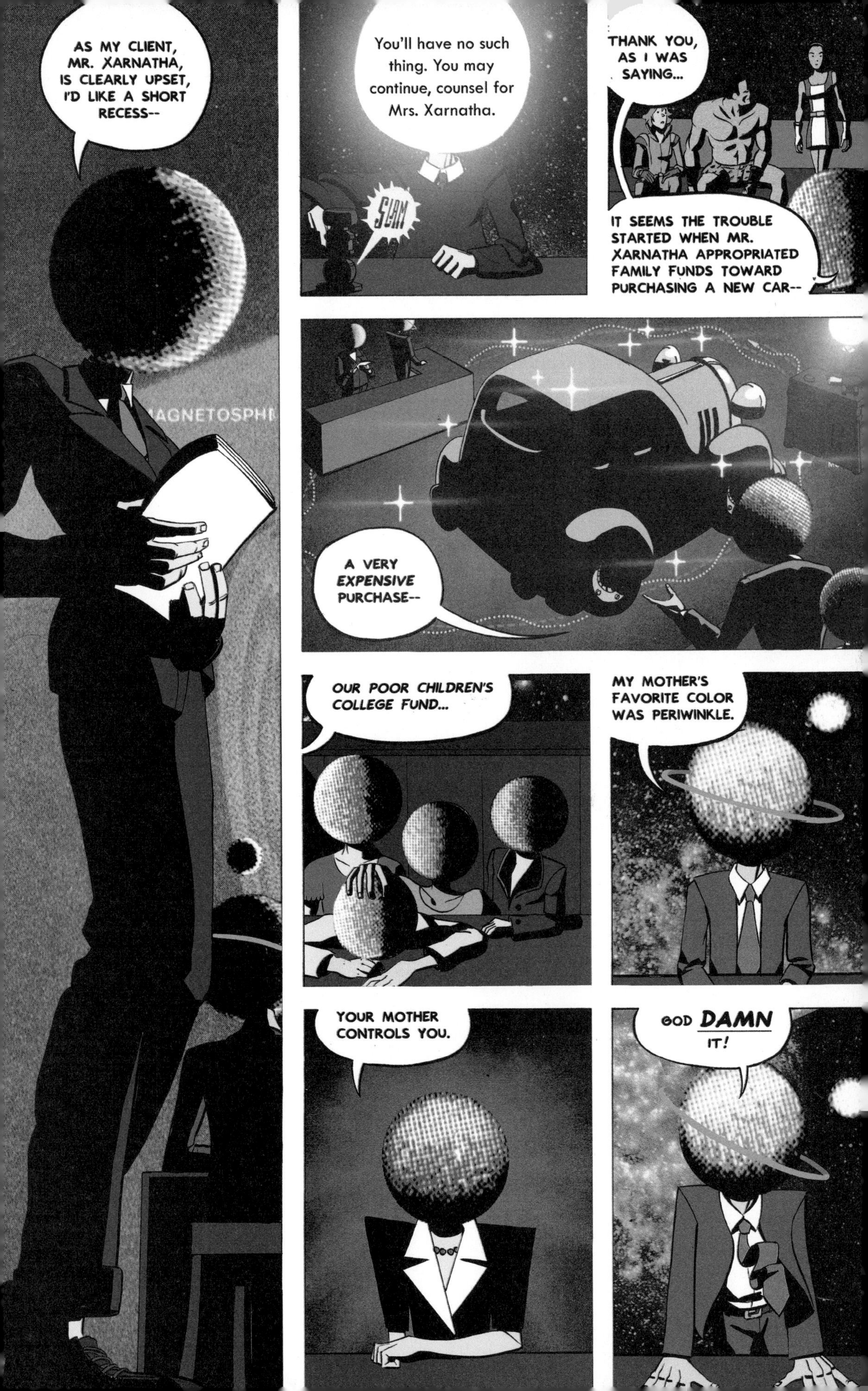
AS MY CLIENT, MR. XARNATHA, IS CLEARLY UPSET, I'D LIKE A SHORT RECESS--
SLAM
You'll have no such thing. You may continue, counsel for Mrs. Xarnatha.
THANK YOU, AS I WAS SAYING...
IT SEEMS THE TROUBLE STARTED WHEN MR. XARNATHA APPROPRIATED FAMILY FUNDS TOWARD PURCHASING A NEW CAR--
A VERY *EXPENSIVE* PURCHASE--
OUR POOR CHILDREN'S COLLEGE FUND...
MY MOTHER'S FAVORITE COLOR WAS PERIWINKLE.
YOUR MOTHER CONTROLS YOU.
GOD **DAMN** IT!

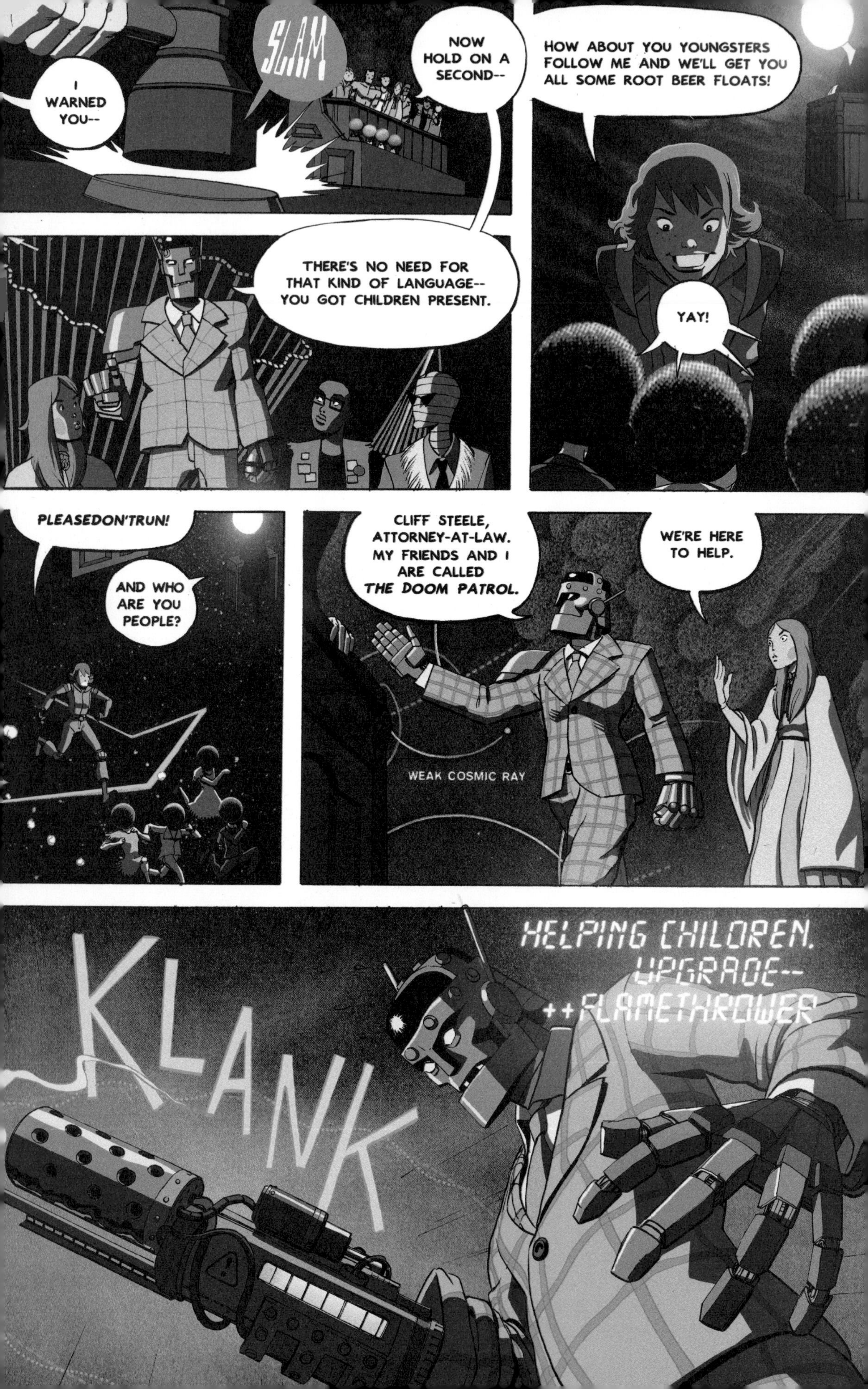
I WARNED YOU--
SLAM
NOW HOLD ON A SECOND--
THERE'S NO NEED FOR THAT KIND OF LANGUAGE-- YOU GOT CHILDREN PRESENT.
HOW ABOUT YOU YOUNGSTERS FOLLOW ME AND WE'LL GET YOU ALL SOME ROOT BEER FLOATS!
YAY!
PLEASEDON'TRUN!
AND WHO ARE YOU PEOPLE?
CLIFF STEELE, ATTORNEY-AT-LAW. MY FRIENDS AND I ARE CALLED THE DOOM PATROL.
WE'RE HERE TO HELP.
WEAK COSMIC RAY
KLANK
HELPING CHILDREN. UPGRADE-- ++FLAMETHROWER

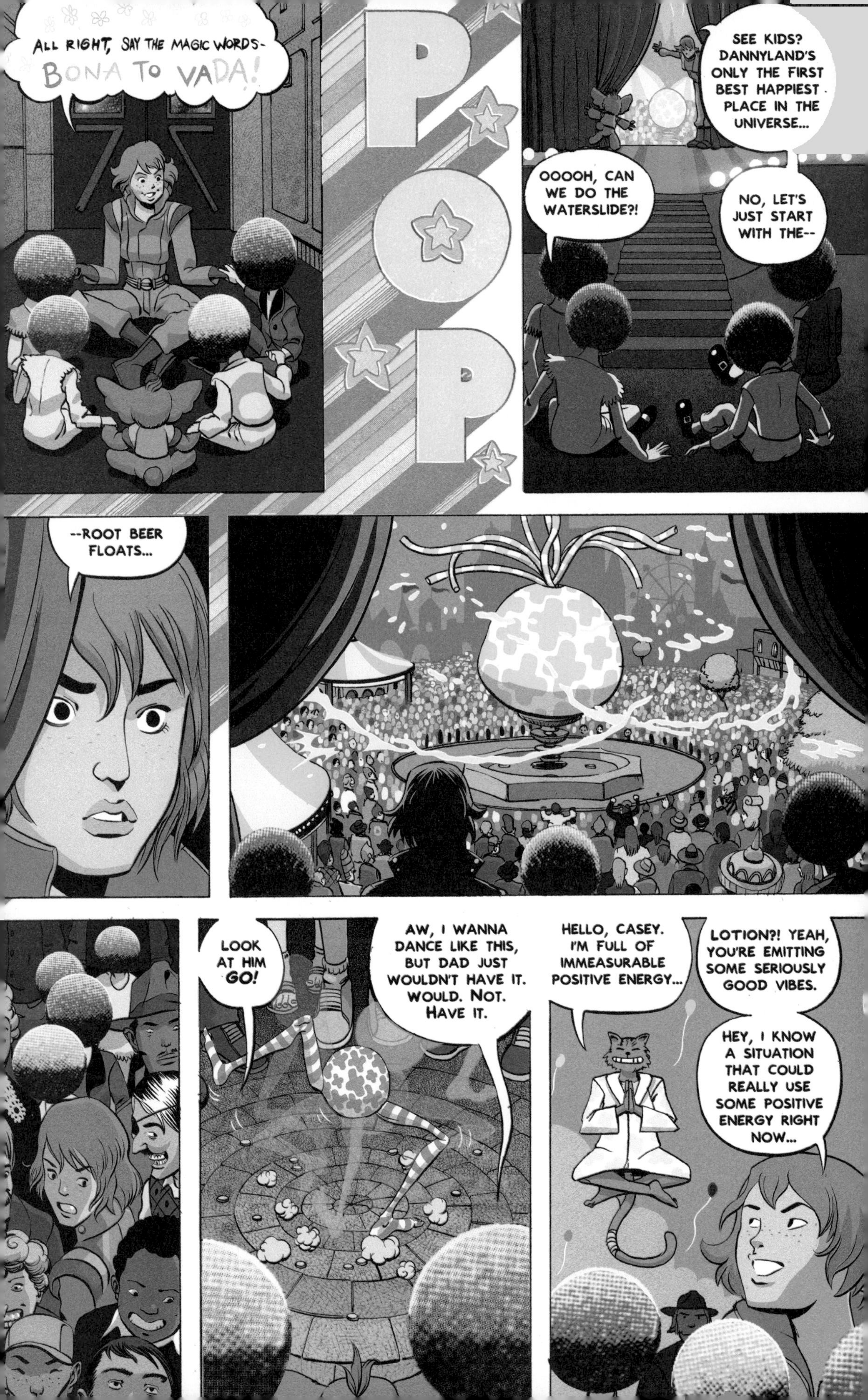
ALL RIGHT, SAY THE MAGIC WORDS-
BONA TO VADA!
POP
SEE KIDS? DANNYLAND'S ONLY THE FIRST BEST HAPPIEST PLACE IN THE UNIVERSE...
OOOOH, CAN WE DO THE WATERSLIDE?!
NO, LET'S JUST START WITH THE--
--ROOT BEER FLOATS...
LOOK AT HIM GO!
AW, I WANNA DANCE LIKE THIS, BUT DAD JUST WOULDN'T HAVE IT. WOULD. NOT. HAVE IT.
HELLO, CASEY. I'M FULL OF IMMEASURABLE POSITIVE ENERGY...
LOTION?! YEAH, YOU'RE EMITTING SOME SERIOUSLY GOOD VIBES.
HEY, I KNOW A SITUATION THAT COULD REALLY USE SOME POSITIVE ENERGY RIGHT NOW...

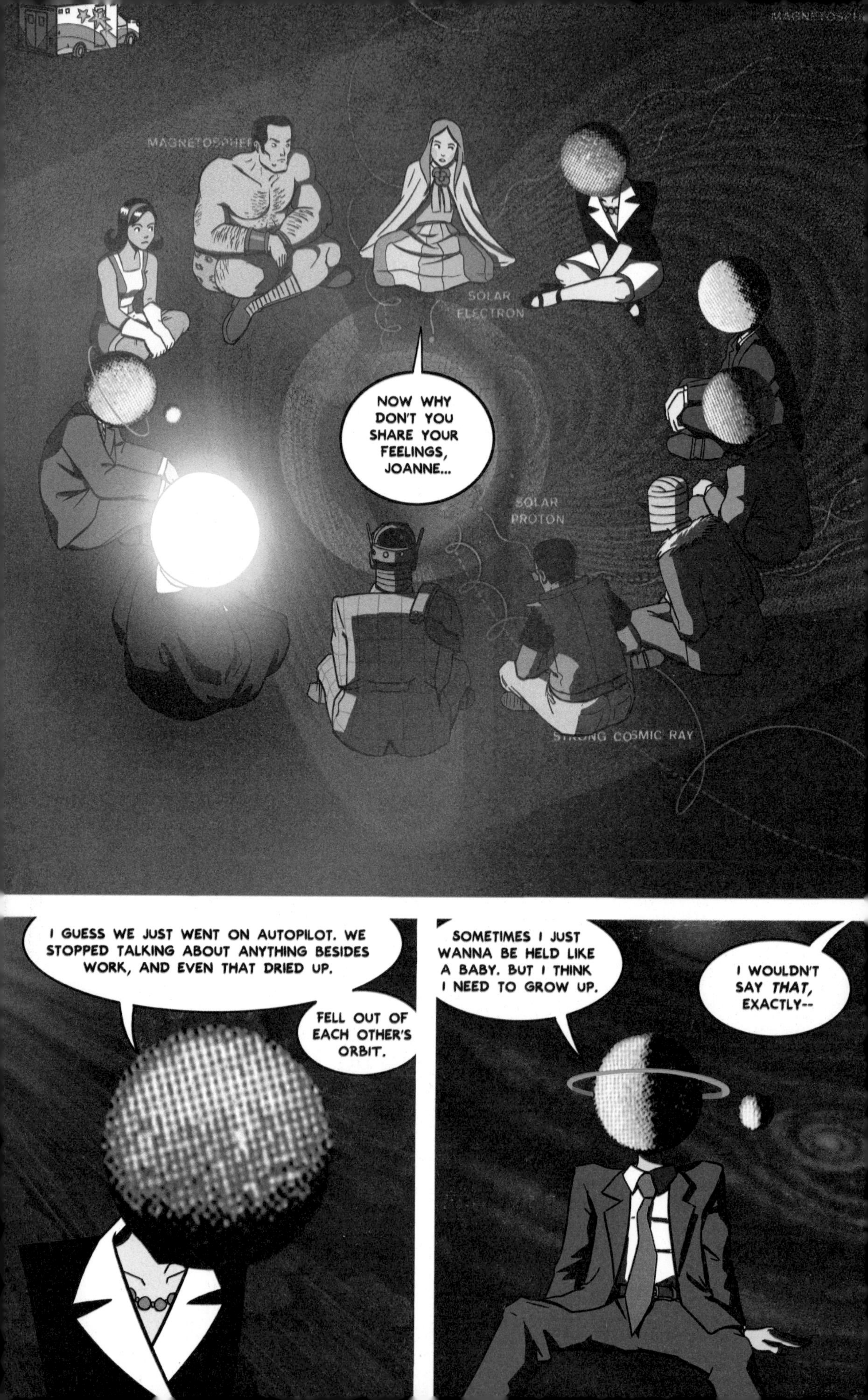
SOLAR ELECTRON
NOW WHY DON'T YOU SHARE YOUR FEELINGS, JOANNE...
SOLAR PROTON
COSMIC RAY
I GUESS WE JUST WENT ON AUTOPILOT. WE STOPPED TALKING ABOUT ANYTHING BESIDES WORK, AND EVEN THAT DRIED UP.
FELL OUT OF EACH OTHER'S ORBIT.
SOMETIMES I JUST WANNA BE HELD LIKE A BABY. BUT I THINK I NEED TO GROW UP.
I WOULDN'T SAY *THAT*, EXACTLY--

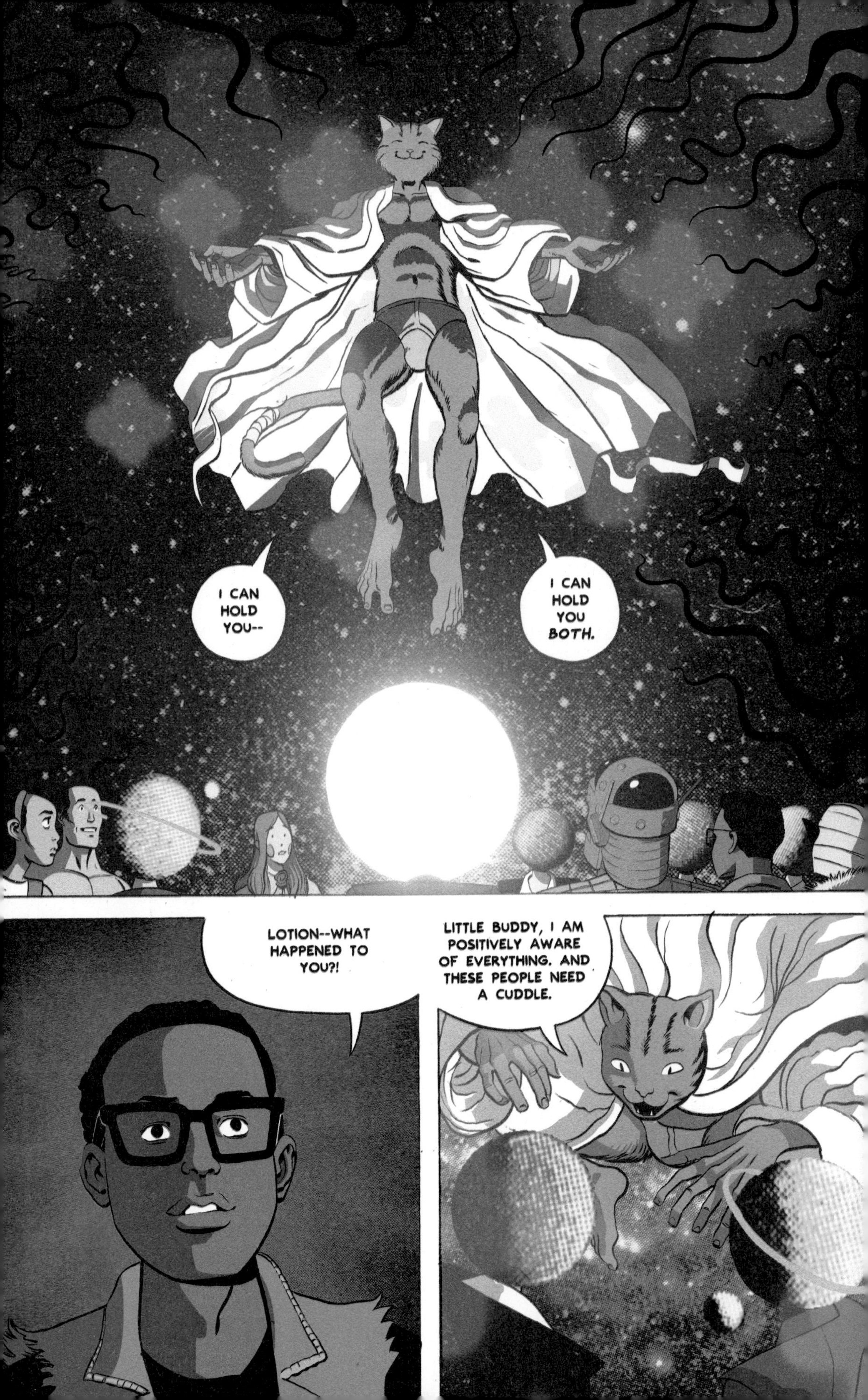
I CAN HOLD YOU--
I CAN HOLD YOU BOTH.
LOTION--WHAT HAPPENED TO YOU?!
LITTLE BUDDY, I AM POSITIVELY AWARE OF EVERYTHING. AND THESE PEOPLE NEED A CUDDLE.

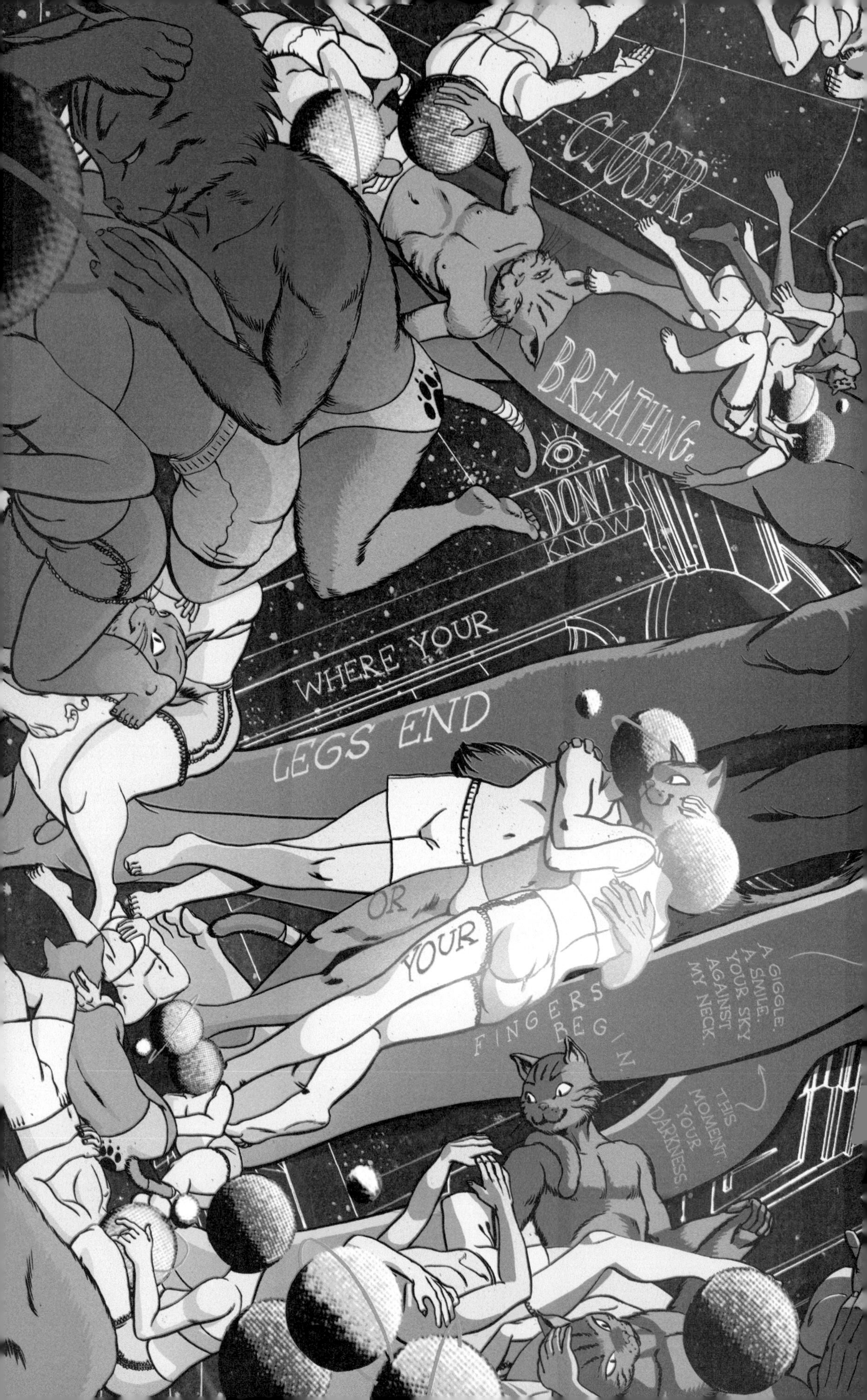

CLOSER.
BREATHING.
DONT KNOW
WHERE YOUR
LEGS END
OR YOUR
FINGERS BEGIN.
A GIGGLE. A SMILE. YOUR SKY AGAINST MY NECK.
THIS MOMENT. YOUR DARKNESS.

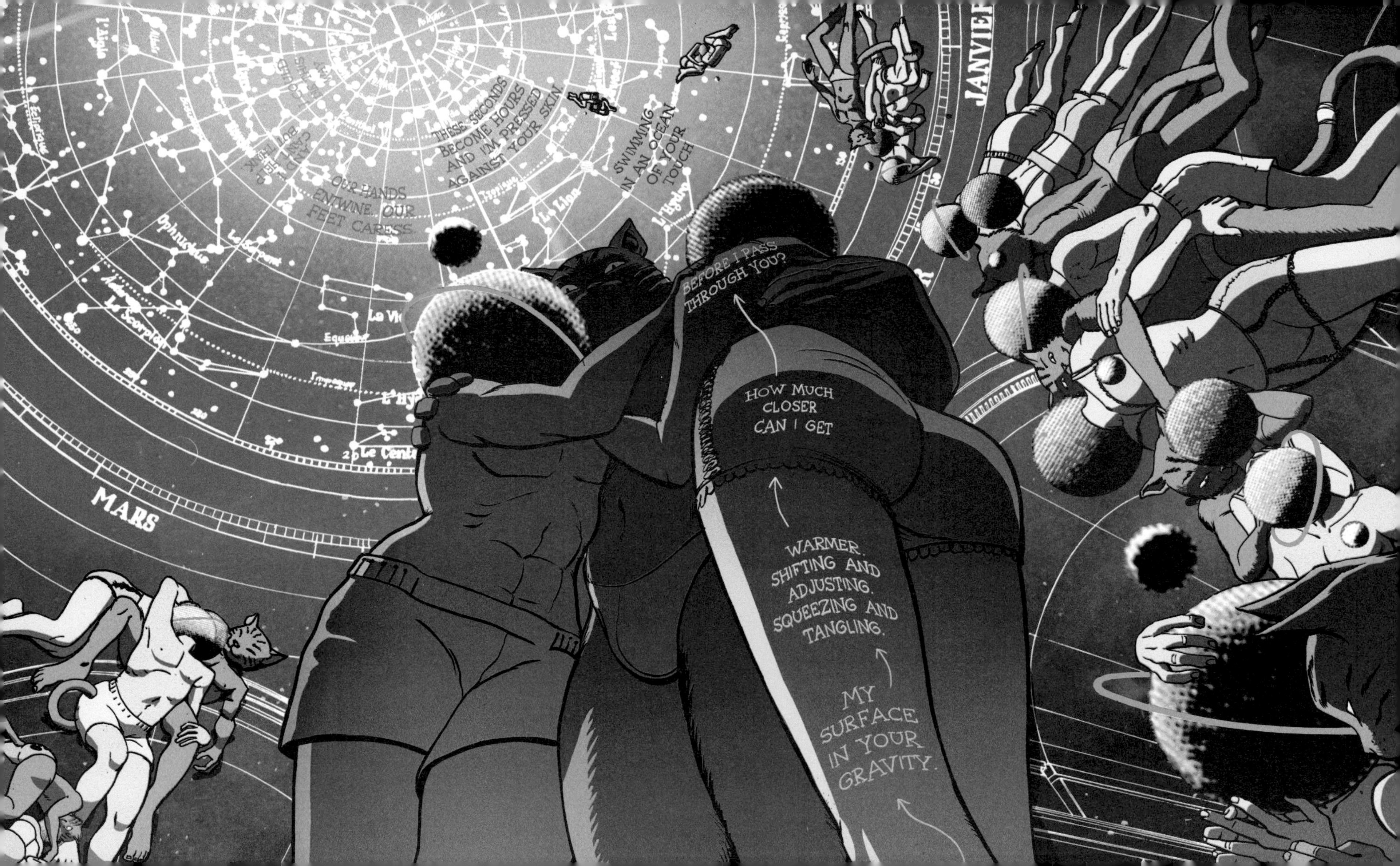

MY SURFACE IN YOUR GRAVITY.
WARMER. SHIFTING AND ADJUSTING. SQUEEZING AND TANGLING.
HOW MUCH CLOSER CAN I GET
BEFORE I PASS THROUGH YOU?
OUR HANDS ENTWINE. OUR FEET CARESS.
AND I CAN'T HELP BUT THINK
I COULD DIE THIS WAY
THESE SECONDS BECOME HOURS AND I'M PRESSED AGAINST YOUR SKIN
SWIMMING IN AN OCEAN OF YOUR TOUCH
MARS
JANVIER

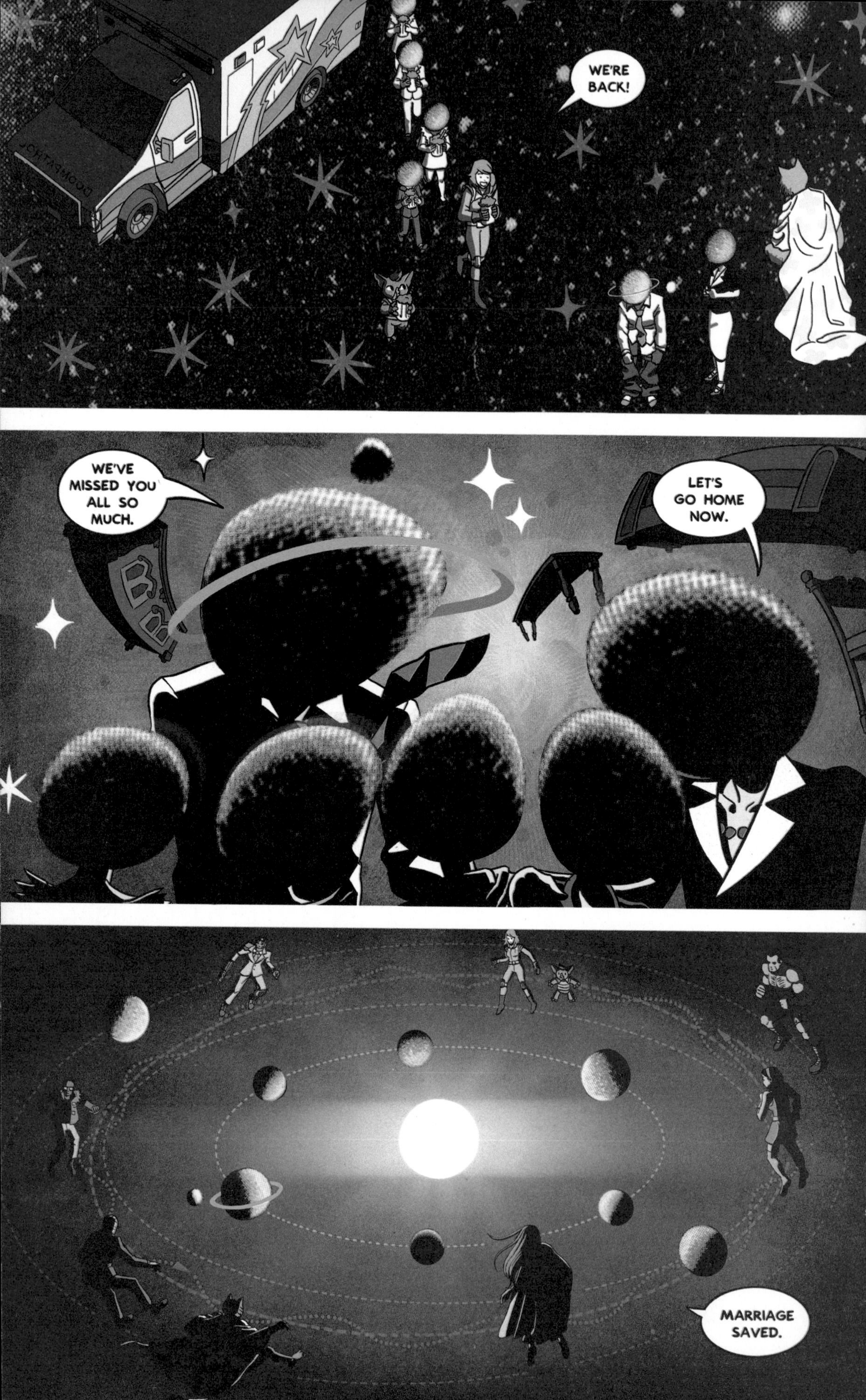
WE'RE BACK!
WE'VE MISSED YOU ALL SO MUCH.
LET'S GO HOME NOW.
MARRIAGE SAVED.

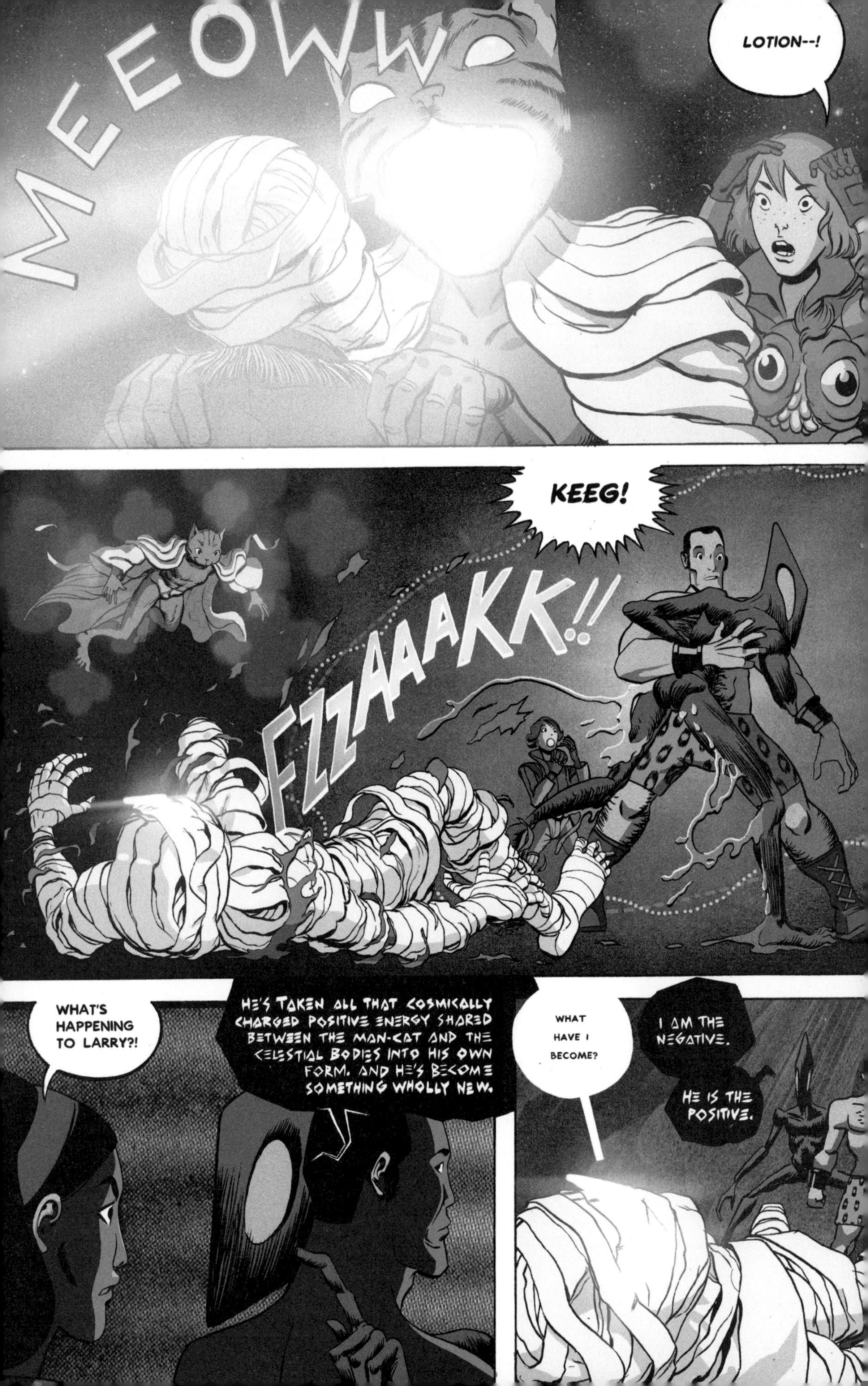
MEEOWW
LOTION--!
KEEG!
FZZAAAKK!!
WHAT'S HAPPENING TO LARRY?!
HE'S TAKEN ALL THAT COSMICALLY CHARGED POSITIVE ENERGY SHARED BETWEEN THE MAN-CAT AND THE CELESTIAL BODIES INTO HIS OWN FORM. AND HE'S BECOME SOMETHING WHOLLY NEW.
WHAT HAVE I BECOME?
I AM THE NEGATIVE.
HE IS THE POSITIVE.

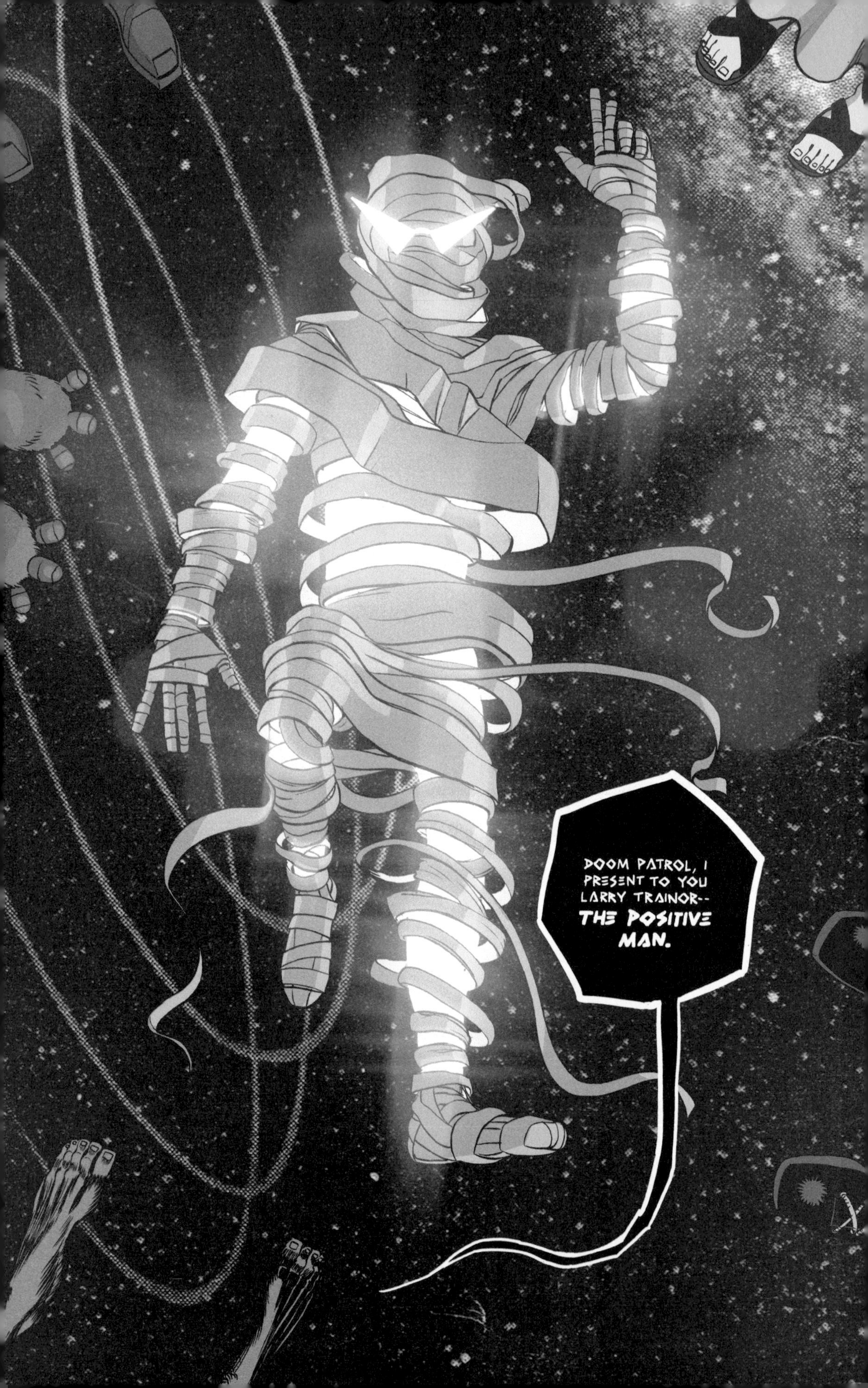
DOOM PATROL, I PRESENT TO YOU LARRY TRAINOR-- THE POSITIVE MAN.

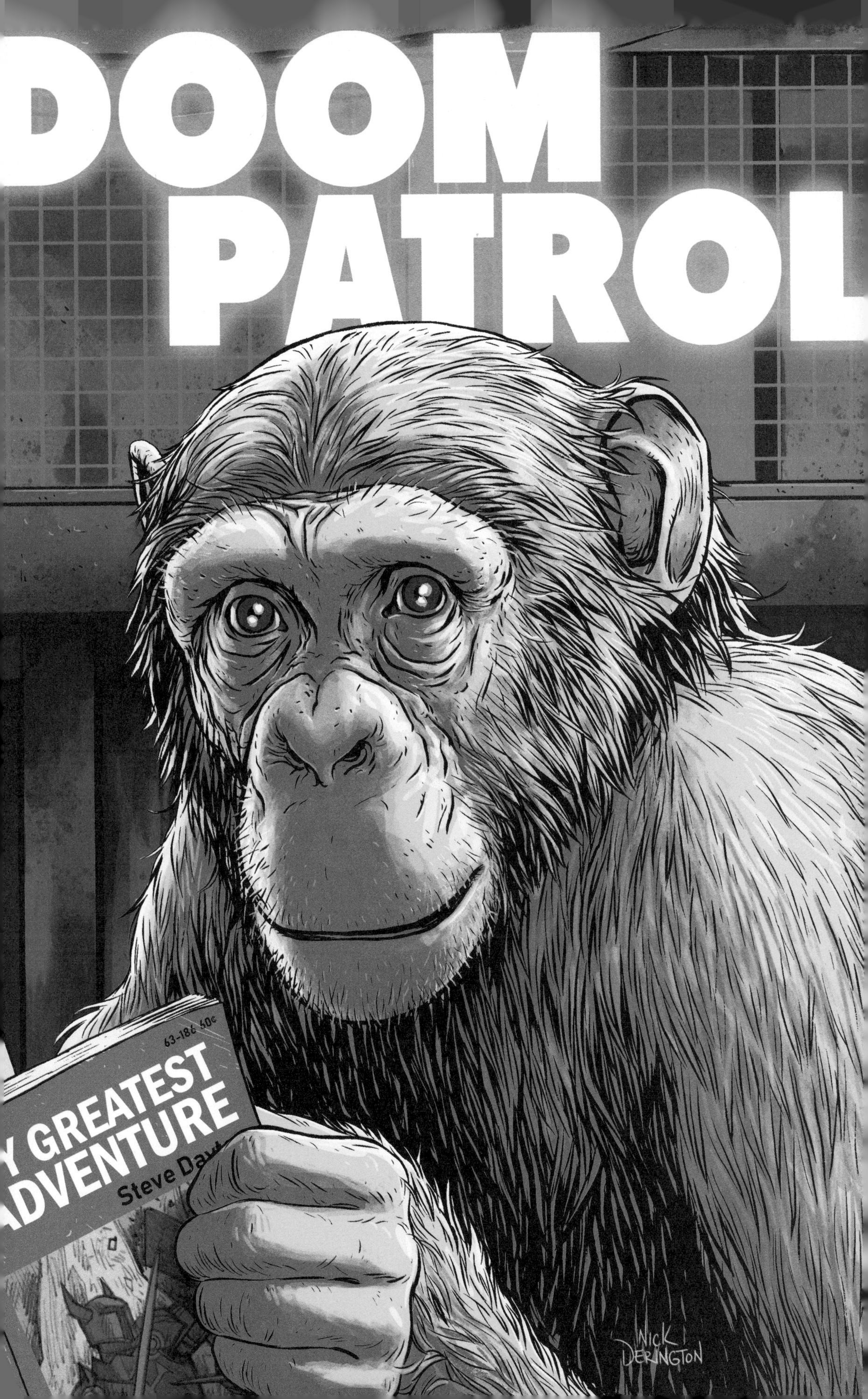
DOOM PATROL
63-186 50¢
Y GREATEST
ADVENTURE
Steve Dayt
NICK DERINGTON

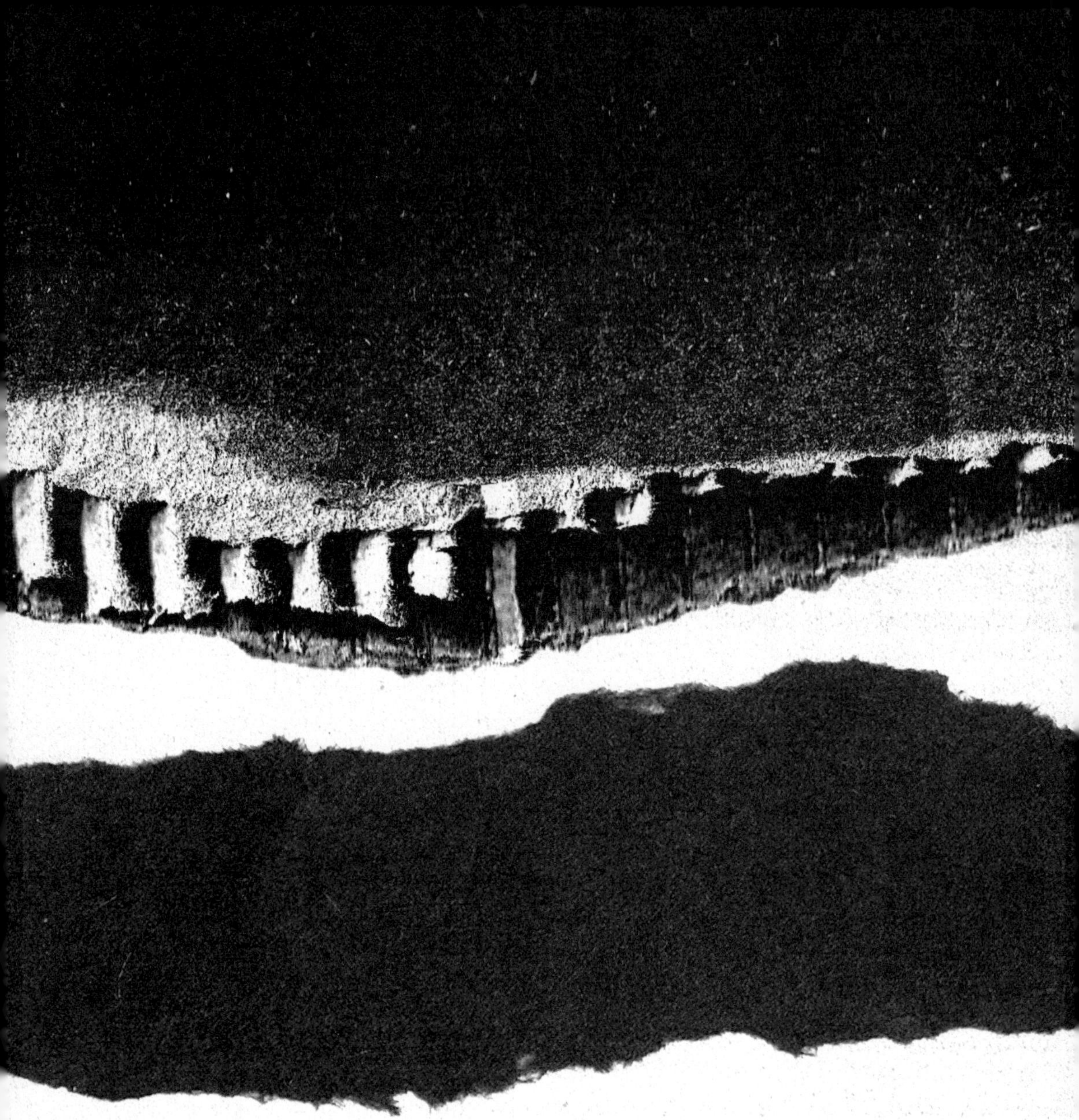

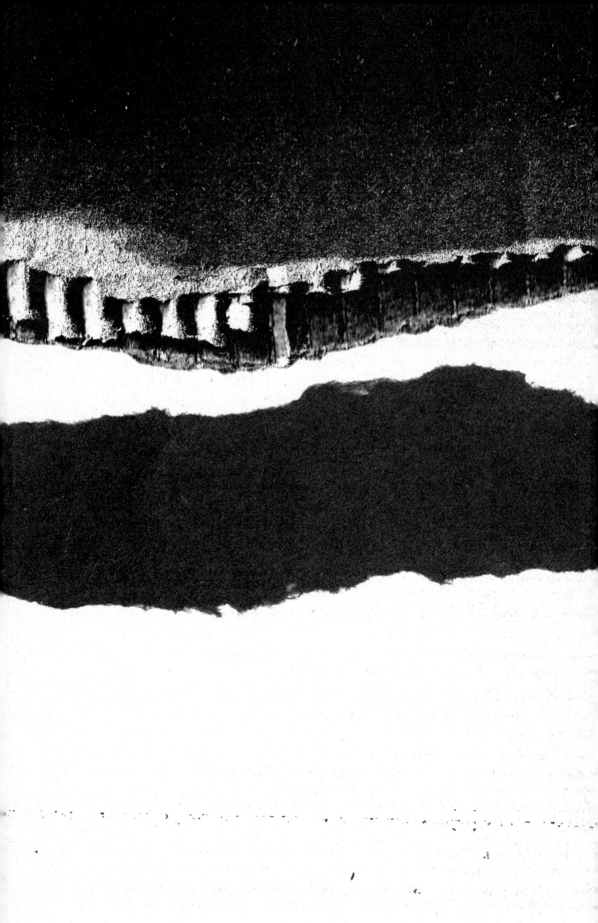

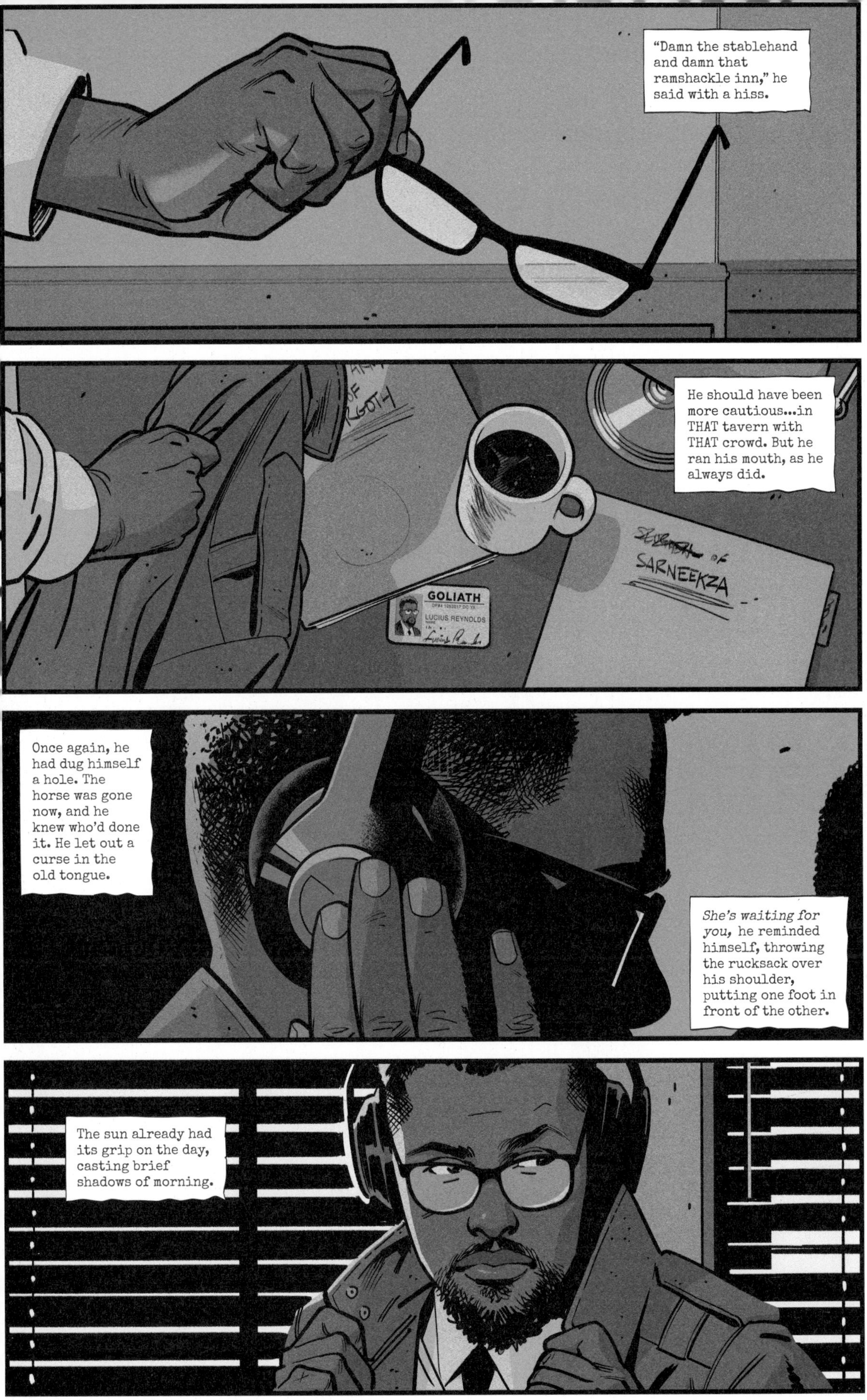
"Damn the stablehand and damn that ramshackle inn," he said with a hiss.
He should have been more cautious...in THAT tavern with THAT crowd. But he ran his mouth, as he always did.
SARNEEKZA
GOLIATH
LUCIUS REYNOLDS
Once again, he had dug himself a hole. The horse was gone now, and he knew who'd done it. He let out a curse in the old tongue.
She's waiting for you, he reminded himself, throwing the rucksack over his shoulder, putting one foot in front of the other.
The sun already had its grip on the day, casting brief shadows of morning.

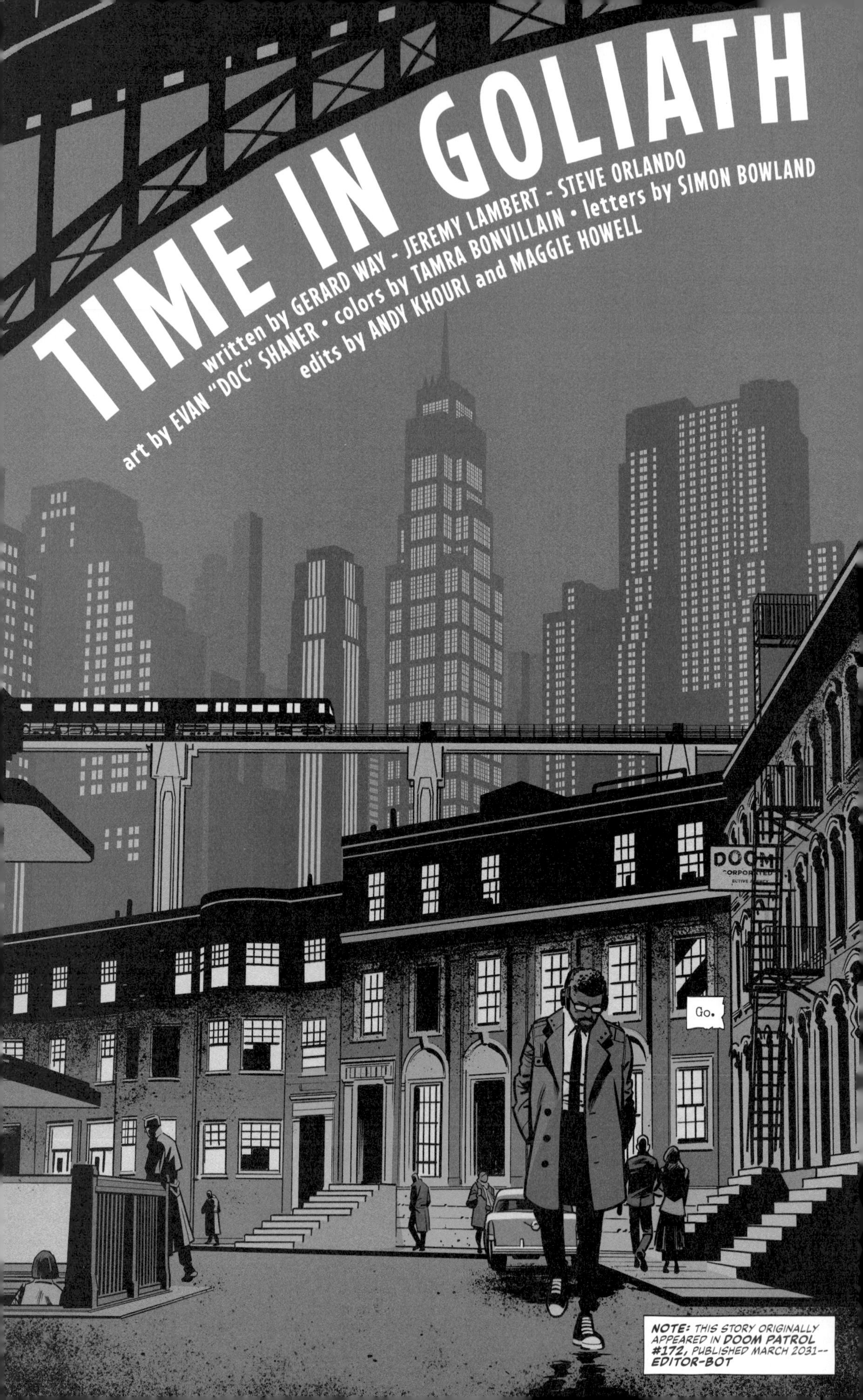
TIME IN GOLIATH
written by GERARD WAY - JEREMY LAMBERT - STEVE ORLANDO
art by EVAN "DOC" SHANER • colors by TAMRA BONVILLAIN • letters by SIMON BOWLAND
edits by ANDY KHOURI and MAGGIE HOWELL
DOOM
Go.
NOTE: THIS STORY ORIGINALLY APPEARED IN DOOM PATROL #172, PUBLISHED MARCH 2031-- EDITOR-BOT

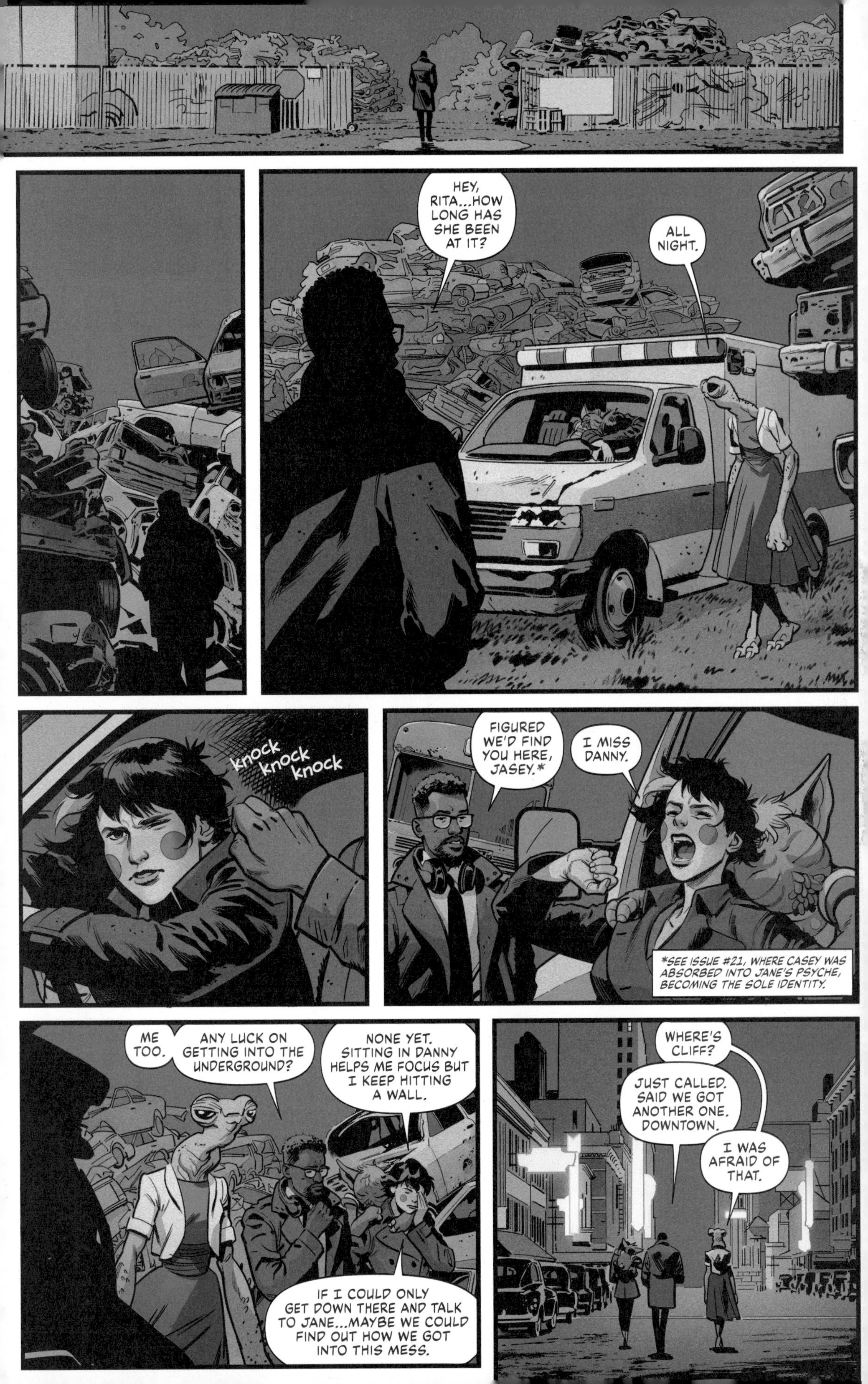
HEY, RITA...HOW LONG HAS SHE BEEN AT IT?
ALL NIGHT.
knock knock knock
FIGURED WE'D FIND YOU HERE, JASEY.*
I MISS DANNY.
*SEE ISSUE #21, WHERE CASEY WAS ABSORBED INTO JANE'S PSYCHE, BECOMING THE SOLE IDENTITY.
ME TOO.
ANY LUCK ON GETTING INTO THE UNDERGROUND?
NONE YET. SITTING IN DANNY HELPS ME FOCUS BUT I KEEP HITTING A WALL.
IF I COULD ONLY GET DOWN THERE AND TALK TO JANE...MAYBE WE COULD FIND OUT HOW WE GOT INTO THIS MESS.
WHERE'S CLIFF?
JUST CALLED. SAID WE GOT ANOTHER ONE. DOWNTOWN.
I WAS AFRAID OF THAT.

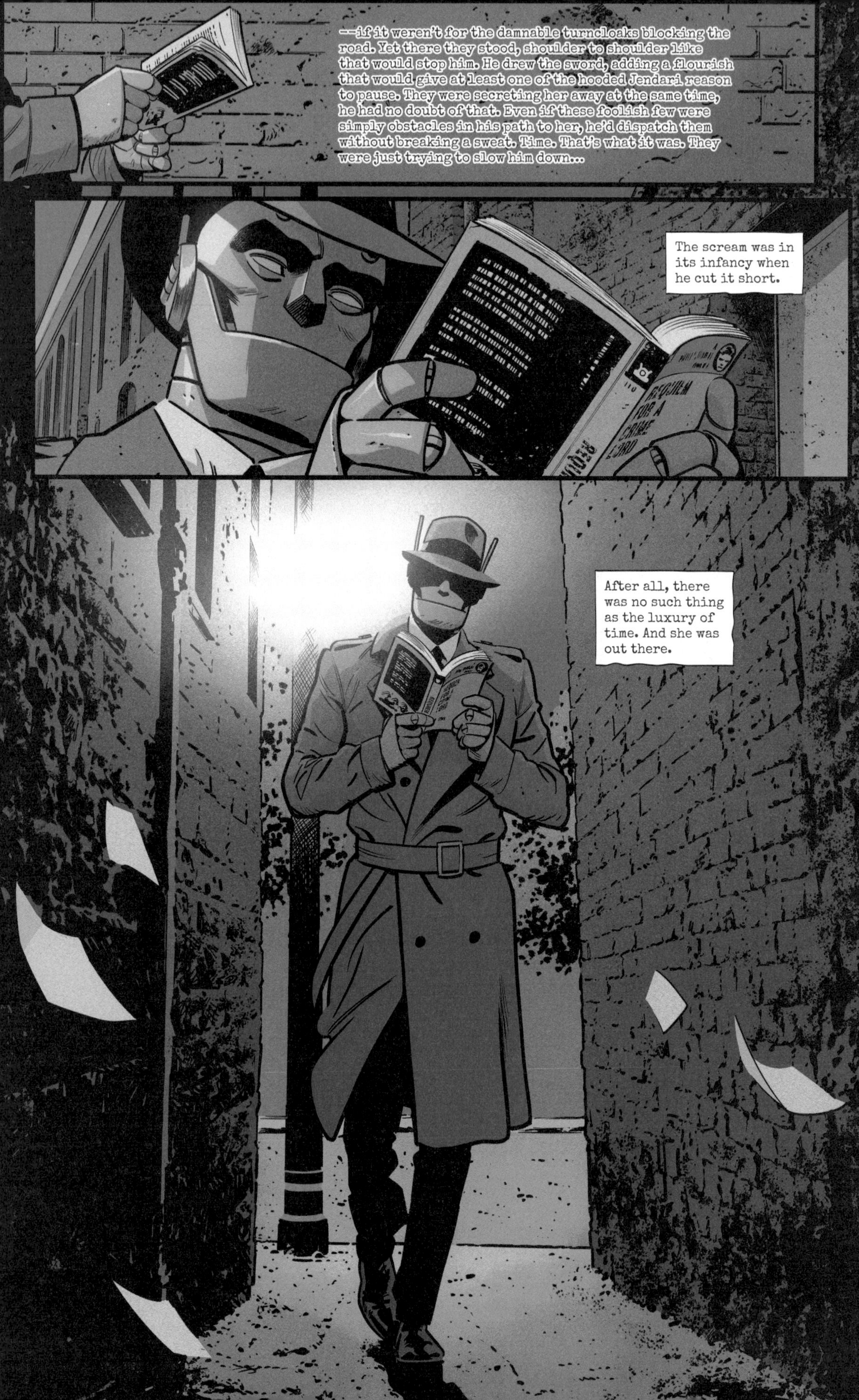
--if it weren't for the damnable turncloaks blocking the road. Yet there they stood, shoulder to shoulder like that would stop him. He drew the sword, adding a flourish that would give at least one of the hooded Jendari reason to pause. They were secreting her away at the same time, he had no doubt of that. Even if these foolish few were simply obstacles in his path to her, he'd dispatch them without breaking a sweat. Time. That's what it was. They were just trying to slow him down...
The scream was in its infancy when he cut it short.
REQUIEM FOR A CRIME LORD
After all, there was no such thing as the luxury of time. And she was out there.

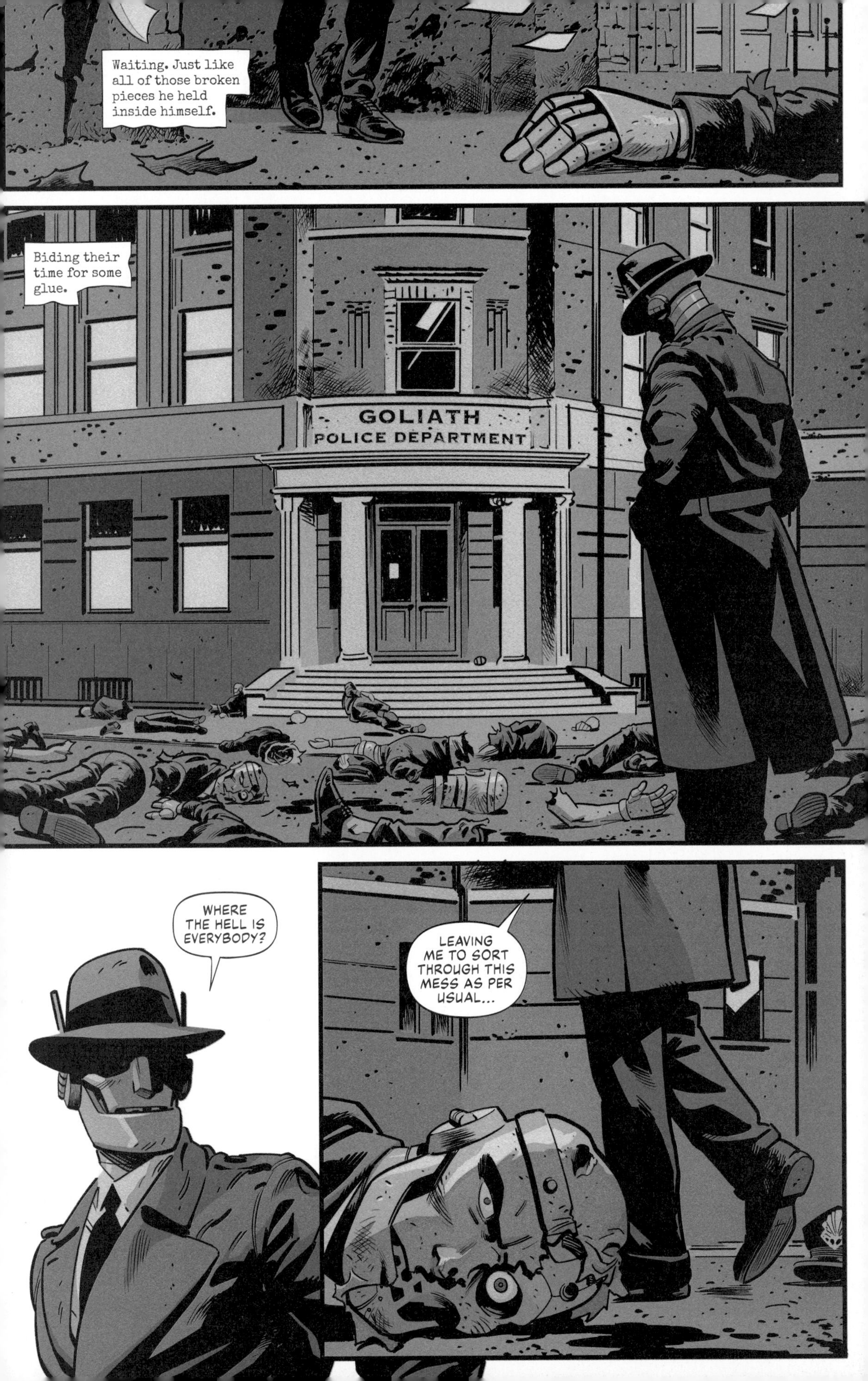
Waiting. Just like all of those broken pieces he held inside himself.
Biding their time for some glue.
GOLIATH POLICE DEPARTMENT
WHERE THE HELL IS EVERYBODY?
LEAVING ME TO SORT THROUGH THIS MESS AS PER USUAL...

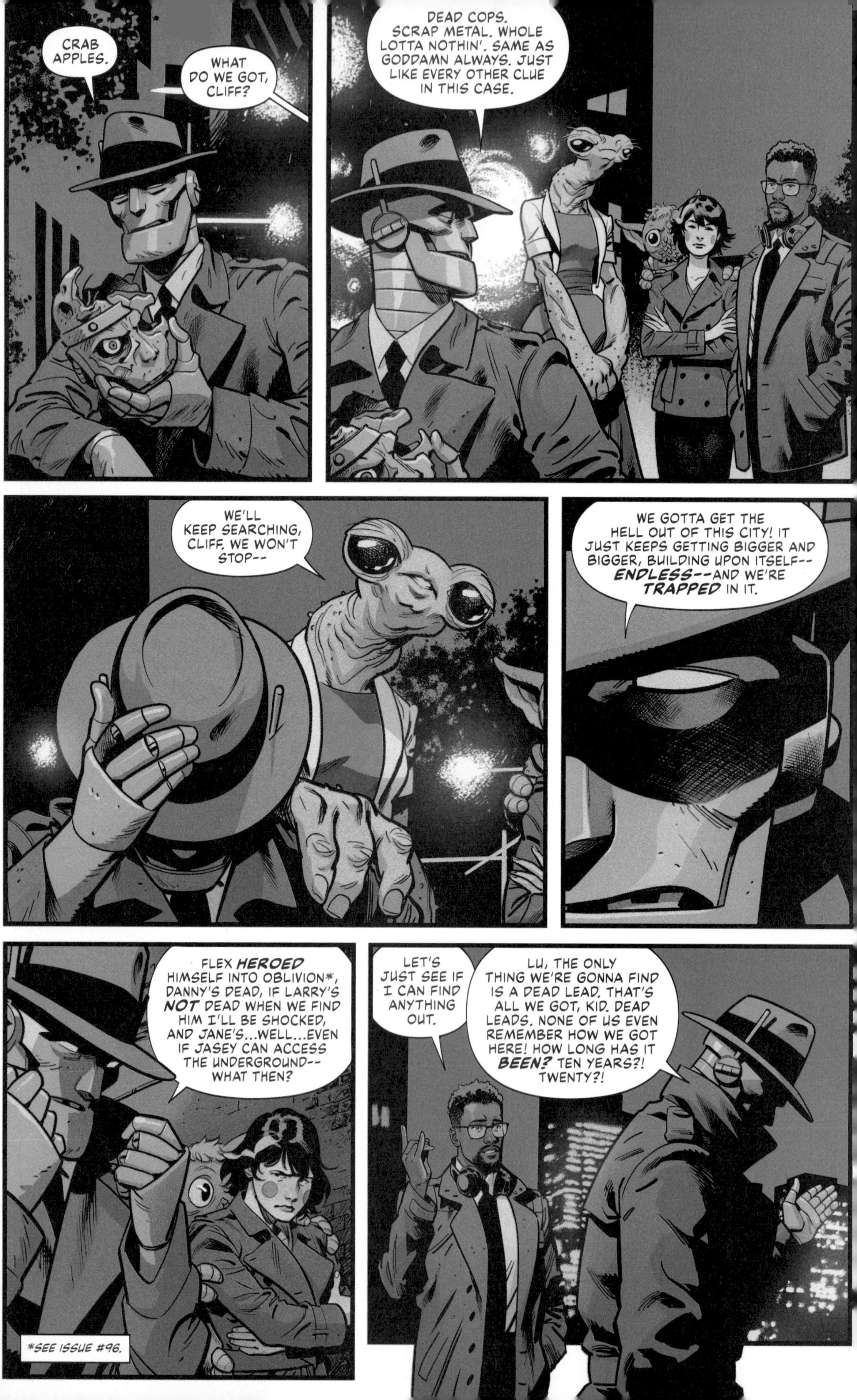
CRAB APPLES.
WHAT DO WE GOT, CLIFF?
DEAD COPS. SCRAP METAL. WHOLE LOTTA NOTHIN'. SAME AS GODDAMN ALWAYS. JUST LIKE EVERY OTHER CLUE IN THIS CASE.
WE'LL KEEP SEARCHING, CLIFF. WE WON'T STOP--
WE GOTTA GET THE HELL OUT OF THIS CITY! IT JUST KEEPS GETTING BIGGER AND BIGGER, BUILDING UPON ITSELF-- ENDLESS--AND WE'RE TRAPPED IN IT.
FLEX HEROED HIMSELF INTO OBLIVION*, DANNY'S DEAD, IF LARRY'S NOT DEAD WHEN WE FIND HIM I'LL BE SHOCKED, AND JANE'S...WELL...EVEN IF JASEY CAN ACCESS THE UNDERGROUND-- WHAT THEN?
*SEE ISSUE #96.
LET'S JUST SEE IF I CAN FIND ANYTHING OUT.
LU, THE ONLY THING WE'RE GONNA FIND IS A DEAD LEAD. THAT'S ALL WE GOT, KID. DEAD LEADS. NONE OF US EVEN REMEMBER HOW WE GOT HERE! HOW LONG HAS IT BEEN? TEN YEARS?! TWENTY?!

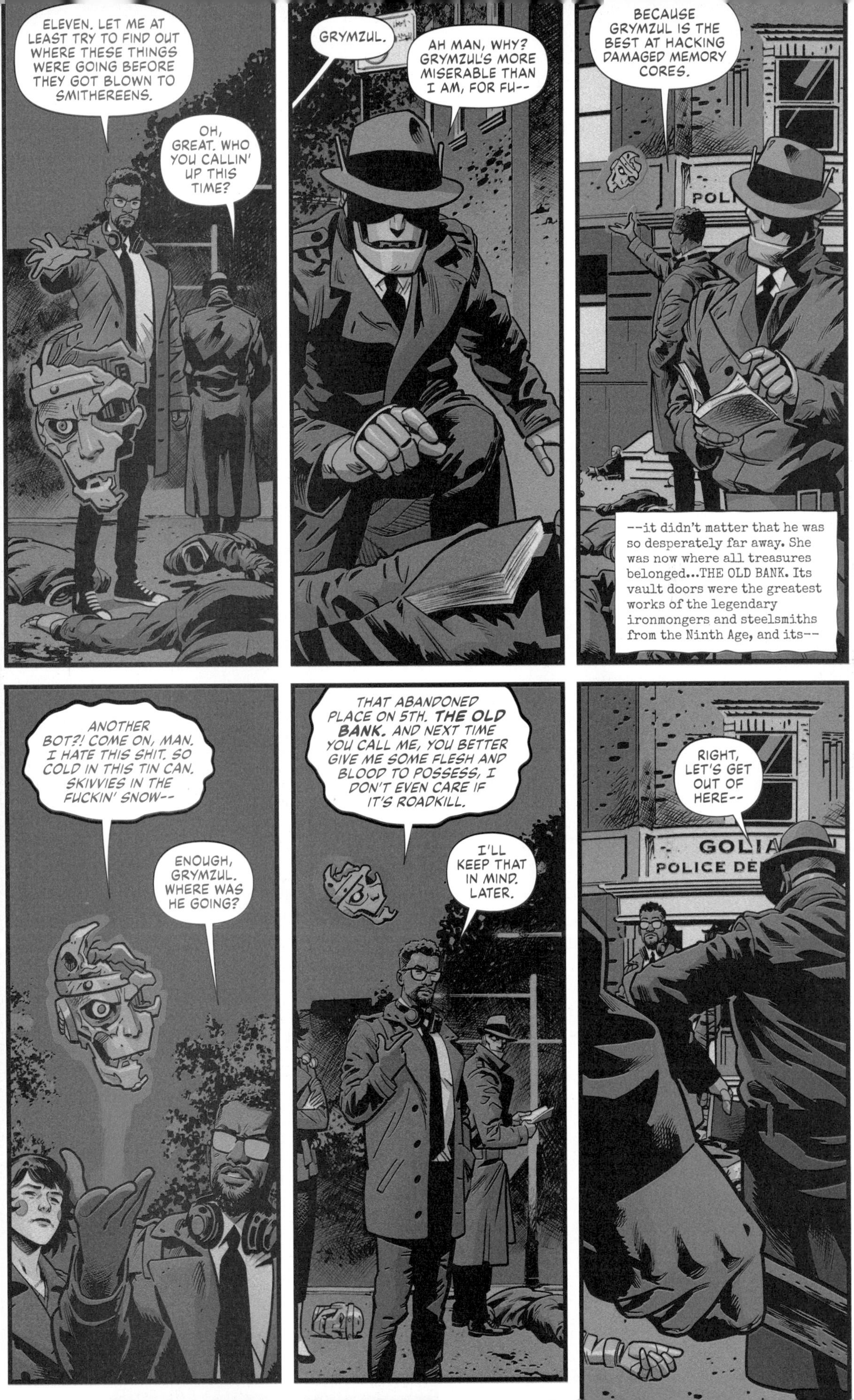
ELEVEN. LET ME AT LEAST TRY TO FIND OUT WHERE THESE THINGS WERE GOING BEFORE THEY GOT BLOWN TO SMITHEREENS.
OH, GREAT. WHO YOU CALLIN' UP THIS TIME?
GRYMZUL.
AH MAN, WHY? GRYMZUL'S MORE MISERABLE THAN I AM, FOR FU--
BECAUSE GRYMZUL IS THE BEST AT HACKING DAMAGED MEMORY CORES.
POLI
--it didn't matter that he was so desperately far away. She was now where all treasures belonged...THE OLD BANK. Its vault doors were the greatest works of the legendary ironmongers and steelsmiths from the Ninth Age, and its--
ANOTHER BOT?! COME ON, MAN. I HATE THIS SHIT. SO COLD IN THIS TIN CAN. SKIVVIES IN THE FUCKIN' SNOW--
ENOUGH, GRYMZUL. WHERE WAS HE GOING?
THAT ABANDONED PLACE ON 5TH. THE OLD BANK. AND NEXT TIME YOU CALL ME, YOU BETTER GIVE ME SOME FLESH AND BLOOD TO POSSESS, I DON'T EVEN CARE IF IT'S ROADKILL.
I'LL KEEP THAT IN MIND. LATER.
RIGHT, LET'S GET OUT OF HERE--
GOLIA
POLICE DE

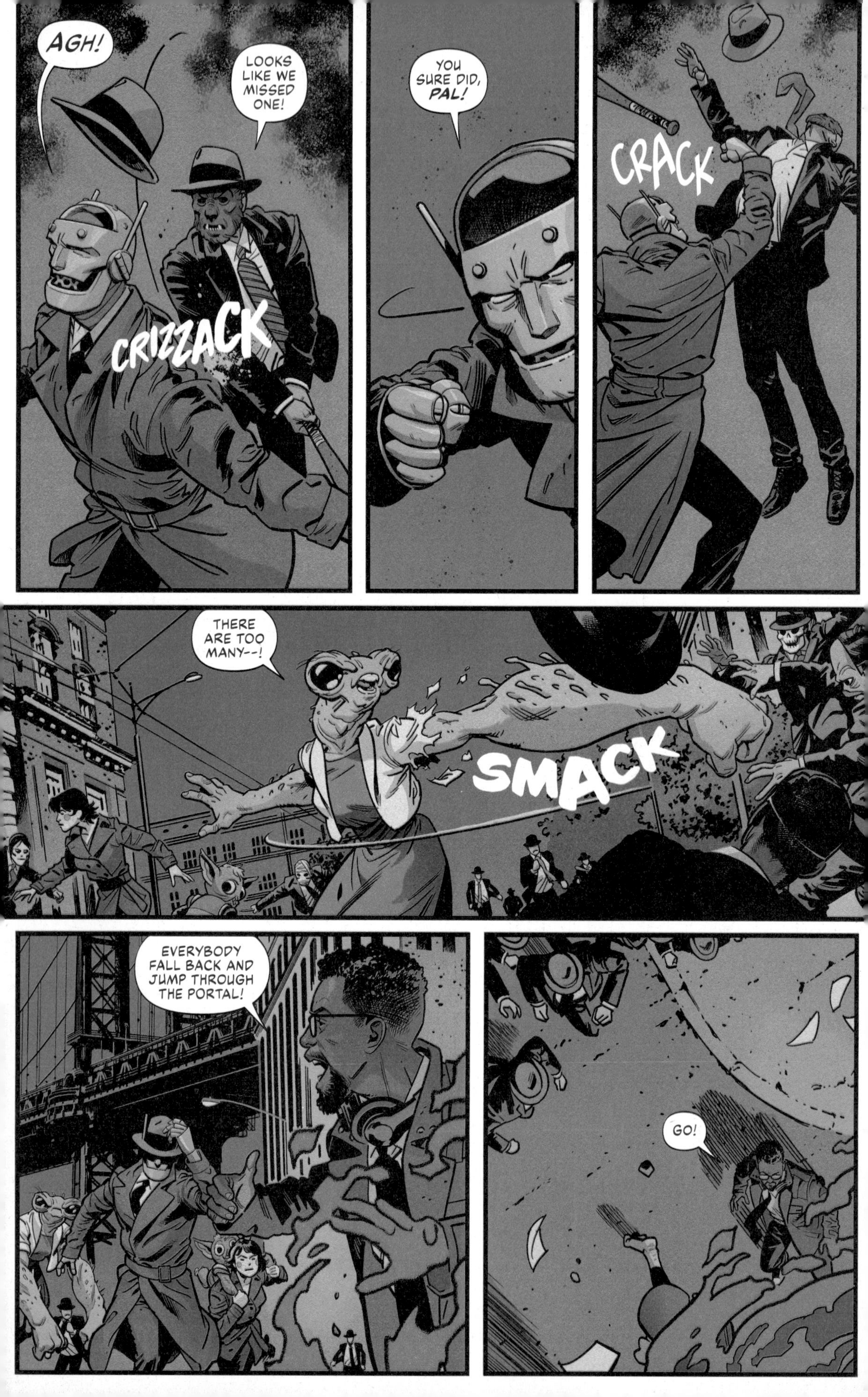
AGH!
LOOKS LIKE WE MISSED ONE!
CRIZZACK
YOU SURE DID, PAL!
CRACK
THERE ARE TOO MANY--!
SMACK
EVERYBODY FALL BACK AND JUMP THROUGH THE PORTAL!
GO!

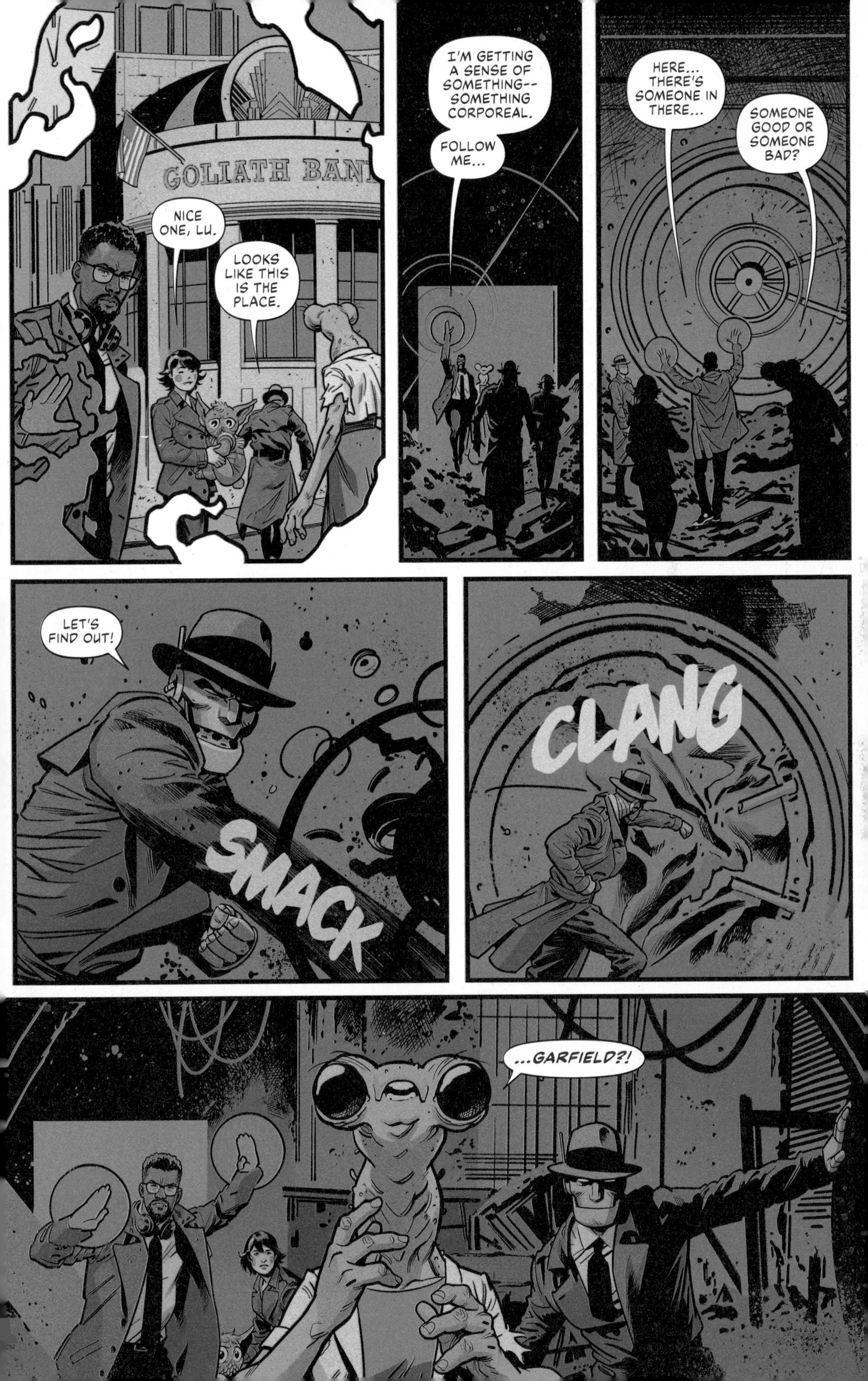
GOLIATH BANK
NICE ONE, LU.
LOOKS LIKE THIS IS THE PLACE.
I'M GETTING A SENSE OF SOMETHING--SOMETHING CORPOREAL.
FOLLOW ME...
HERE... THERE'S SOMEONE IN THERE...
SOMEONE GOOD OR SOMEONE BAD?
LET'S FIND OUT!
SMACK
CLANG
...GARFIELD?!

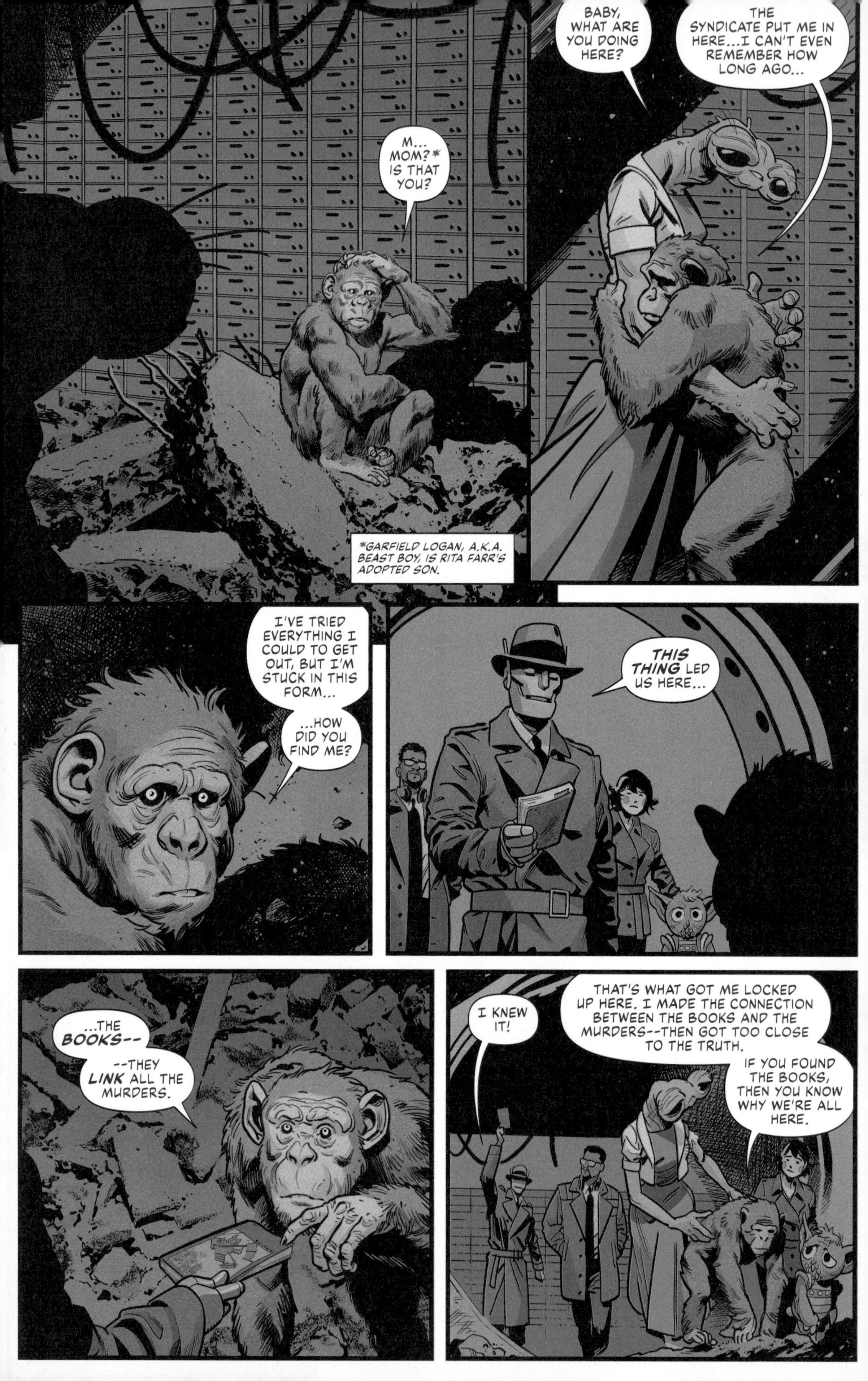
M... MOM?* IS THAT YOU?
*GARFIELD LOGAN, A.K.A. BEAST BOY, IS RITA FARR'S ADOPTED SON.
BABY, WHAT ARE YOU DOING HERE?
THE SYNDICATE PUT ME IN HERE...I CAN'T EVEN REMEMBER HOW LONG AGO...
I'VE TRIED EVERYTHING I COULD TO GET OUT, BUT I'M STUCK IN THIS FORM...
...HOW DID YOU FIND ME?
THIS THING LED US HERE...
...THE BOOKS--
--THEY LINK ALL THE MURDERS.
I KNEW IT!
THAT'S WHAT GOT ME LOCKED UP HERE. I MADE THE CONNECTION BETWEEN THE BOOKS AND THE MURDERS--THEN GOT TOO CLOSE TO THE TRUTH.
IF YOU FOUND THE BOOKS, THEN YOU KNOW WHY WE'RE ALL HERE.

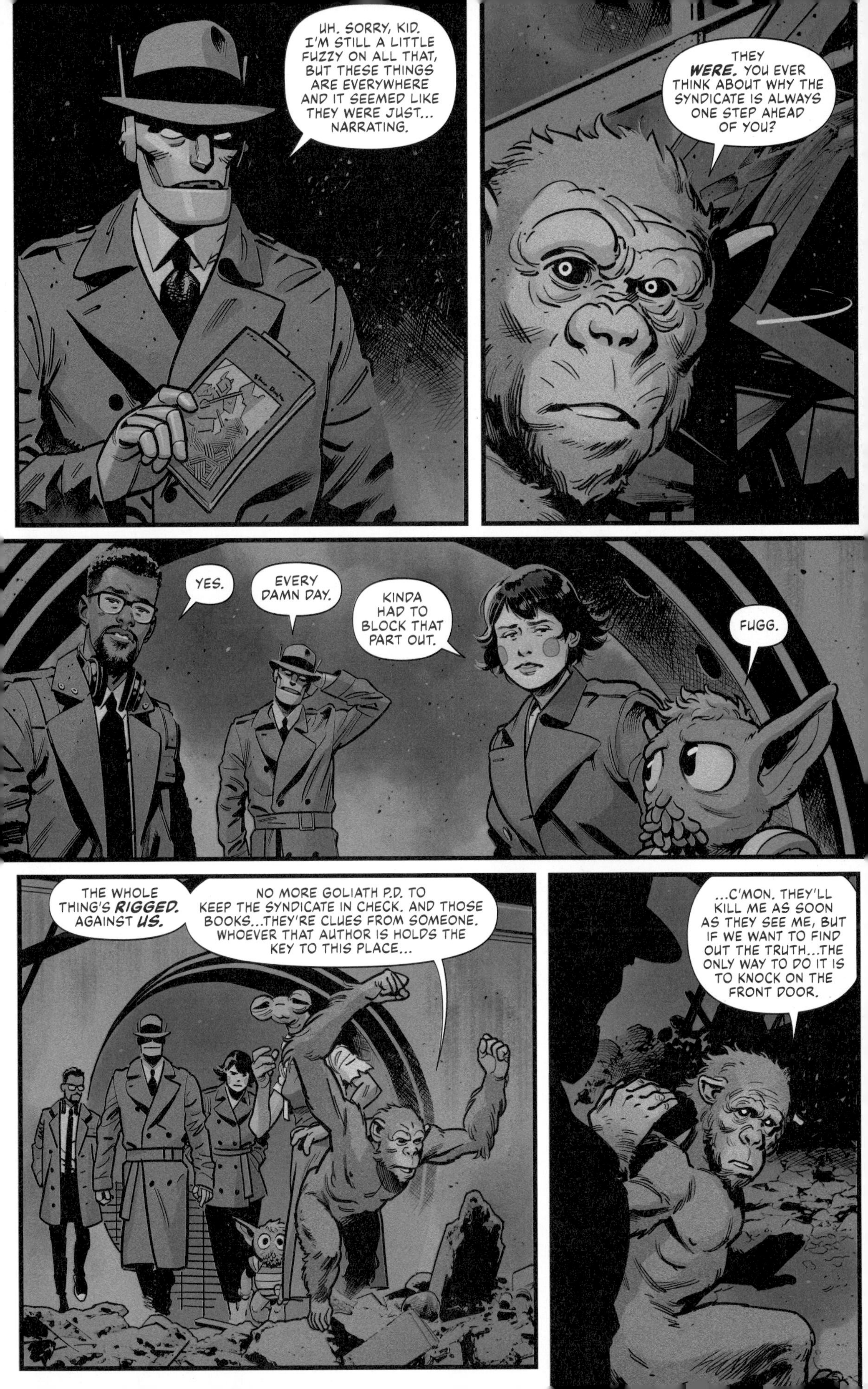
UH. SORRY, KID. I'M STILL A LITTLE FUZZY ON ALL THAT, BUT THESE THINGS ARE EVERYWHERE AND IT SEEMED LIKE THEY WERE JUST... NARRATING.
THEY *WERE.* YOU EVER THINK ABOUT WHY THE SYNDICATE IS ALWAYS ONE STEP AHEAD OF YOU?
YES.
EVERY DAMN DAY.
KINDA HAD TO BLOCK THAT PART OUT.
FUGG.
THE WHOLE THING'S *RIGGED.* AGAINST *US.*
NO MORE GOLIATH P.D. TO KEEP THE SYNDICATE IN CHECK. AND THOSE BOOKS...THEY'RE CLUES FROM SOMEONE. WHOEVER THAT AUTHOR IS HOLDS THE KEY TO THIS PLACE...
...C'MON. THEY'LL KILL ME AS SOON AS THEY SEE ME, BUT IF WE WANT TO FIND OUT THE TRUTH...THE ONLY WAY TO DO IT IS TO KNOCK ON THE FRONT DOOR.

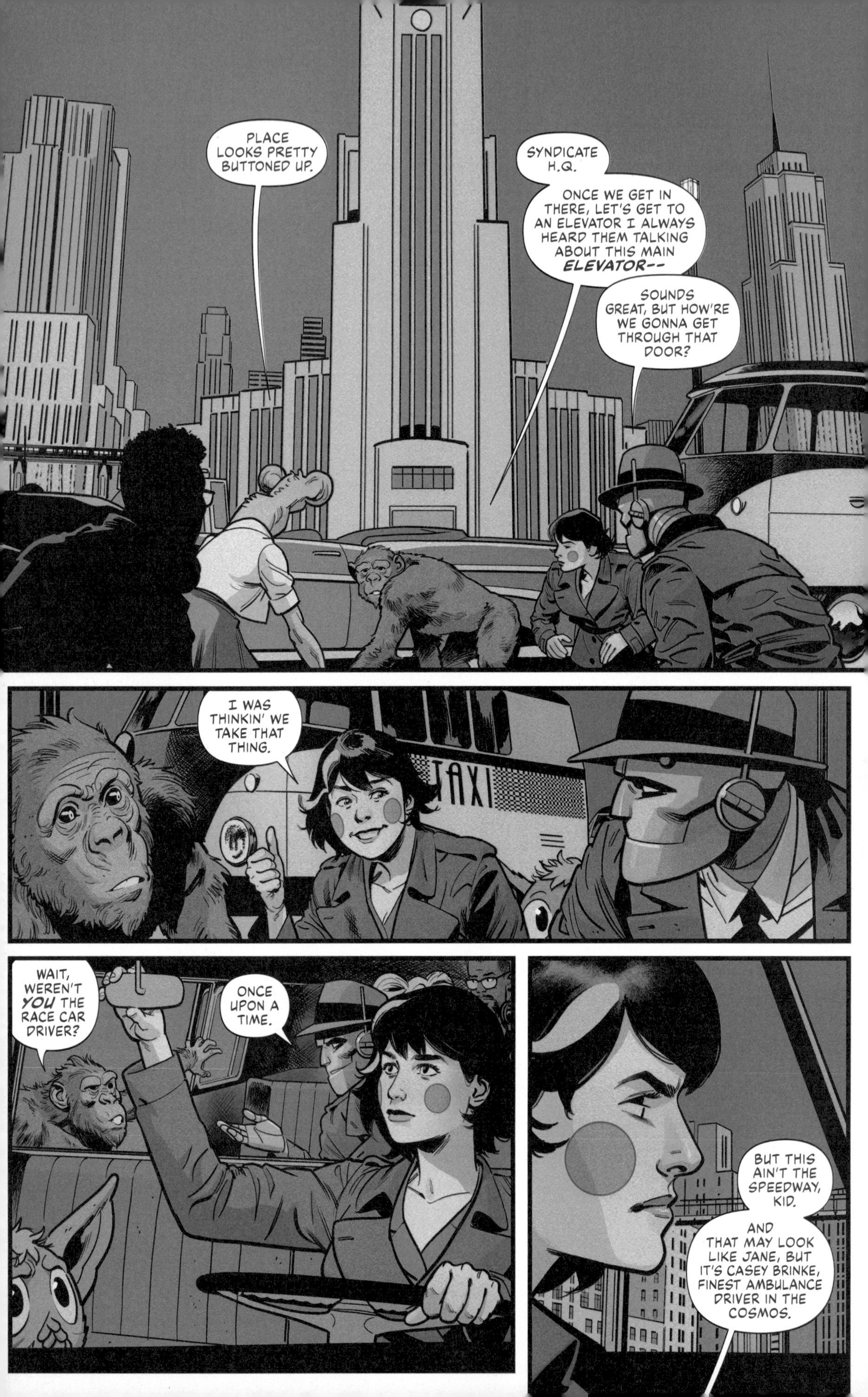
PLACE LOOKS PRETTY BUTTONED UP.
SYNDICATE H.Q.
ONCE WE GET IN THERE, LET'S GET TO AN ELEVATOR I ALWAYS HEARD THEM TALKING ABOUT THIS MAIN *ELEVATOR--*
SOUNDS GREAT, BUT HOW'RE WE GONNA GET THROUGH THAT DOOR?
I WAS THINKIN' WE TAKE THAT THING.
TAXI
WAIT, WEREN'T *YOU* THE RACE CAR DRIVER?
ONCE UPON A TIME.
BUT THIS AIN'T THE SPEEDWAY, KID.
AND THAT MAY LOOK LIKE JANE, BUT IT'S CASEY BRINKE, FINEST AMBULANCE DRIVER IN THE COSMOS.

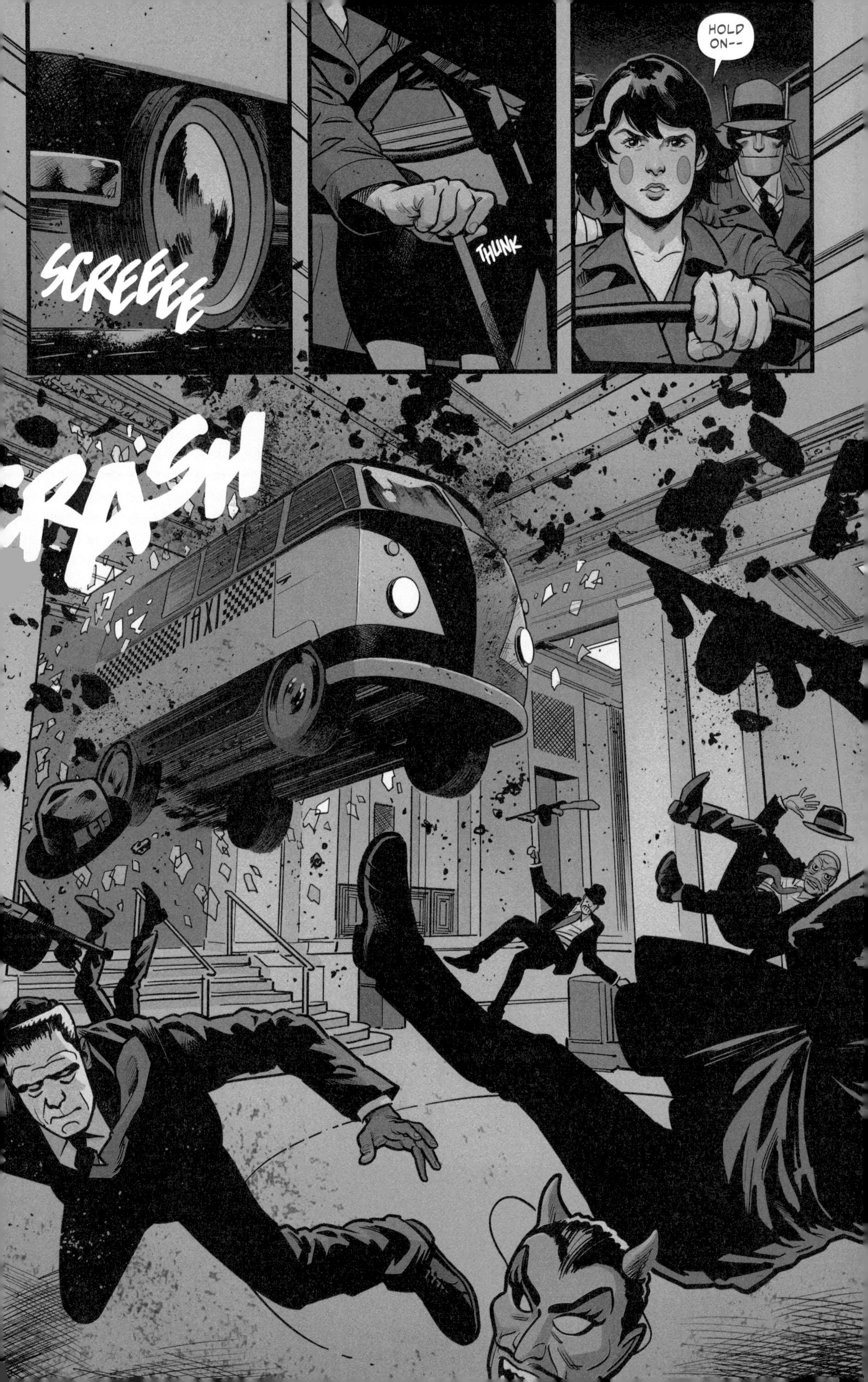
SCREEEEE
THUNK
HOLD ON--
CRASH
TAXI

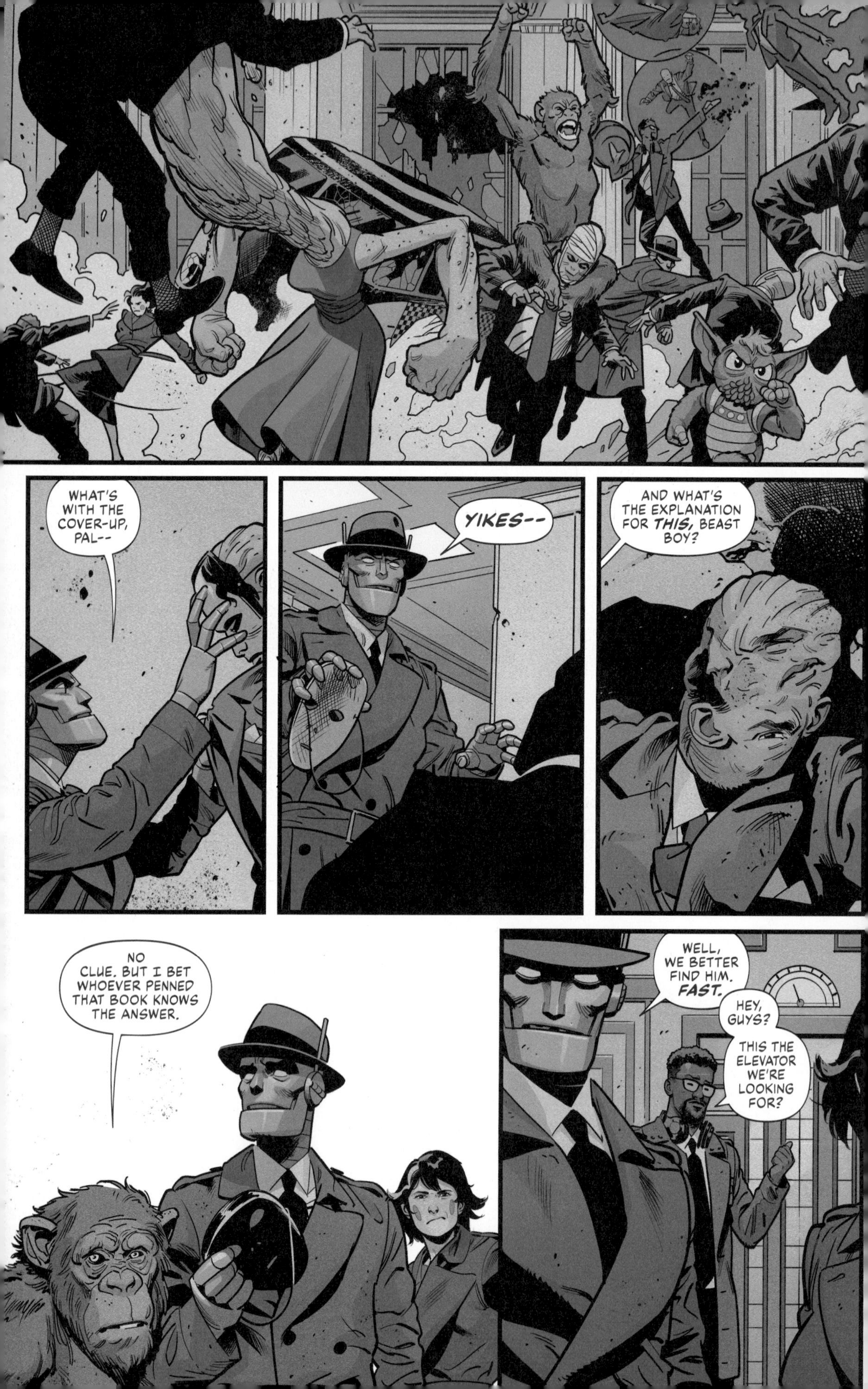
WHAT'S WITH THE COVER-UP, PAL--
YIKES--
AND WHAT'S THE EXPLANATION FOR THIS, BEAST BOY?
NO CLUE. BUT I BET WHOEVER PENNED THAT BOOK KNOWS THE ANSWER.
WELL, WE BETTER FIND HIM. FAST.
HEY, GUYS?
THIS THE ELEVATOR WE'RE LOOKING FOR?

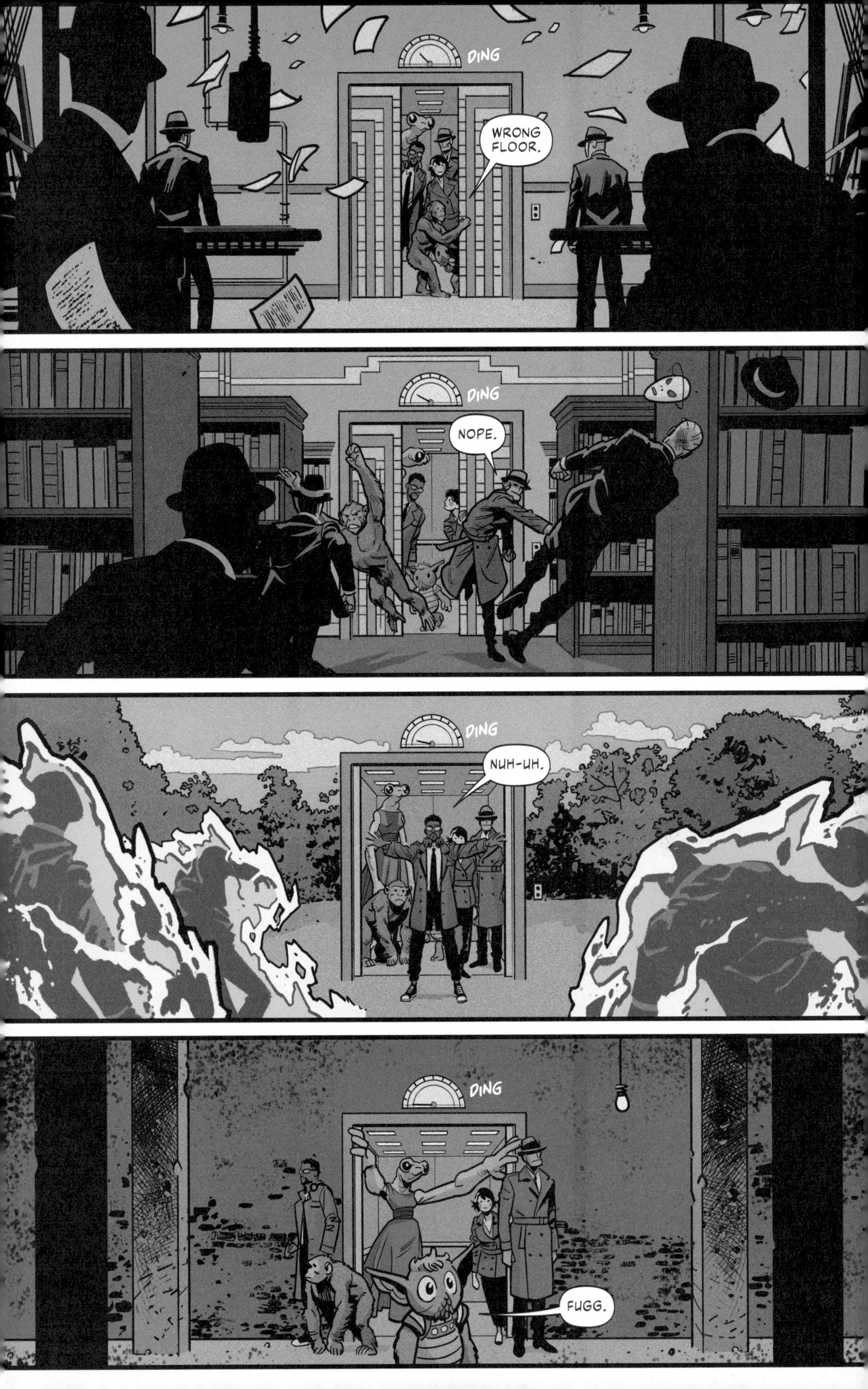
DING
WRONG FLOOR.
DING
NOPE.
DING
NUH-UH.
DING
FUGG.

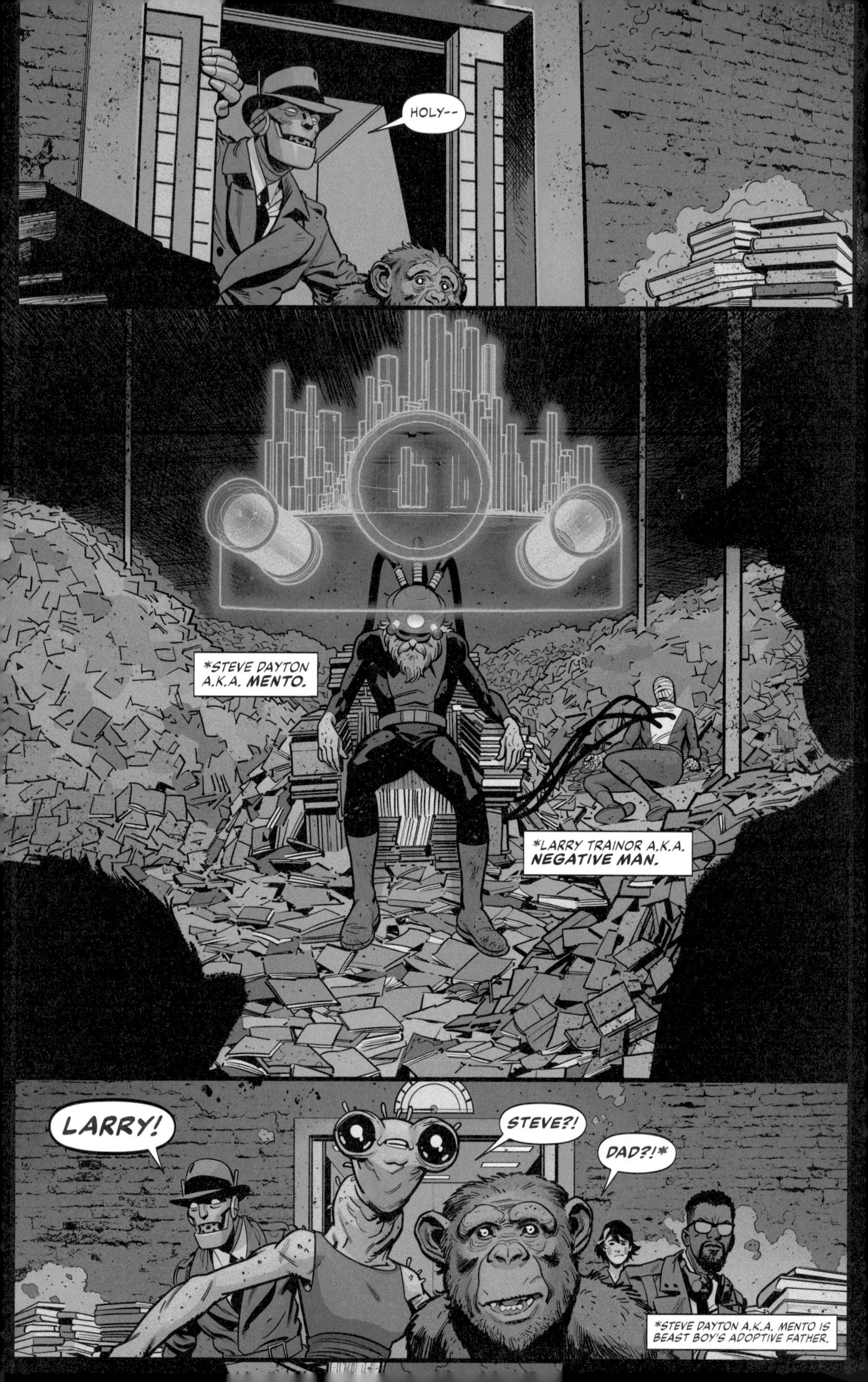
HOLY--
*STEVE DAYTON A.K.A. MENTO.
*LARRY TRAINOR A.K.A. NEGATIVE MAN.
LARRY!
STEVE?!
DAD?!*
*STEVE DAYTON A.K.A. MENTO IS BEAST BOY'S ADOPTIVE FATHER.

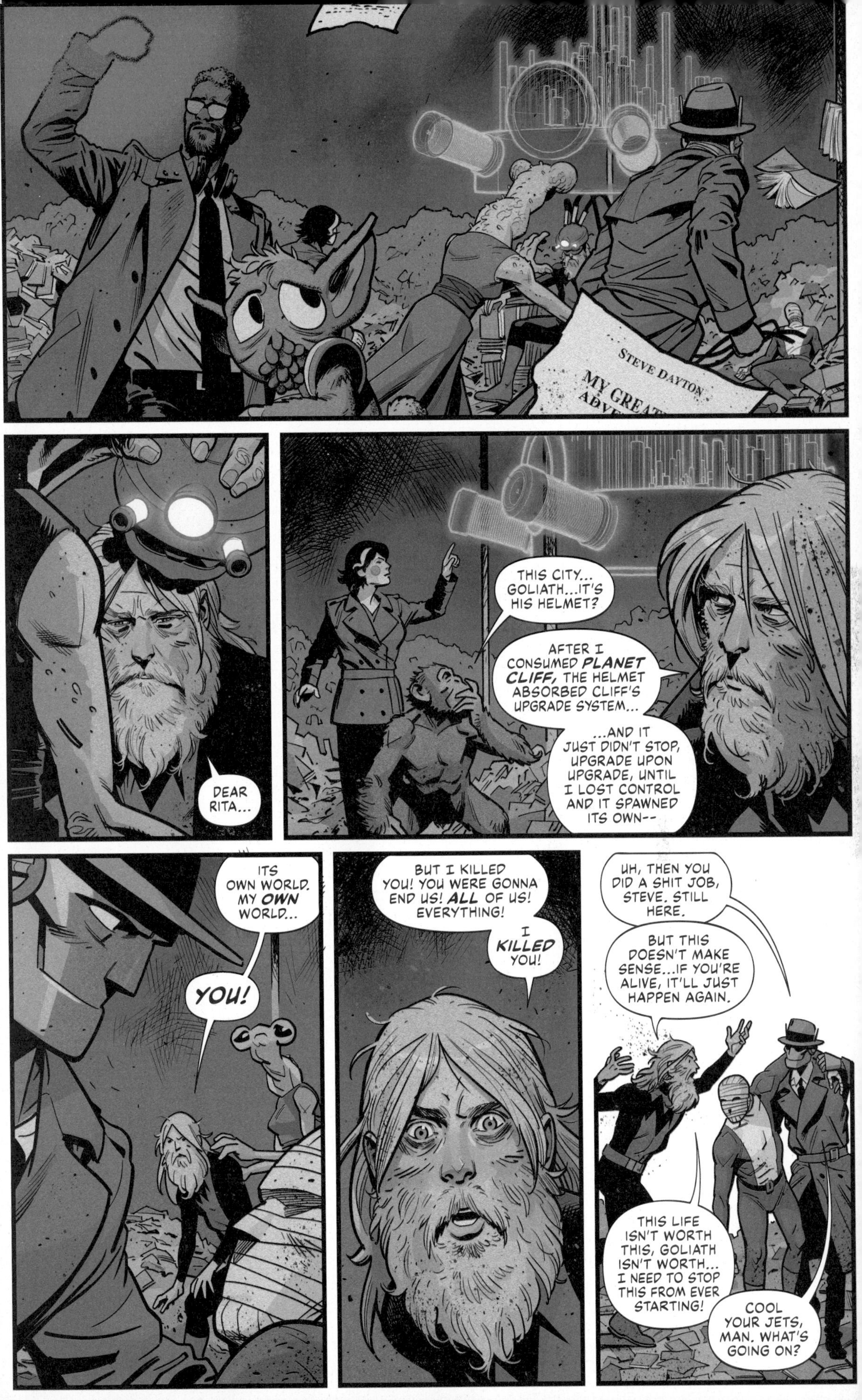
STEVE DAYTON
MY GREAT
ADVE
DEAR RITA...
THIS CITY... GOLIATH...IT'S HIS HELMET?
AFTER I CONSUMED PLANET CLIFF, THE HELMET ABSORBED CLIFF'S UPGRADE SYSTEM...
...AND IT JUST DIDN'T STOP, UPGRADE UPON UPGRADE, UNTIL I LOST CONTROL AND IT SPAWNED ITS OWN--
ITS OWN WORLD. MY OWN WORLD...
YOU!
BUT I KILLED YOU! YOU WERE GONNA END US! ALL OF US! EVERYTHING!
I KILLED YOU!
UH, THEN YOU DID A SHIT JOB, STEVE. STILL HERE.
BUT THIS DOESN'T MAKE SENSE...IF YOU'RE ALIVE, IT'LL JUST HAPPEN AGAIN.
THIS LIFE ISN'T WORTH THIS, GOLIATH ISN'T WORTH... I NEED TO STOP THIS FROM EVER STARTING!
COOL YOUR JETS, MAN. WHAT'S GOING ON?

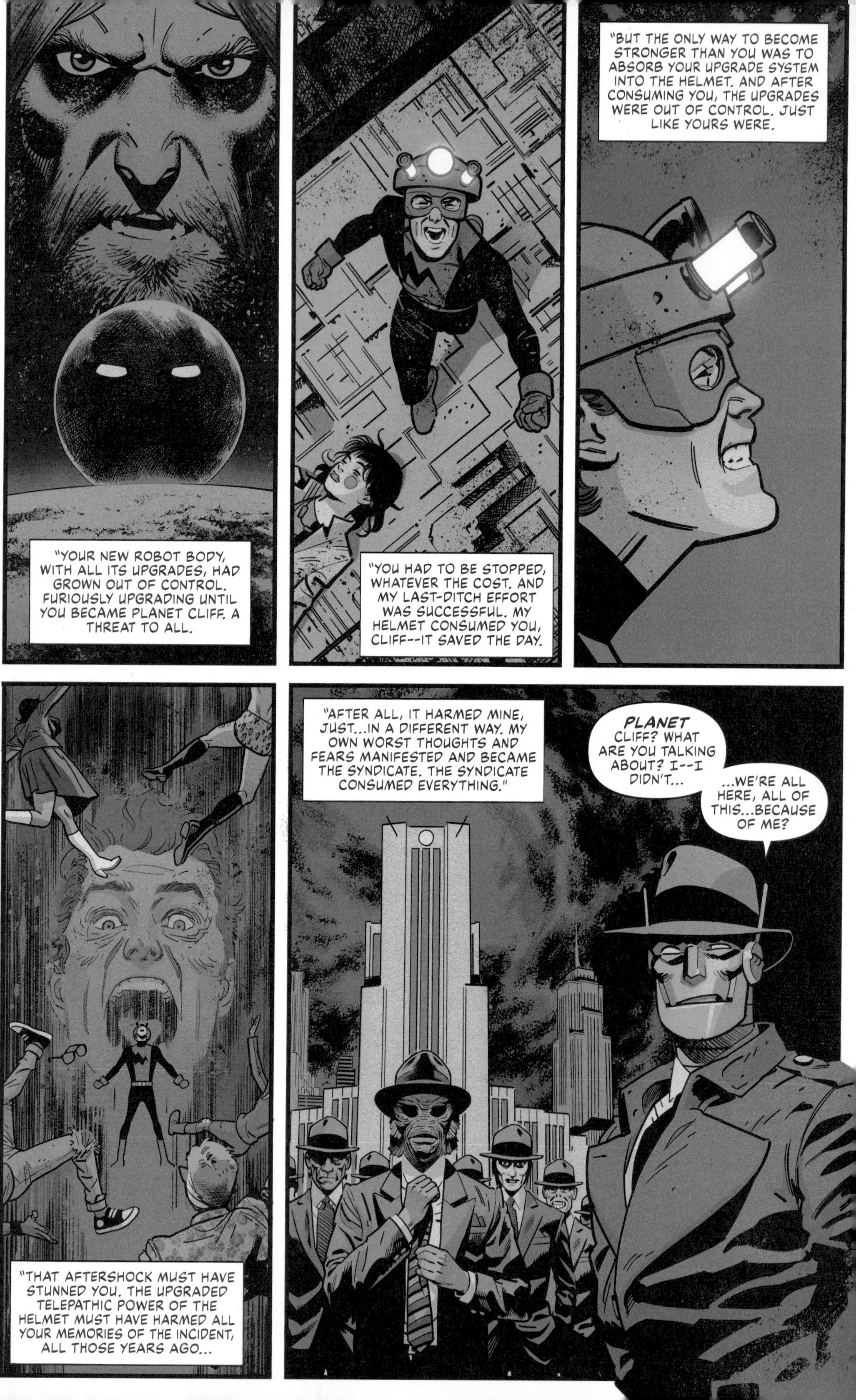
"YOUR NEW ROBOT BODY, WITH ALL ITS UPGRADES, HAD GROWN OUT OF CONTROL. FURIOUSLY UPGRADING UNTIL YOU BECAME PLANET CLIFF. A THREAT TO ALL.
"YOU HAD TO BE STOPPED, WHATEVER THE COST. AND MY LAST-DITCH EFFORT WAS SUCCESSFUL. MY HELMET CONSUMED YOU, CLIFF--IT SAVED THE DAY.
"BUT THE ONLY WAY TO BECOME STRONGER THAN YOU WAS TO ABSORB YOUR UPGRADE SYSTEM INTO THE HELMET. AND AFTER CONSUMING YOU, THE UPGRADES WERE OUT OF CONTROL. JUST LIKE YOURS WERE.
"THAT AFTERSHOCK MUST HAVE STUNNED YOU. THE UPGRADED TELEPATHIC POWER OF THE HELMET MUST HAVE HARMED ALL YOUR MEMORIES OF THE INCIDENT, ALL THOSE YEARS AGO...
"AFTER ALL, IT HARMED MINE, JUST...IN A DIFFERENT WAY. MY OWN WORST THOUGHTS AND FEARS MANIFESTED AND BECAME THE SYNDICATE. THE SYNDICATE CONSUMED EVERYTHING."
PLANET CLIFF? WHAT ARE YOU TALKING ABOUT? I--I DIDN'T...
...WE'RE ALL HERE, ALL OF THIS...BECAUSE OF ME?

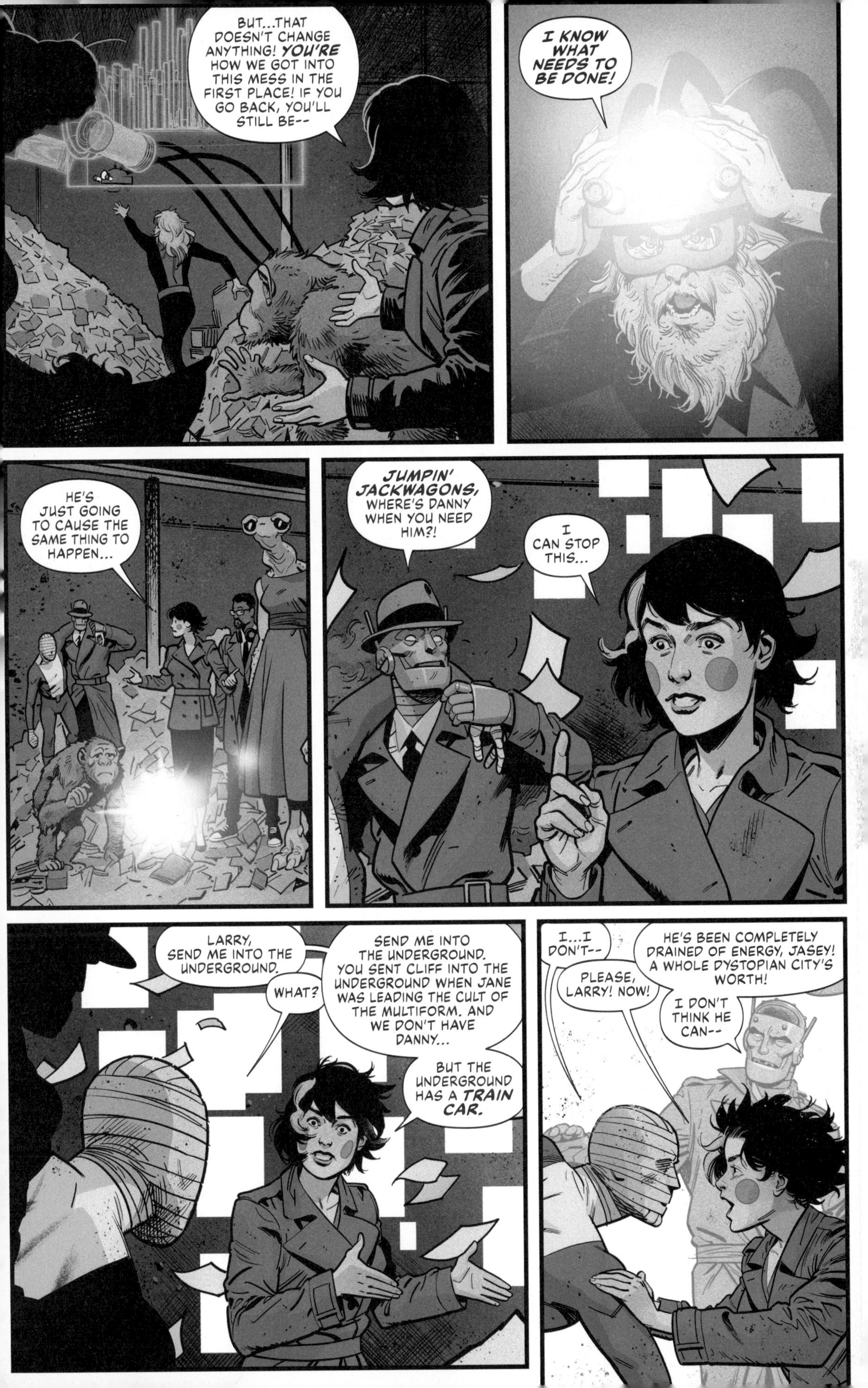
BUT...THAT DOESN'T CHANGE ANYTHING! YOU'RE HOW WE GOT INTO THIS MESS IN THE FIRST PLACE! IF YOU GO BACK, YOU'LL STILL BE--
I KNOW WHAT NEEDS TO BE DONE!
HE'S JUST GOING TO CAUSE THE SAME THING TO HAPPEN...
JUMPIN' JACKWAGONS, WHERE'S DANNY WHEN YOU NEED HIM?!
I CAN STOP THIS...
LARRY, SEND ME INTO THE UNDERGROUND.
WHAT?
SEND ME INTO THE UNDERGROUND. YOU SENT CLIFF INTO THE UNDERGROUND WHEN JANE WAS LEADING THE CULT OF THE MULTIFORM. AND WE DON'T HAVE DANNY...
BUT THE UNDERGROUND HAS A TRAIN CAR.
I...I DON'T--
PLEASE, LARRY! NOW!
HE'S BEEN COMPLETELY DRAINED OF ENERGY, JASEY! A WHOLE DYSTOPIAN CITY'S WORTH!
I DON'T THINK HE CAN--

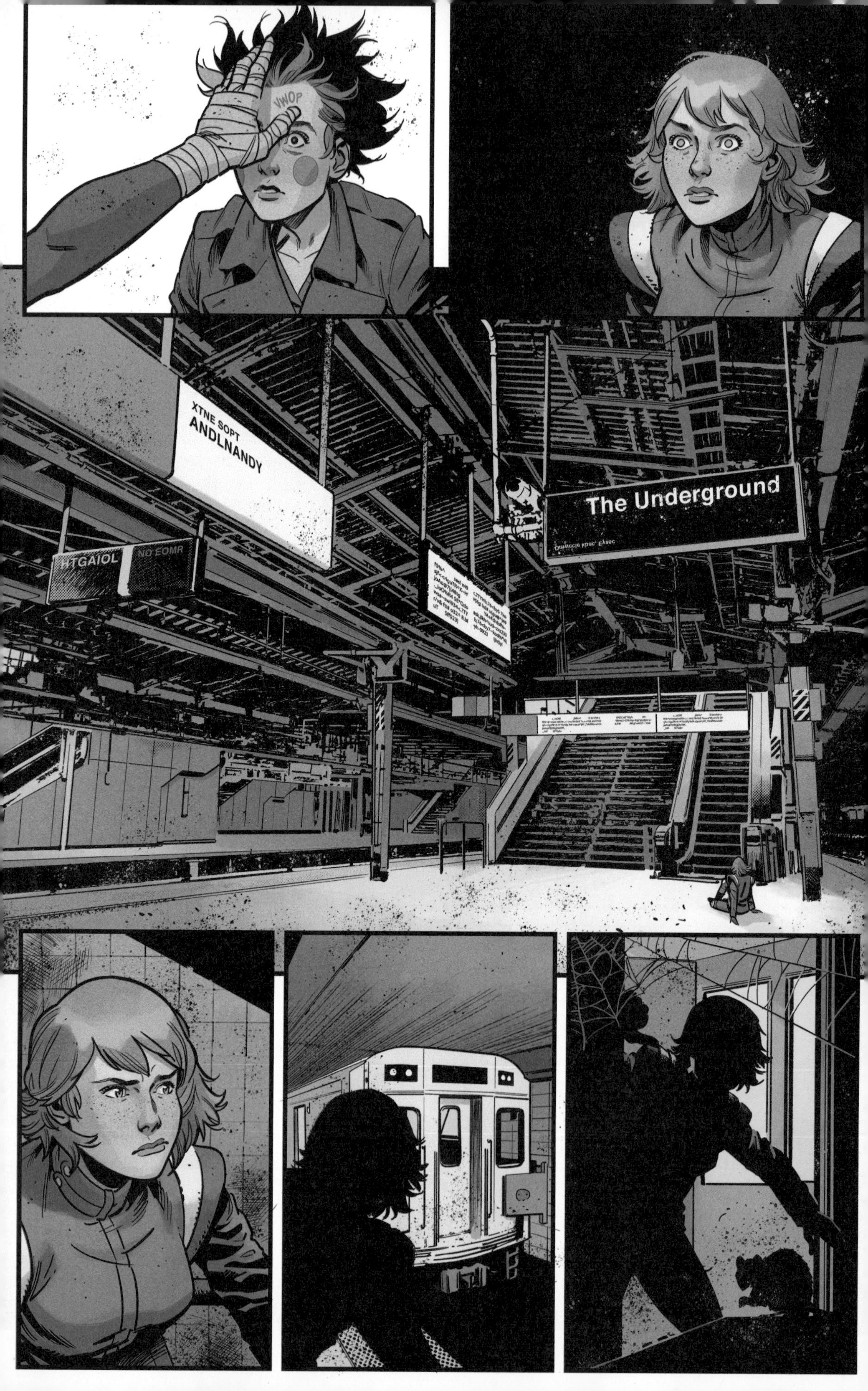
VWOP
XTNE SOPT
ANDLNANDY
HTGAIOL
NO EOMR
The Underground

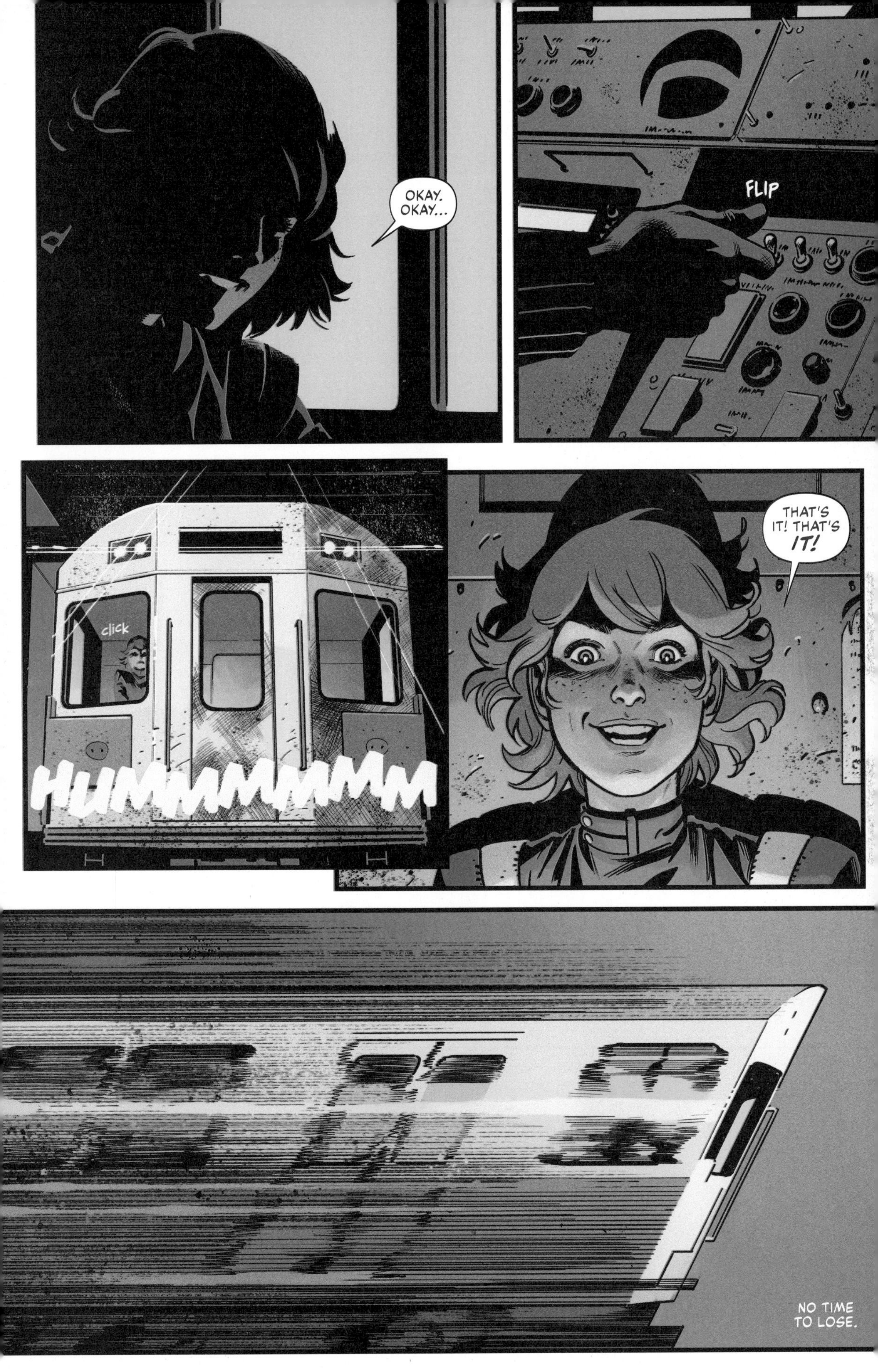
OKAY. OKAY...
FLIP
click
HUMMMMMMM
THAT'S IT! THAT'S IT!
NO TIME TO LOSE.

HE'LL
GET THERE
FIRST...

BUT I CAN
DO THIS.

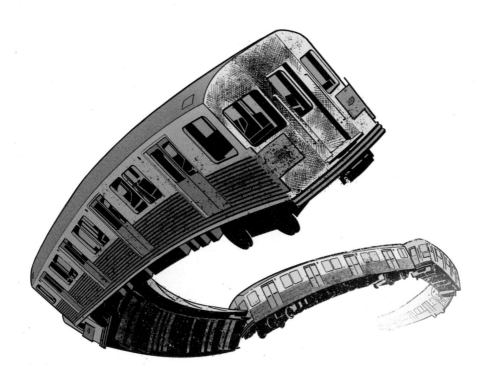

I CAN SEND JANE
A MESSAGE...AND
I CAN SAVE US.

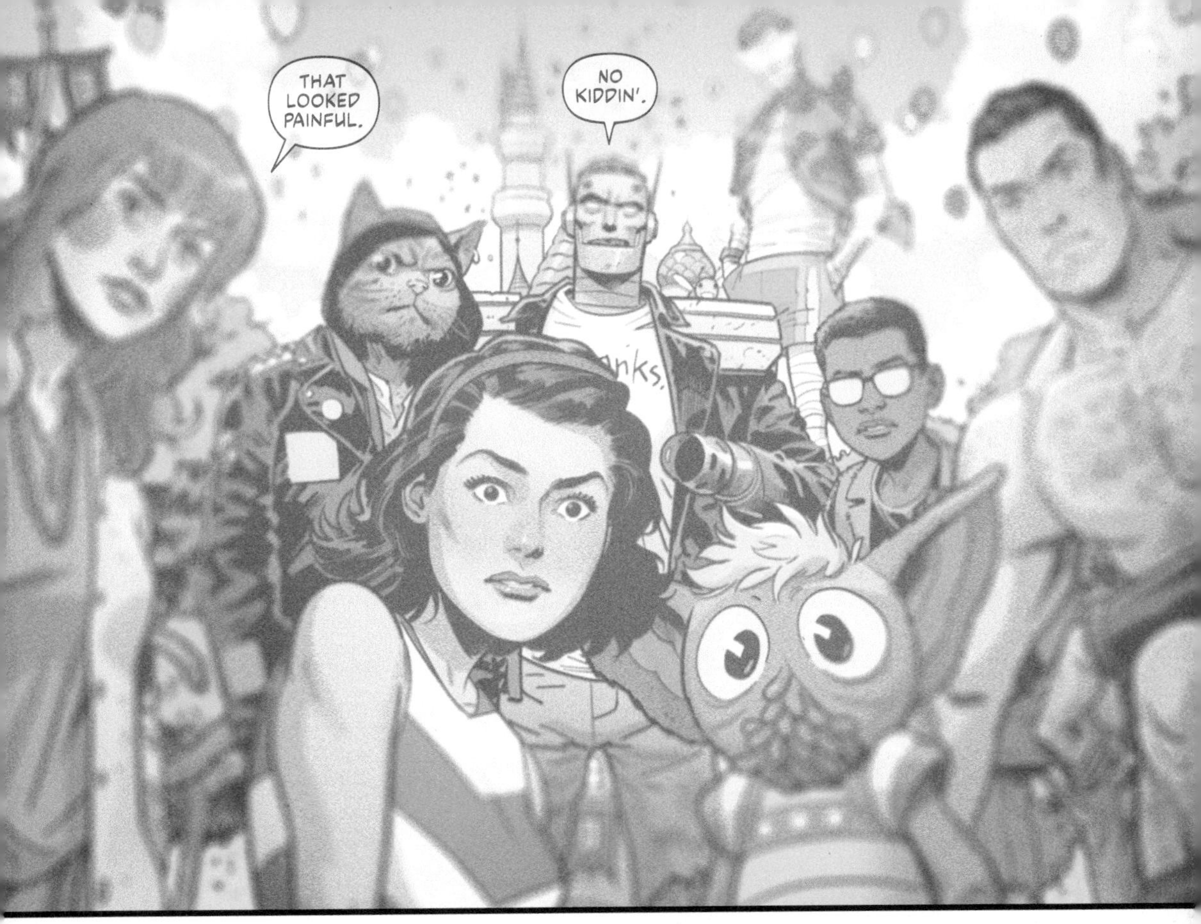
THAT LOOKED PAINFUL.
NO KIDDIN'.

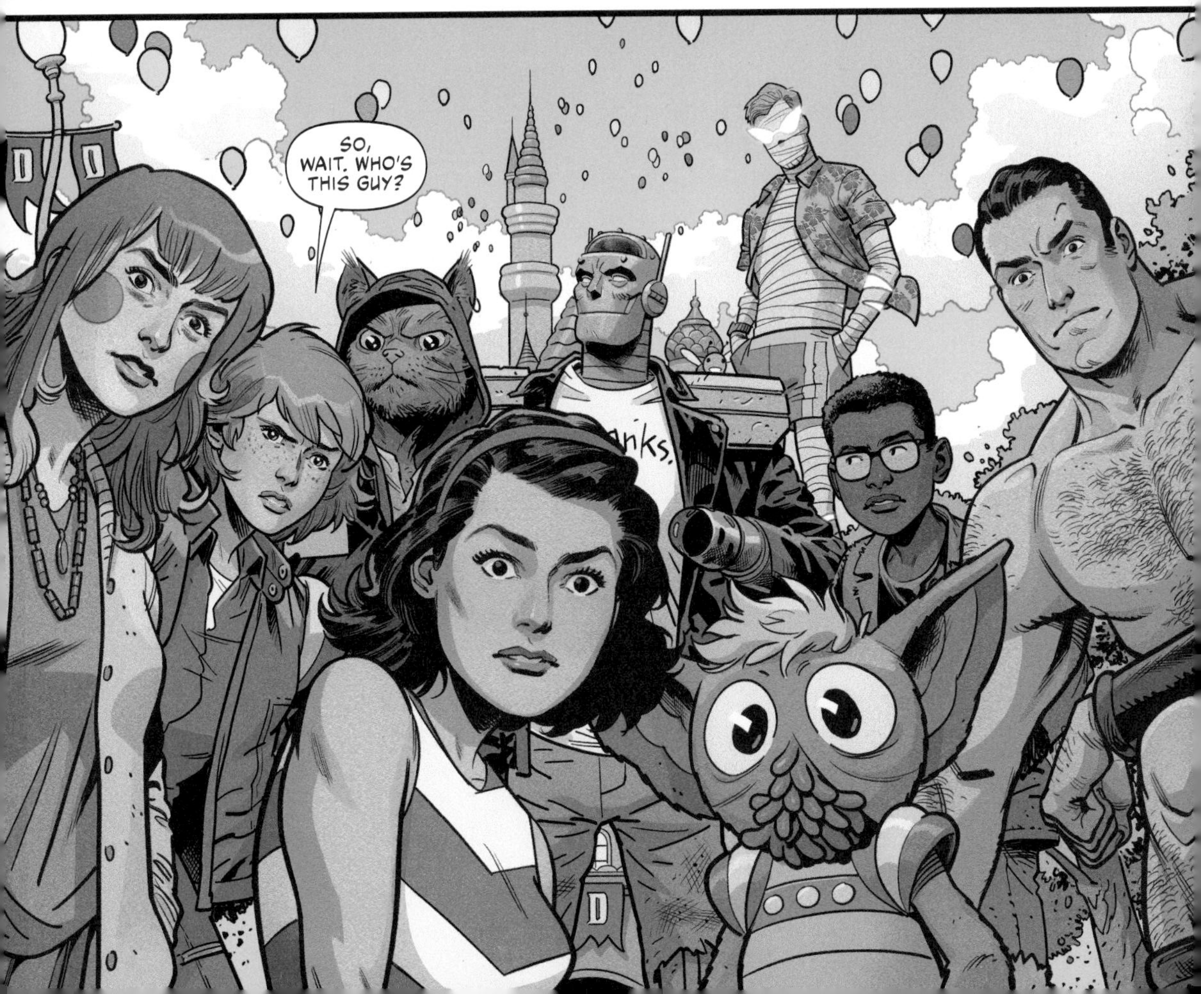
SO, WAIT. WHO'S THIS GUY?

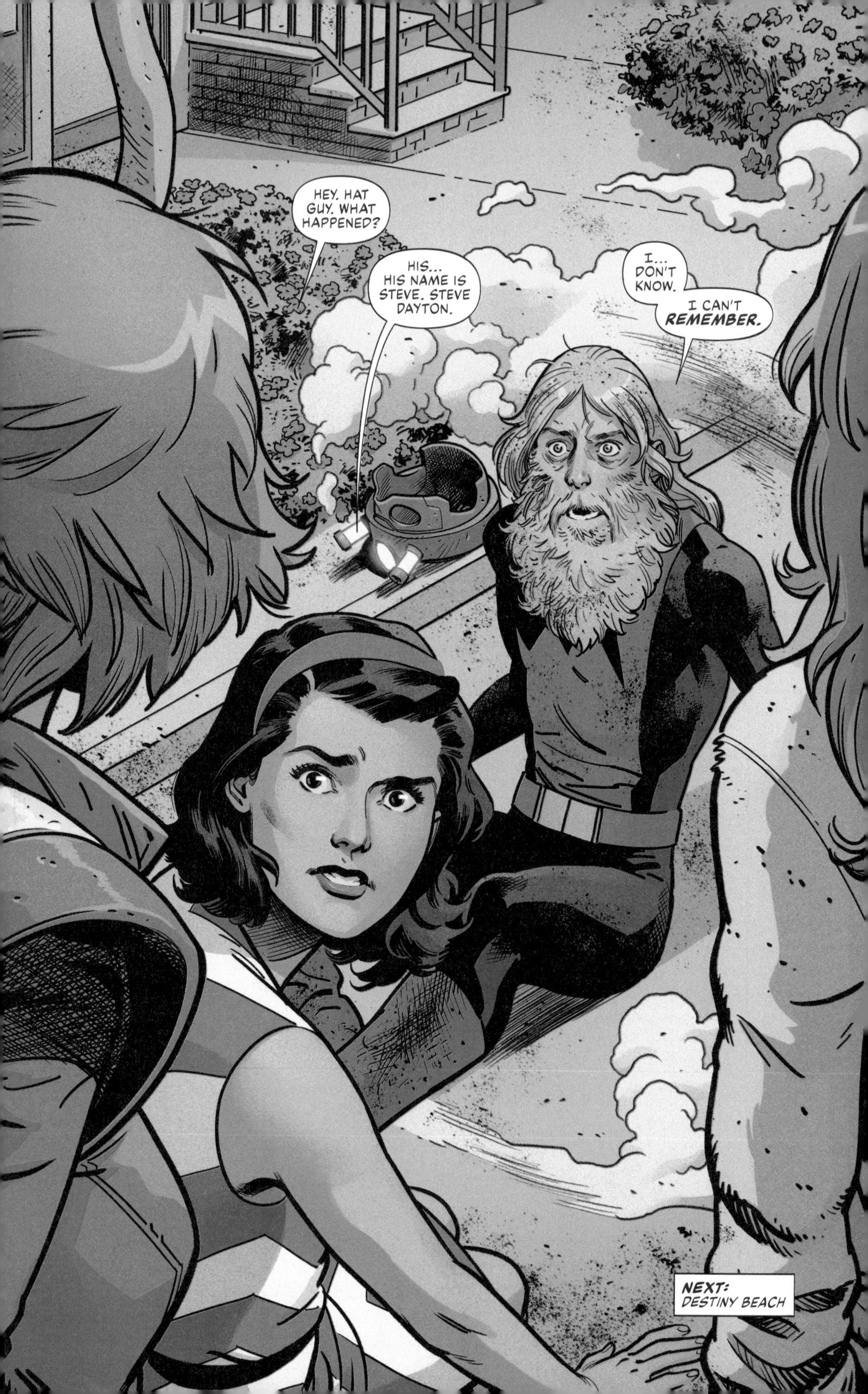
HEY. HAT GUY. WHAT HAPPENED?
HIS... HIS NAME IS STEVE. STEVE DAYTON.
I... DON'T KNOW.
I CAN'T **REMEMBER.**
NEXT: DESTINY BEACH

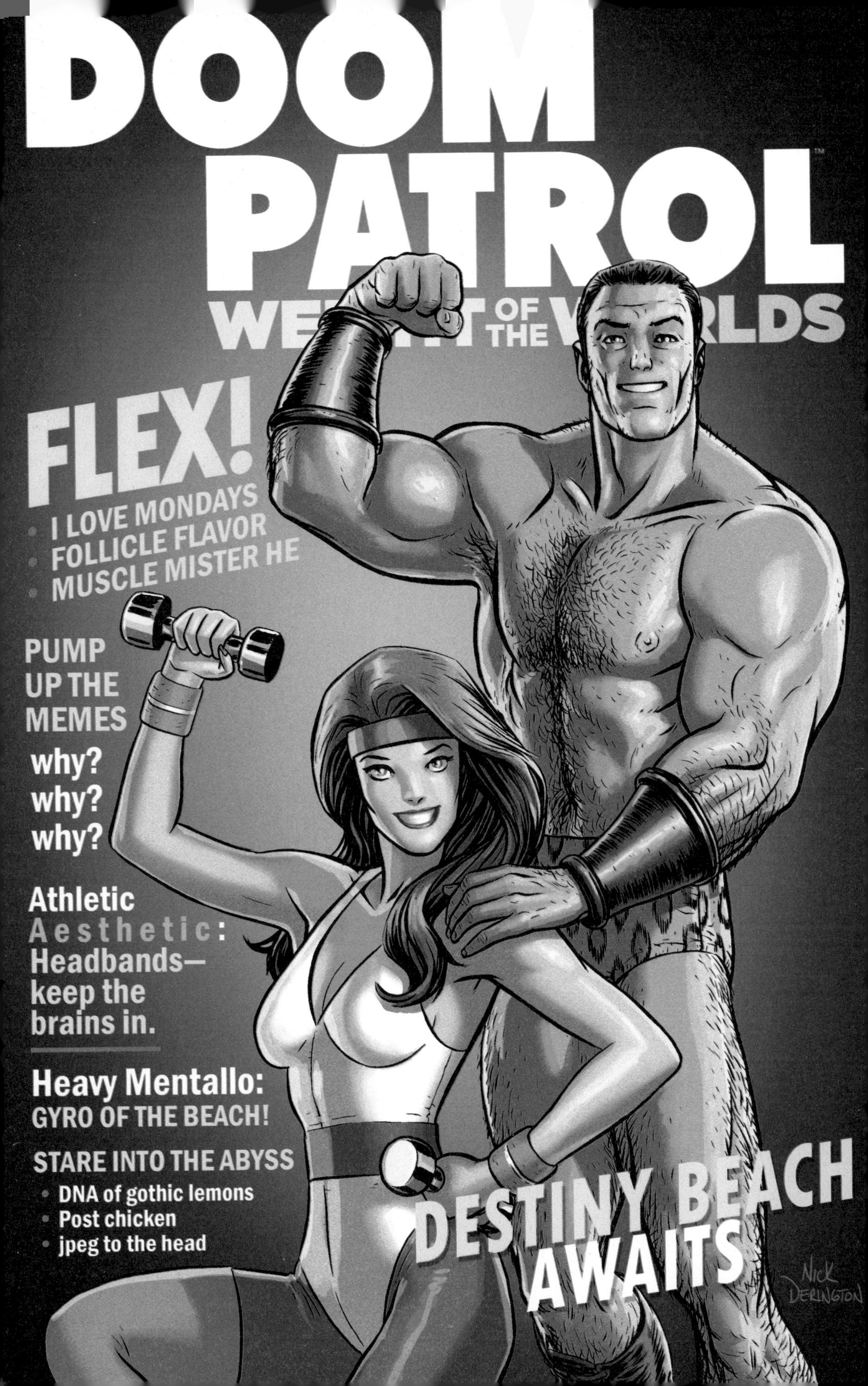
DOOM PATROL™
WE
OF THE
RLDS
FLEX!
• I LOVE MONDAYS
• FOLLICLE FLAVOR
• MUSCLE MISTER HE
PUMP UP THE MEMES
why?
why?
why?
Athletic Aesthetic: Headbands—keep the brains in.
Heavy Mentallo: GYRO OF THE BEACH!
STARE INTO THE ABYSS
• DNA of gothic lemons
• Post chicken
• jpeg to the head
DESTINY BEACH AWAITS
NICK DERINGTON

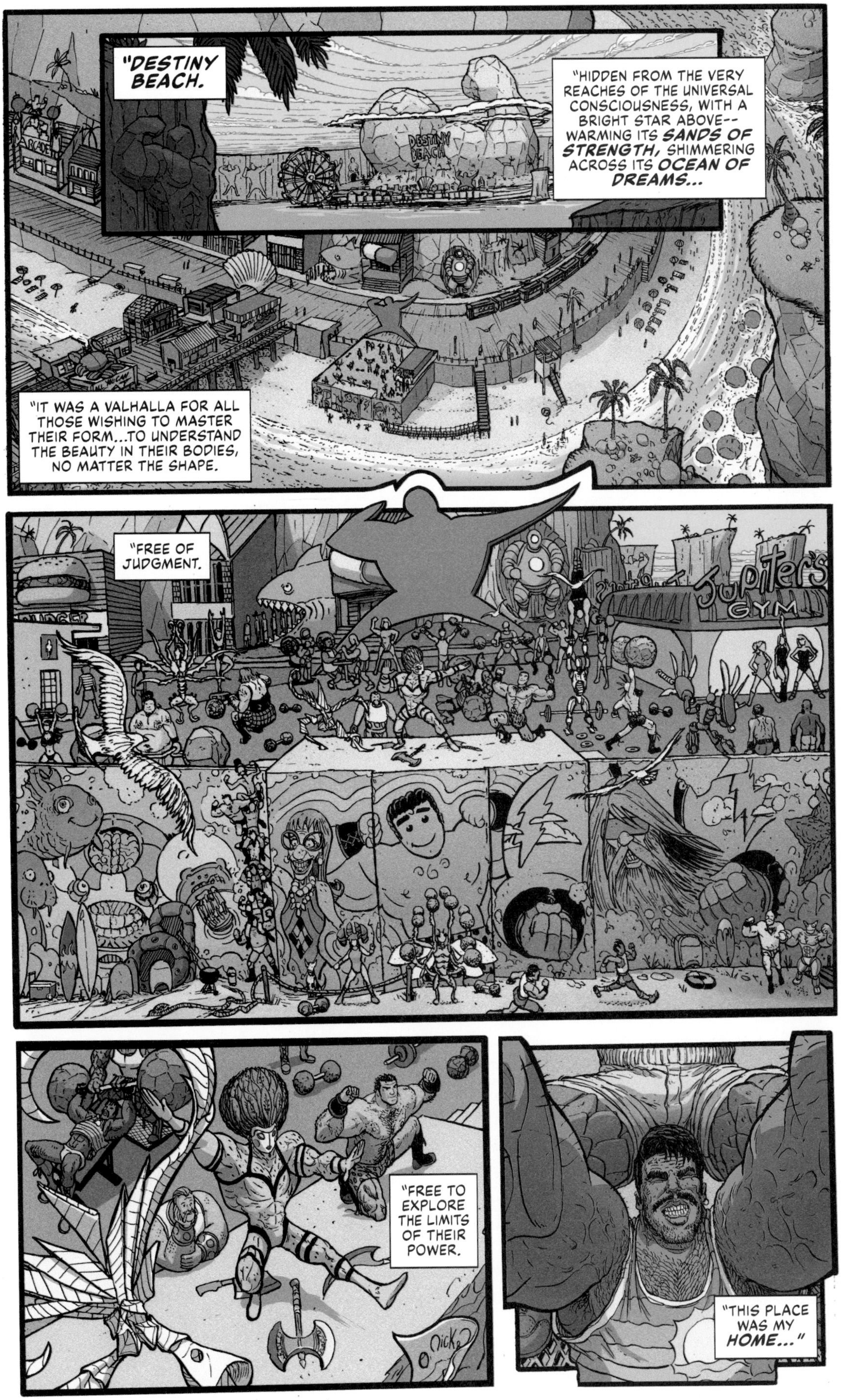
"DESTINY BEACH.
DESTINY BEACH
"HIDDEN FROM THE VERY REACHES OF THE UNIVERSAL CONSCIOUSNESS, WITH A BRIGHT STAR ABOVE--WARMING ITS ***SANDS OF STRENGTH,*** SHIMMERING ACROSS ITS ***OCEAN OF DREAMS...***
"IT WAS A VALHALLA FOR ALL THOSE WISHING TO MASTER THEIR FORM...TO UNDERSTAND THE BEAUTY IN THEIR BODIES, NO MATTER THE SHAPE.
"FREE OF JUDGMENT.
Jupiters
GYM
"FREE TO EXPLORE THE LIMITS OF THEIR POWER.
"THIS PLACE WAS MY ***HOME...***"

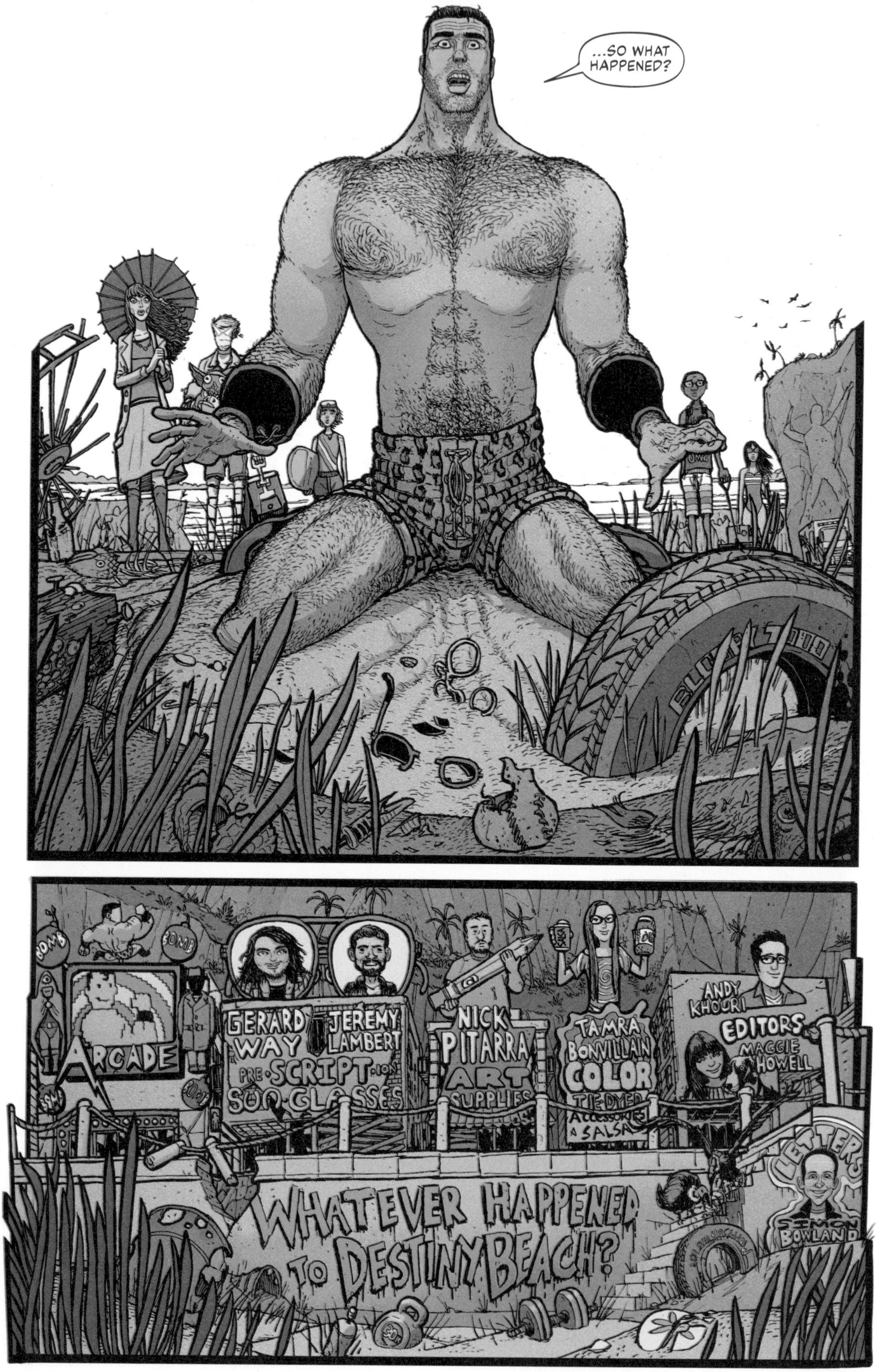
...SO WHAT HAPPENED?
BOMB
BOMB
ARCADE
GERARD WAY
JEREMY LAMBERT
PRE-SCRIPT-ION SUN-GLASSES
NICK PITARRA
ART SUPPLIES
TAMRA BONVILLAIN
COLOR
TIE-DYED ACCESSORIES & SALSA
ANDY KHOURI
EDITORS
MAGGIE HOWELL
LETTERS
SIMON BOWLAND
WHATEVER HAPPENED TO DESTINY BEACH?

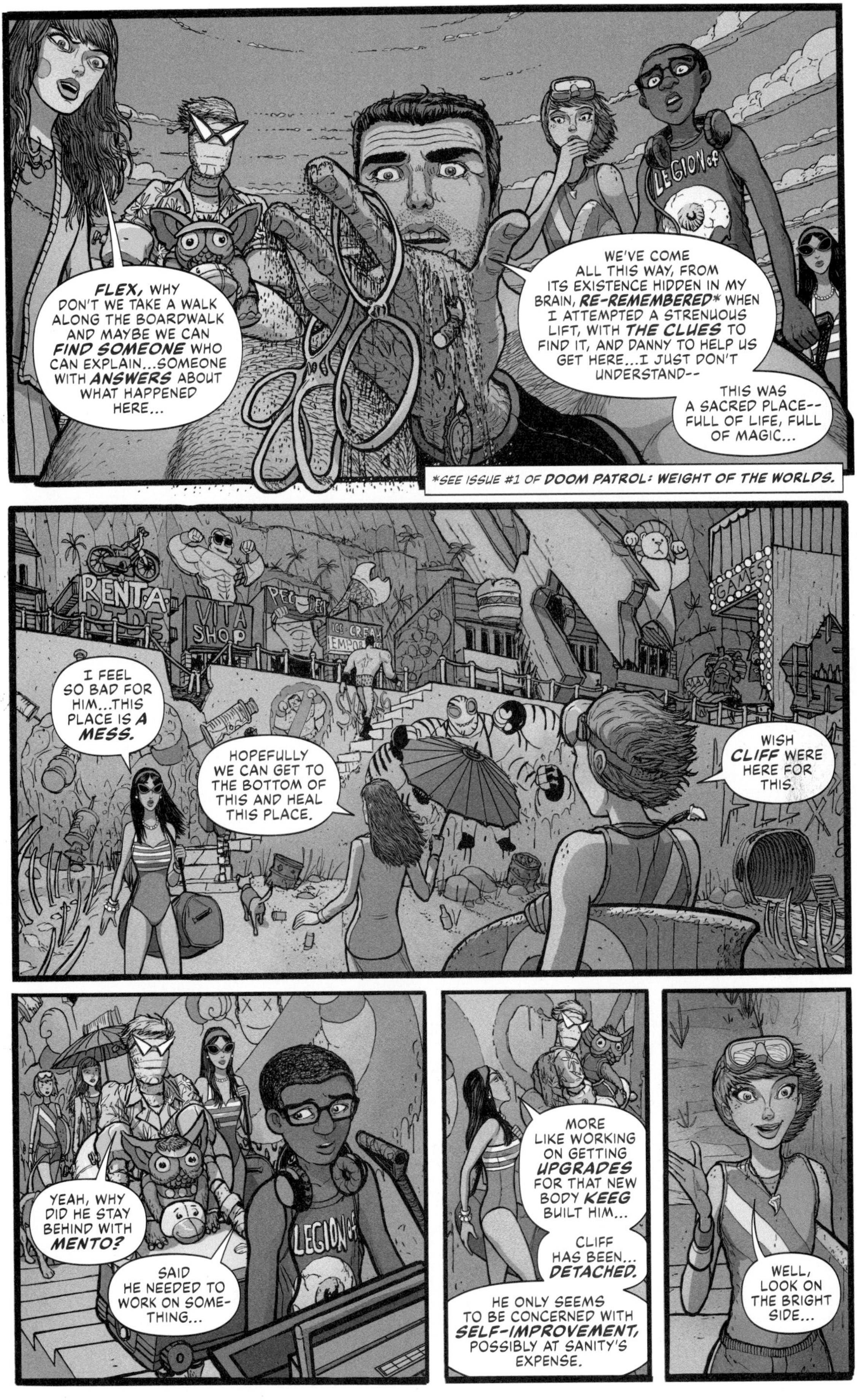
FLEX, WHY DON'T WE TAKE A WALK ALONG THE BOARDWALK AND MAYBE WE CAN FIND SOMEONE WHO CAN EXPLAIN...SOMEONE WITH ANSWERS ABOUT WHAT HAPPENED HERE...
WE'VE COME ALL THIS WAY, FROM ITS EXISTENCE HIDDEN IN MY BRAIN, RE-REMEMBERED* WHEN I ATTEMPTED A STRENUOUS LIFT, WITH THE CLUES TO FIND IT, AND DANNY TO HELP US GET HERE...I JUST DON'T UNDERSTAND--
THIS WAS A SACRED PLACE--FULL OF LIFE, FULL OF MAGIC...
*SEE ISSUE #1 OF DOOM PATROL: WEIGHT OF THE WORLDS.
RENT-A-RIDE
VITA SHOP
ICE CREAM EMPOR
GAMES
I FEEL SO BAD FOR HIM...THIS PLACE IS A MESS.
HOPEFULLY WE CAN GET TO THE BOTTOM OF THIS AND HEAL THIS PLACE.
WISH CLIFF WERE HERE FOR THIS.
YEAH, WHY DID HE STAY BEHIND WITH MENTO?
SAID HE NEEDED TO WORK ON SOME-THING...
MORE LIKE WORKING ON GETTING UPGRADES FOR THAT NEW BODY KEEG BUILT HIM...
CLIFF HAS BEEN... DETACHED.
HE ONLY SEEMS TO BE CONCERNED WITH SELF-IMPROVEMENT, POSSIBLY AT SANITY'S EXPENSE.
WELL, LOOK ON THE BRIGHT SIDE...

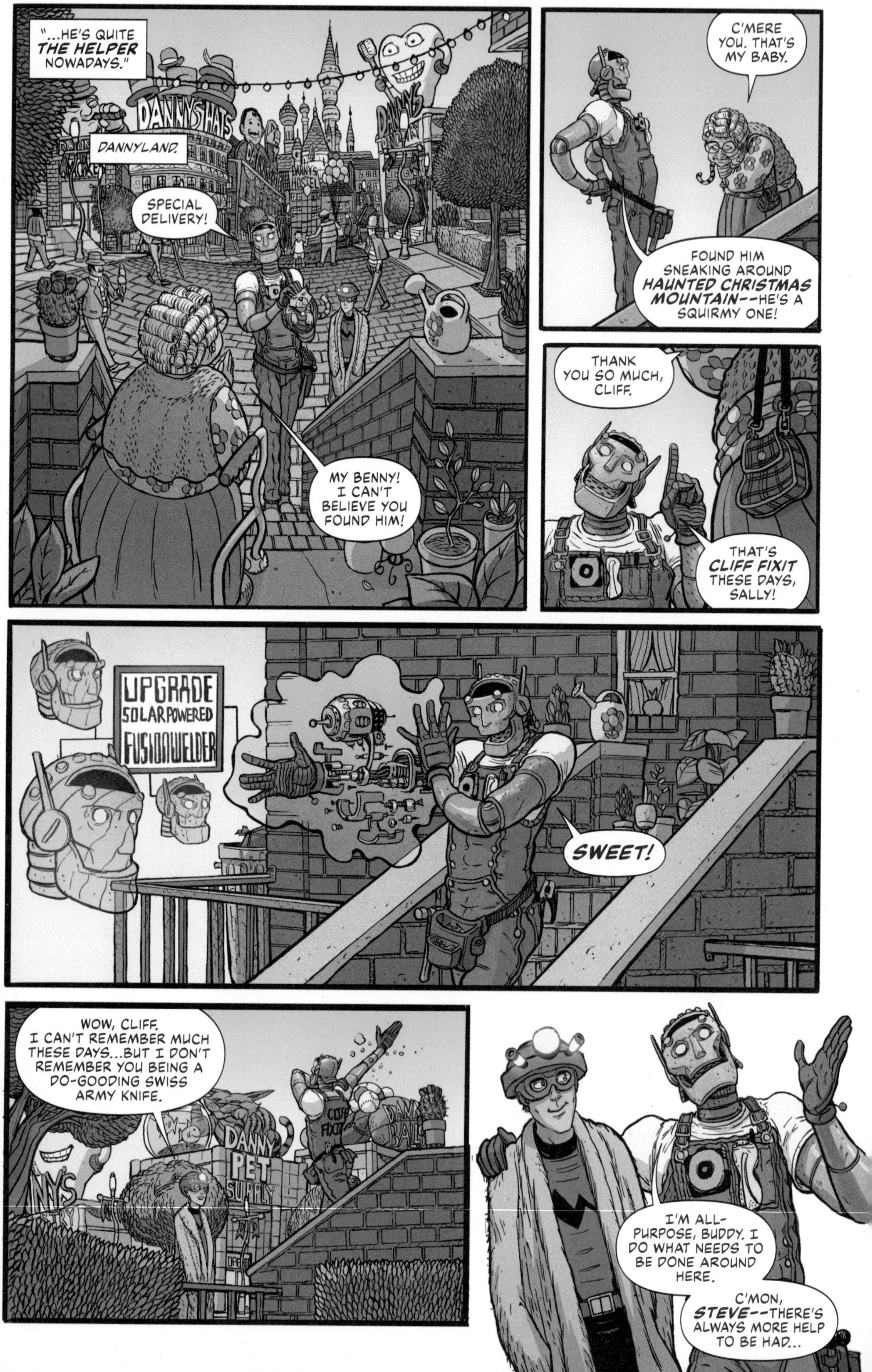
"...HE'S QUITE THE HELPER NOWADAYS."
DANNY'S HATS
DANNY'S HOSTEL
DANNYLAND.
SPECIAL DELIVERY!
MY BENNY! I CAN'T BELIEVE YOU FOUND HIM!
C'MERE YOU. THAT'S MY BABY.
FOUND HIM SNEAKING AROUND HAUNTED CHRISTMAS MOUNTAIN--HE'S A SQUIRMY ONE!
THANK YOU SO MUCH, CLIFF.
THAT'S CLIFF FIXIT THESE DAYS, SALLY!
UPGRADE SOLAR POWERED FUSIONWELDER
SWEET!
WOW, CLIFF. I CAN'T REMEMBER MUCH THESE DAYS...BUT I DON'T REMEMBER YOU BEING A DO-GOODING SWISS ARMY KNIFE.
DANNY PET SUPPLY
I'M ALL-PURPOSE, BUDDY. I DO WHAT NEEDS TO BE DONE AROUND HERE.
C'MON, STEVE--THERE'S ALWAYS MORE HELP TO BE HAD...

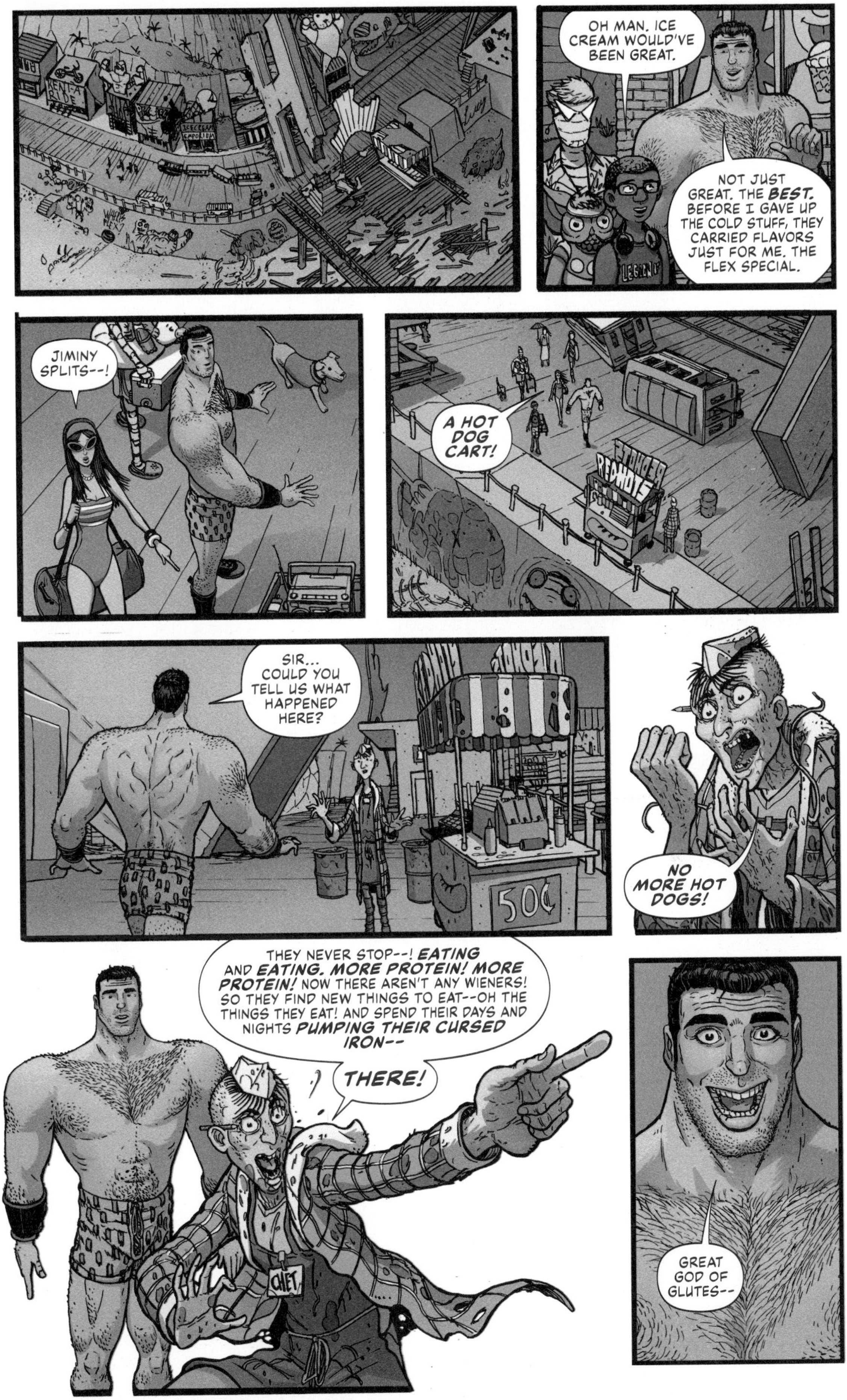
OH MAN. ICE CREAM WOULD'VE BEEN GREAT.
NOT JUST GREAT. THE **BEST.** BEFORE I GAVE UP THE COLD STUFF, THEY CARRIED FLAVORS JUST FOR ME. THE FLEX SPECIAL.
JIMINY SPLITS--!
A HOT DOG CART!
SIR... COULD YOU TELL US WHAT HAPPENED HERE?
50¢
NO MORE HOT DOGS!
THEY NEVER STOP--! ***EATING*** AND ***EATING. MORE PROTEIN! MORE PROTEIN!*** NOW THERE AREN'T ANY WIENERS! SO THEY FIND NEW THINGS TO EAT--OH THE THINGS THEY EAT! AND SPEND THEIR DAYS AND NIGHTS ***PUMPING THEIR CURSED IRON--***
THERE!
CHET
GREAT GOD OF GLUTES--

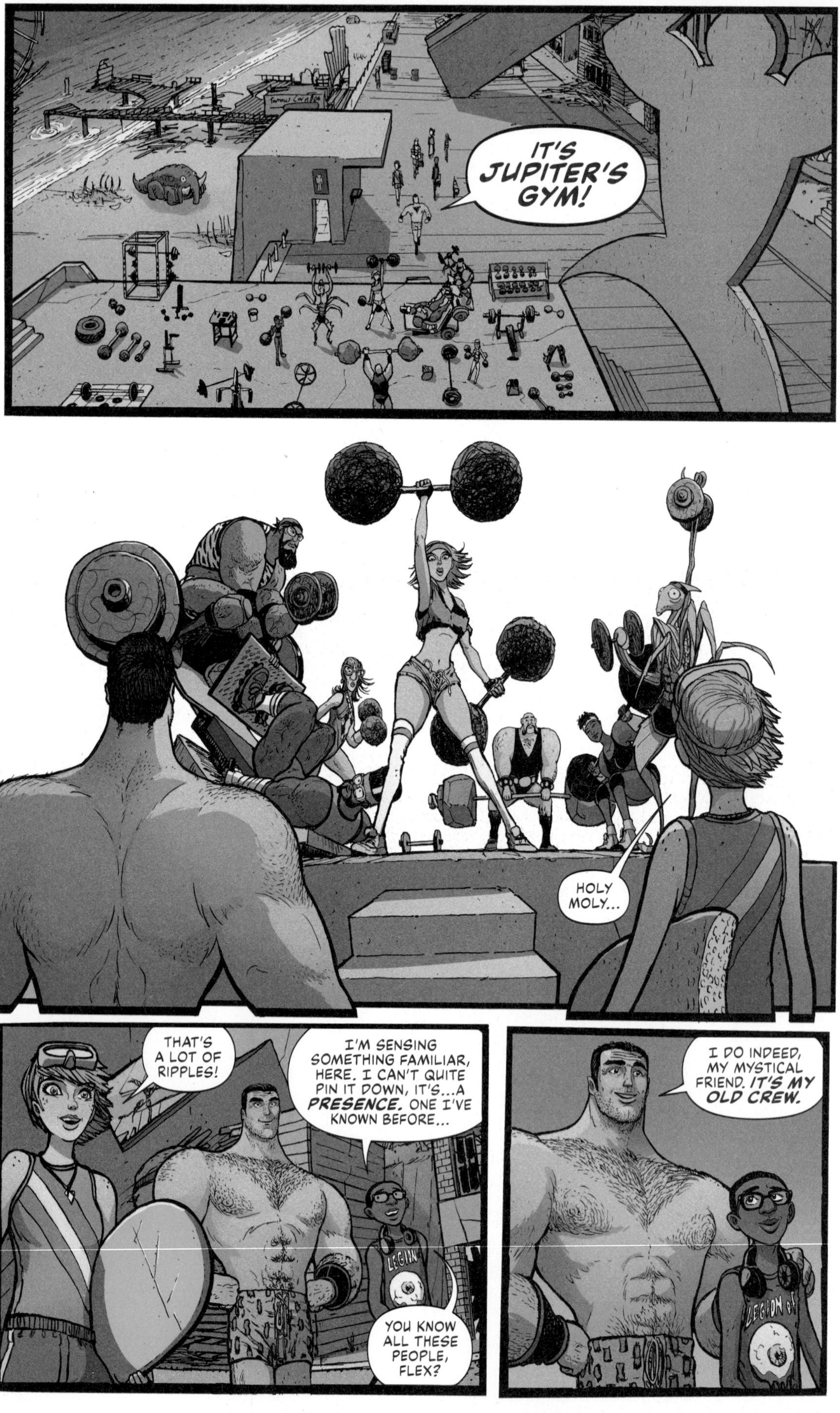
IT'S JUPITER'S GYM!
HOLY MOLY...
THAT'S A LOT OF RIPPLES!
I'M SENSING SOMETHING FAMILIAR, HERE. I CAN'T QUITE PIN IT DOWN, IT'S...A *PRESENCE.* ONE I'VE KNOWN BEFORE...
YOU KNOW ALL THESE PEOPLE, FLEX?
I DO INDEED, MY MYSTICAL FRIEND. *IT'S MY OLD CREW.*
LEGION OF

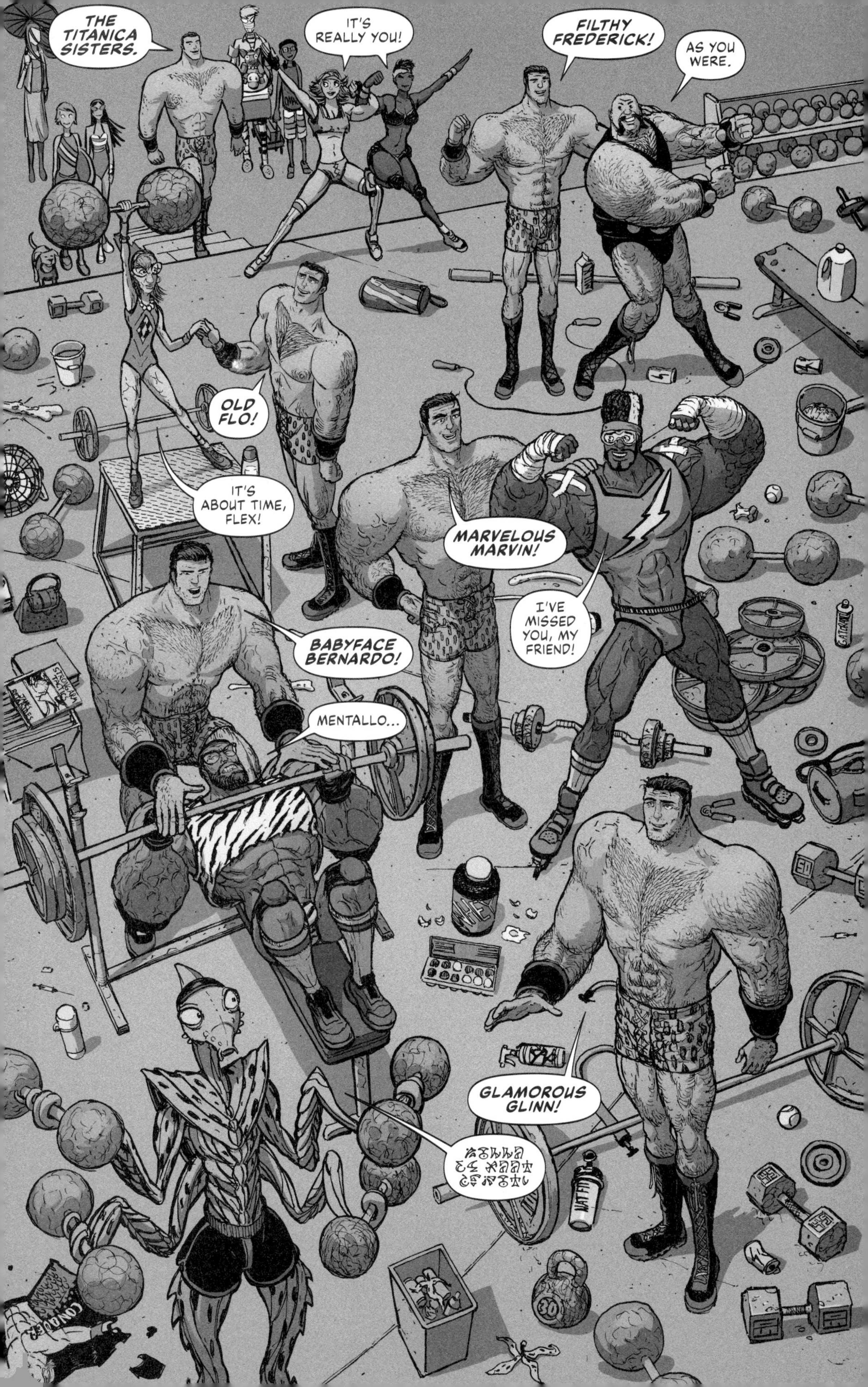
THE TITANICA SISTERS.
IT'S REALLY YOU!
FILTHY FREDERICK!
AS YOU WERE.
OLD FLO!
IT'S ABOUT TIME, FLEX!
MARVELOUS MARVIN!
I'VE MISSED YOU, MY FRIEND!
BABYFACE BERNARDO!
MENTALLO...
GLAMOROUS GLINN!

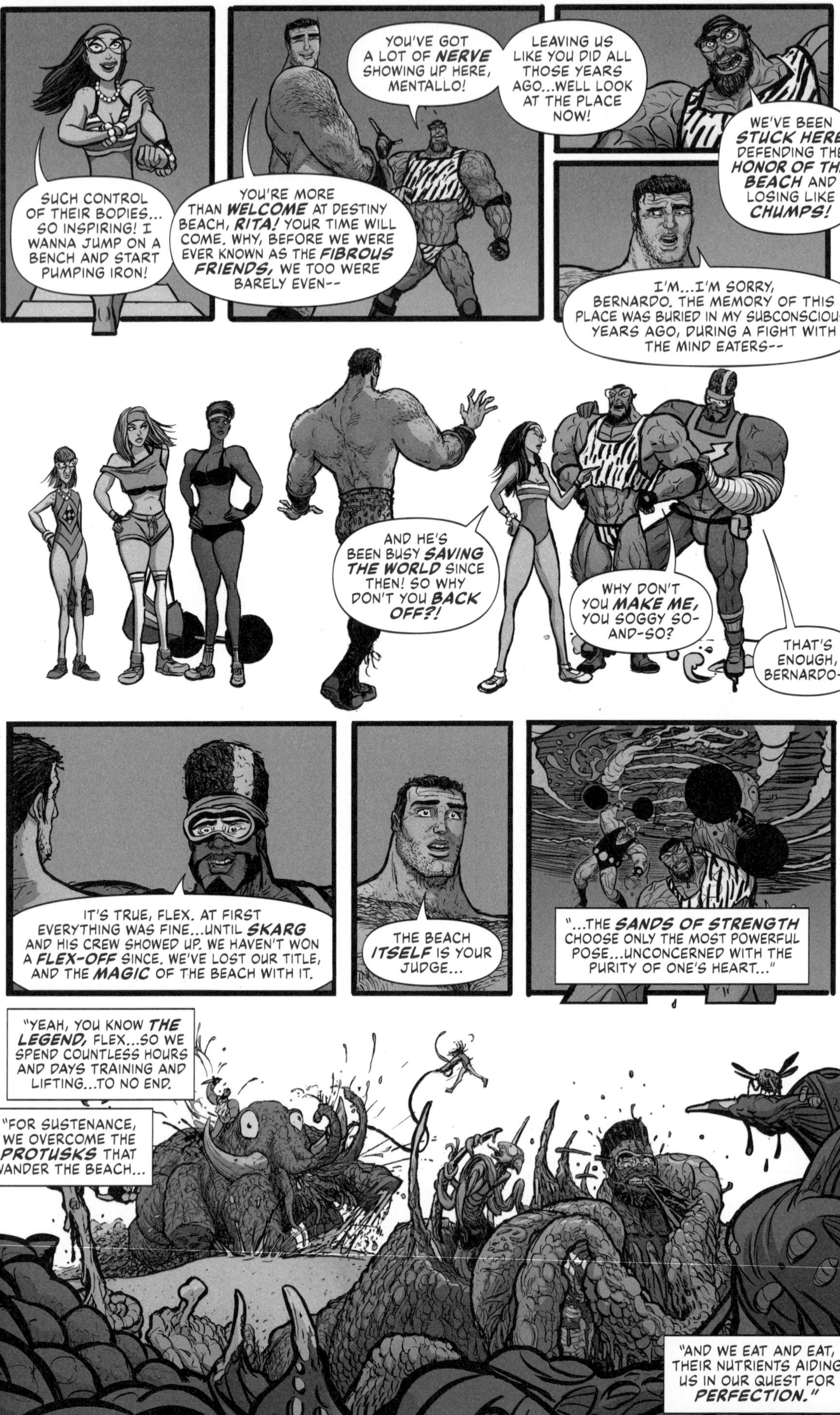
SUCH CONTROL OF THEIR BODIES... SO INSPIRING! I WANNA JUMP ON A BENCH AND START PUMPING IRON!
YOU'RE MORE THAN WELCOME AT DESTINY BEACH, RITA! YOUR TIME WILL COME. WHY, BEFORE WE WERE EVER KNOWN AS THE FIBROUS FRIENDS, WE TOO WERE BARELY EVEN--
YOU'VE GOT A LOT OF NERVE SHOWING UP HERE, MENTALLO!
LEAVING US LIKE YOU DID ALL THOSE YEARS AGO...WELL LOOK AT THE PLACE NOW!
WE'VE BEEN STUCK HERE DEFENDING THE HONOR OF THE BEACH AND LOSING LIKE CHUMPS!
I'M...I'M SORRY, BERNARDO. THE MEMORY OF THIS PLACE WAS BURIED IN MY SUBCONSCIOUS, YEARS AGO, DURING A FIGHT WITH THE MIND EATERS--
AND HE'S BEEN BUSY SAVING THE WORLD SINCE THEN! SO WHY DON'T YOU BACK OFF?!
WHY DON'T YOU MAKE ME, YOU SOGGY SO-AND-SO?
THAT'S ENOUGH, BERNARDO--
IT'S TRUE, FLEX. AT FIRST EVERYTHING WAS FINE...UNTIL SKARG AND HIS CREW SHOWED UP. WE HAVEN'T WON A FLEX-OFF SINCE. WE'VE LOST OUR TITLE, AND THE MAGIC OF THE BEACH WITH IT.
THE BEACH ITSELF IS YOUR JUDGE...
"...THE SANDS OF STRENGTH CHOOSE ONLY THE MOST POWERFUL POSE...UNCONCERNED WITH THE PURITY OF ONE'S HEART..."
"YEAH, YOU KNOW THE LEGEND, FLEX...SO WE SPEND COUNTLESS HOURS AND DAYS TRAINING AND LIFTING...TO NO END.
"FOR SUSTENANCE, WE OVERCOME THE PROTUSKS THAT WANDER THE BEACH...
"AND WE EAT AND EAT, THEIR NUTRIENTS AIDING US IN OUR QUEST FOR PERFECTION."

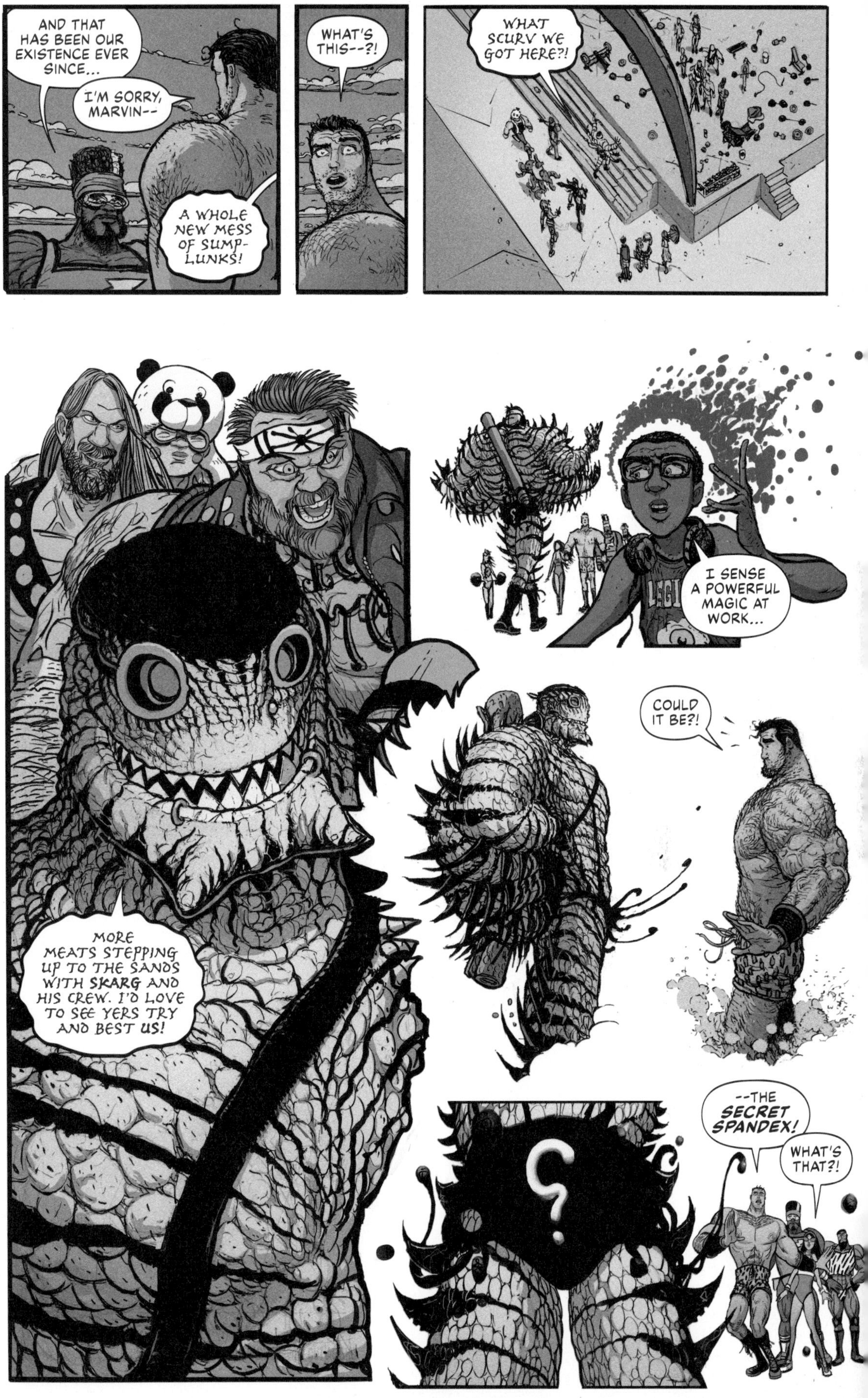
AND THAT HAS BEEN OUR EXISTENCE EVER SINCE...
I'M SORRY, MARVIN--
A WHOLE NEW MESS OF SUMP-LUNKS!
WHAT'S THIS--?!
WHAT SCURV WE GOT HERE?!
MORE MEATS STEPPING UP TO THE SANDS WITH SKARG AND HIS CREW. I'D LOVE TO SEE YERS TRY AND BEST US!
I SENSE A POWERFUL MAGIC AT WORK...
COULD IT BE?!
--THE SECRET SPANDEX!
WHAT'S THAT?!

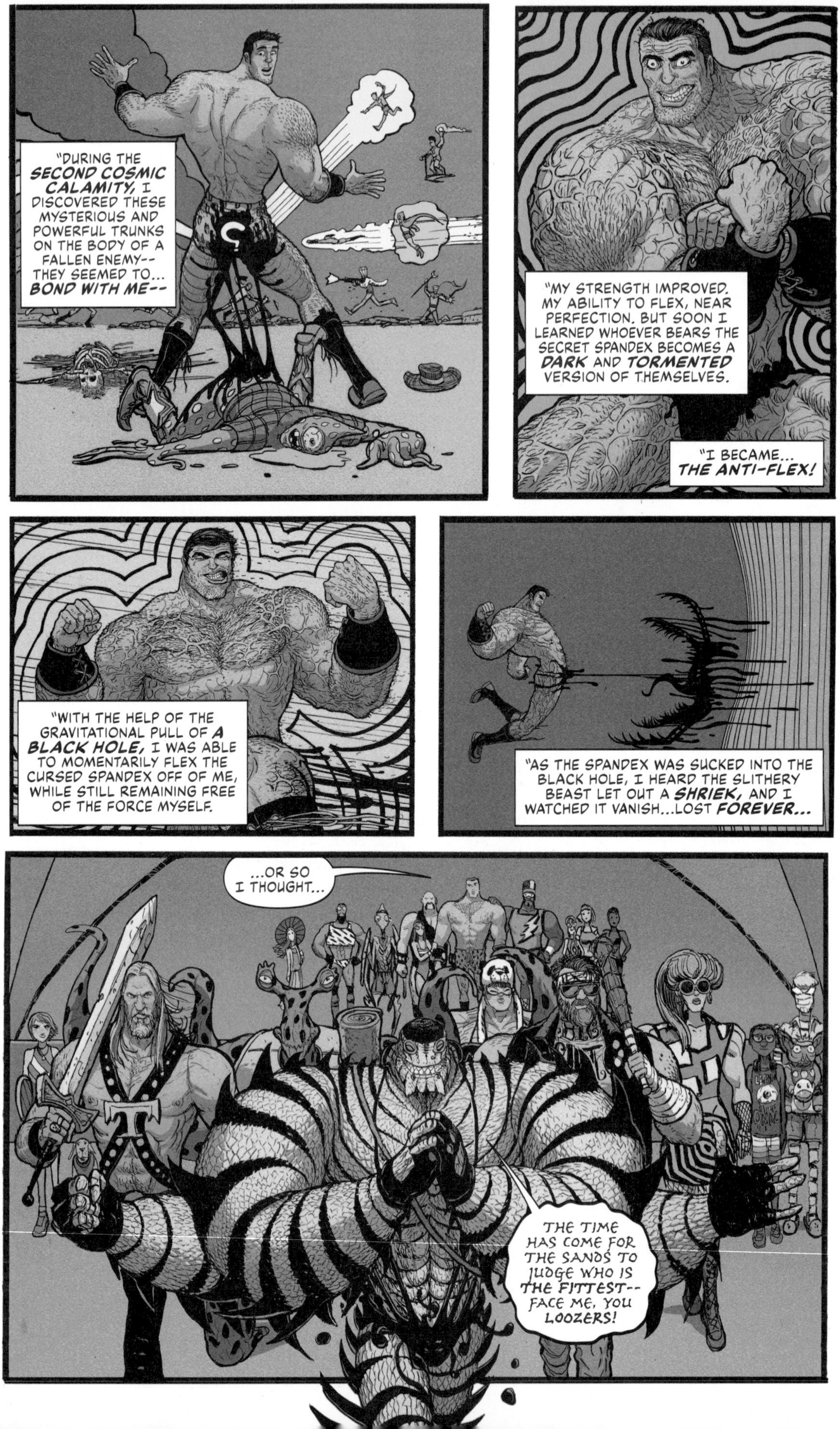
"DURING THE SECOND COSMIC CALAMITY, I DISCOVERED THESE MYSTERIOUS AND POWERFUL TRUNKS ON THE BODY OF A FALLEN ENEMY-- THEY SEEMED TO... BOND WITH ME--
"MY STRENGTH IMPROVED. MY ABILITY TO FLEX, NEAR PERFECTION. BUT SOON I LEARNED WHOEVER BEARS THE SECRET SPANDEX BECOMES A DARK AND TORMENTED VERSION OF THEMSELVES.
"I BECAME... THE ANTI-FLEX!
"WITH THE HELP OF THE GRAVITATIONAL PULL OF A BLACK HOLE, I WAS ABLE TO MOMENTARILY FLEX THE CURSED SPANDEX OFF OF ME, WHILE STILL REMAINING FREE OF THE FORCE MYSELF.
"AS THE SPANDEX WAS SUCKED INTO THE BLACK HOLE, I HEARD THE SLITHERY BEAST LET OUT A SHRIEK, AND I WATCHED IT VANISH...LOST FOREVER...
...OR SO I THOUGHT...
THE TIME HAS COME FOR THE SANDS TO JUDGE WHO IS THE FITTEST-- FACE ME, YOU LOOZERS!

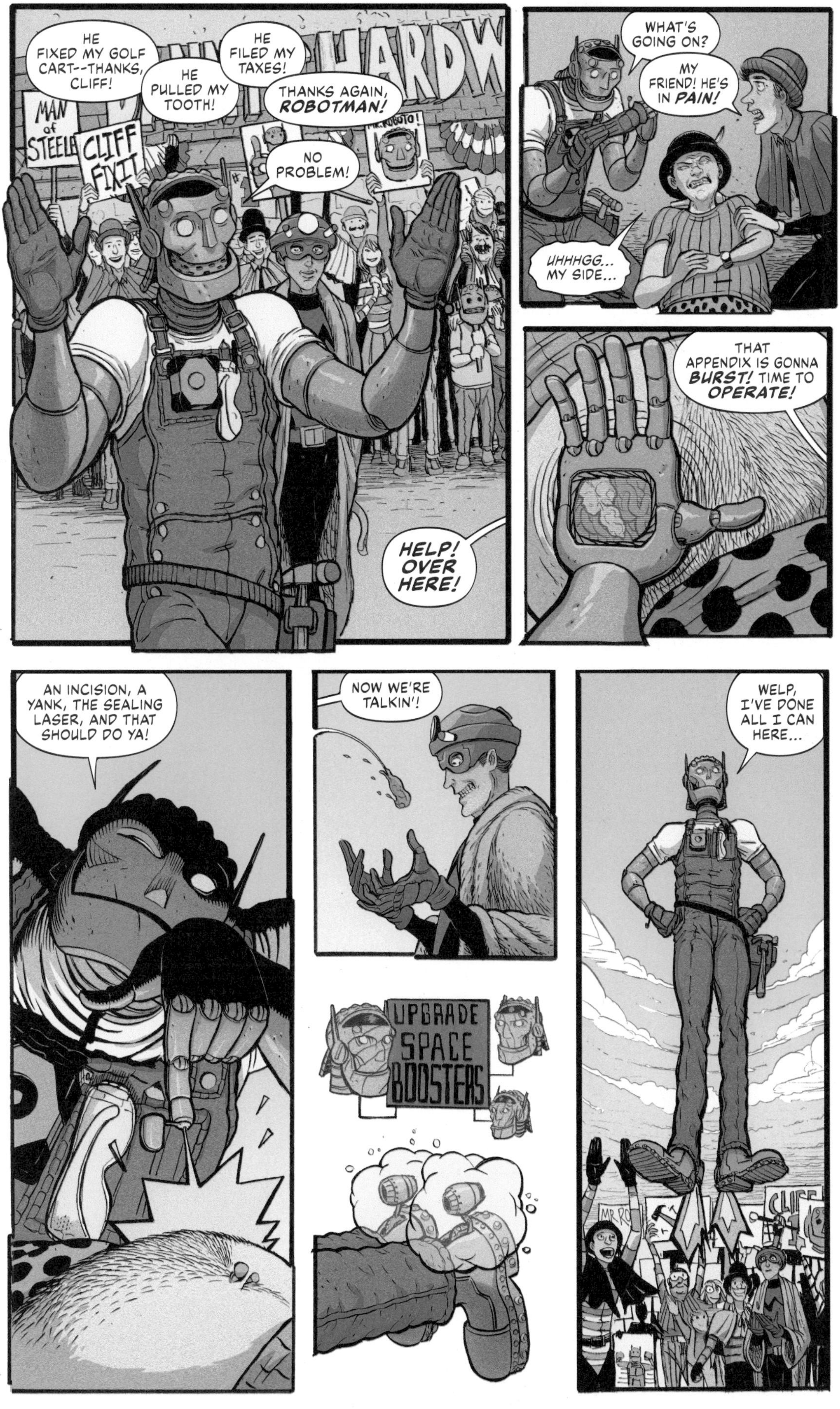
HARDW
MAN of STEEL
CLIFF FIX-IT
MR. ROBOTO!
HE FIXED MY GOLF CART--THANKS, CLIFF!
HE PULLED MY TOOTH!
HE FILED MY TAXES!
THANKS AGAIN, ROBOTMAN!
NO PROBLEM!
HELP! OVER HERE!
WHAT'S GOING ON?
MY FRIEND! HE'S IN PAIN!
UHHHGG... MY SIDE...
THAT APPENDIX IS GONNA BURST! TIME TO OPERATE!
AN INCISION, A YANK, THE SEALING LASER, AND THAT SHOULD DO YA!
NOW WE'RE TALKIN'!
UPGRADE SPACE BOOSTERS
WELP, I'VE DONE ALL I CAN HERE...

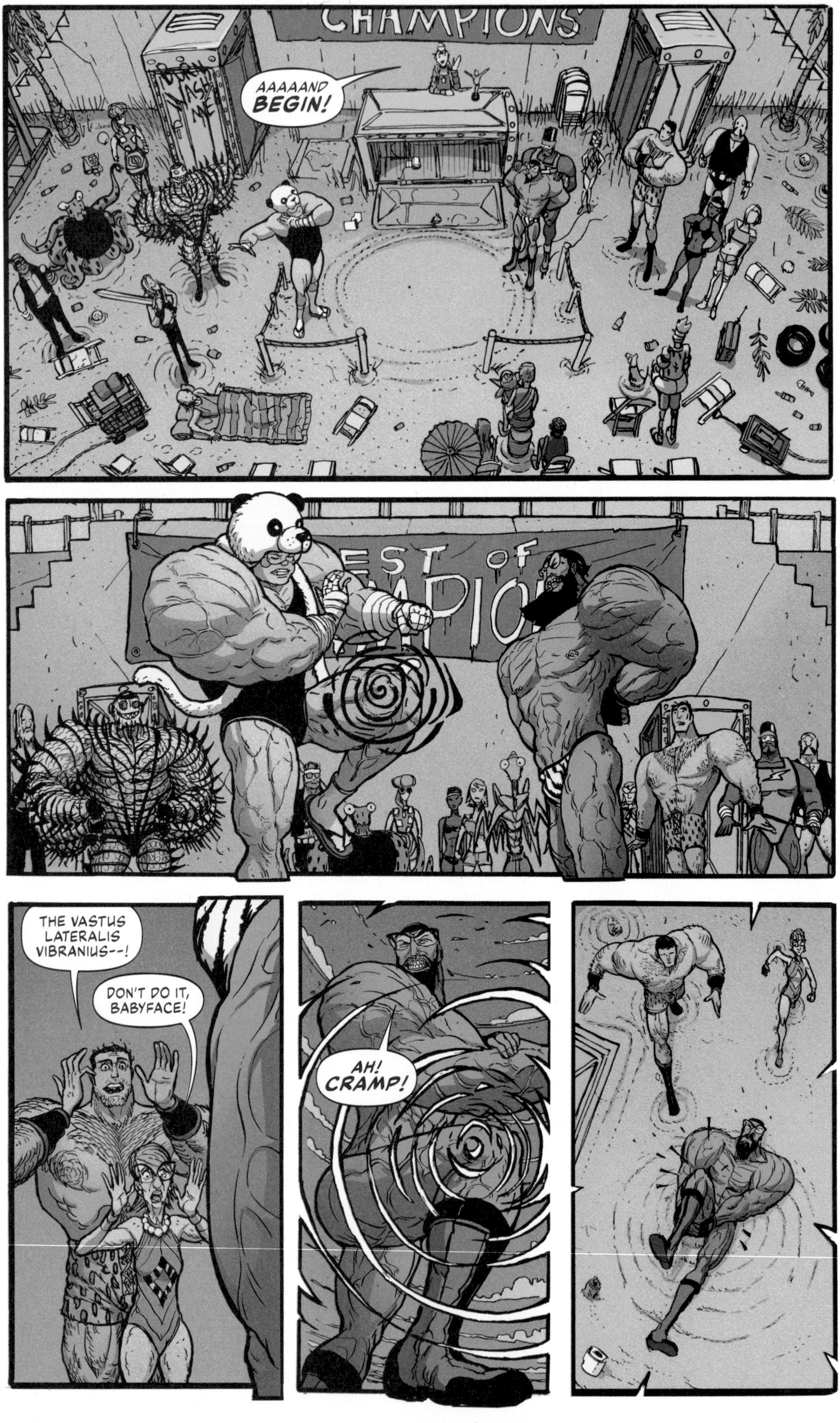
CHAMPIONS
AAAAAND BEGIN!
EST OF
THE VASTUS LATERALIS VIBRANIUS--!
DON'T DO IT, BABYFACE!
AH! CRAMP!

HIS LEG--!

IT'S CRAMPING INWARD--*HE'S GOING TO CRAMP HIMSELF INTO INFINITY!*

WE NEED TO GET *THE CABANA-MAN*--HIS MAGIC HANDS COULD SAVE BERNARDO'S *LIFE!*

WHO'S THE CABANA-MAN?!

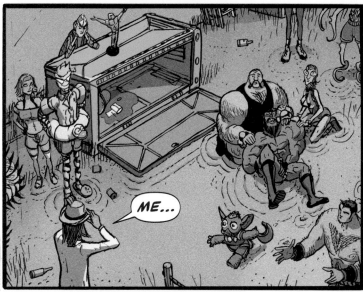

ME...

I'M THE CABANA-MAN.

RICARDO!

THANK YOU, MY LITTLE FRIEND.

HOW ARE YOU EVEN ALIVE?!

MY *ESSENCE* DRIFTED INTO SPACE, ACROSS THE HEAVENS, MIXING WITH STAR MATTER AND MOONBEAMS...EVENTUALLY IT DRIFTED TO THIS PLACE, DESTINY BEACH, AND I WAS BORN ANEW AMONG THE SANDS...

...TO USE MY MAGIC HANDS AGAIN TO SAVE THE LIVES OF ALL WHO NEEDED *SENSUAL HEALING.*

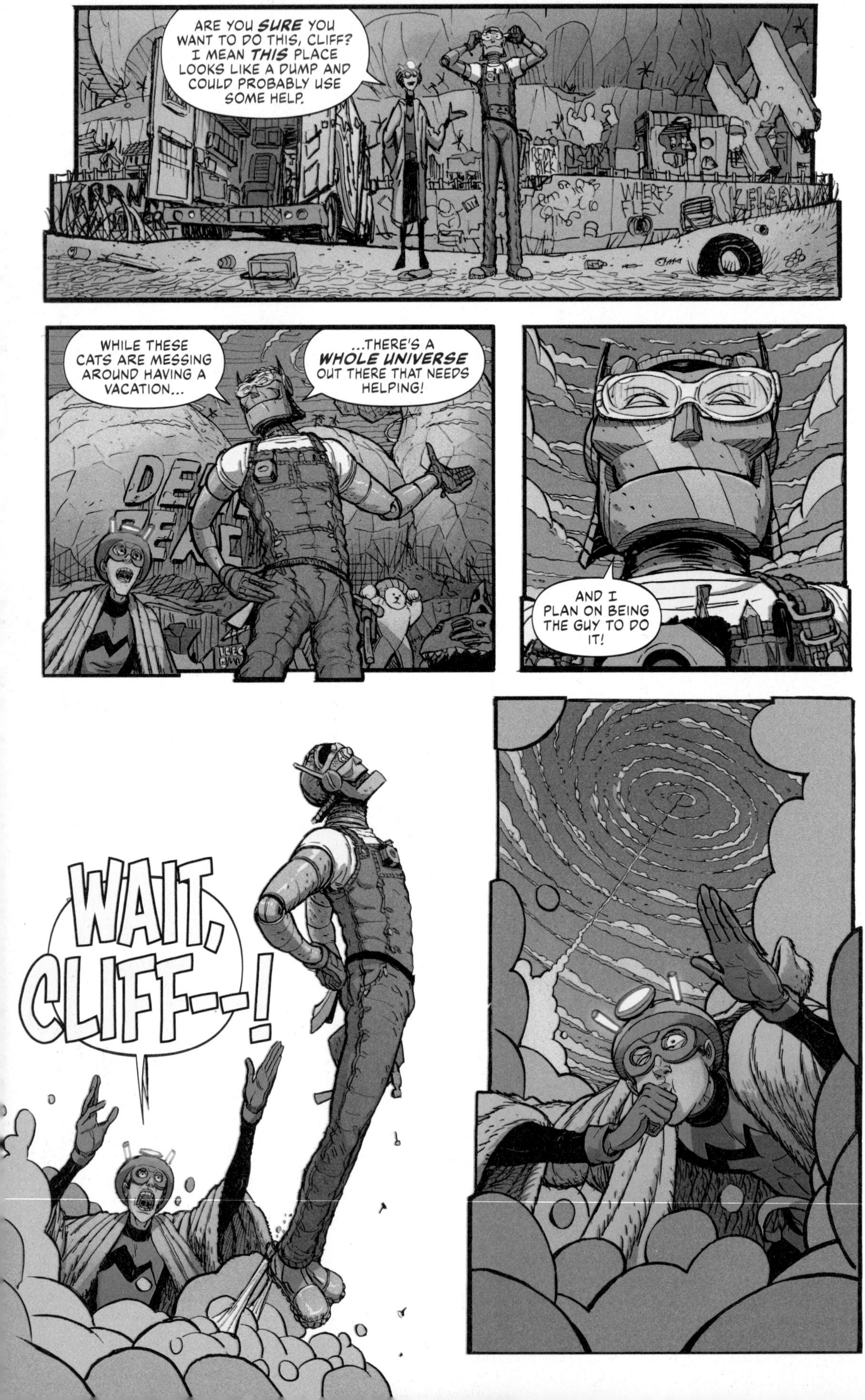
ARE YOU *SURE* YOU WANT TO DO THIS, CLIFF? I MEAN *THIS* PLACE LOOKS LIKE A DUMP AND COULD PROBABLY USE SOME HELP.
RENTAL BIKK
WHERE'S FLEX
WHILE THESE CATS ARE MESSING AROUND HAVING A VACATION...
...THERE'S A *WHOLE UNIVERSE* OUT THERE THAT NEEDS HELPING!
AND I PLAN ON BEING THE GUY TO DO IT!
WAIT, CLIFF--!

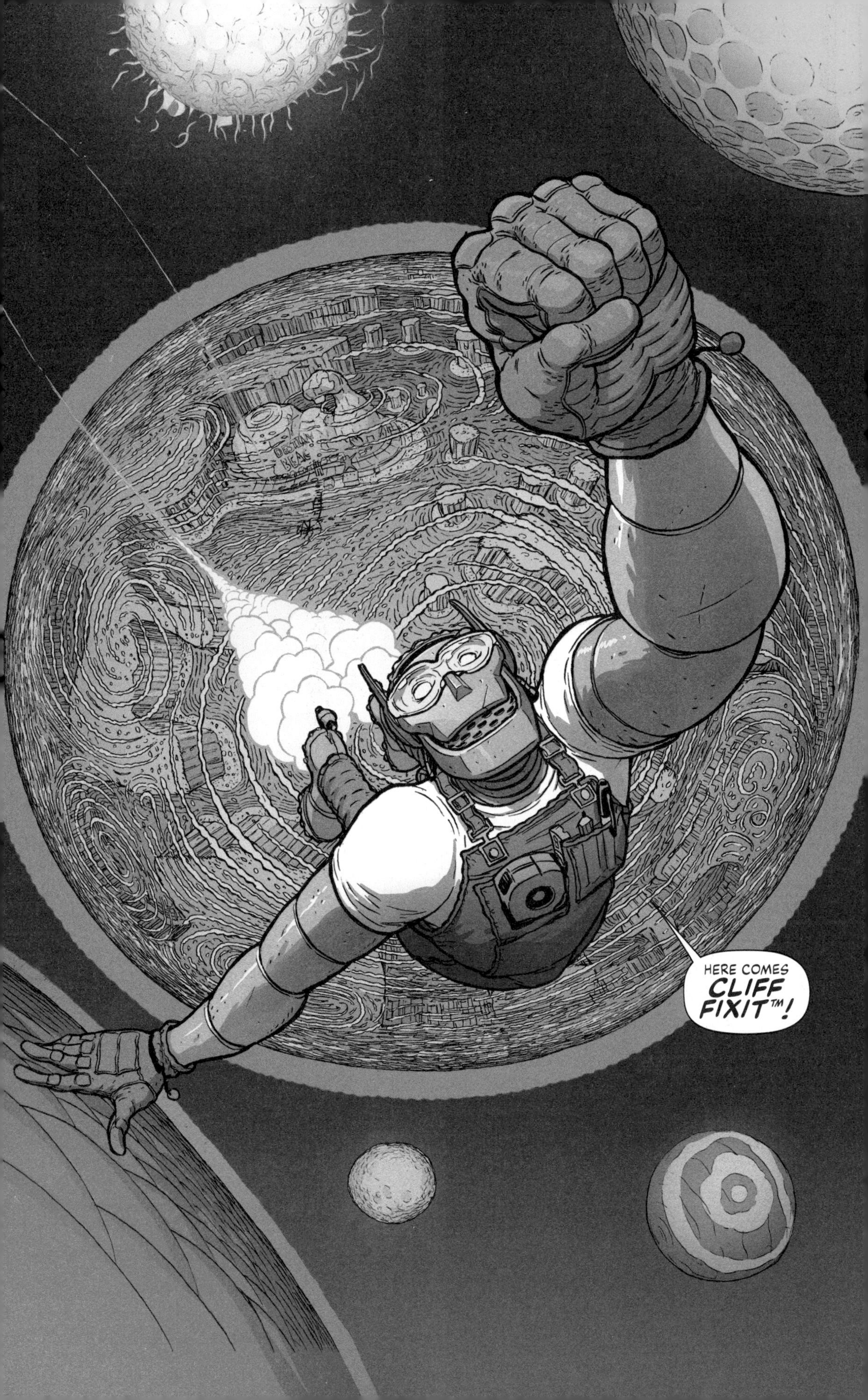
HERE COMES
CLIFF
FIXIT™!

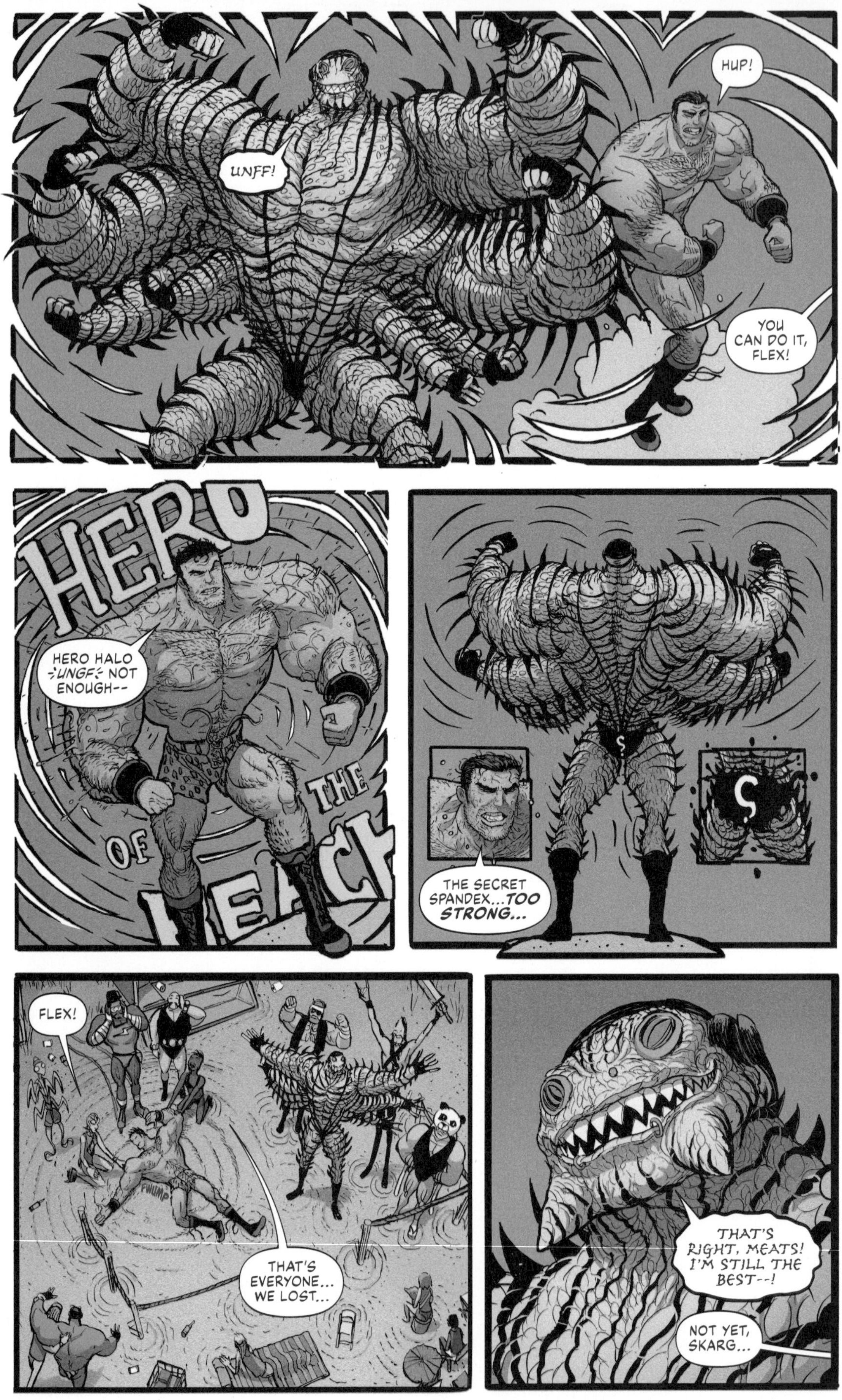

UNFF!
HUP!
YOU CAN DO IT, FLEX!
HERO
HERO HALO -UNGF- NOT ENOUGH--
THE
OF
THE SECRET SPANDEX...TOO STRONG...
FLEX!
FWUMP
THAT'S EVERYONE... WE LOST...
THAT'S RIGHT, MEATS! I'M STILL THE BEST--!
NOT YET, SKARG...

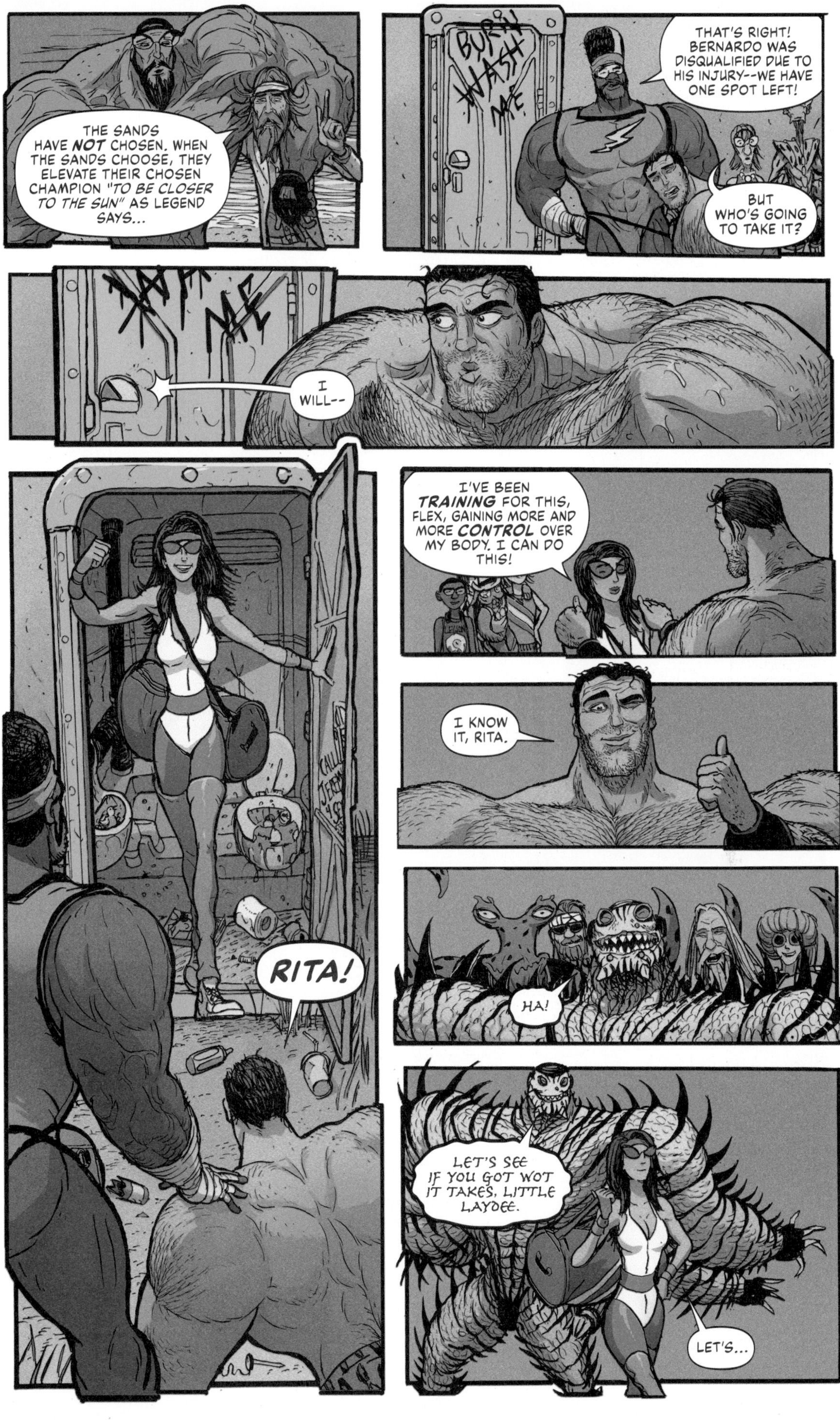
THE SANDS HAVE NOT CHOSEN. WHEN THE SANDS CHOOSE, THEY ELEVATE THEIR CHOSEN CHAMPION "TO BE CLOSER TO THE SUN" AS LEGEND SAYS...
BURN WASH ME
THAT'S RIGHT! BERNARDO WAS DISQUALIFIED DUE TO HIS INJURY--WE HAVE ONE SPOT LEFT!
BUT WHO'S GOING TO TAKE IT?
I WILL--
RITA!
I'VE BEEN TRAINING FOR THIS, FLEX, GAINING MORE AND MORE CONTROL OVER MY BODY. I CAN DO THIS!
I KNOW IT, RITA.
HA!
LET'S SEE IF YOU GOT WOT IT TAKES, LITTLE LAYDEE.
LET'S...

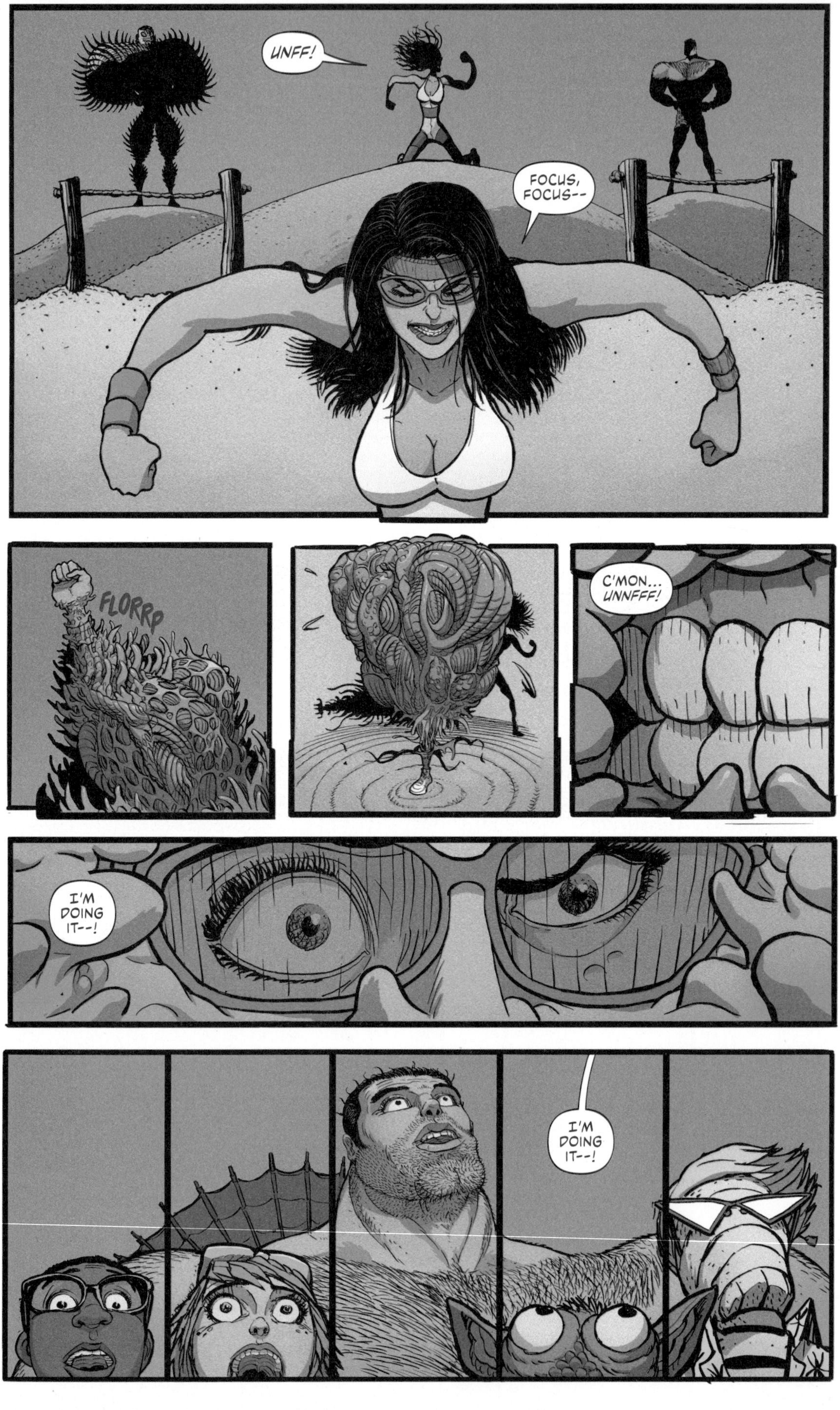
UNFF!
FOCUS, FOCUS--
FLORRP
C'MON... UNNFFF!
I'M DOING IT--!
I'M DOING IT--!

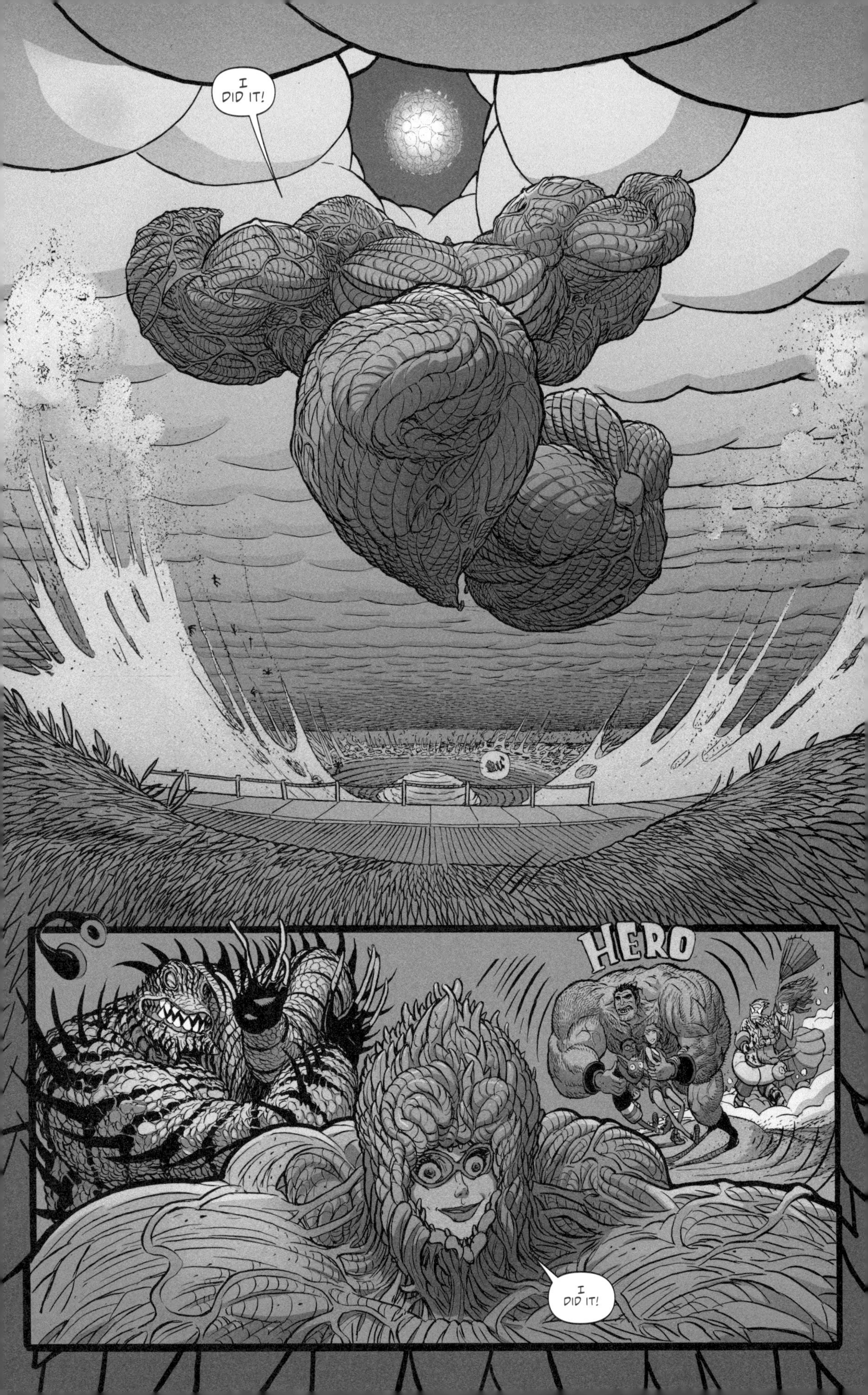
I DID IT!
HERO
I DID IT!

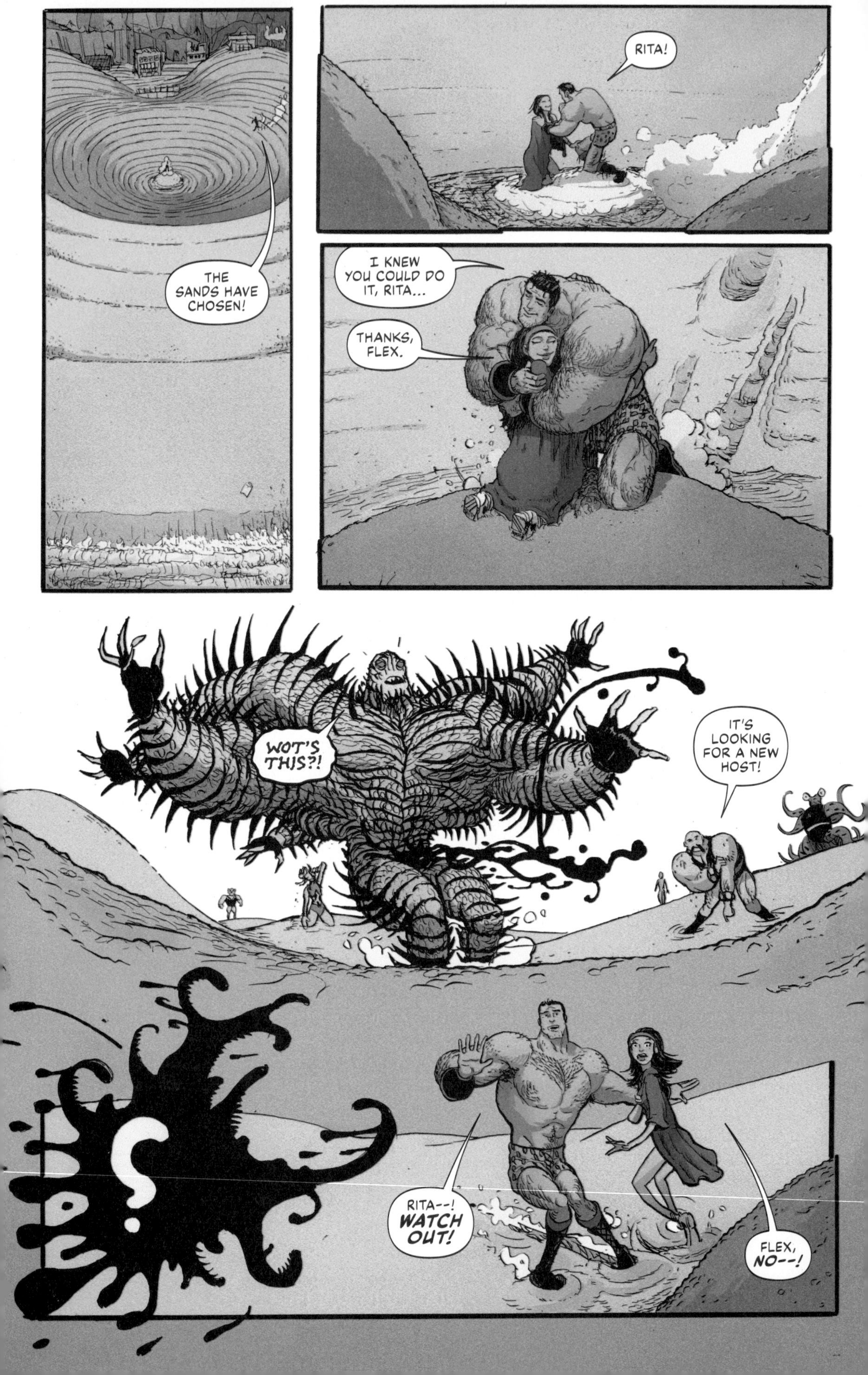
THE SANDS HAVE CHOSEN!
RITA!
I KNEW YOU COULD DO IT, RITA...
THANKS, FLEX.
WOT'S THIS?!
IT'S LOOKING FOR A NEW HOST!
RITA--! WATCH OUT!
FLEX, NO--!

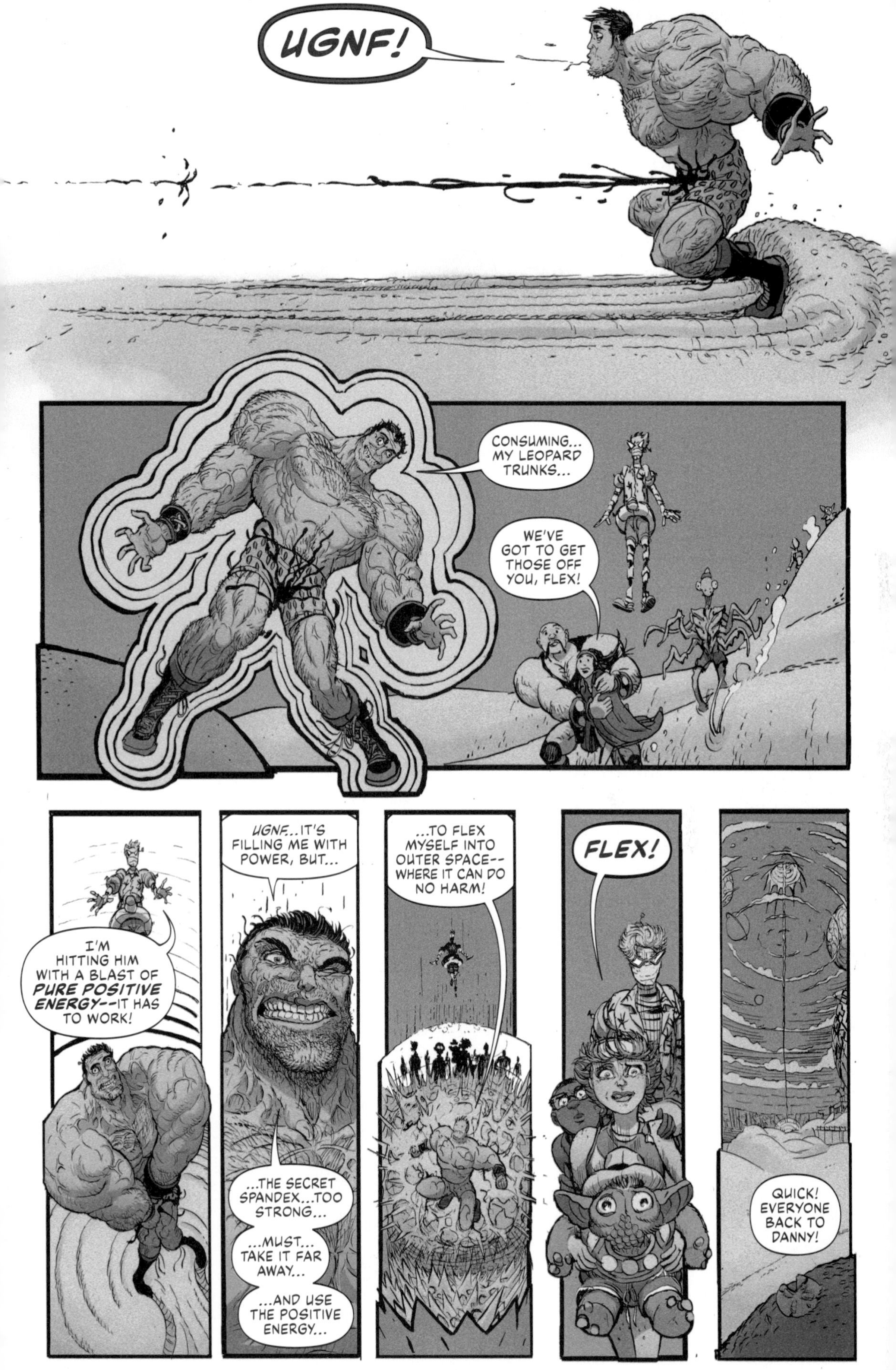
UGNF!
CONSUMING... MY LEOPARD TRUNKS...
WE'VE GOT TO GET THOSE OFF YOU, FLEX!
I'M HITTING HIM WITH A BLAST OF PURE POSITIVE ENERGY--IT HAS TO WORK!
UGNF... IT'S FILLING ME WITH POWER, BUT...
...THE SECRET SPANDEX...TOO STRONG...
...MUST... TAKE IT FAR AWAY...
...AND USE THE POSITIVE ENERGY...
...TO FLEX MYSELF INTO OUTER SPACE-- WHERE IT CAN DO NO HARM!
FLEX!
QUICK! EVERYONE BACK TO DANNY!

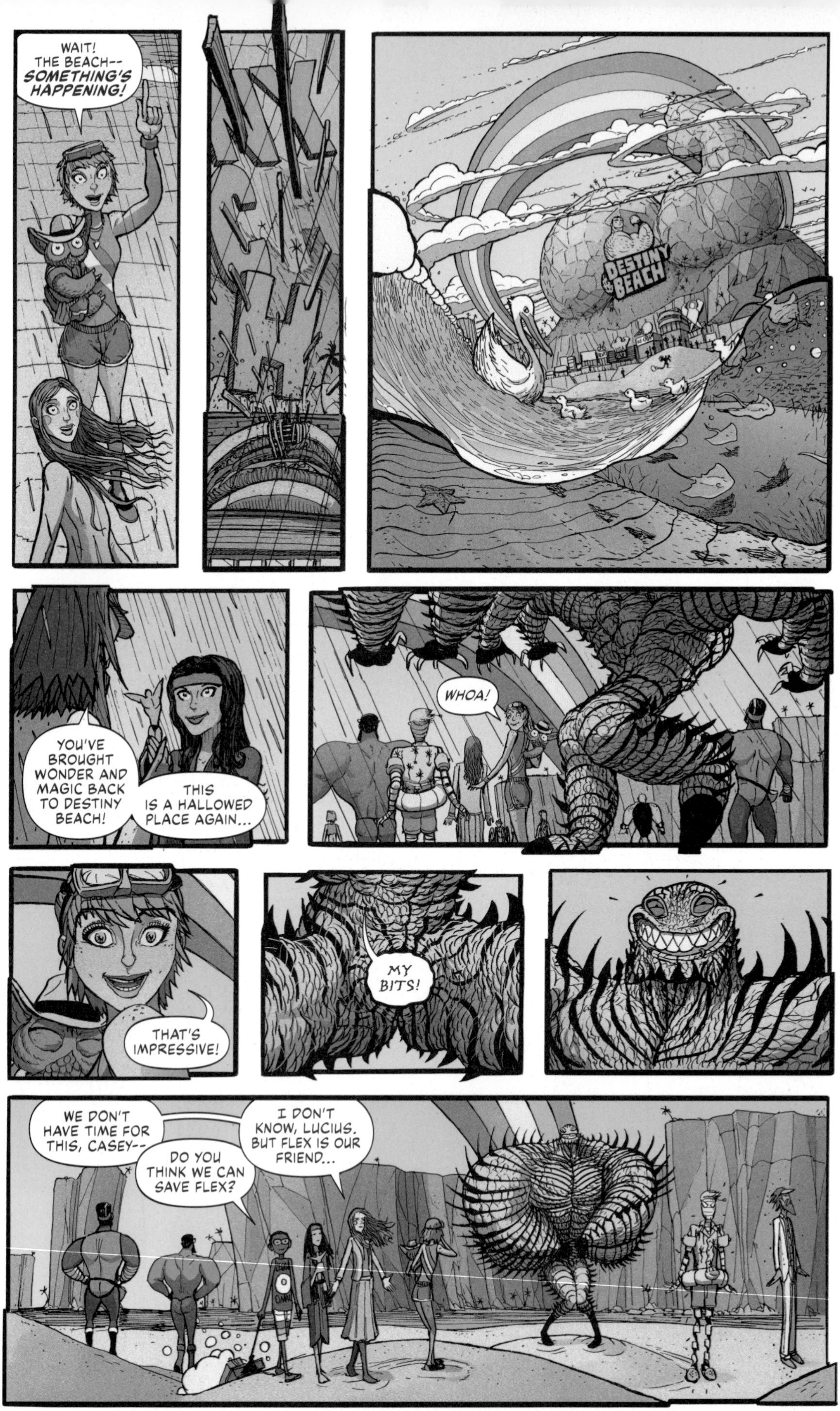
WAIT! THE BEACH-- SOMETHING'S HAPPENING!
DESTINY BEACH
YOU'VE BROUGHT WONDER AND MAGIC BACK TO DESTINY BEACH!
THIS IS A HALLOWED PLACE AGAIN...
WHOA!
THAT'S IMPRESSIVE!
MY BITS!
WE DON'T HAVE TIME FOR THIS, CASEY--
DO YOU THINK WE CAN SAVE FLEX?
I DON'T KNOW, LUCIUS. BUT FLEX IS OUR FRIEND...

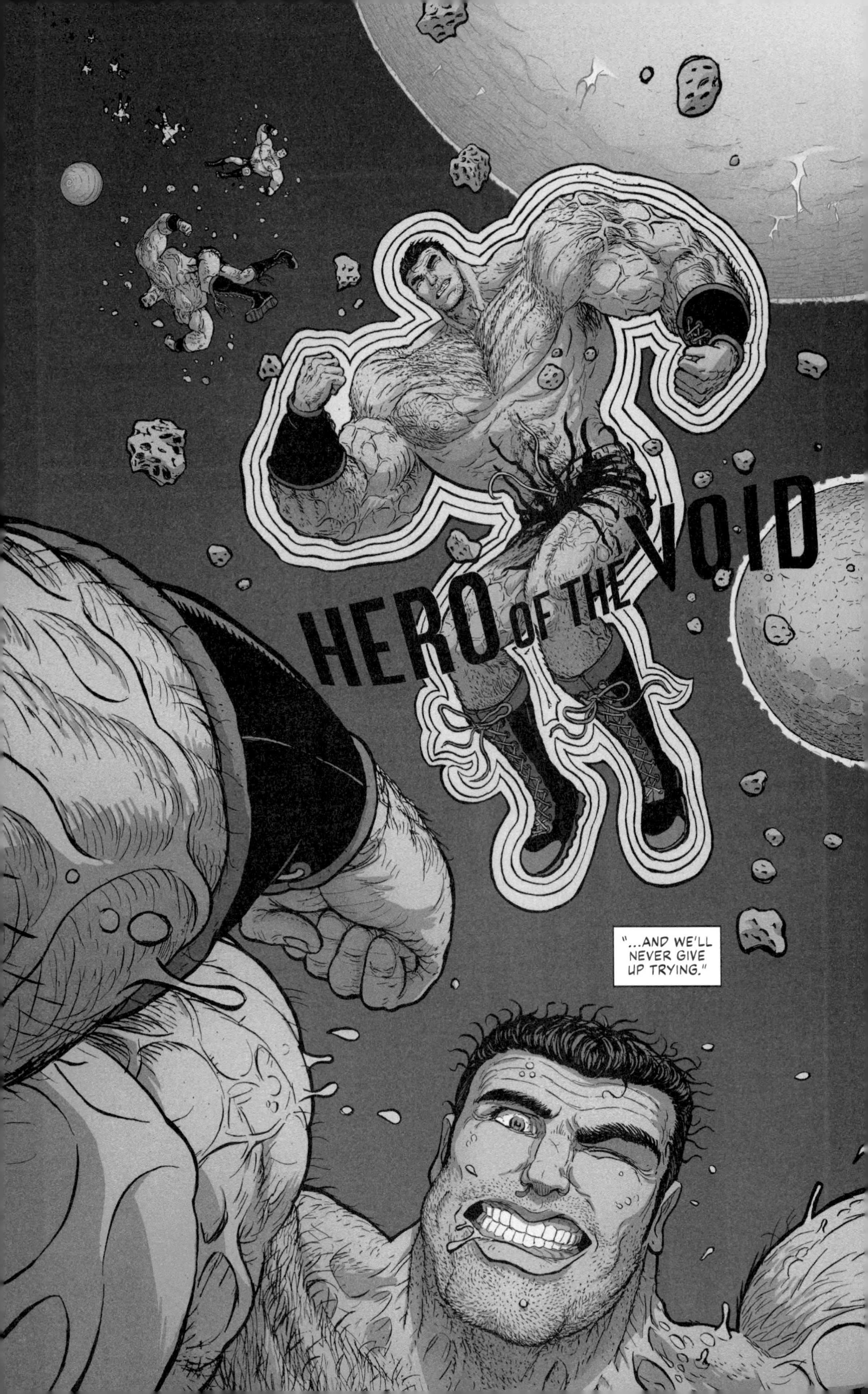
HERO OF THE VOID
"...AND WE'LL NEVER GIVE UP TRYING."

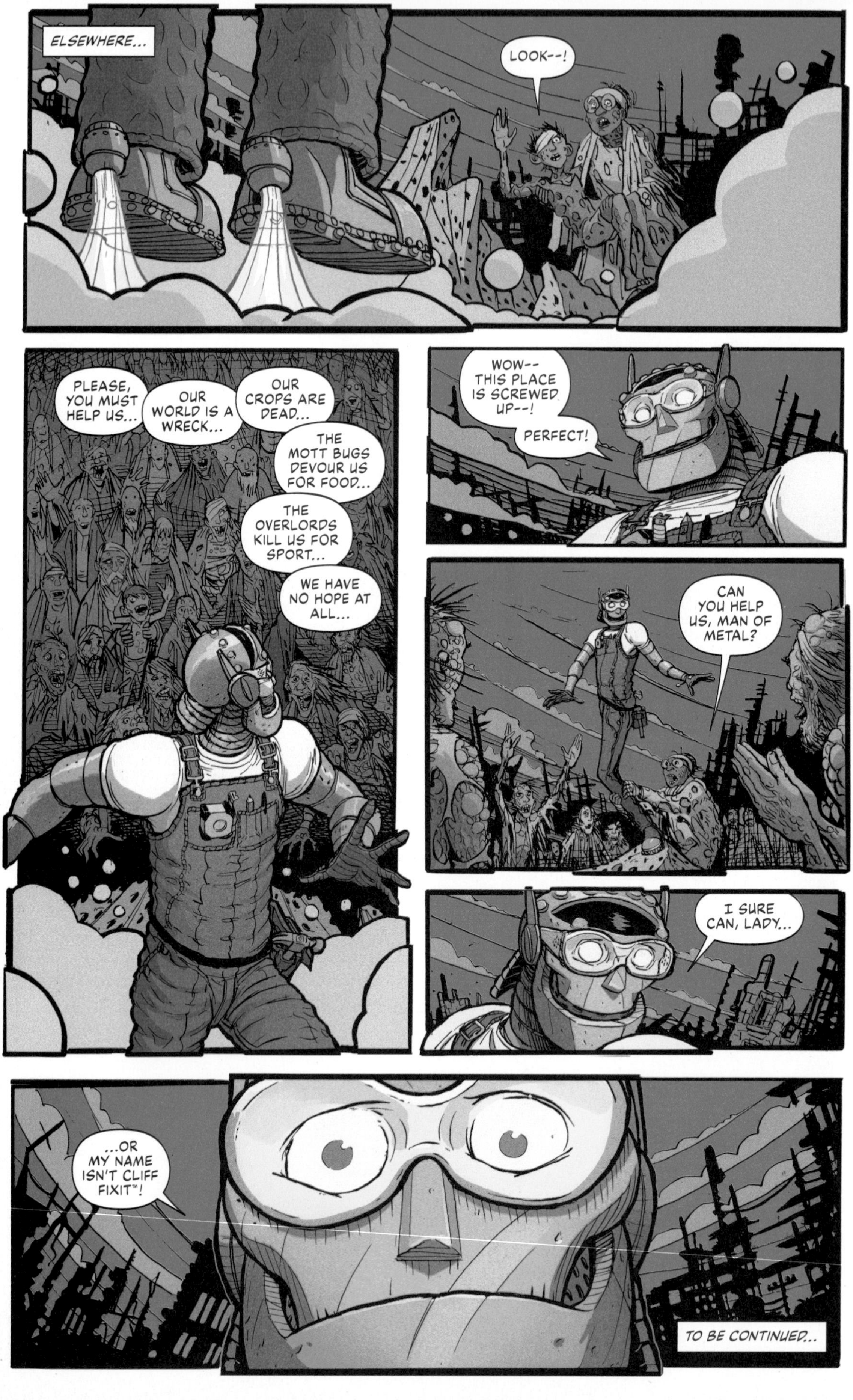
ELSEWHERE...
LOOK--!
PLEASE, YOU MUST HELP US...
OUR WORLD IS A WRECK...
OUR CROPS ARE DEAD...
THE MOTT BUGS DEVOUR US FOR FOOD...
THE OVERLORDS KILL US FOR SPORT...
WE HAVE NO HOPE AT ALL...
WOW-- THIS PLACE IS SCREWED UP--!
PERFECT!
CAN YOU HELP US, MAN OF METAL?
I SURE CAN, LADY...
...OR MY NAME ISN'T CLIFF FIXIT™!
TO BE CONTINUED...

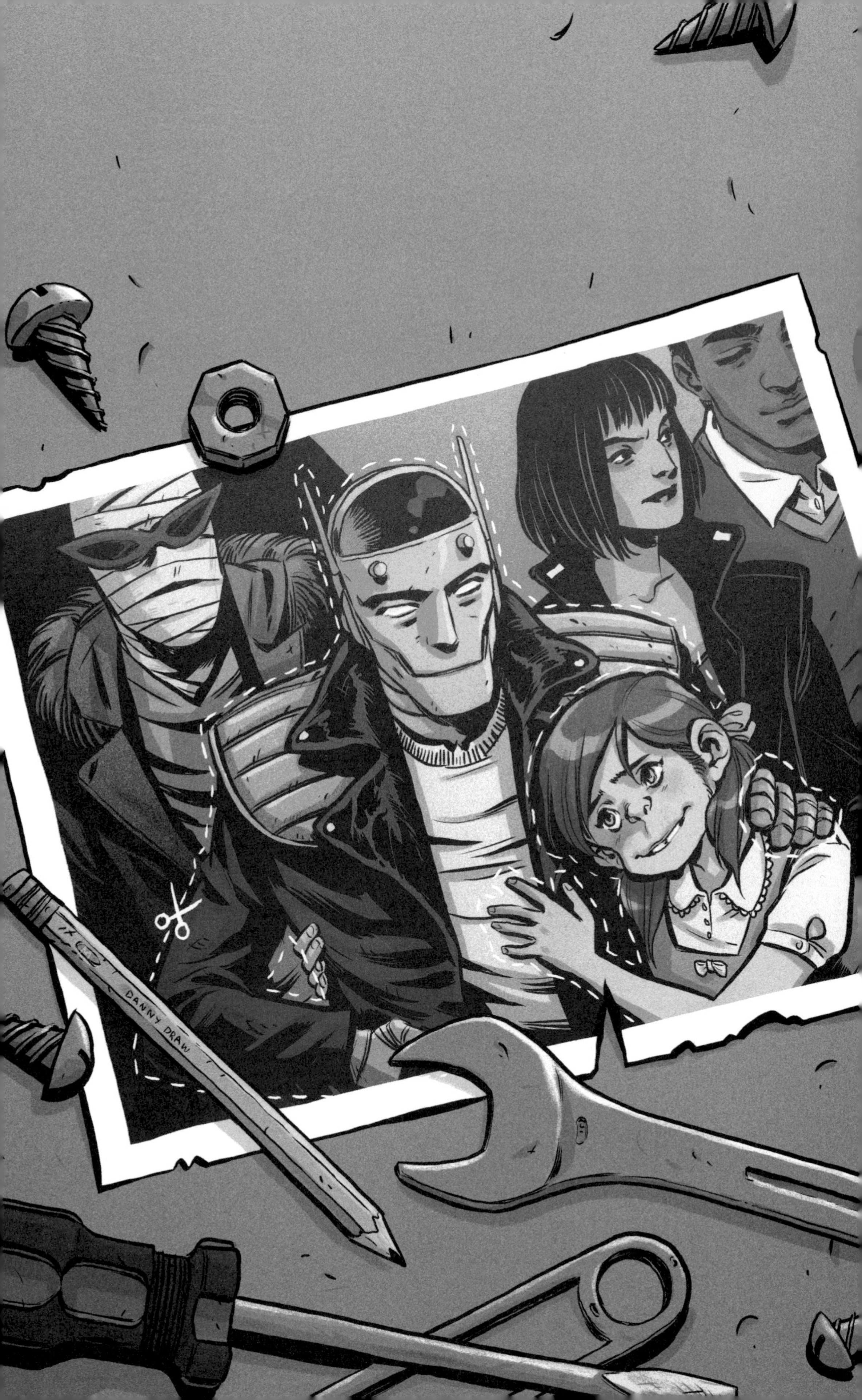
DANNY DRAW

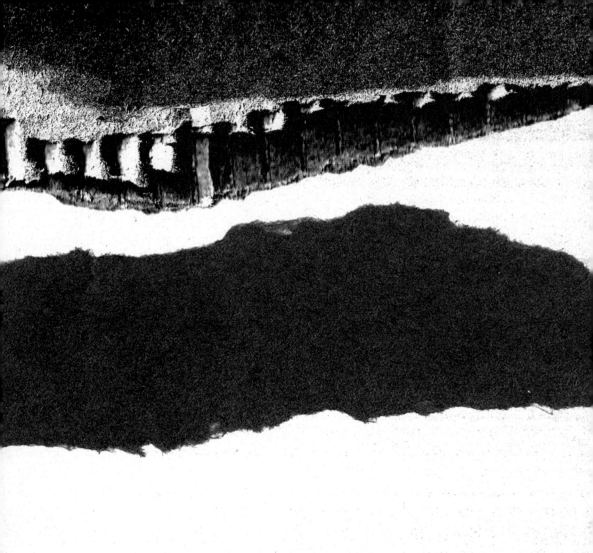

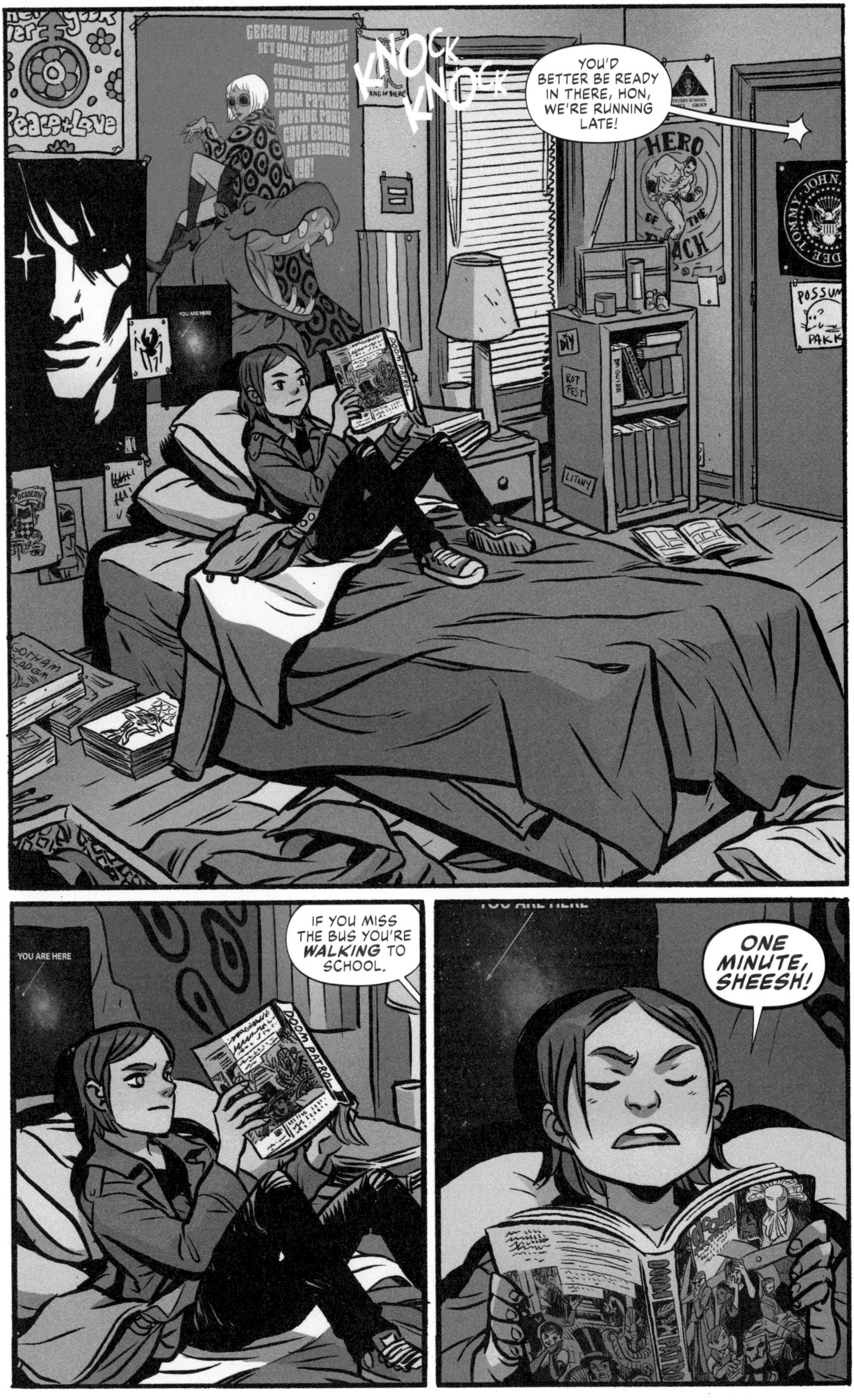
KNOCK KNOCK
YOU'D BETTER BE READY IN THERE, HON, WE'RE RUNNING LATE!
IF YOU MISS THE BUS YOU'RE WALKING TO SCHOOL.
ONE MINUTE, SHEESH!

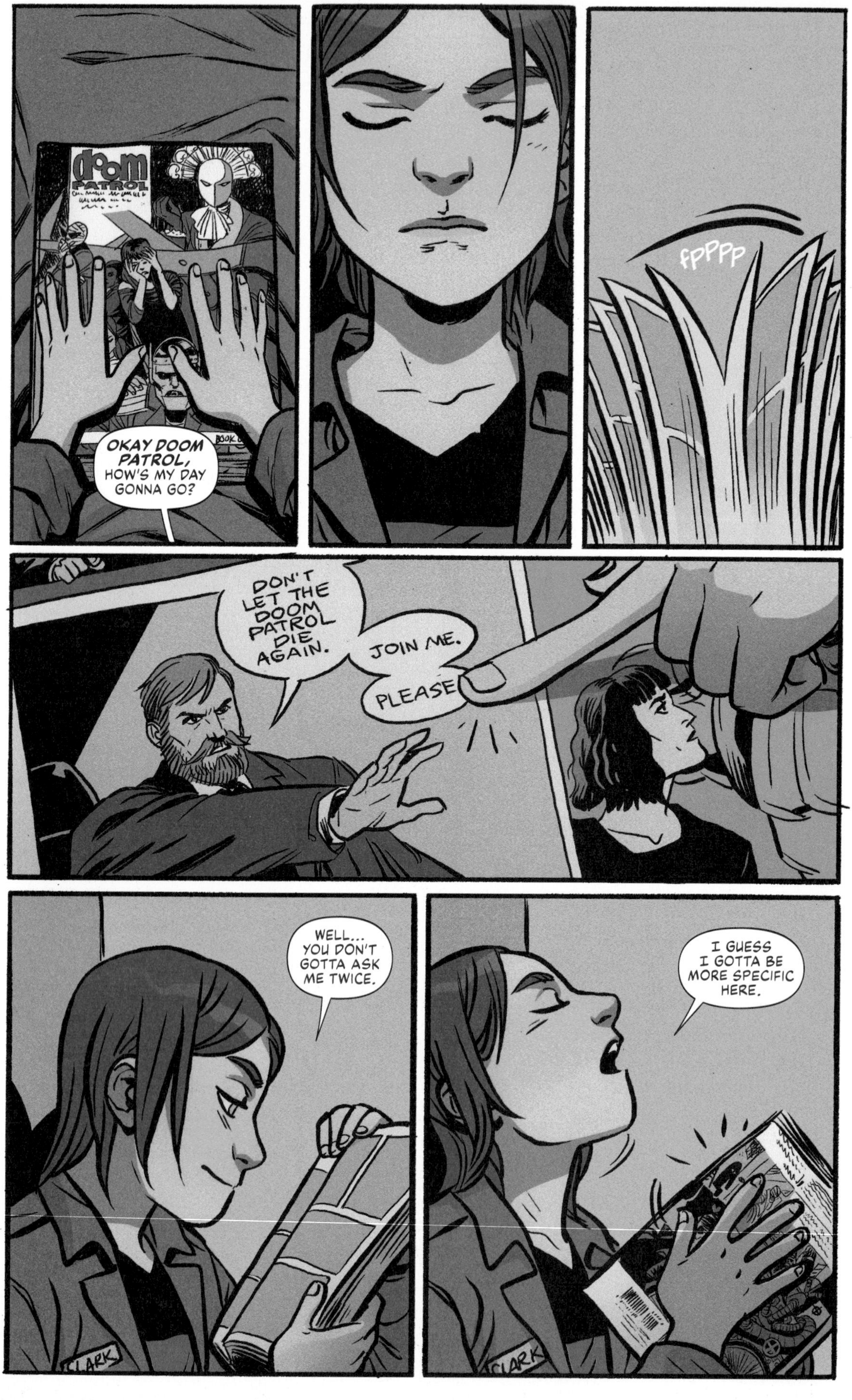
OKAY DOOM PATROL, HOW'S MY DAY GONNA GO?
FPPPP
DON'T LET THE DOOM PATROL DIE AGAIN.
JOIN ME.
PLEASE
WELL... YOU DON'T GOTTA ASK ME TWICE.
I GUESS I GOTTA BE MORE SPECIFIC HERE.

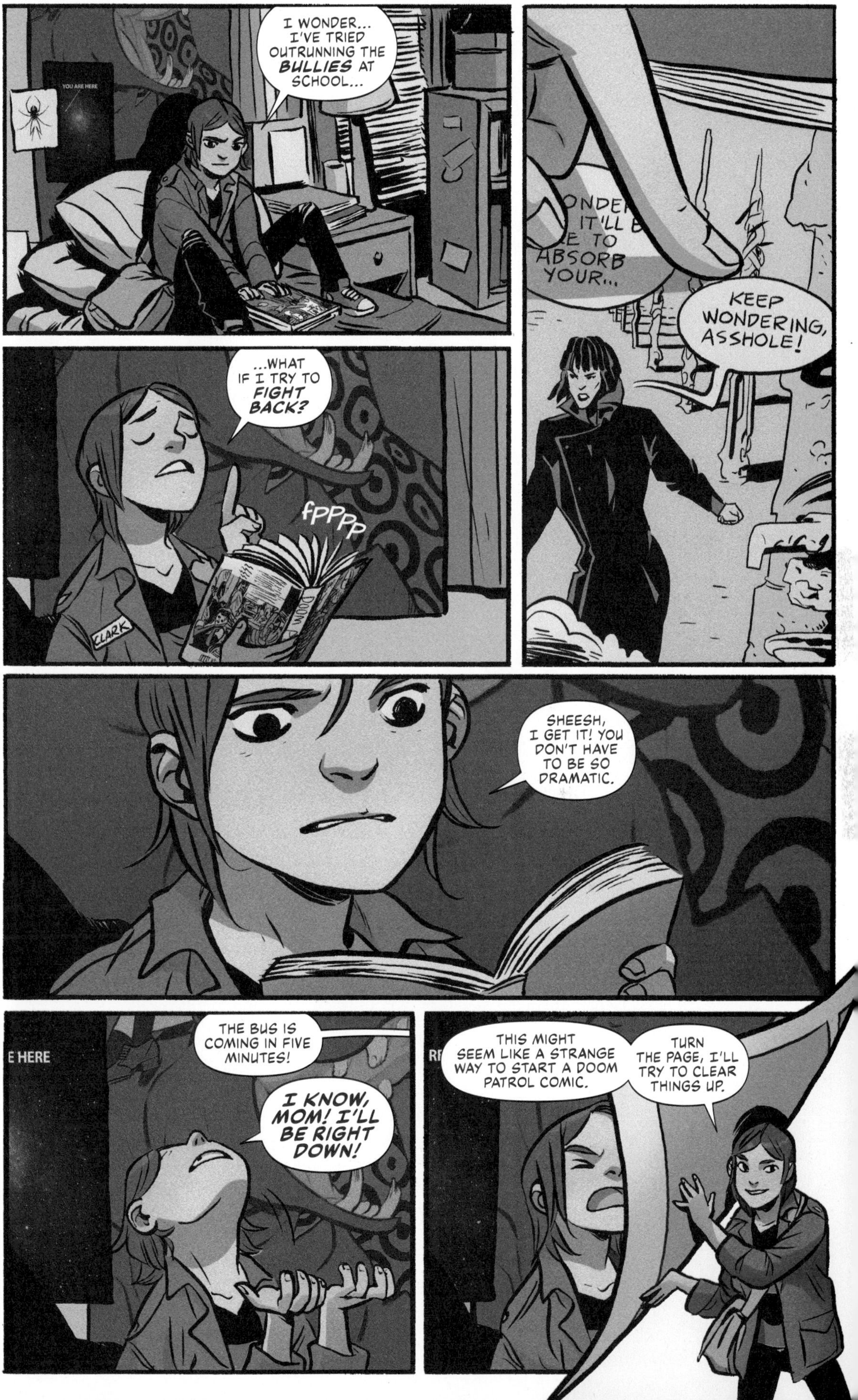
YOU ARE HERE
I WONDER... I'VE TRIED OUTRUNNING THE BULLIES AT SCHOOL...
ONDER IT'LL B E TO ABSORB YOUR...
KEEP WONDERING, ASSHOLE!
...WHAT IF I TRY TO FIGHT BACK?
fPPPP
CLARK
DOOM
SHEESH, I GET IT! YOU DON'T HAVE TO BE SO DRAMATIC.
E HERE
THE BUS IS COMING IN FIVE MINUTES!
I KNOW, MOM! I'LL BE RIGHT DOWN!
THIS MIGHT SEEM LIKE A STRANGE WAY TO START A DOOM PATROL COMIC.
TURN THE PAGE, I'LL TRY TO CLEAR THINGS UP.

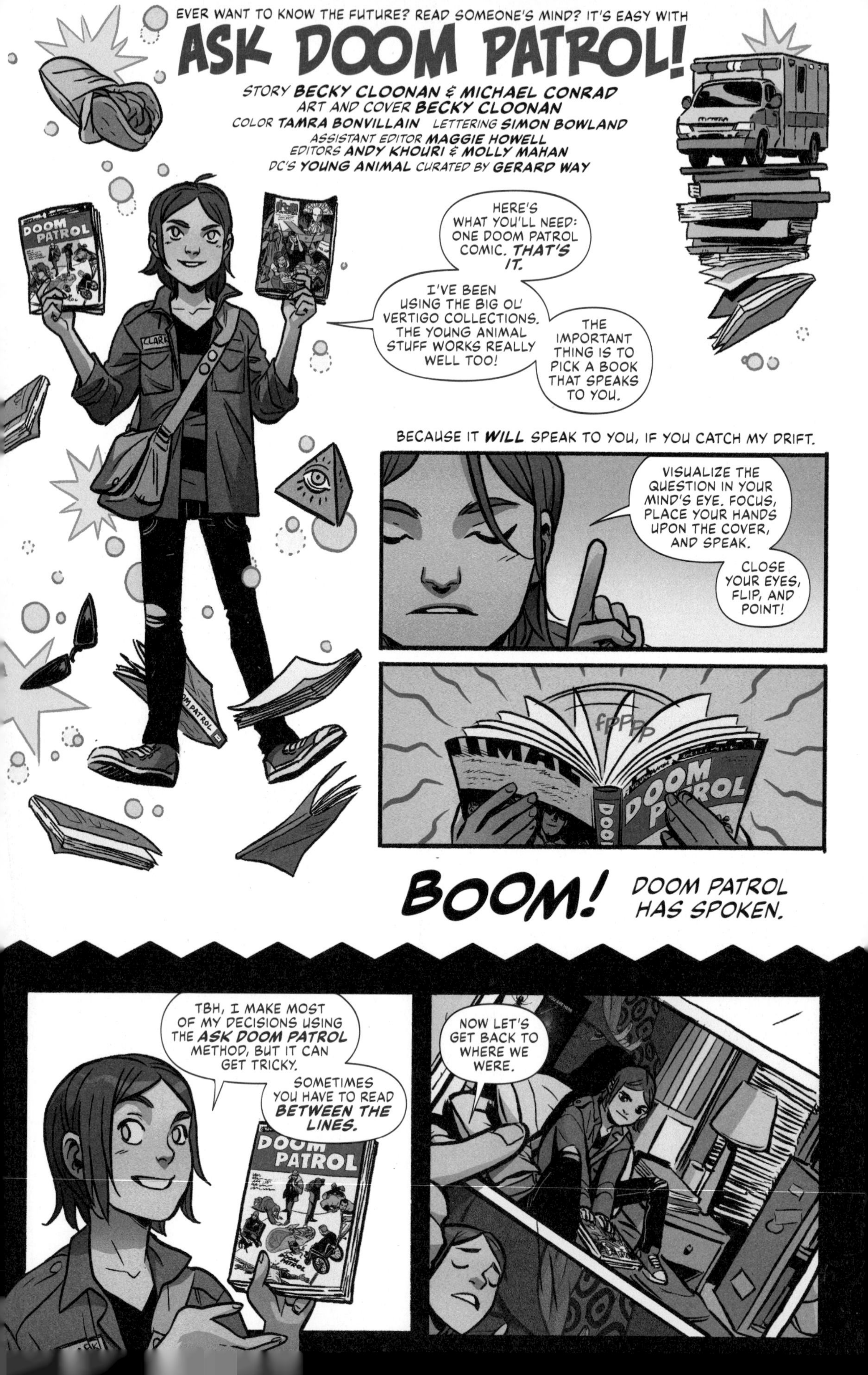
EVER WANT TO KNOW THE FUTURE? READ SOMEONE'S MIND? IT'S EASY WITH
ASK DOOM PATROL!
STORY BECKY CLOONAN & MICHAEL CONRAD
ART AND COVER BECKY CLOONAN
COLOR TAMRA BONVILLAIN LETTERING SIMON BOWLAND
ASSISTANT EDITOR MAGGIE HOWELL
EDITORS ANDY KHOURI & MOLLY MAHAN
DC'S YOUNG ANIMAL CURATED BY GERARD WAY
HERE'S WHAT YOU'LL NEED: ONE DOOM PATROL COMIC. THAT'S IT.
I'VE BEEN USING THE BIG OL' VERTIGO COLLECTIONS. THE YOUNG ANIMAL STUFF WORKS REALLY WELL TOO!
THE IMPORTANT THING IS TO PICK A BOOK THAT SPEAKS TO YOU.
BECAUSE IT WILL SPEAK TO YOU, IF YOU CATCH MY DRIFT.
VISUALIZE THE QUESTION IN YOUR MIND'S EYE. FOCUS, PLACE YOUR HANDS UPON THE COVER, AND SPEAK.
CLOSE YOUR EYES, FLIP, AND POINT!
fPPPP
BOOM! DOOM PATROL HAS SPOKEN.
TBH, I MAKE MOST OF MY DECISIONS USING THE ASK DOOM PATROL METHOD, BUT IT CAN GET TRICKY.
SOMETIMES YOU HAVE TO READ BETWEEN THE LINES.
NOW LET'S GET BACK TO WHERE WE WERE.

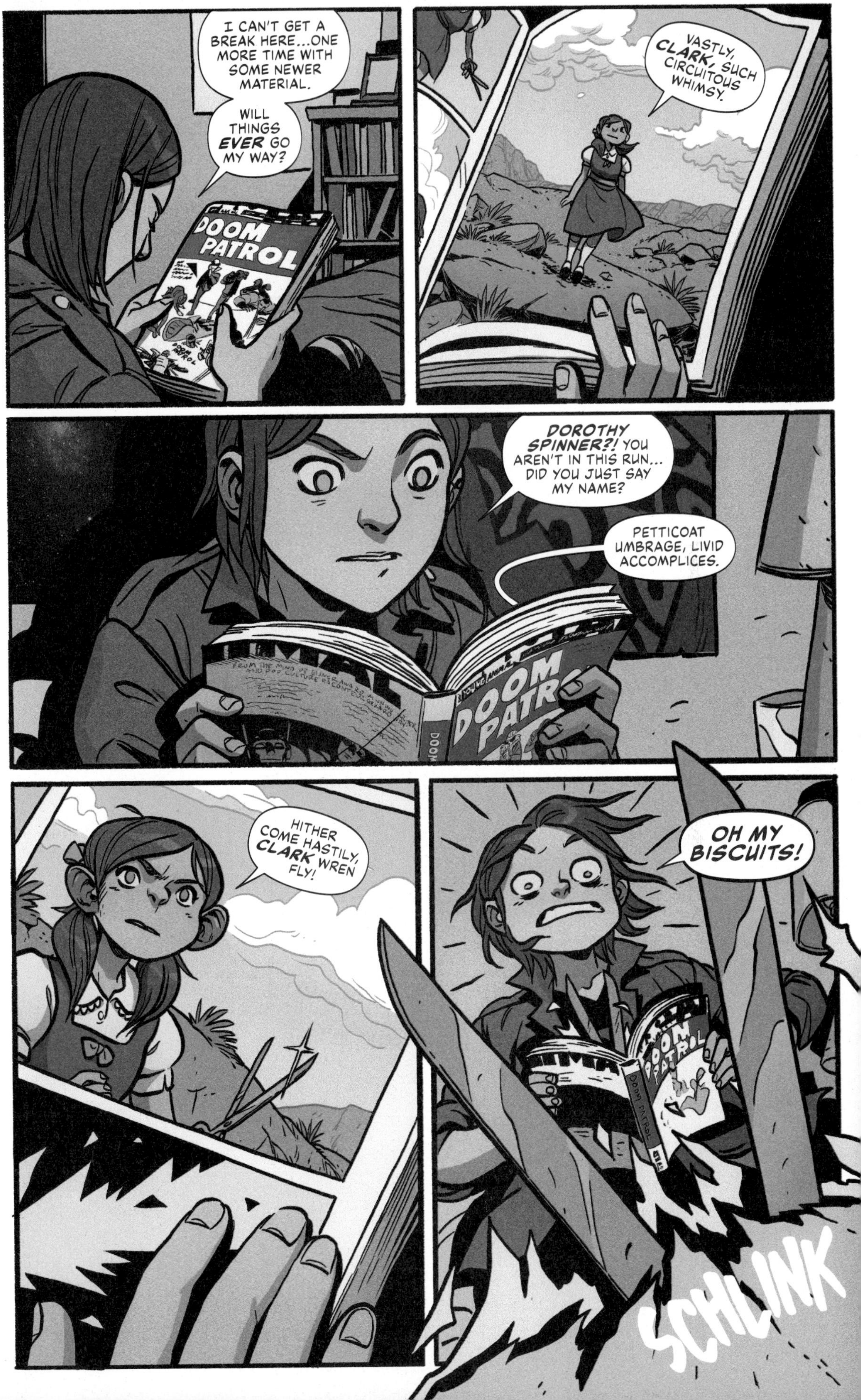
I CAN'T GET A BREAK HERE...ONE MORE TIME WITH SOME NEWER MATERIAL.
WILL THINGS EVER GO MY WAY?
DOOM PATROL
VASTLY, CLARK, SUCH CIRCUITOUS WHIMSY.
DOROTHY SPINNER?! YOU AREN'T IN THIS RUN... DID YOU JUST SAY MY NAME?
PETTICOAT UMBRAGE, LIVID ACCOMPLICES.
DOOM PATROL
HITHER COME HASTILY, CLARK WREN FLY!
OH MY BISCUITS!
DOOM PATROL
SCHLINK

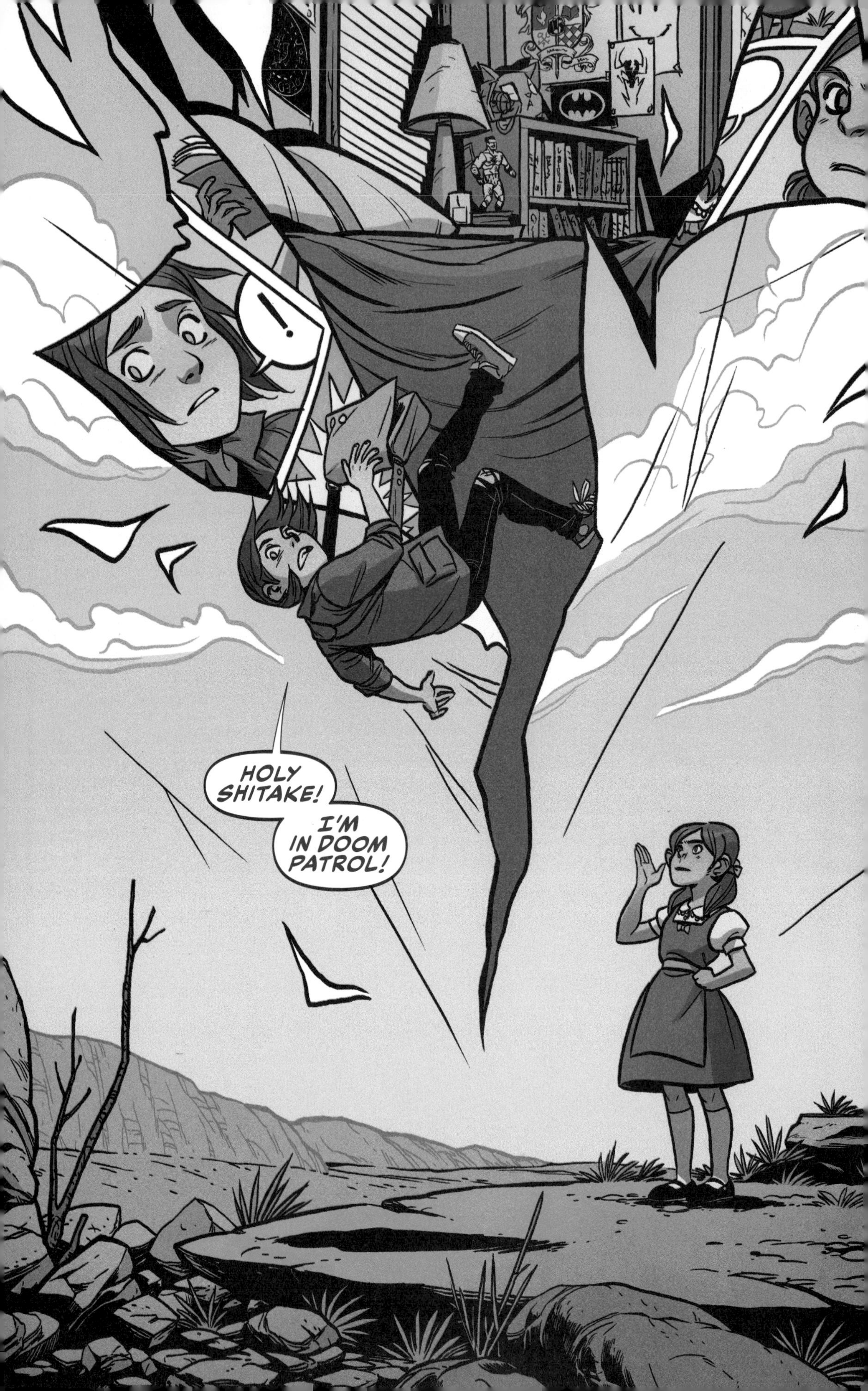
!
HOLY SHITAKE!
I'M IN DOOM PATROL!

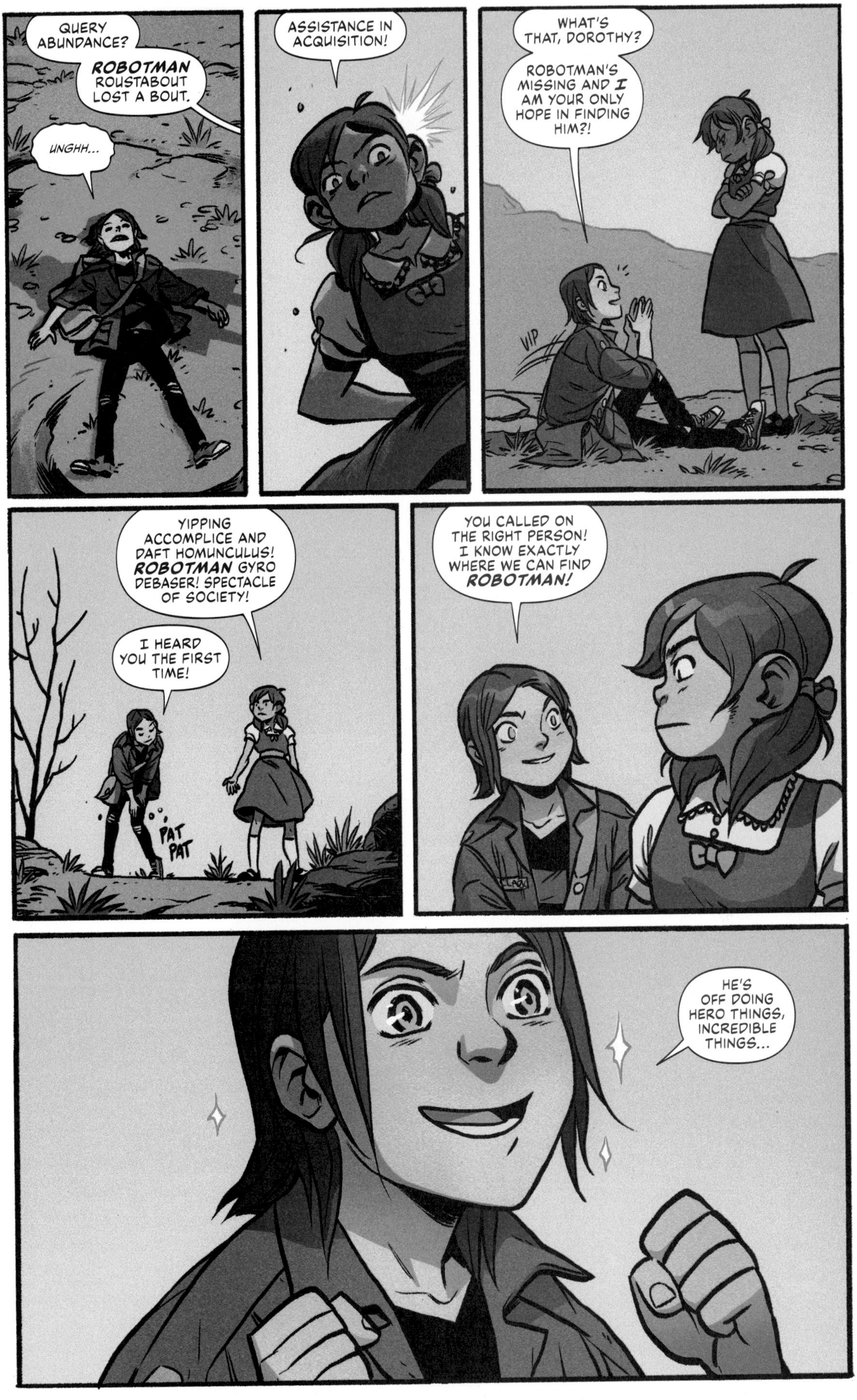
QUERY ABUNDANCE?
ROBOTMAN ROUSTABOUT LOST A BOUT.
UNGHH...
ASSISTANCE IN ACQUISITION!
WHAT'S THAT, DOROTHY?
ROBOTMAN'S MISSING AND I AM YOUR ONLY HOPE IN FINDING HIM?!
VIP
YIPPING ACCOMPLICE AND DAFT HOMUNCULUS! ROBOTMAN GYRO DEBASER! SPECTACLE OF SOCIETY!
I HEARD YOU THE FIRST TIME!
PAT PAT
YOU CALLED ON THE RIGHT PERSON! I KNOW EXACTLY WHERE WE CAN FIND ROBOTMAN!
HE'S OFF DOING HERO THINGS, INCREDIBLE THINGS...

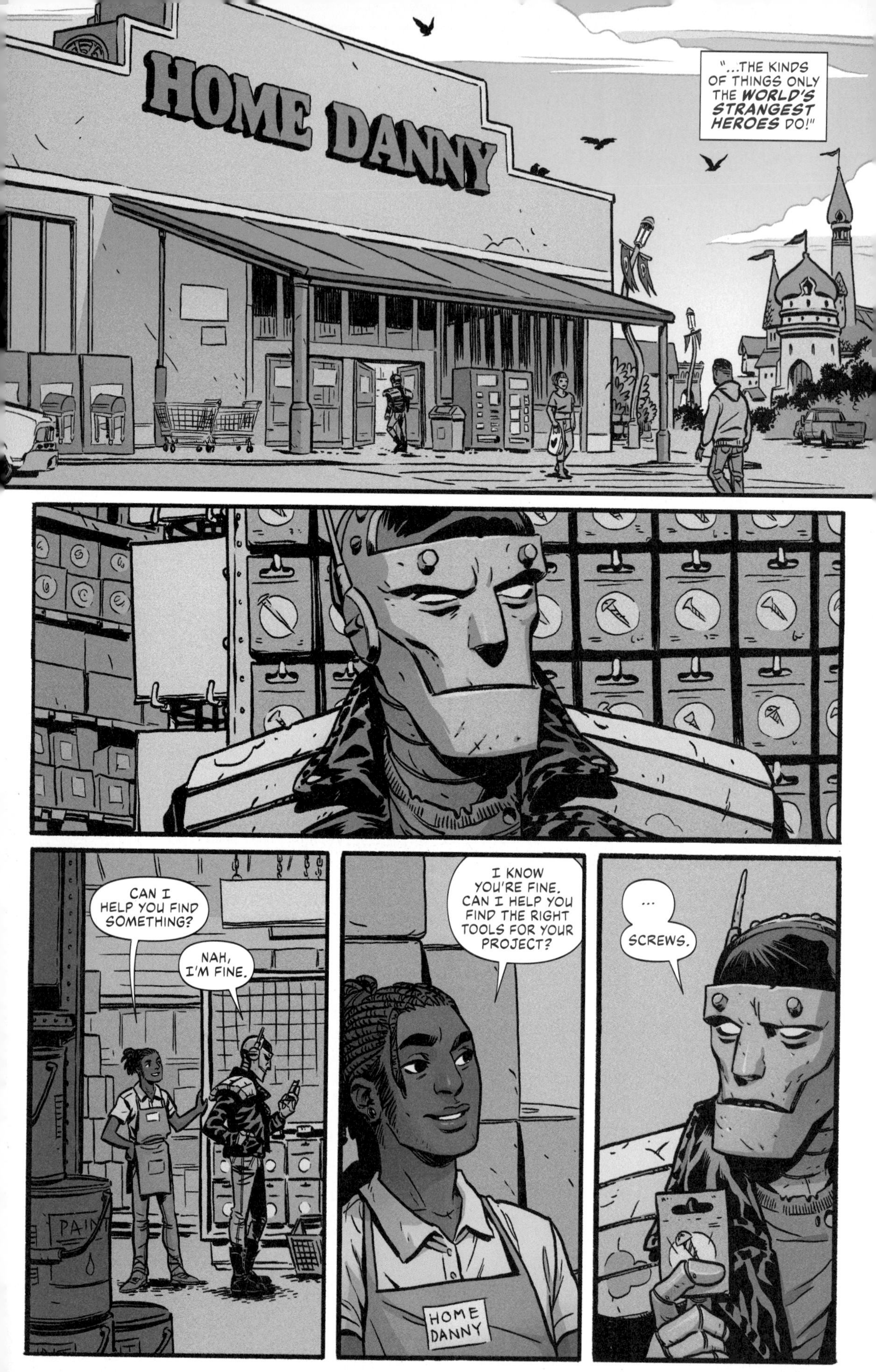

HOME DANNY
"...THE KINDS OF THINGS ONLY THE WORLD'S STRANGEST HEROES DO!"
CAN I HELP YOU FIND SOMETHING?
NAH, I'M FINE.
PAINT
I KNOW YOU'RE FINE. CAN I HELP YOU FIND THE RIGHT TOOLS FOR YOUR PROJECT?
HOME DANNY
...
SCREWS.

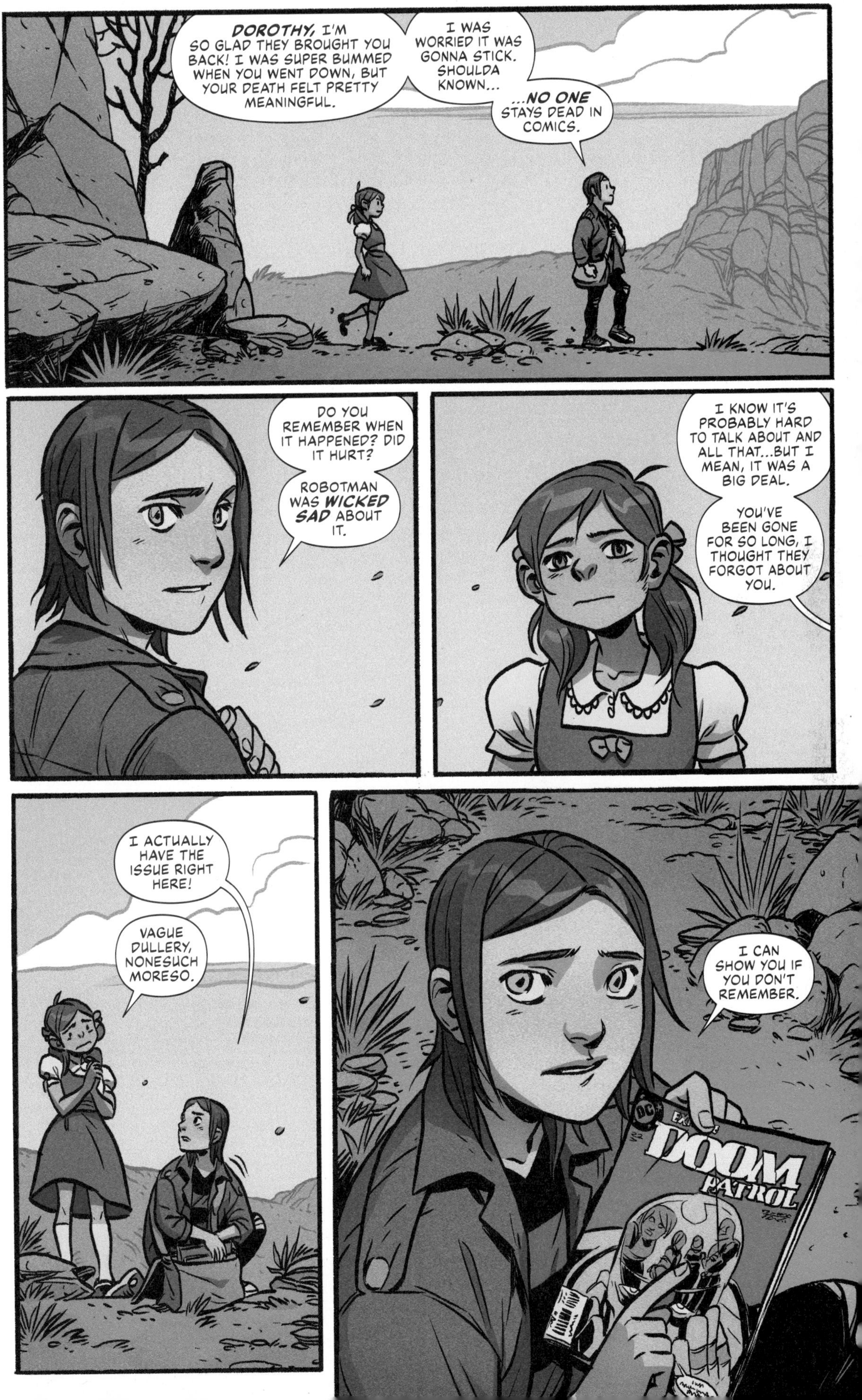
DOROTHY, I'M SO GLAD THEY BROUGHT YOU BACK! I WAS SUPER BUMMED WHEN YOU WENT DOWN, BUT YOUR DEATH FELT PRETTY MEANINGFUL.
I WAS WORRIED IT WAS GONNA STICK. SHOULDA KNOWN...
...NO ONE STAYS DEAD IN COMICS.
DO YOU REMEMBER WHEN IT HAPPENED? DID IT HURT?
ROBOTMAN WAS WICKED SAD ABOUT IT.
I KNOW IT'S PROBABLY HARD TO TALK ABOUT AND ALL THAT...BUT I MEAN, IT WAS A BIG DEAL.
YOU'VE BEEN GONE FOR SO LONG, I THOUGHT THEY FORGOT ABOUT YOU.
I ACTUALLY HAVE THE ISSUE RIGHT HERE!
VAGUE DULLERY, NONESUCH MORESO.
I CAN SHOW YOU IF YOU DON'T REMEMBER.
DOOM PATROL

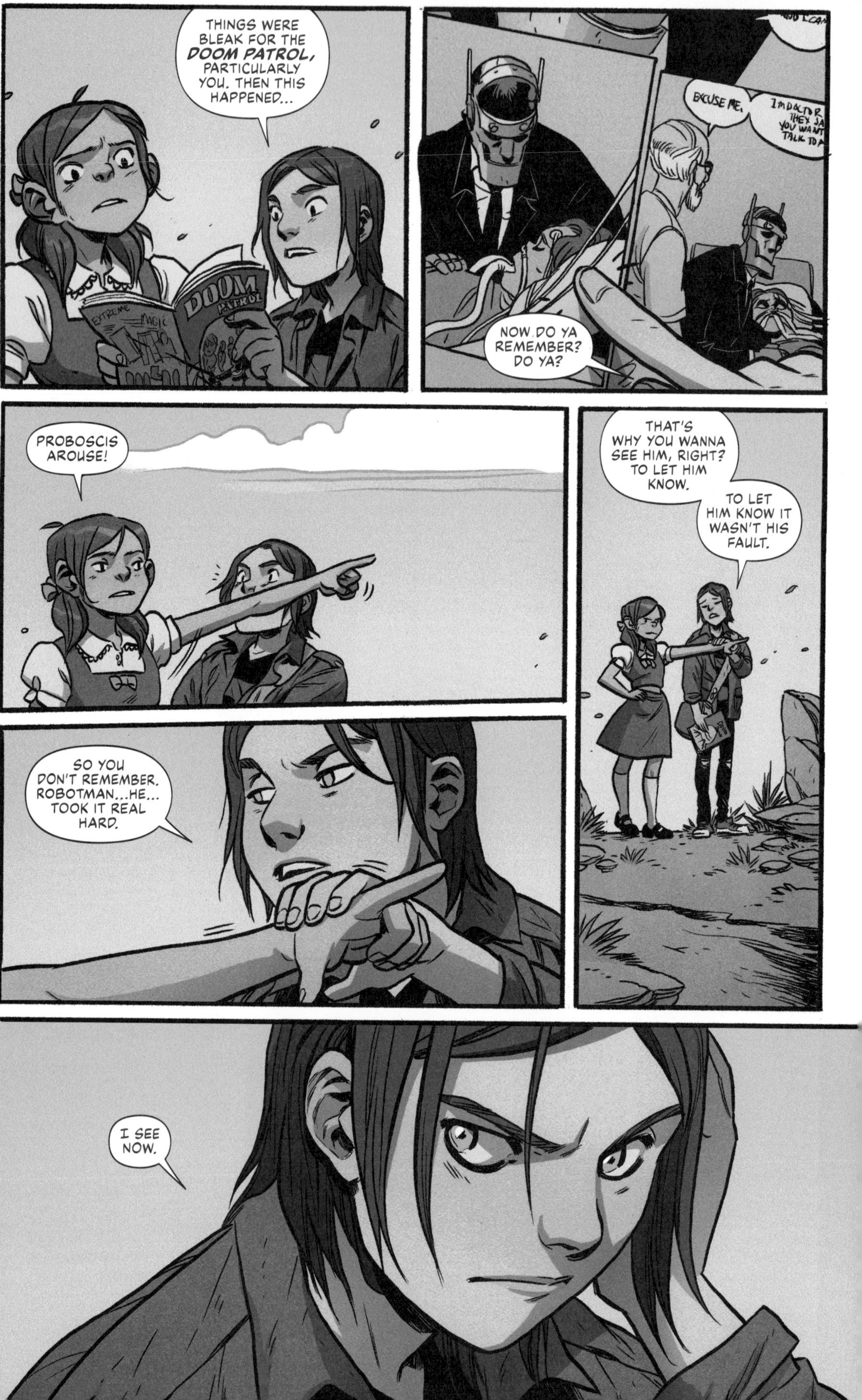
THINGS WERE BLEAK FOR THE DOOM PATROL, PARTICULARLY YOU. THEN THIS HAPPENED...
DOOM PATROL
EXTREME MAGIC
EXCUSE ME.
NOW. DO YA REMEMBER? DO YA?
PROBOSCIS AROUSE!
SO YOU DON'T REMEMBER. ROBOTMAN...HE... TOOK IT REAL HARD.
THAT'S WHY YOU WANNA SEE HIM, RIGHT? TO LET HIM KNOW.
TO LET HIM KNOW IT WASN'T HIS FAULT.
I SEE NOW.

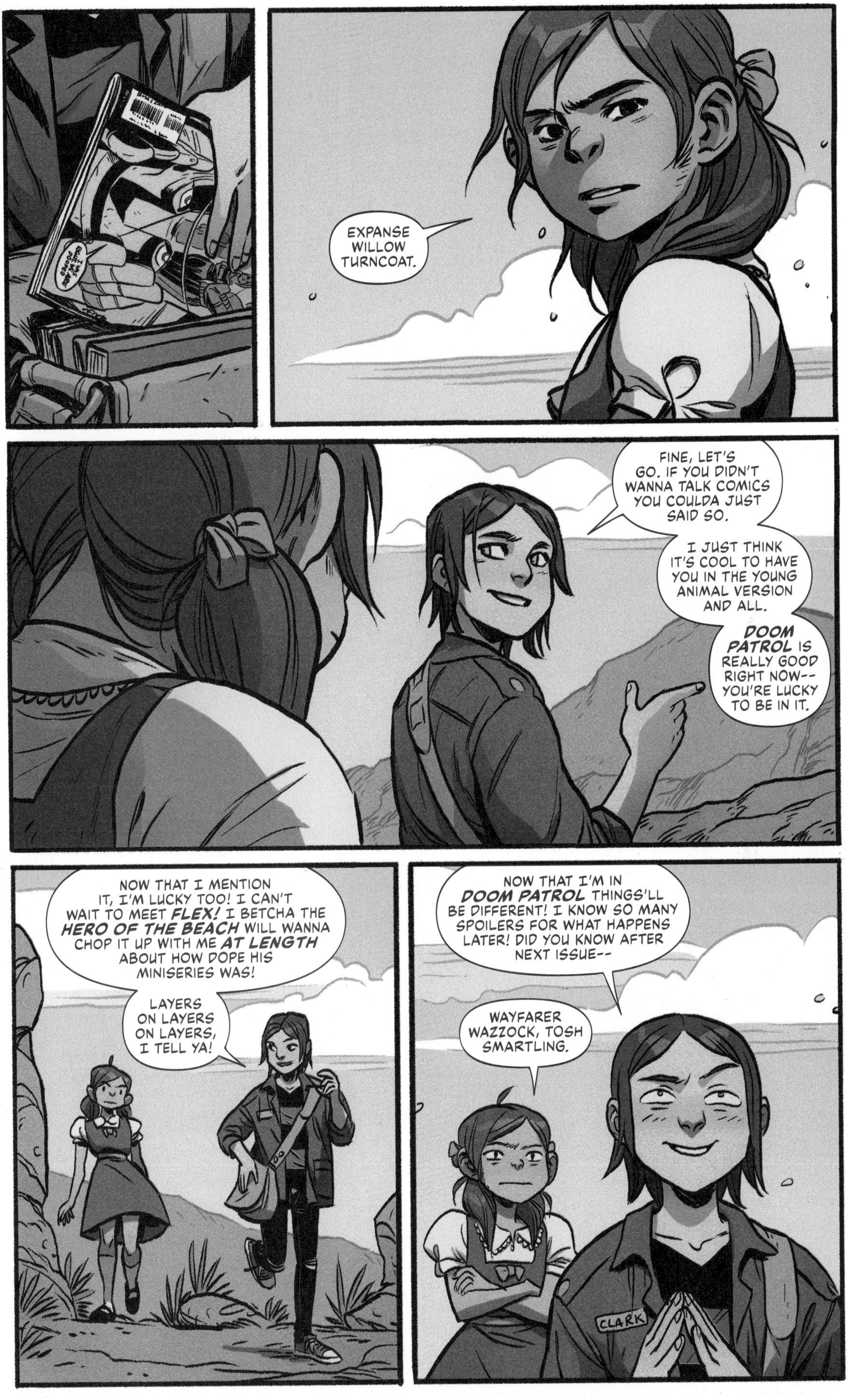
EXPANSE WILLOW TURNCOAT.
FINE, LET'S GO. IF YOU DIDN'T WANNA TALK COMICS YOU COULDA JUST SAID SO.
I JUST THINK IT'S COOL TO HAVE YOU IN THE YOUNG ANIMAL VERSION AND ALL.
DOOM PATROL IS REALLY GOOD RIGHT NOW-- YOU'RE LUCKY TO BE IN IT.
NOW THAT I MENTION IT, I'M LUCKY TOO! I CAN'T WAIT TO MEET FLEX! I BETCHA THE HERO OF THE BEACH WILL WANNA CHOP IT UP WITH ME AT LENGTH ABOUT HOW DOPE HIS MINISERIES WAS!
LAYERS ON LAYERS ON LAYERS, I TELL YA!
NOW THAT I'M IN DOOM PATROL THINGS'LL BE DIFFERENT! I KNOW SO MANY SPOILERS FOR WHAT HAPPENS LATER! DID YOU KNOW AFTER NEXT ISSUE--
WAYFARER WAZZOCK, TOSH SMARTLING.
CLARK

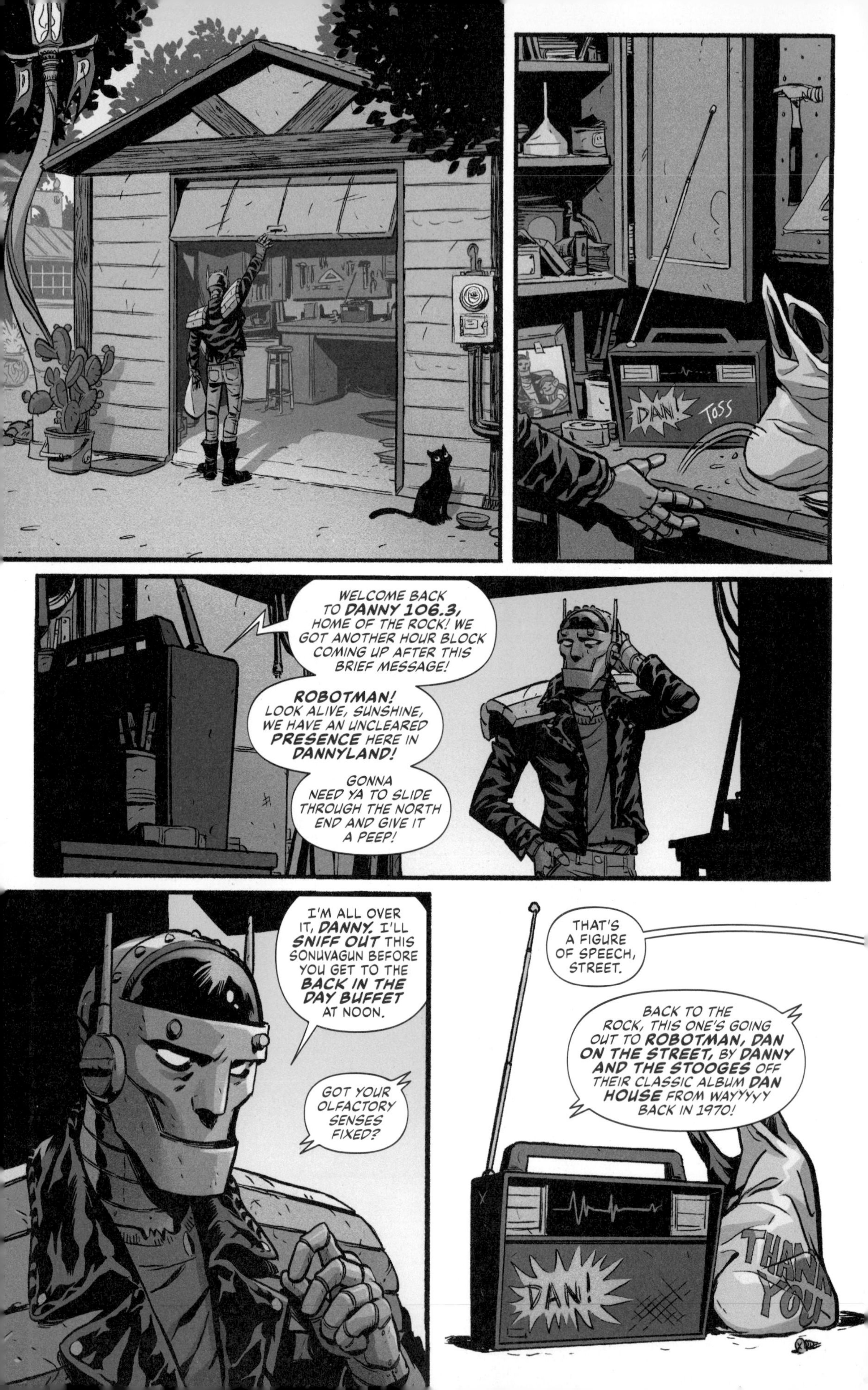
DAN!
TOSS
WELCOME BACK TO DANNY 106.3, HOME OF THE ROCK! WE GOT ANOTHER HOUR BLOCK COMING UP AFTER THIS BRIEF MESSAGE!
ROBOTMAN! LOOK ALIVE, SUNSHINE, WE HAVE AN UNCLEARED PRESENCE HERE IN DANNYLAND!
GONNA NEED YA TO SLIDE THROUGH THE NORTH END AND GIVE IT A PEEP!
I'M ALL OVER IT, DANNY. I'LL SNIFF OUT THIS SONUVAGUN BEFORE YOU GET TO THE BACK IN THE DAY BUFFET AT NOON.
GOT YOUR OLFACTORY SENSES FIXED?
THAT'S A FIGURE OF SPEECH, STREET.
BACK TO THE ROCK, THIS ONE'S GOING OUT TO ROBOTMAN, DAN ON THE STREET, BY DANNY AND THE STOOGES OFF THEIR CLASSIC ALBUM DAN HOUSE FROM WAYYYYY BACK IN 1970!
DAN!
THANK YOU

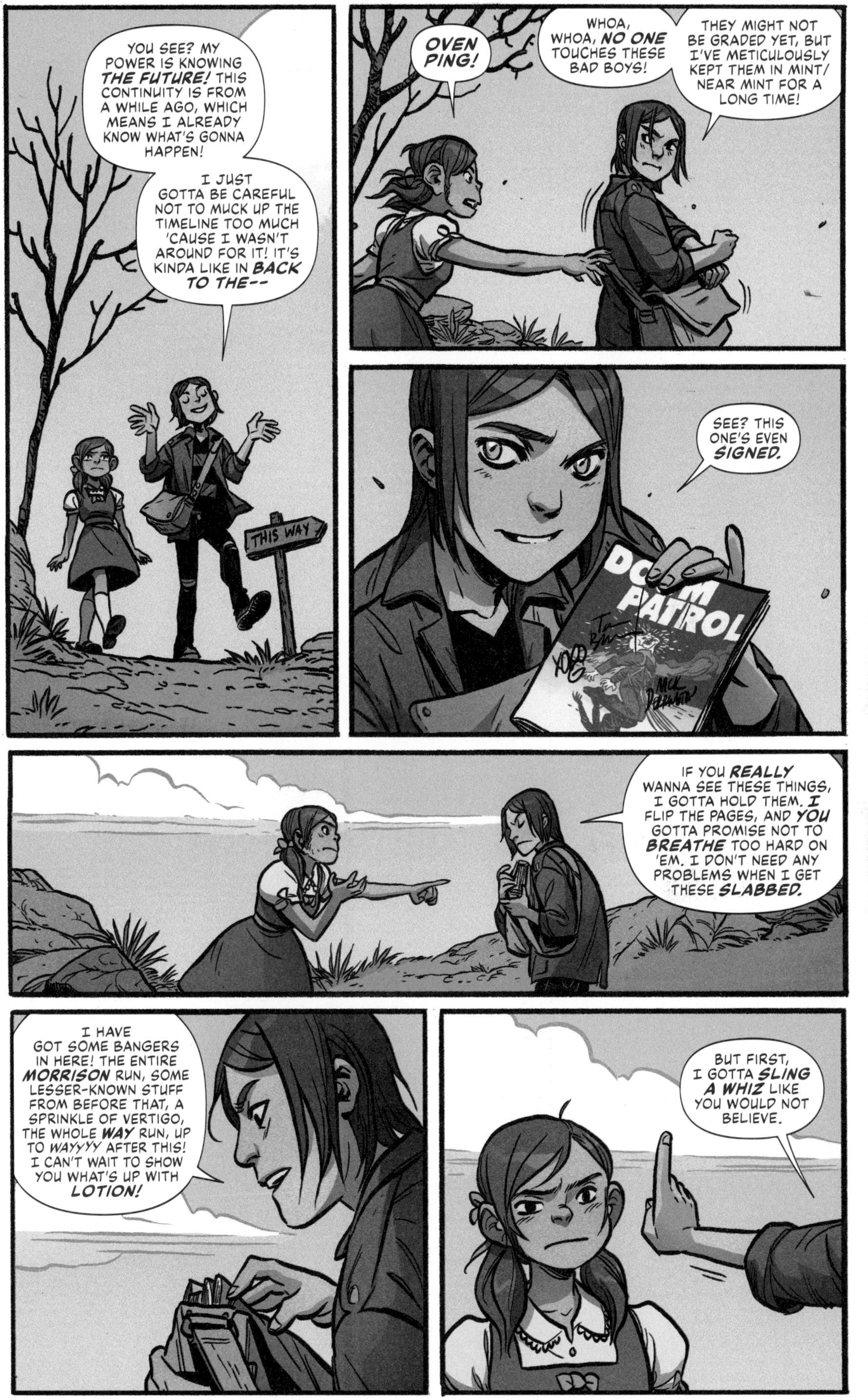
YOU SEE? MY POWER IS KNOWING THE FUTURE! THIS CONTINUITY IS FROM A WHILE AGO, WHICH MEANS I ALREADY KNOW WHAT'S GONNA HAPPEN!
I JUST GOTTA BE CAREFUL NOT TO MUCK UP THE TIMELINE TOO MUCH 'CAUSE I WASN'T AROUND FOR IT! IT'S KINDA LIKE IN BACK TO THE--
THIS WAY
OVEN PING!
WHOA, WHOA, NO ONE TOUCHES THESE BAD BOYS!
THEY MIGHT NOT BE GRADED YET, BUT I'VE METICULOUSLY KEPT THEM IN MINT/NEAR MINT FOR A LONG TIME!
SEE? THIS ONE'S EVEN SIGNED.
DOOM PATROL
IF YOU REALLY WANNA SEE THESE THINGS, I GOTTA HOLD THEM. I FLIP THE PAGES, AND YOU GOTTA PROMISE NOT TO BREATHE TOO HARD ON 'EM. I DON'T NEED ANY PROBLEMS WHEN I GET THESE SLABBED.
I HAVE GOT SOME BANGERS IN HERE! THE ENTIRE MORRISON RUN, SOME LESSER-KNOWN STUFF FROM BEFORE THAT, A SPRINKLE OF VERTIGO, THE WHOLE WAY RUN, UP TO WAYYYY AFTER THIS! I CAN'T WAIT TO SHOW YOU WHAT'S UP WITH LOTION!
BUT FIRST, I GOTTA SLING A WHIZ LIKE YOU WOULD NOT BELIEVE.

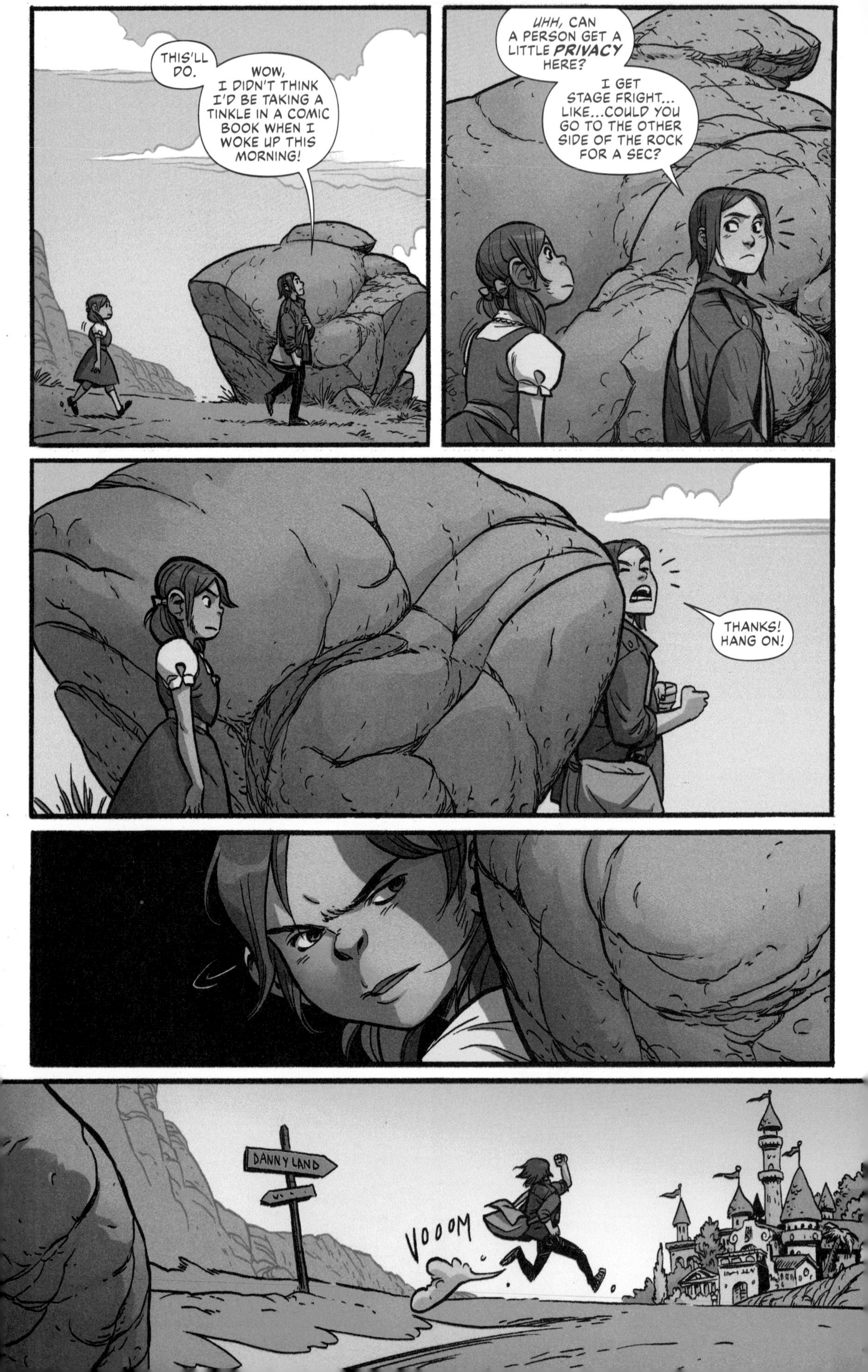
THIS'LL DO.
WOW, I DIDN'T THINK I'D BE TAKING A TINKLE IN A COMIC BOOK WHEN I WOKE UP THIS MORNING!
UHH, CAN A PERSON GET A LITTLE PRIVACY HERE?
I GET STAGE FRIGHT... LIKE...COULD YOU GO TO THE OTHER SIDE OF THE ROCK FOR A SEC?
THANKS! HANG ON!
DANNY LAND
VOOOM

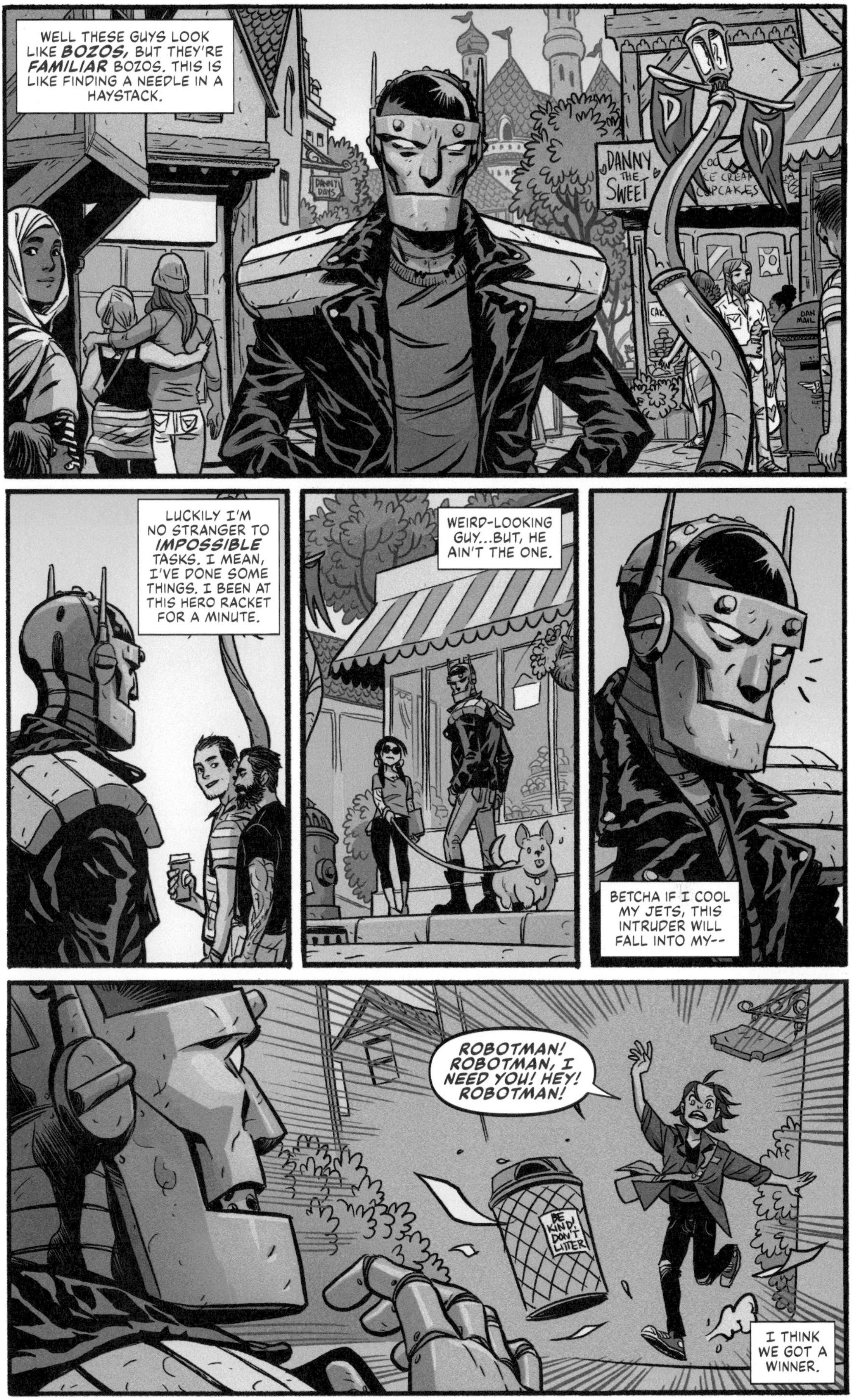
WELL THESE GUYS LOOK LIKE BOZOS, BUT THEY'RE FAMILIAR BOZOS. THIS IS LIKE FINDING A NEEDLE IN A HAYSTACK.
DANNY THE SWEET
LUCKILY I'M NO STRANGER TO IMPOSSIBLE TASKS. I MEAN, I'VE DONE SOME THINGS. I BEEN AT THIS HERO RACKET FOR A MINUTE.
WEIRD-LOOKING GUY...BUT, HE AIN'T THE ONE.
BETCHA IF I COOL MY JETS, THIS INTRUDER WILL FALL INTO MY--
ROBOTMAN! ROBOTMAN, I NEED YOU! HEY! ROBOTMAN!
BE KIND! DON'T LITTER
I THINK WE GOT A WINNER.

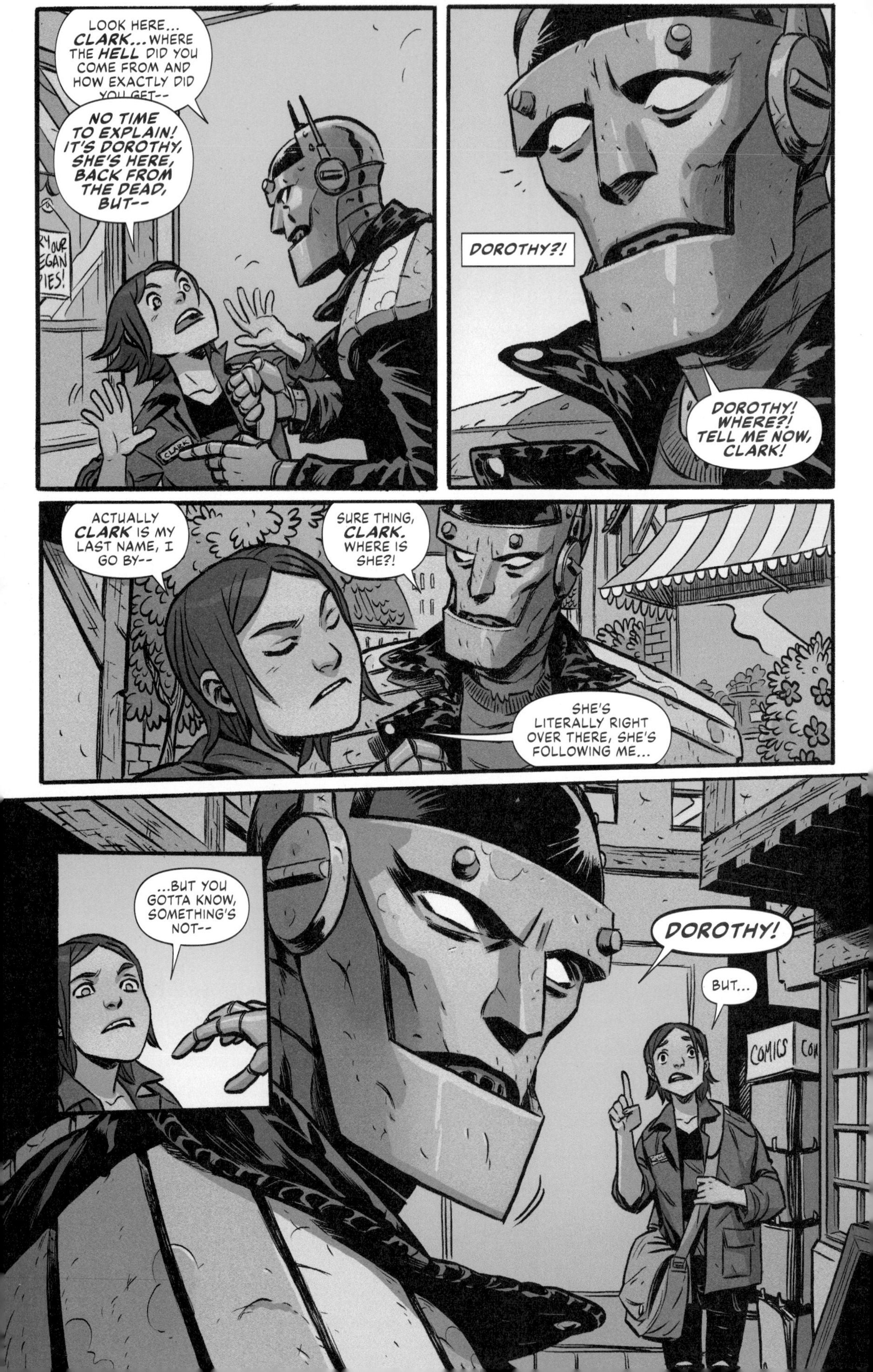
LOOK HERE... CLARK... WHERE THE HELL DID YOU COME FROM AND HOW EXACTLY DID YOU GET--
NO TIME TO EXPLAIN! IT'S DOROTHY, SHE'S HERE, BACK FROM THE DEAD, BUT--
DOROTHY?!
DOROTHY! WHERE?! TELL ME NOW, CLARK!
ACTUALLY CLARK IS MY LAST NAME, I GO BY--
SURE THING, CLARK. WHERE IS SHE?!
SHE'S LITERALLY RIGHT OVER THERE, SHE'S FOLLOWING ME...
...BUT YOU GOTTA KNOW, SOMETHING'S NOT--
DOROTHY!
BUT...
COMICS

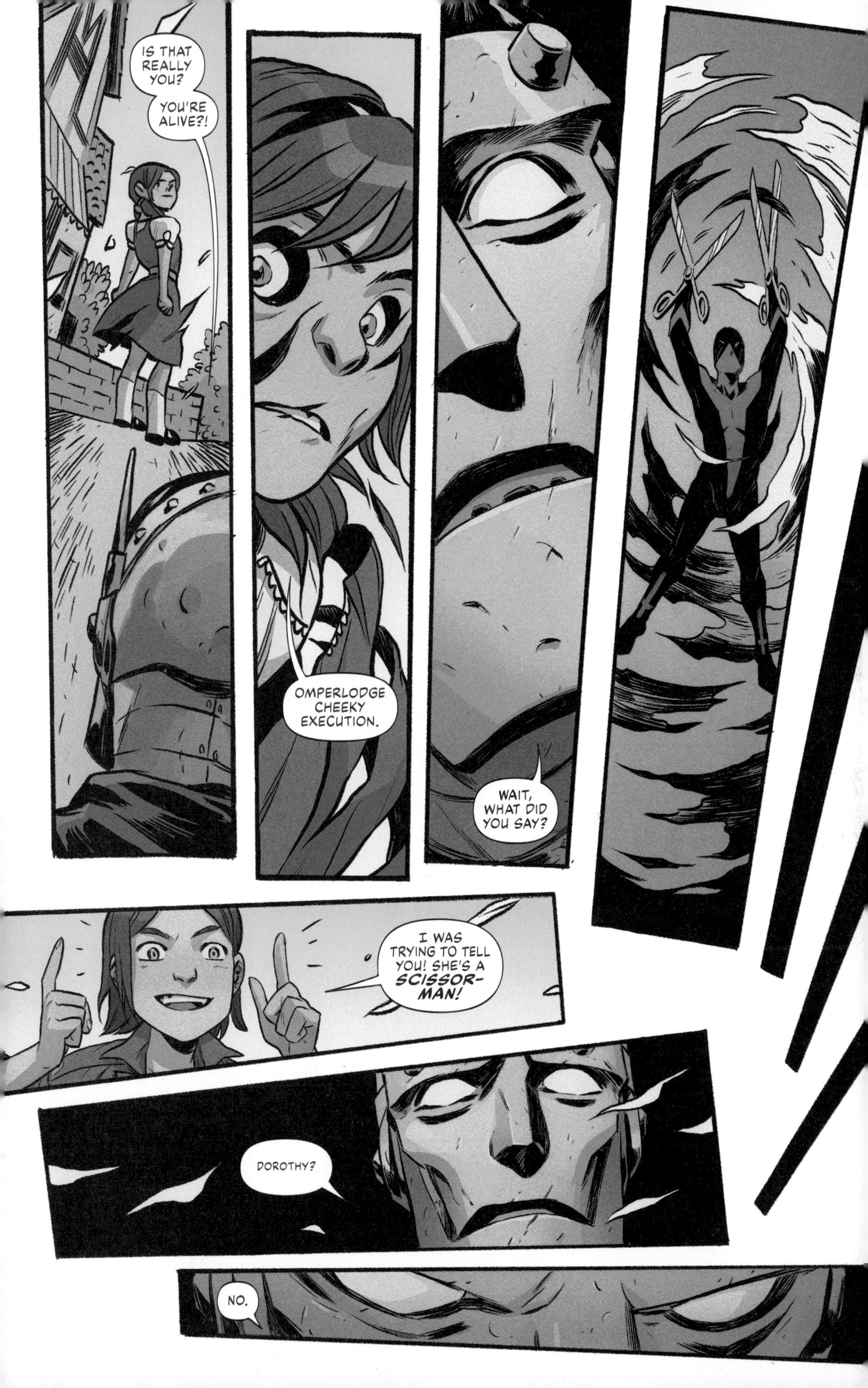

IS THAT REALLY YOU?
YOU'RE ALIVE?!
OMPERLODGE CHEEKY EXECUTION.
WAIT, WHAT DID YOU SAY?
I WAS TRYING TO TELL YOU! SHE'S A SCISSOR-MAN!
DOROTHY?
NO.

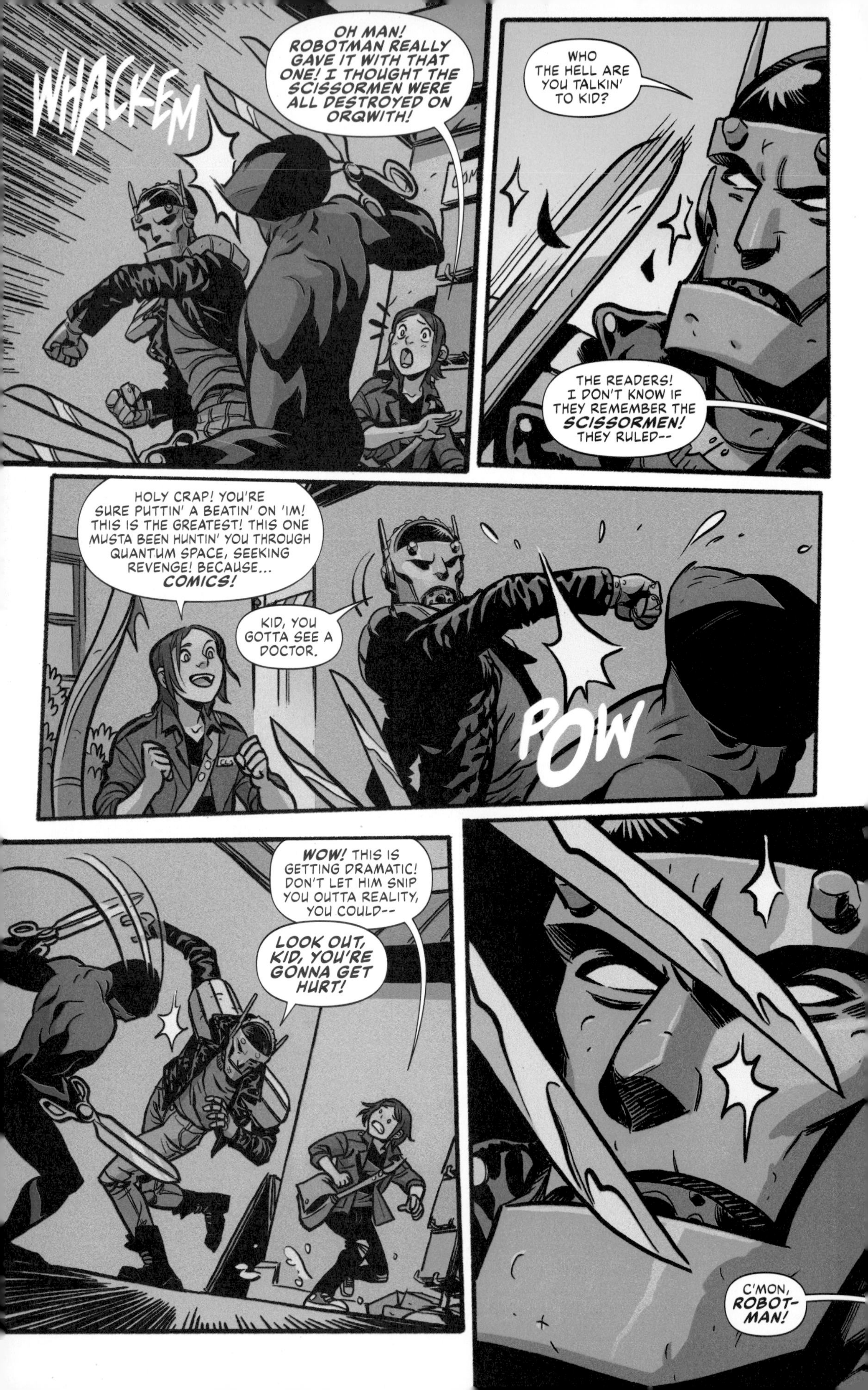
WHACKEM
OH MAN! ROBOTMAN REALLY GAVE IT WITH THAT ONE! I THOUGHT THE SCISSORMEN WERE ALL DESTROYED ON ORQWITH!
WHO THE HELL ARE YOU TALKIN' TO KID?
THE READERS! I DON'T KNOW IF THEY REMEMBER THE SCISSORMEN! THEY RULED--
HOLY CRAP! YOU'RE SURE PUTTIN' A BEATIN' ON 'IM! THIS IS THE GREATEST! THIS ONE MUSTA BEEN HUNTIN' YOU THROUGH QUANTUM SPACE, SEEKING REVENGE! BECAUSE... COMICS!
KID, YOU GOTTA SEE A DOCTOR.
POW
WOW! THIS IS GETTING DRAMATIC! DON'T LET HIM SNIP YOU OUTTA REALITY, YOU COULD--
LOOK OUT, KID, YOU'RE GONNA GET HURT!
C'MON, ROBOT-MAN!

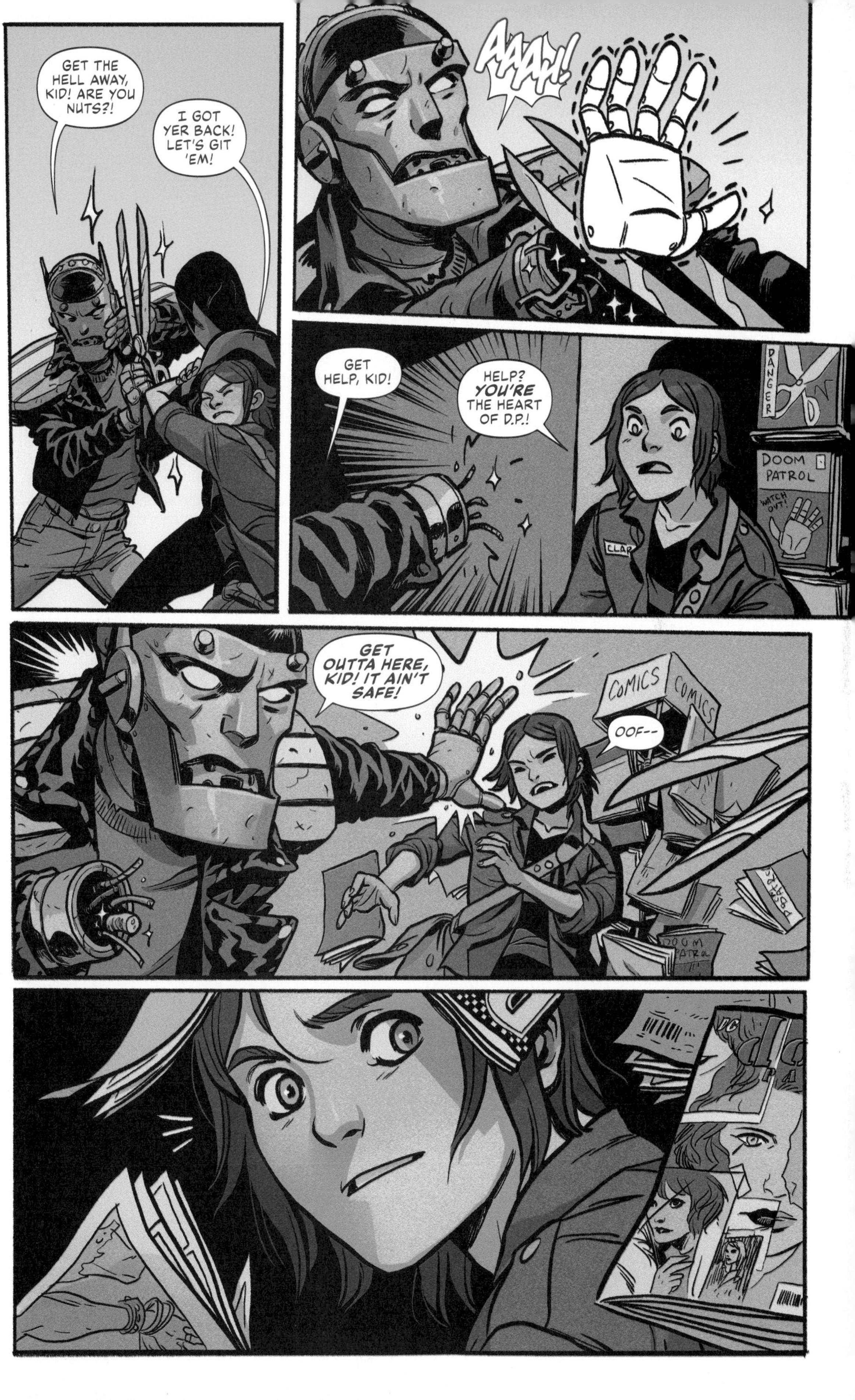
GET THE HELL AWAY, KID! ARE YOU NUTS?!
I GOT YER BACK! LET'S GIT 'EM!
AAAH!
GET HELP, KID!
HELP? YOU'RE THE HEART OF D.P.!
DANGER
DOOM PATROL
WATCH OUT!
GET OUTTA HERE, KID! IT AIN'T SAFE!
COMICS
COMICS
OOF--
DOOM PATROL

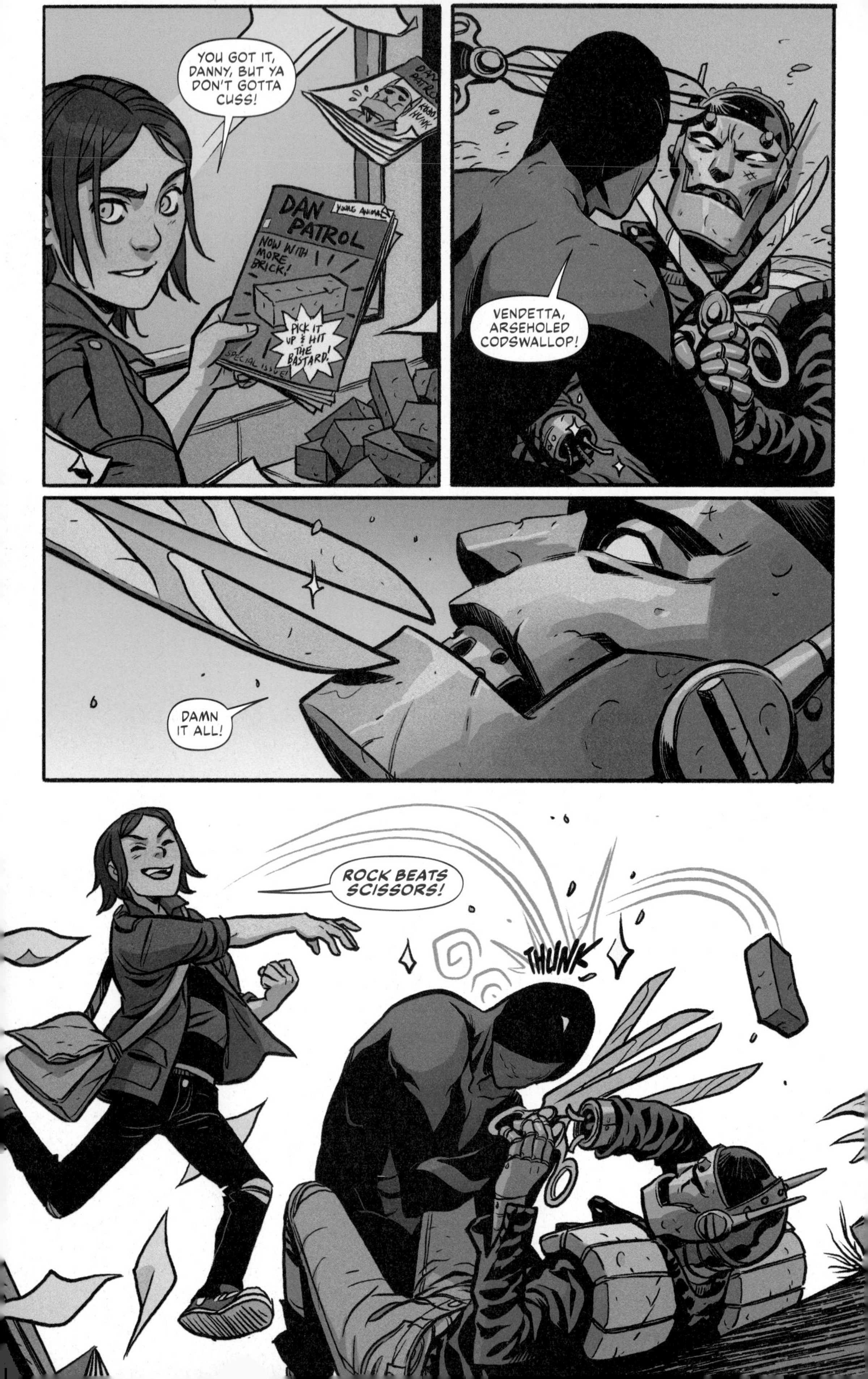
YOU GOT IT, DANNY, BUT YA DON'T GOTTA CUSS!
DAN PATROL
YOUNG ANIMAL
NOW WITH MORE BRICK!
PICK IT UP & HIT THE BASTARD!
SPECIAL ISSUE!
VENDETTA, ARSEHOLED CODSWALLOP!
DAMN IT ALL!
ROCK BEATS SCISSORS!
THUNK

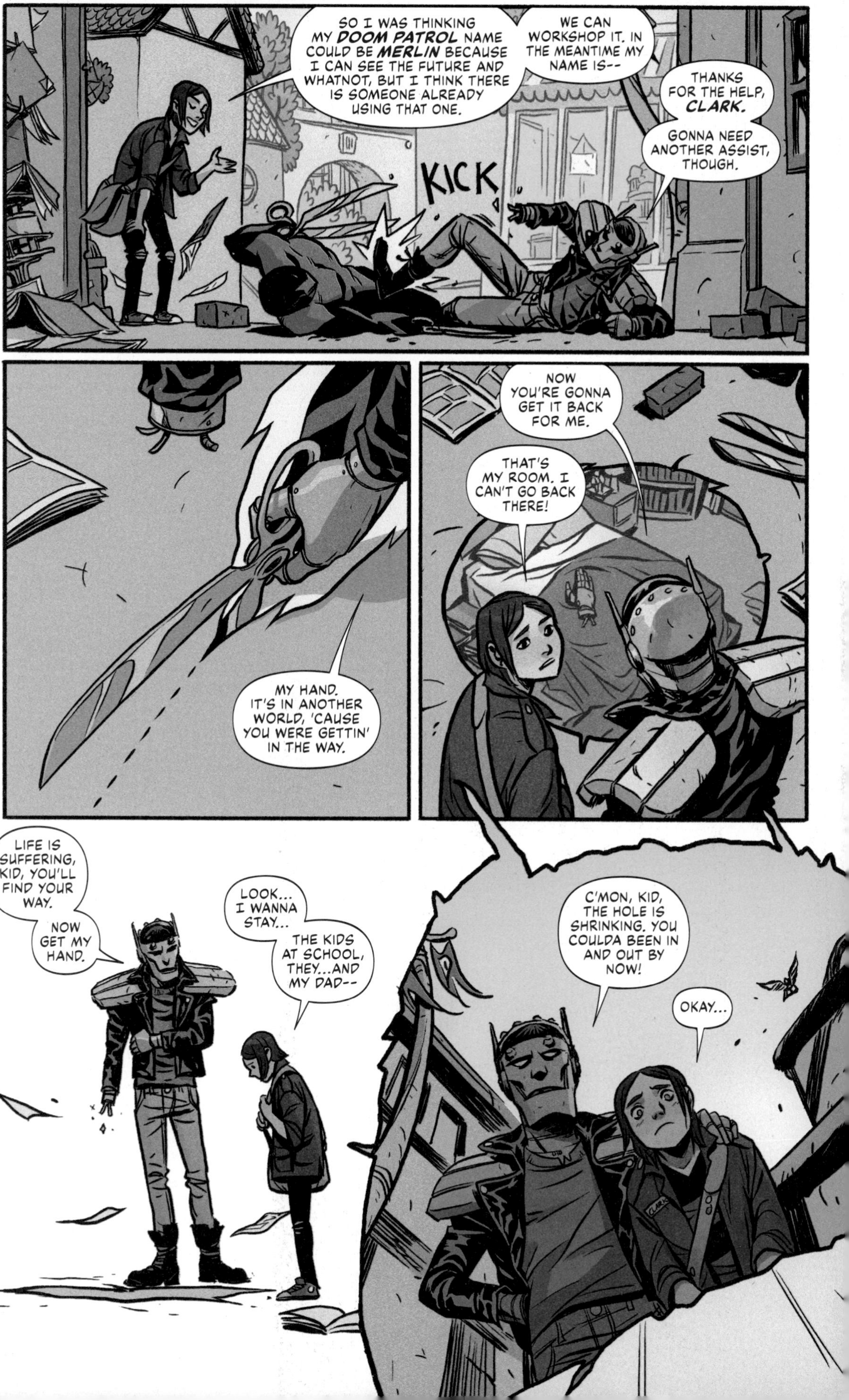
SO I WAS THINKING MY DOOM PATROL NAME COULD BE MERLIN BECAUSE I CAN SEE THE FUTURE AND WHATNOT, BUT I THINK THERE IS SOMEONE ALREADY USING THAT ONE.
WE CAN WORKSHOP IT. IN THE MEANTIME MY NAME IS--
KICK
THANKS FOR THE HELP, CLARK.
GONNA NEED ANOTHER ASSIST, THOUGH.
MY HAND. IT'S IN ANOTHER WORLD, 'CAUSE YOU WERE GETTIN' IN THE WAY.
NOW YOU'RE GONNA GET IT BACK FOR ME.
THAT'S MY ROOM. I CAN'T GO BACK THERE!
LIFE IS SUFFERING, KID, YOU'LL FIND YOUR WAY.
NOW GET MY HAND.
LOOK... I WANNA STAY...
THE KIDS AT SCHOOL, THEY...AND MY DAD--
C'MON, KID, THE HOLE IS SHRINKING. YOU COULDA BEEN IN AND OUT BY NOW!
OKAY...

AAAAAH!

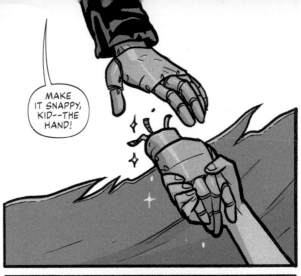

MAKE IT SNAPPY, KID--THE HAND!

FFFIP

GOOD JOB, KID.

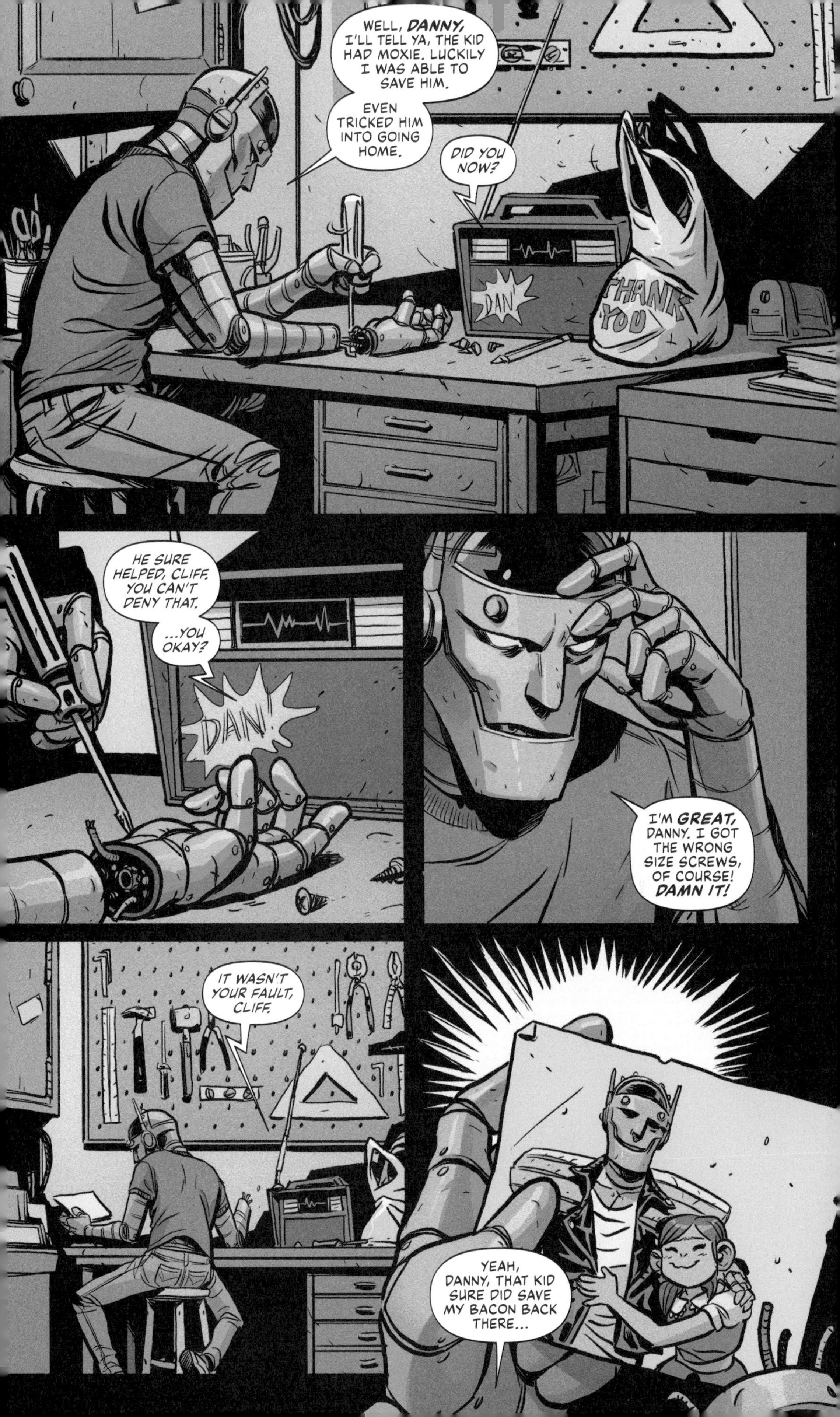
WELL, DANNY, I'LL TELL YA, THE KID HAD MOXIE. LUCKILY I WAS ABLE TO SAVE HIM.
EVEN TRICKED HIM INTO GOING HOME.
DID YOU NOW?
DAN
THANK YOU
HE SURE HELPED, CLIFF. YOU CAN'T DENY THAT.
...YOU OKAY?
DAN
I'M GREAT, DANNY. I GOT THE WRONG SIZE SCREWS, OF COURSE! DAMN IT!
IT WASN'T YOUR FAULT, CLIFF.
YEAH, DANNY, THAT KID SURE DID SAVE MY BACON BACK THERE...

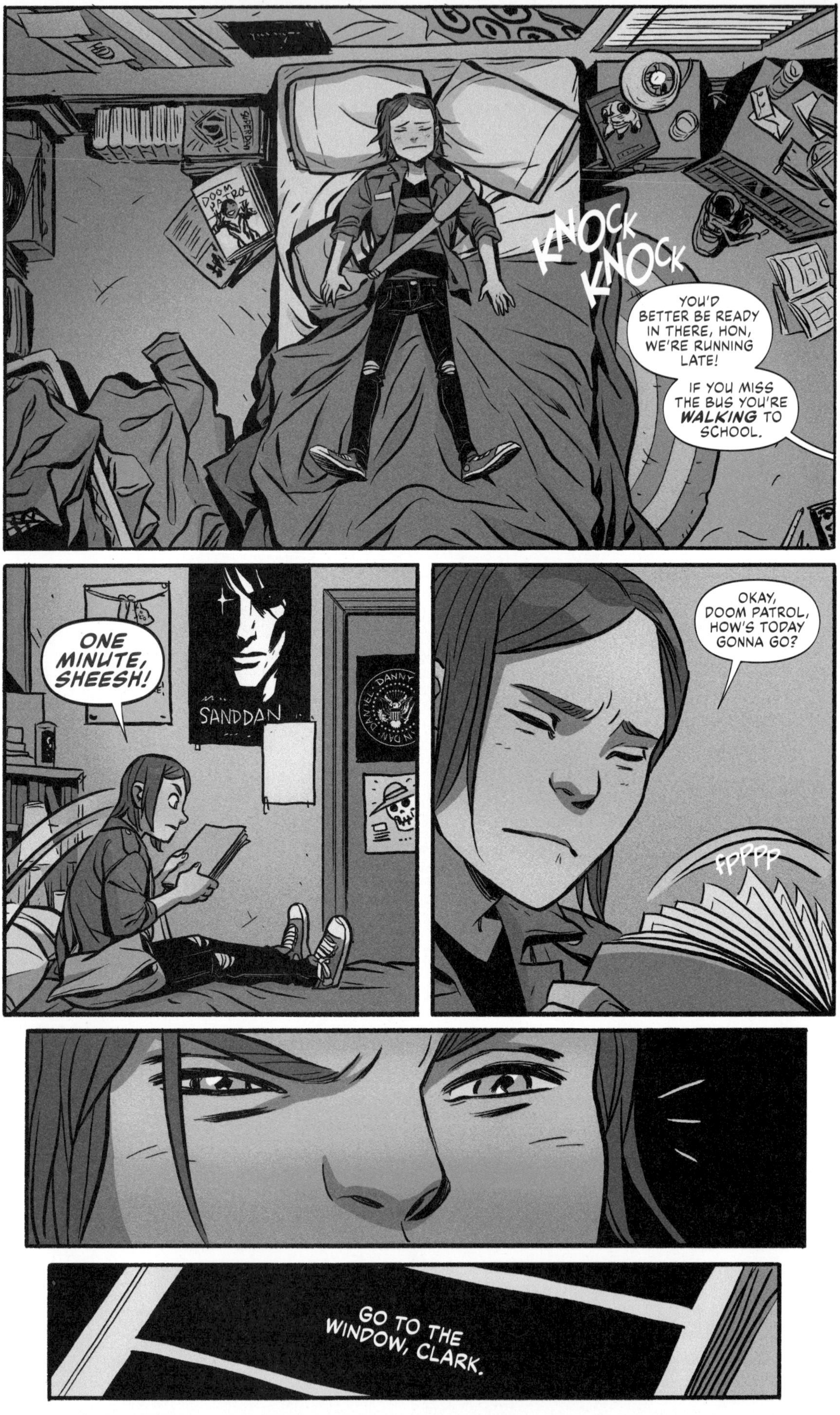
KNOCK KNOCK
YOU'D BETTER BE READY IN THERE, HON, WE'RE RUNNING LATE!
IF YOU MISS THE BUS YOU'RE WALKING TO SCHOOL.
DOOM PATROL
SANDDAN
ONE MINUTE, SHEESH!
OKAY, DOOM PATROL, HOW'S TODAY GONNA GO?
FPPPP
GO TO THE WINDOW, CLARK.

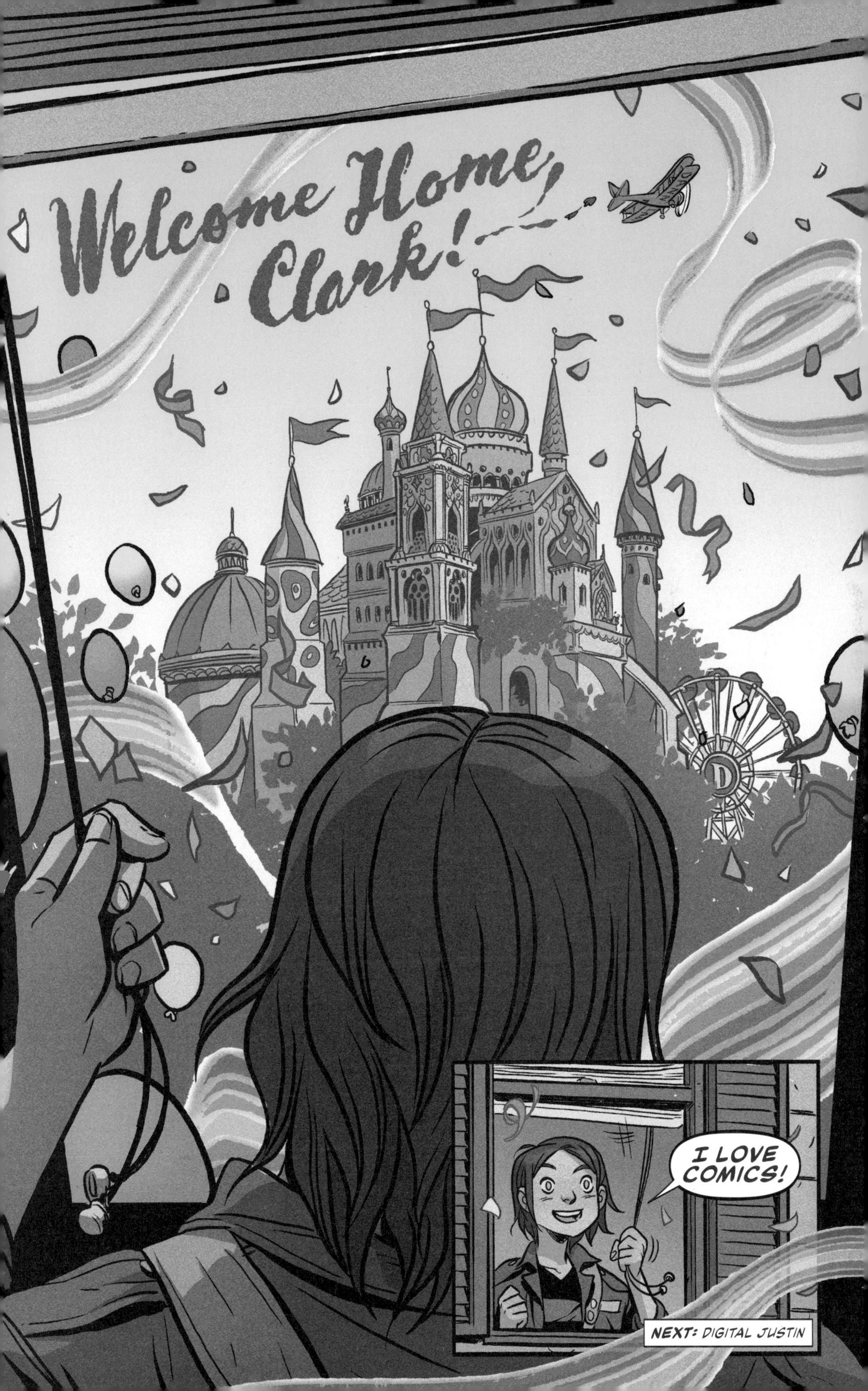
Welcome Home, Clark!
I LOVE COMICS!
NEXT: DIGITAL JUSTIN

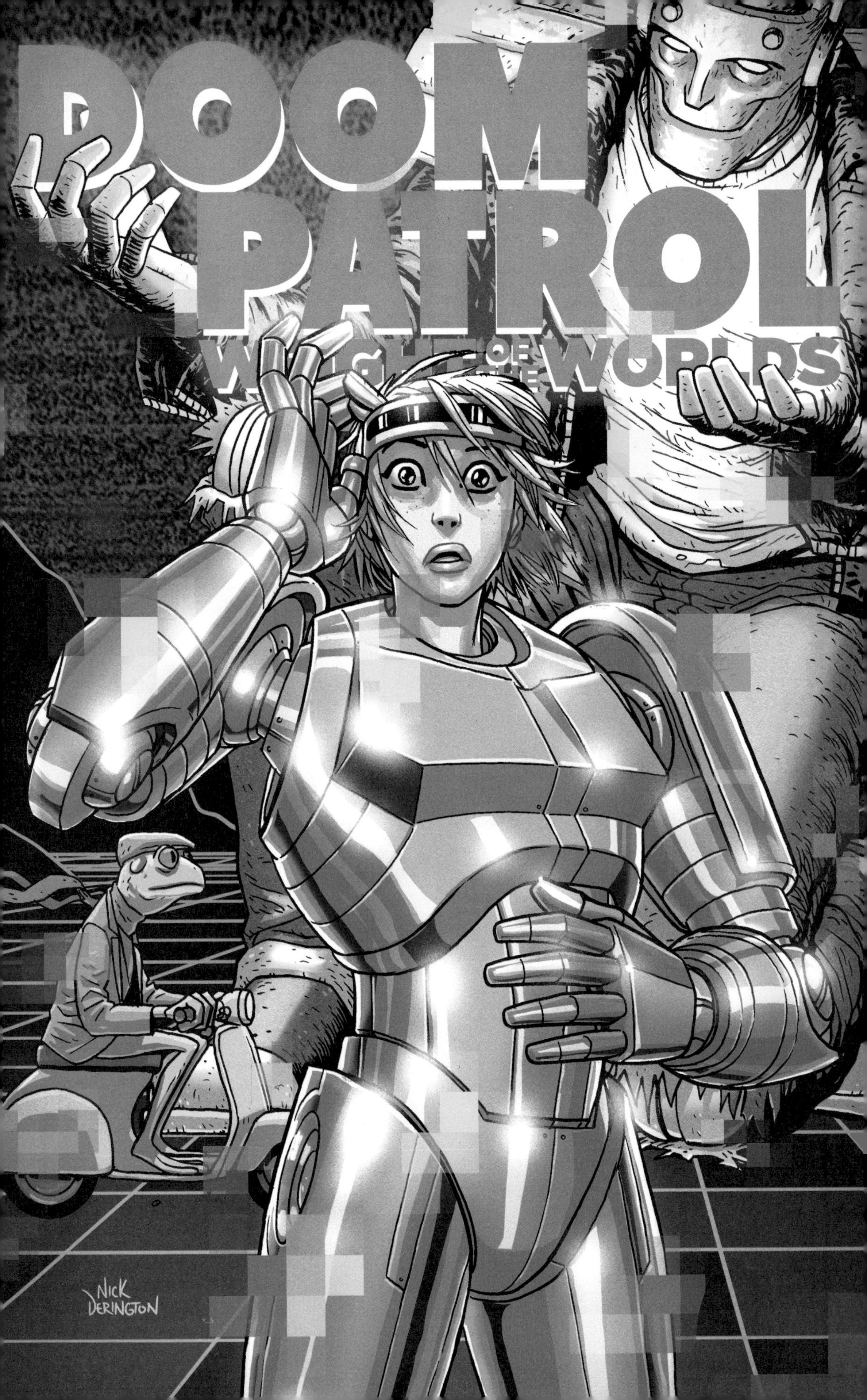
DOOM
PATROL
WORLDS
NICK DERINGTON

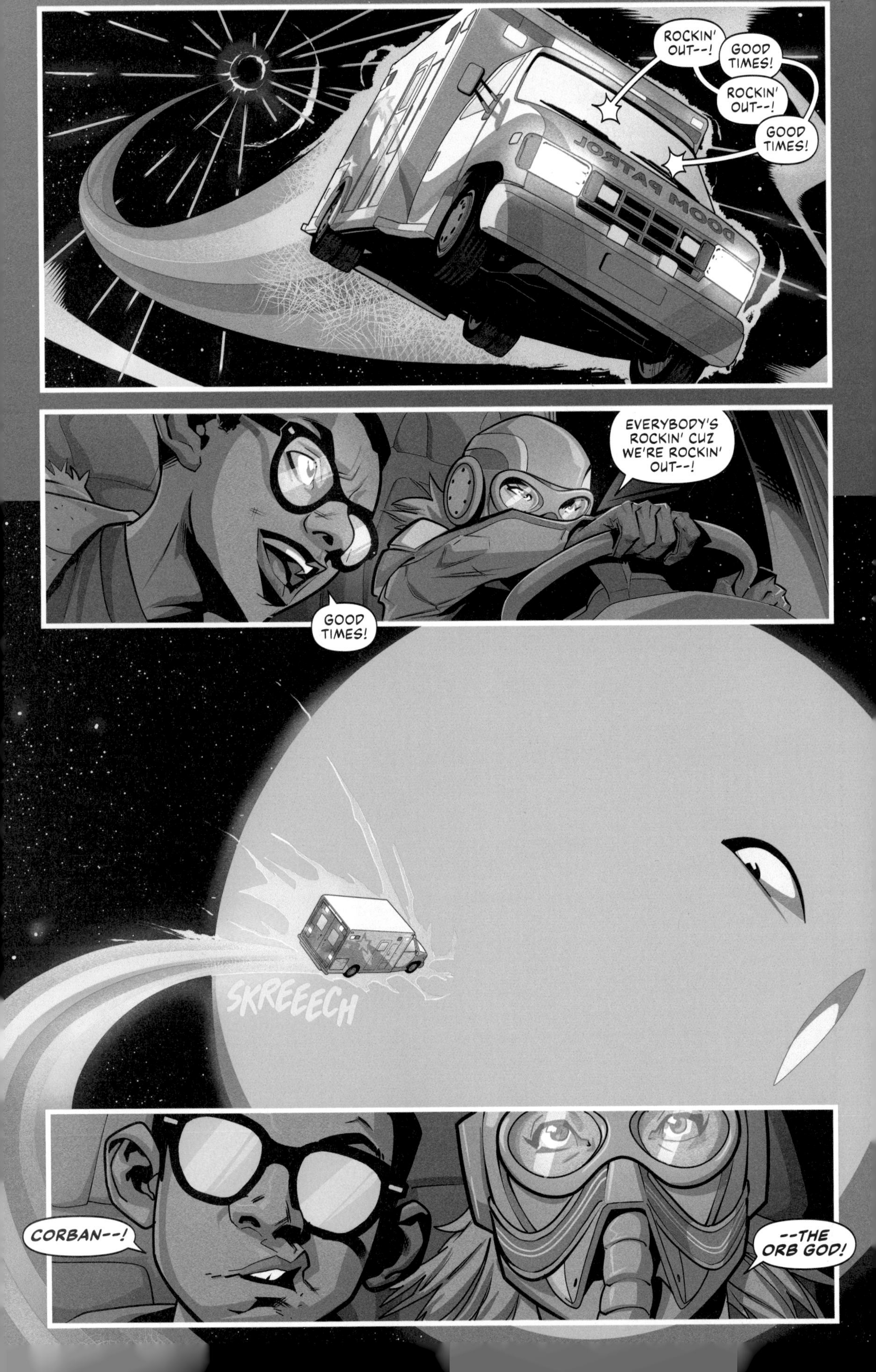
ROCKIN' OUT--!
GOOD TIMES!
ROCKIN' OUT--!
GOOD TIMES!
DOOM PATROL
EVERYBODY'S ROCKIN' CUZ WE'RE ROCKIN' OUT--!
GOOD TIMES!
SKREEEECH
CORBAN--!
--THE ORB GOD!

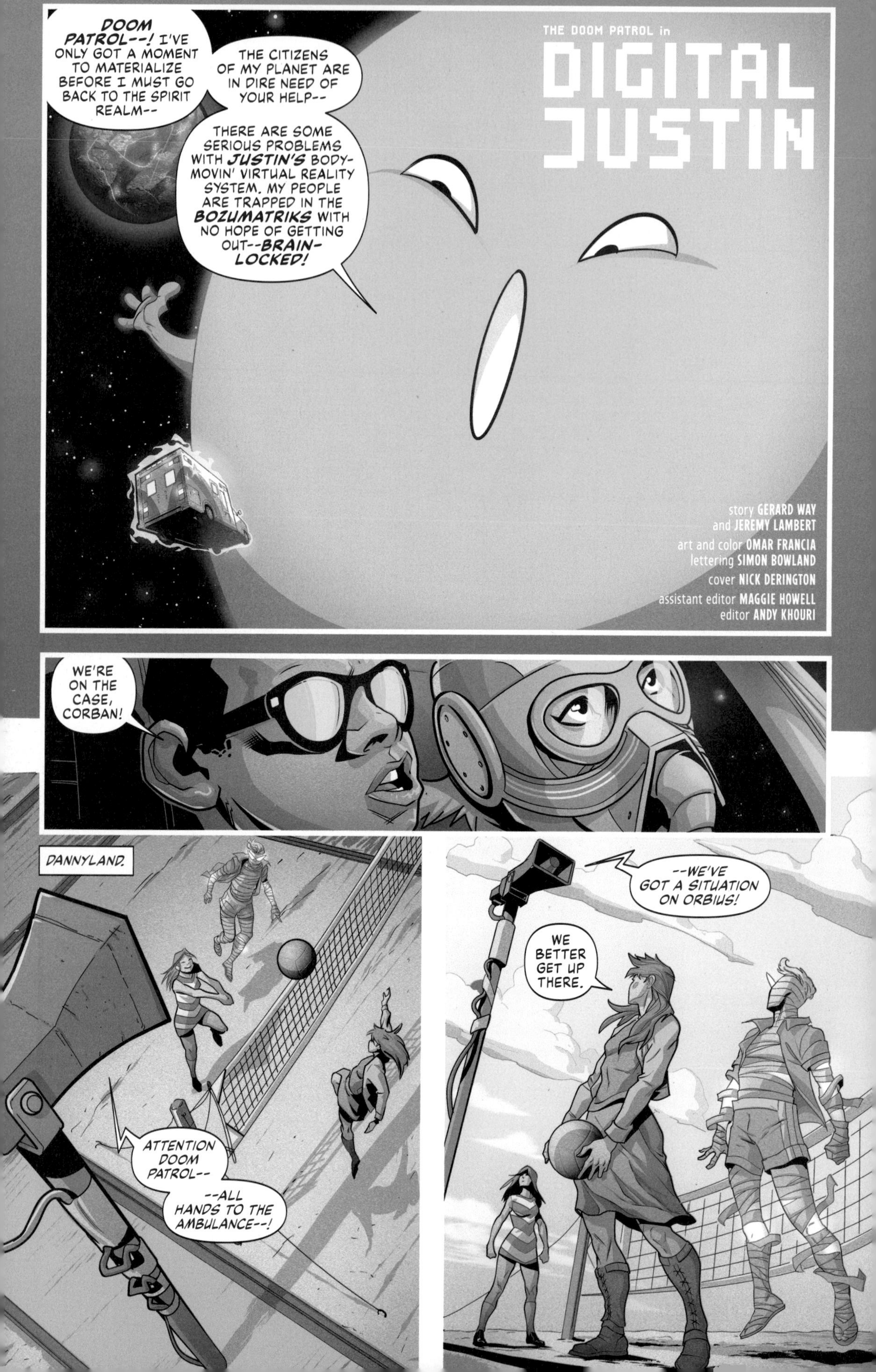
DOOM PATROL--! I'VE ONLY GOT A MOMENT TO MATERIALIZE BEFORE I MUST GO BACK TO THE SPIRIT REALM--
THE CITIZENS OF MY PLANET ARE IN DIRE NEED OF YOUR HELP--
THERE ARE SOME SERIOUS PROBLEMS WITH JUSTIN'S BODY-MOVIN' VIRTUAL REALITY SYSTEM. MY PEOPLE ARE TRAPPED IN THE BOZUMATRIKS WITH NO HOPE OF GETTING OUT--BRAIN-LOCKED!
THE DOOM PATROL in
DIGITAL JUSTIN
story GERARD WAY and JEREMY LAMBERT
art and color OMAR FRANCIA
lettering SIMON BOWLAND
cover NICK DERINGTON
assistant editor MAGGIE HOWELL
editor ANDY KHOURI
WE'RE ON THE CASE, CORBAN!
DANNYLAND.
ATTENTION DOOM PATROL--
--ALL HANDS TO THE AMBULANCE--!
--WE'VE GOT A SITUATION ON ORBIUS!
WE BETTER GET UP THERE.

CORBAN SAID WE SHOULD HEAD INTO THIS MAIN *BMVR* CENTER TO FIND JUSTIN, AND HELP HOWEVER WE CAN...

DEAR ME, THIS *IS* A PROBLEM--

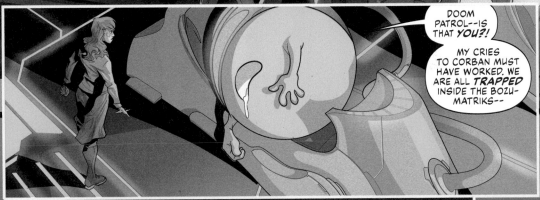

DOOM PATROL--IS THAT *YOU?!*

MY CRIES TO CORBAN MUST HAVE WORKED. WE ARE ALL *TRAPPED* INSIDE THE BOZU-MATRIKS--

--YOU MUST CLIMB ONTO THE *BMVR* AND INTERFACE WITH THE BOZUMATRIKS-- I'LL EXPLAIN THE REST INSIDE--

ALL RIGHT, DOOM PATROL--

READJUSTING

--LET'S JACK IN!

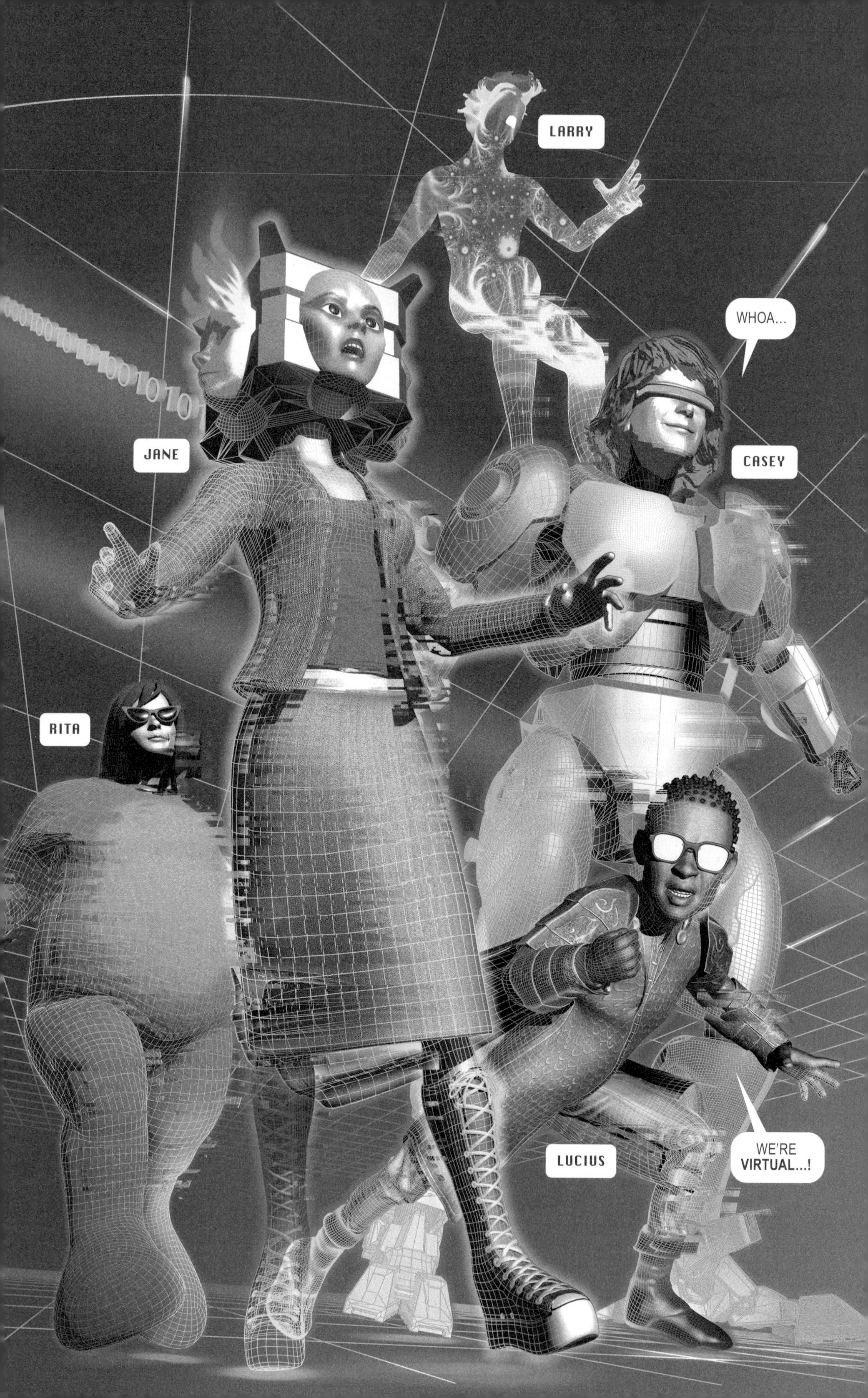
LARRY
WHOA...
JANE
CASEY
RITA
LUCIUS
WE'RE **VIRTUAL...!**

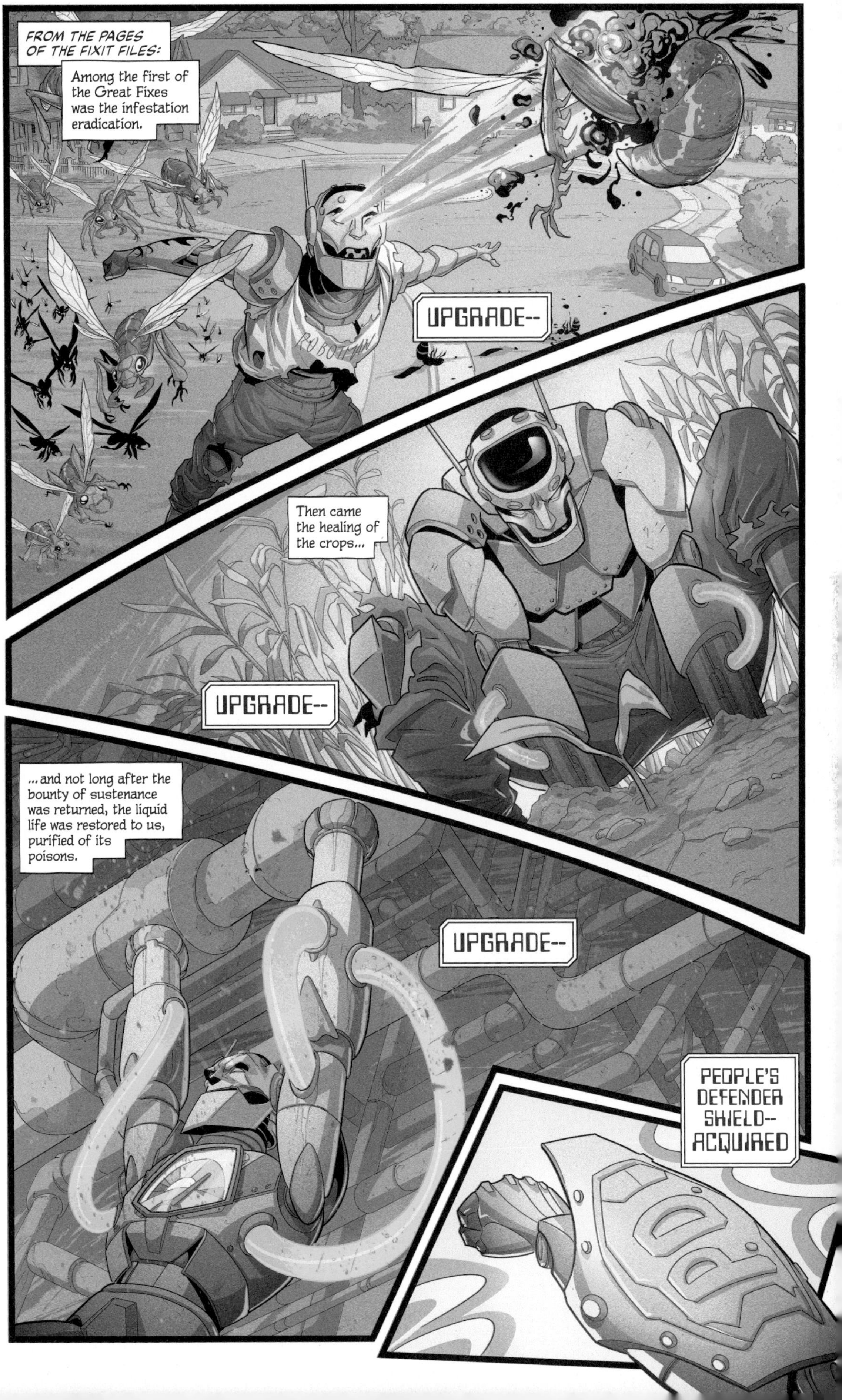
FROM THE PAGES OF THE FIXIT FILES:
Among the first of the Great Fixes was the infestation eradication.
UPGRADE--
Then came the healing of the crops...
UPGRADE--
...and not long after the bounty of sustenance was returned, the liquid life was restored to us, purified of its poisons.
UPGRADE--
PEOPLE'S DEFENDER SHIELD-- ACQUIRED

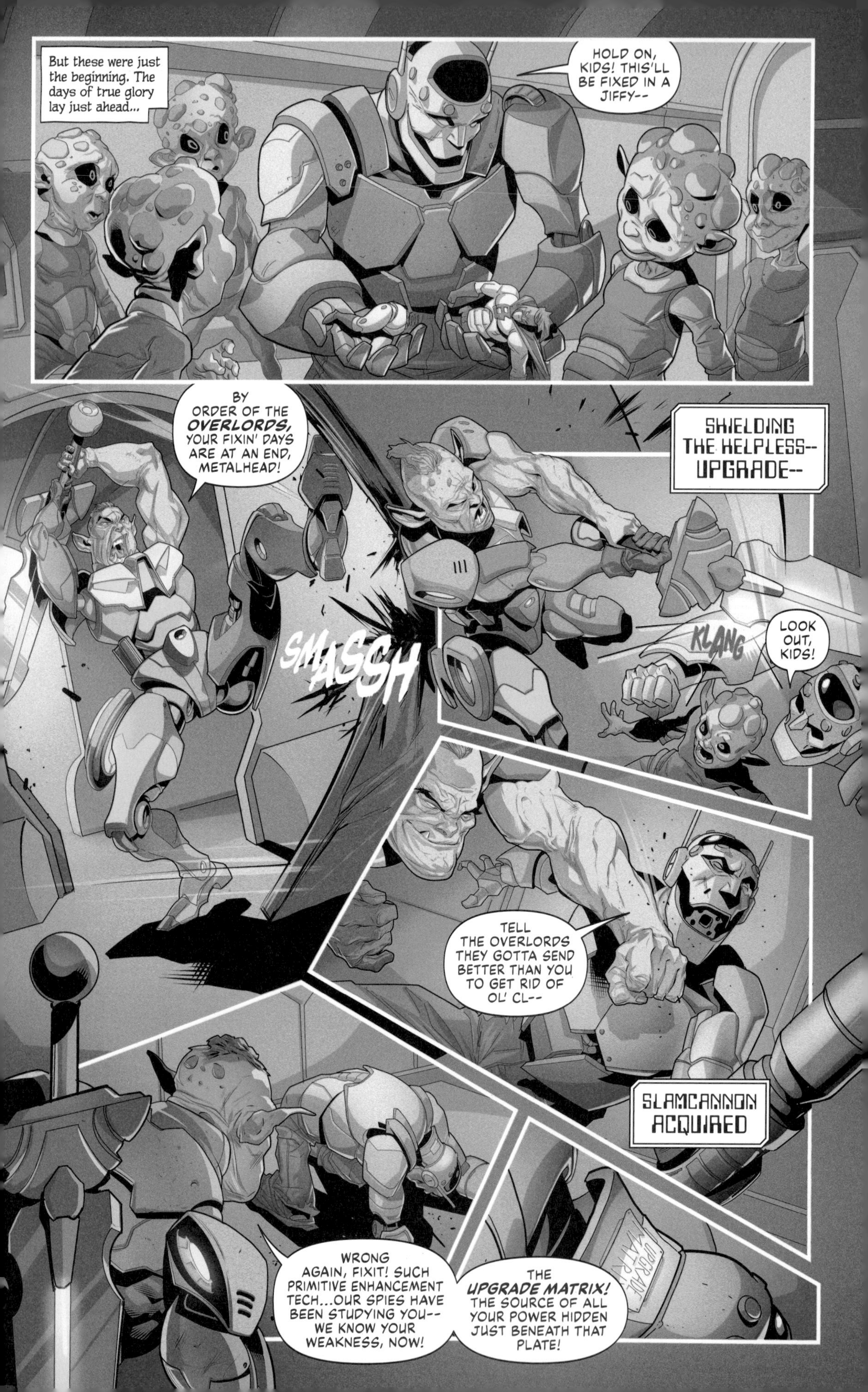
But these were just the beginning. The days of true glory lay just ahead...
HOLD ON, KIDS! THIS'LL BE FIXED IN A JIFFY--
BY ORDER OF THE *OVERLORDS,* YOUR FIXIN' DAYS ARE AT AN END, METALHEAD!
SHIELDING THE HELPLESS-- UPGRADE--
SMASSH
KLANG
LOOK OUT, KIDS!
TELL THE OVERLORDS THEY GOTTA SEND BETTER THAN YOU TO GET RID OF OL' CL--
SLAMCANNON ACQUIRED
WRONG AGAIN, FIXIT! SUCH PRIMITIVE ENHANCEMENT TECH...OUR SPIES HAVE BEEN STUDYING YOU-- WE KNOW YOUR WEAKNESS, NOW!
THE *UPGRADE MATRIX!* THE SOURCE OF ALL YOUR POWER HIDDEN JUST BENEATH THAT PLATE!
UPGRADE MATRIX

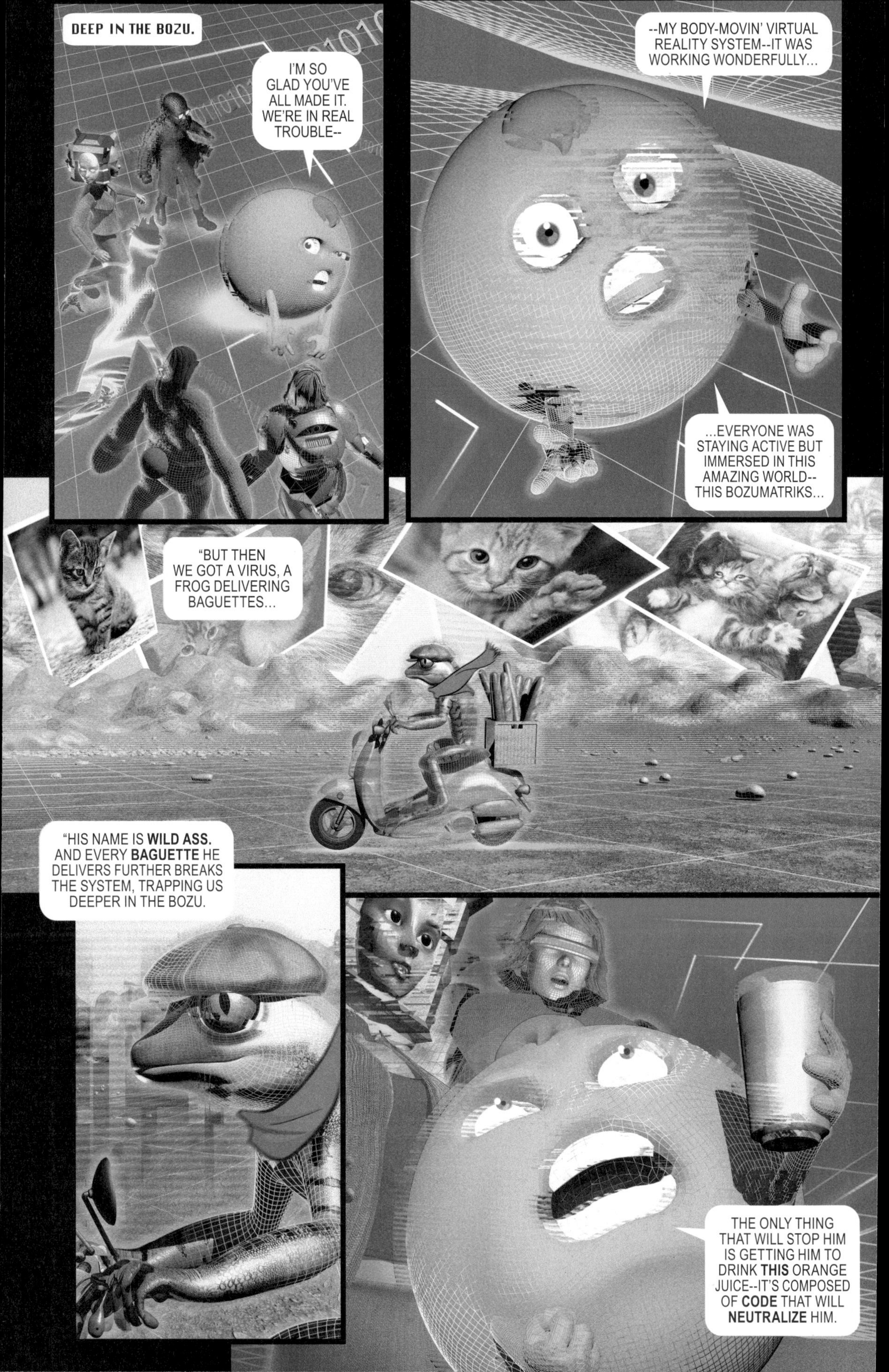
DEEP IN THE BOZU.
I'M SO GLAD YOU'VE ALL MADE IT. WE'RE IN REAL TROUBLE--
--MY BODY-MOVIN' VIRTUAL REALITY SYSTEM--IT WAS WORKING WONDERFULLY...
...EVERYONE WAS STAYING ACTIVE BUT IMMERSED IN THIS AMAZING WORLD--THIS BOZUMATRIKS...
"BUT THEN WE GOT A VIRUS, A FROG DELIVERING BAGUETTES...
"HIS NAME IS **WILD ASS.** AND EVERY **BAGUETTE** HE DELIVERS FURTHER BREAKS THE SYSTEM, TRAPPING US DEEPER IN THE BOZU.
THE ONLY THING THAT WILL STOP HIM IS GETTING HIM TO DRINK **THIS** ORANGE JUICE--IT'S COMPOSED OF **CODE** THAT WILL **NEUTRALIZE** HIM.

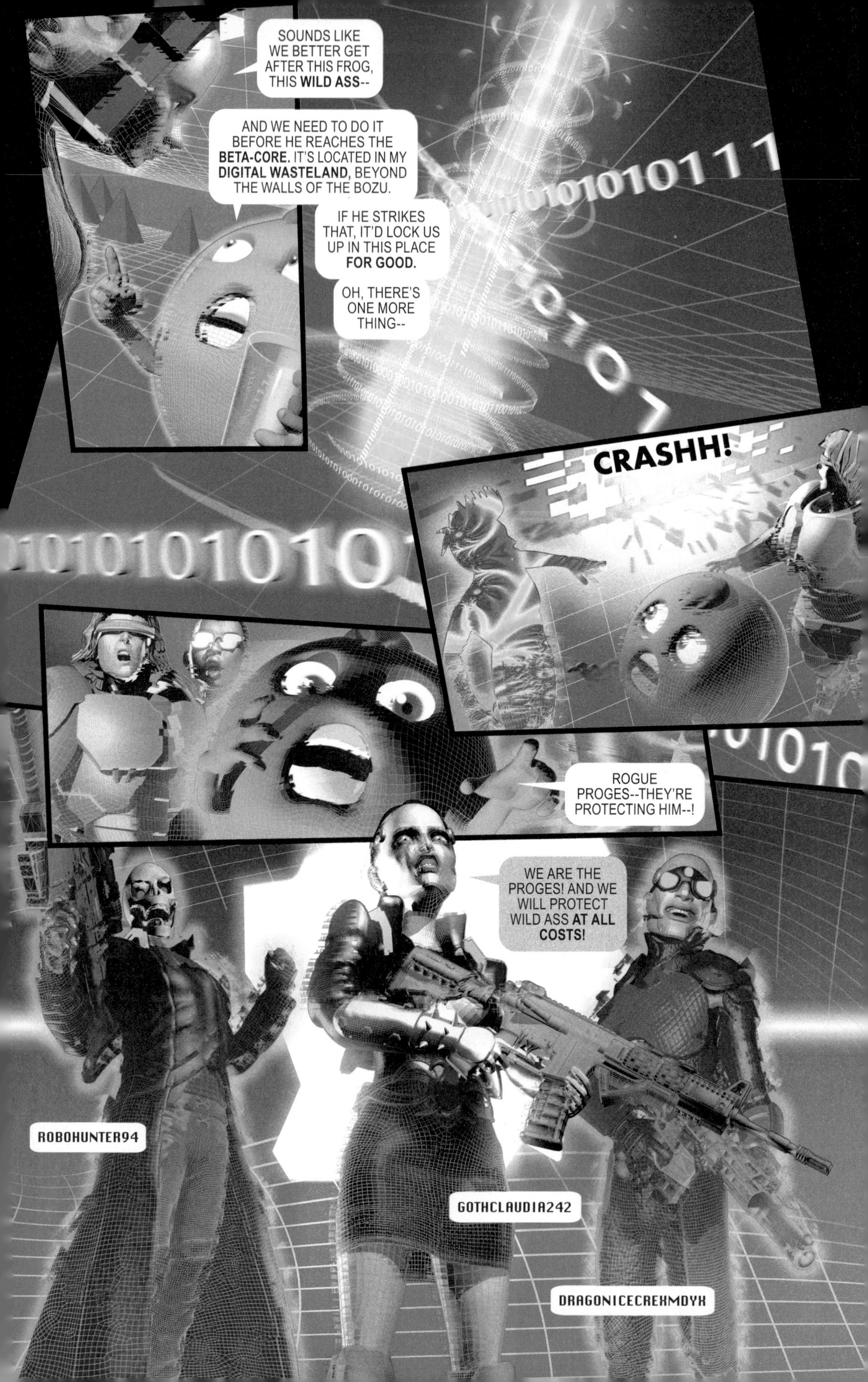

SOUNDS LIKE WE BETTER GET AFTER THIS FROG, THIS **WILD ASS**--
AND WE NEED TO DO IT BEFORE HE REACHES THE **BETA-CORE.** IT'S LOCATED IN MY **DIGITAL WASTELAND**, BEYOND THE WALLS OF THE BOZU.
IF HE STRIKES THAT, IT'D LOCK US UP IN THIS PLACE **FOR GOOD.**
OH, THERE'S ONE MORE THING--
CRASHH!
ROGUE PROGES--THEY'RE PROTECTING HIM--!
WE ARE THE PROGES! AND WE WILL PROTECT WILD ASS **AT ALL COSTS!**
ROBOHUNTER94
GOTHCLAUDIA242
DRAGONICECREAMDYX

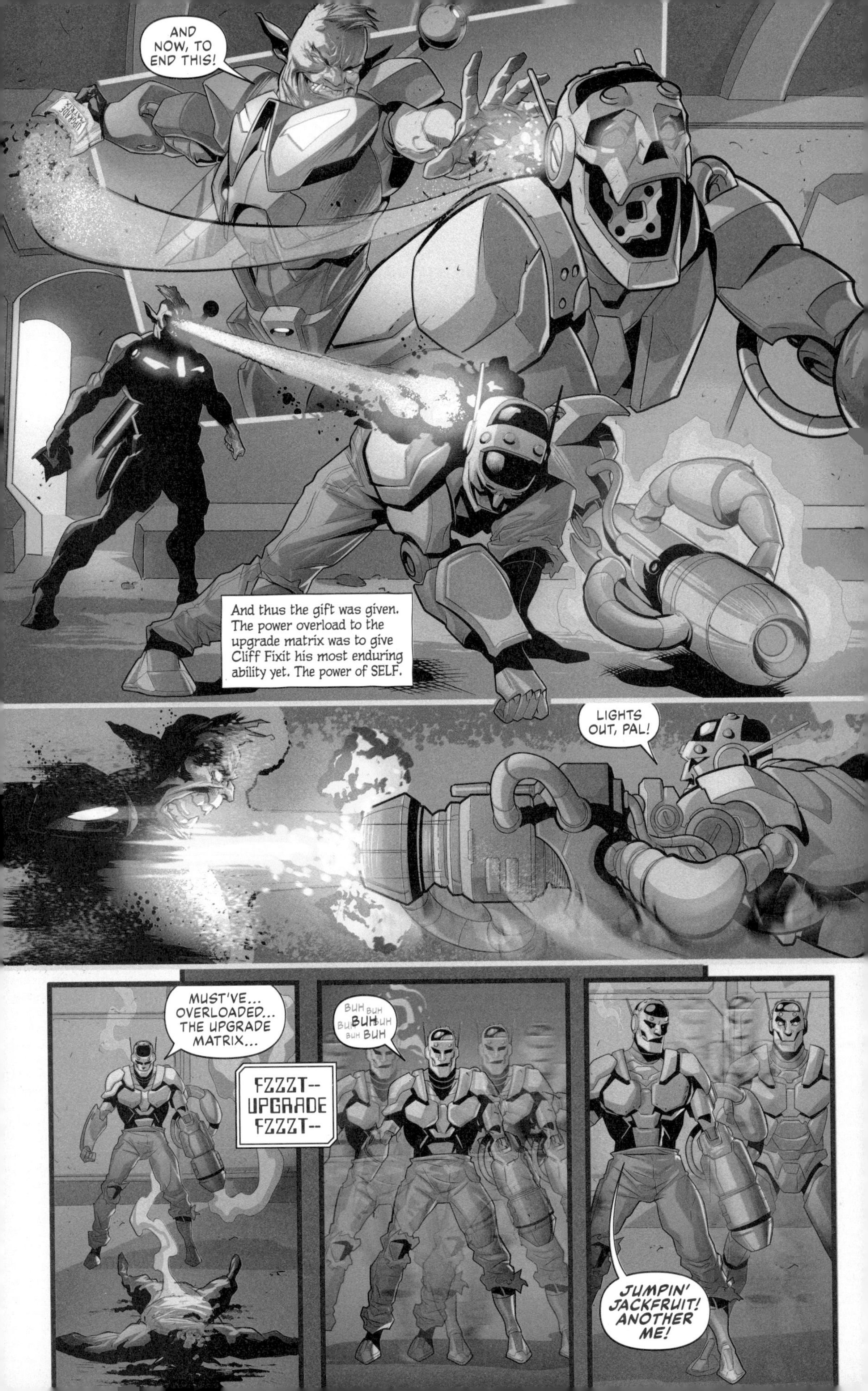
AND NOW, TO END THIS!
And thus the gift was given. The power overload to the upgrade matrix was to give Cliff Fixit his most enduring ability yet. The power of SELF.
LIGHTS OUT, PAL!
MUST'VE... OVERLOADED... THE UPGRADE MATRIX...
FZZZT-- UPGRADE FZZZT--
BUH BUH BUH BUH BUH BUH BUH
JUMPIN' JACKFRUIT! ANOTHER ME!

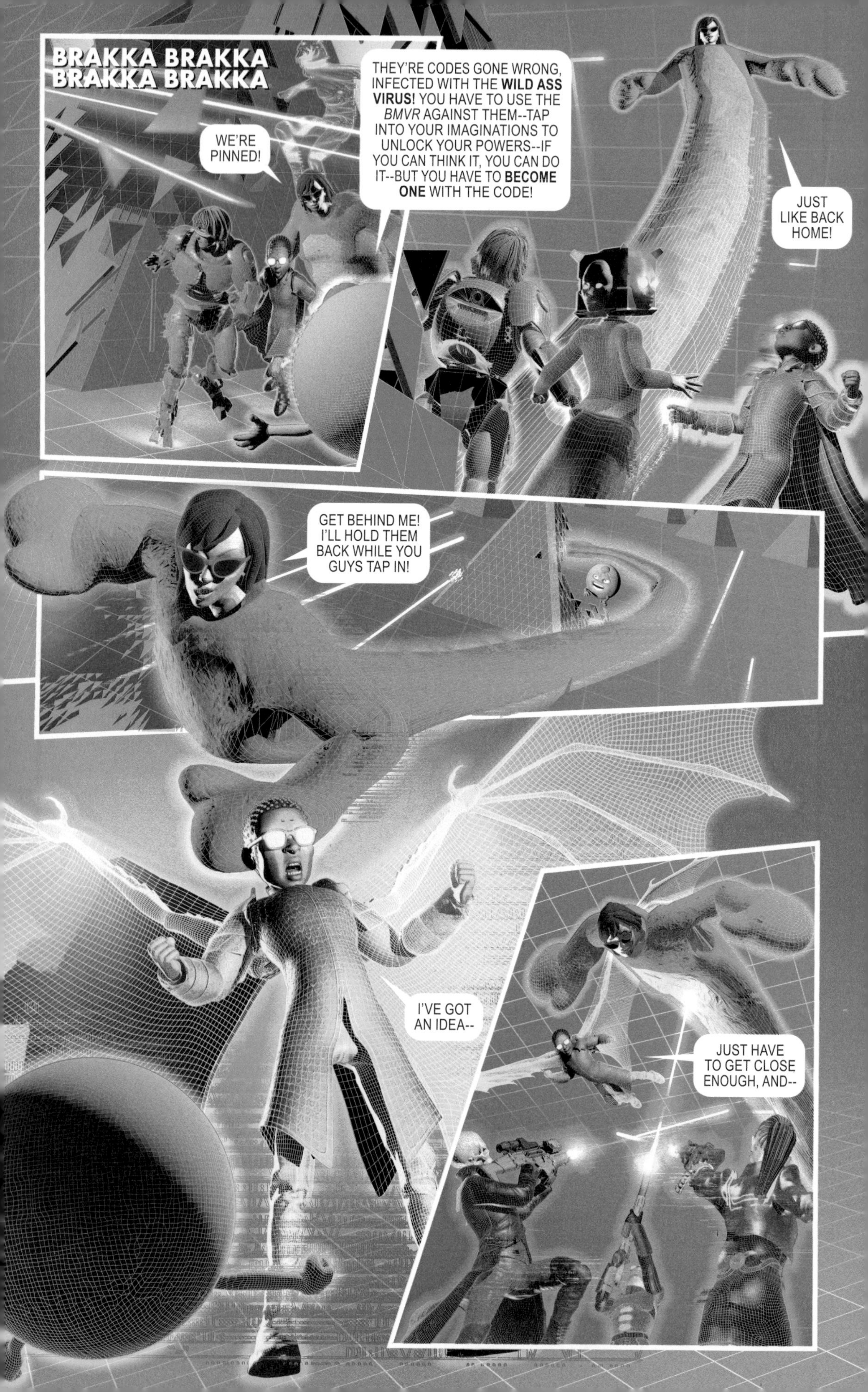
BRAKKA BRAKKA BRAKKA BRAKKA
WE'RE PINNED!
THEY'RE CODES GONE WRONG, INFECTED WITH THE **WILD ASS VIRUS!** YOU HAVE TO USE THE *BMVR* AGAINST THEM--TAP INTO YOUR IMAGINATIONS TO UNLOCK YOUR POWERS--IF YOU CAN THINK IT, YOU CAN DO IT--BUT YOU HAVE TO **BECOME ONE** WITH THE CODE!
JUST LIKE BACK HOME!
GET BEHIND ME! I'LL HOLD THEM BACK WHILE YOU GUYS TAP IN!
I'VE GOT AN IDEA--
JUST HAVE TO GET CLOSE ENOUGH, AND--

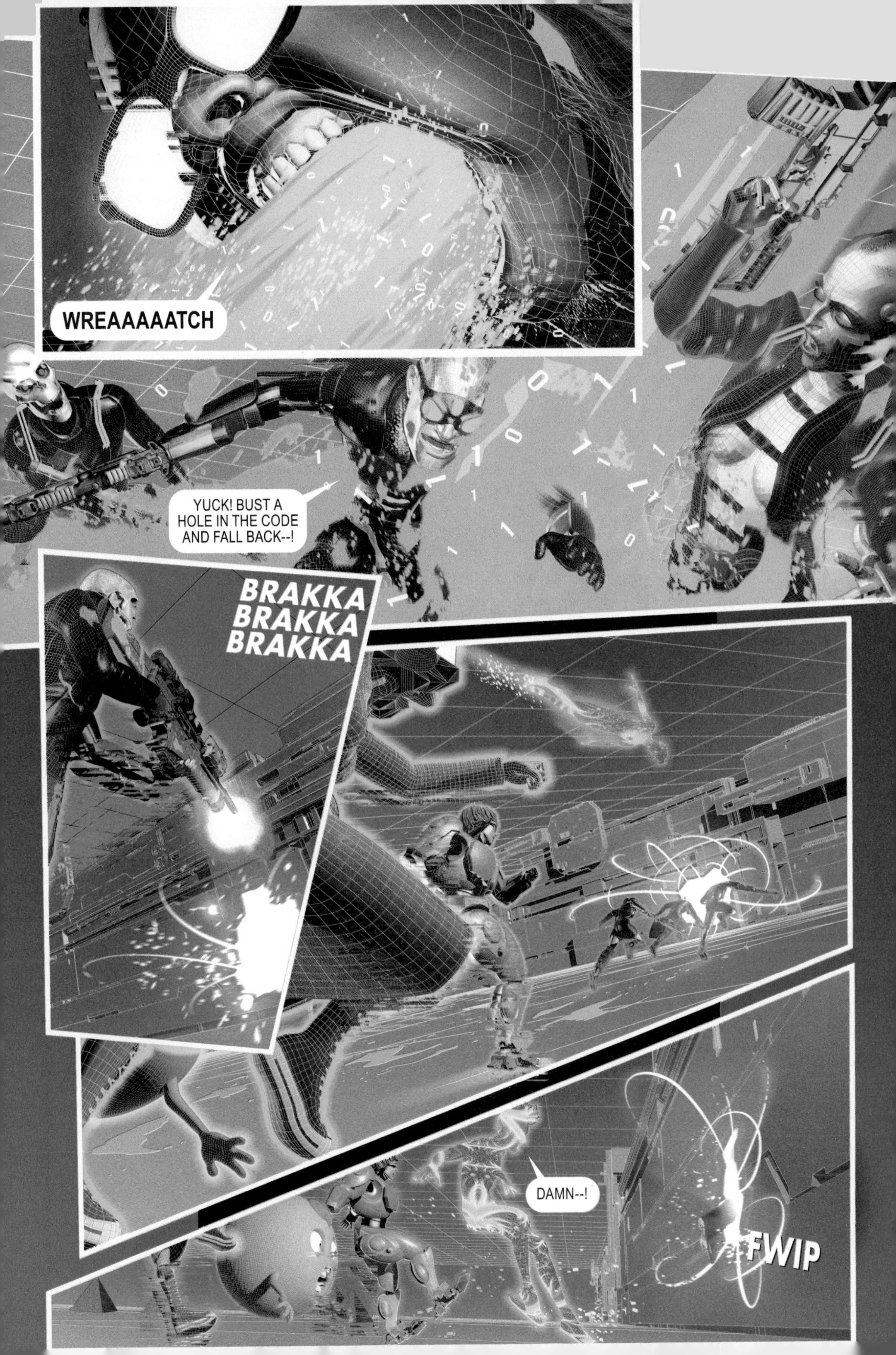
WREAAAAATCH
YUCK! BUST A HOLE IN THE CODE AND FALL BACK--!
BRAKKA BRAKKA BRAKKA
DAMN--!
FWIP

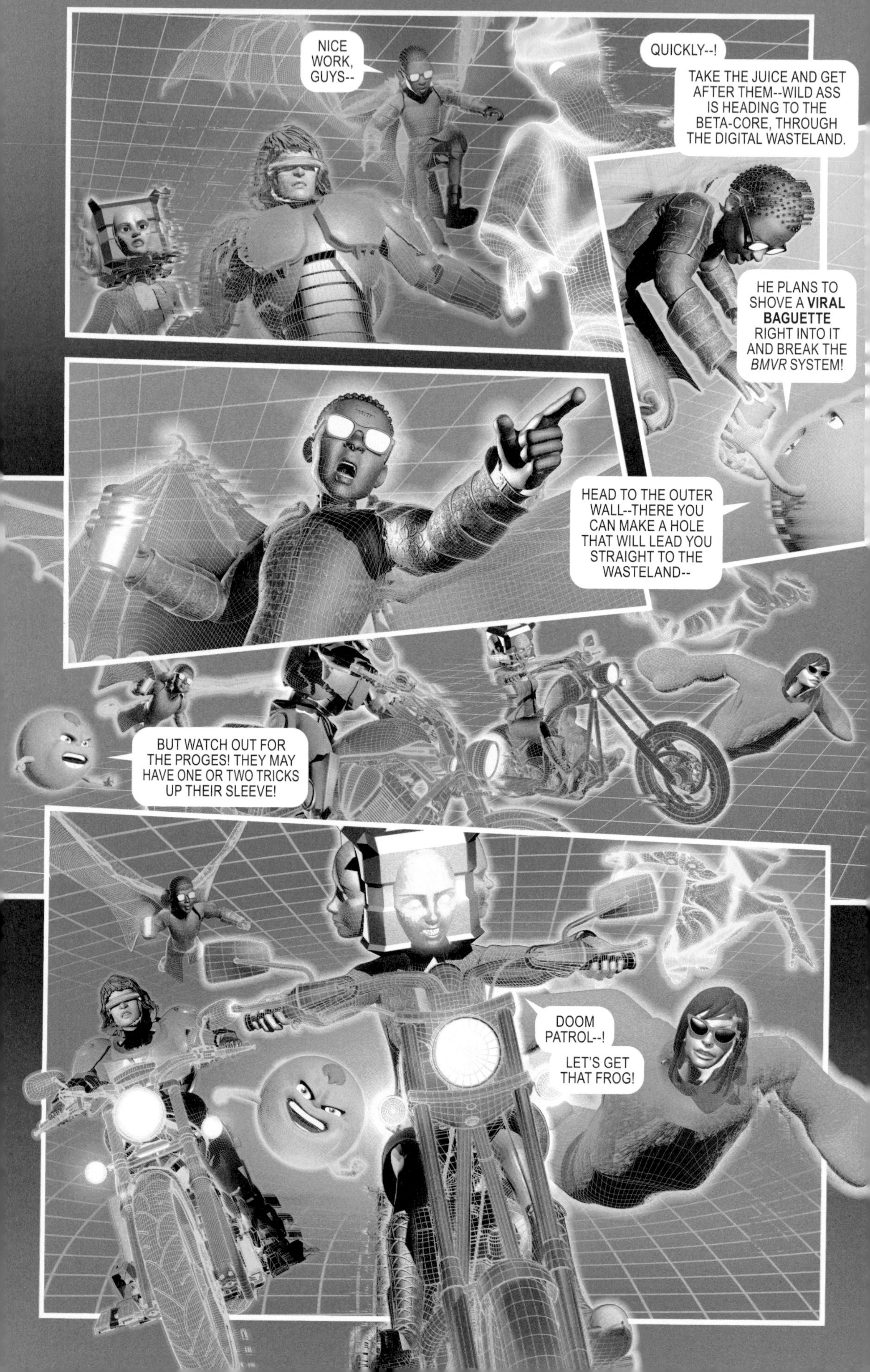
NICE WORK, GUYS--
QUICKLY--!
TAKE THE JUICE AND GET AFTER THEM--WILD ASS IS HEADING TO THE BETA-CORE, THROUGH THE DIGITAL WASTELAND.
HE PLANS TO SHOVE A **VIRAL BAGUETTE** RIGHT INTO IT AND BREAK THE *BMVR* SYSTEM!
HEAD TO THE OUTER WALL--THERE YOU CAN MAKE A HOLE THAT WILL LEAD YOU STRAIGHT TO THE WASTELAND--
BUT WATCH OUT FOR THE PROGES! THEY MAY HAVE ONE OR TWO TRICKS UP THEIR SLEEVE!
DOOM PATROL--!
LET'S GET THAT FROG!

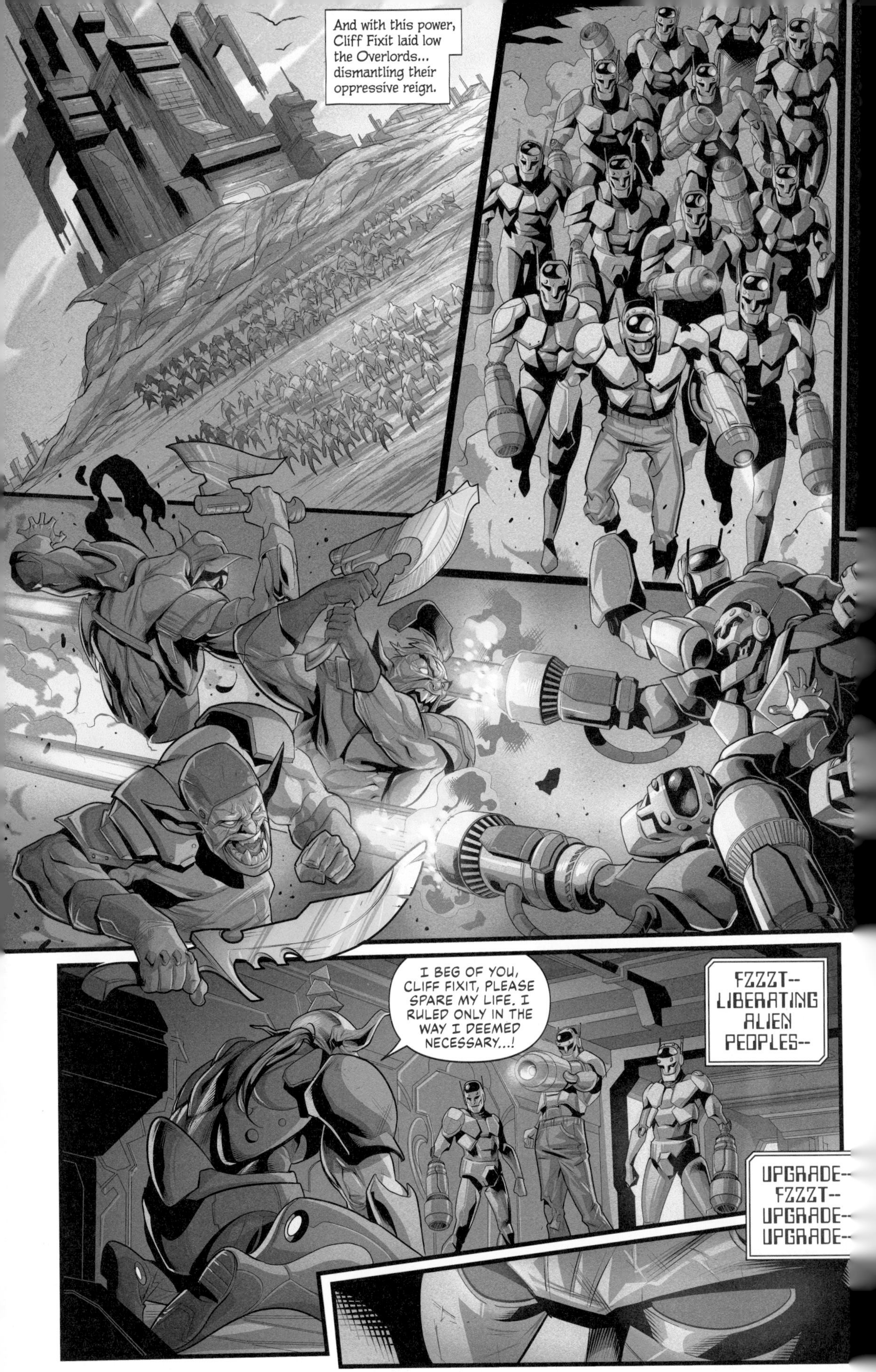

And with this power, Cliff Fixit laid low the Overlords... dismantling their oppressive reign.
I BEG OF YOU, CLIFF FIXIT, PLEASE SPARE MY LIFE. I RULED ONLY IN THE WAY I DEEMED NECESSARY...!
FZZZT-- LIBERATING ALIEN PEOPLES--
UPGRADE-- FZZZT-- UPGRADE-- UPGRADE--

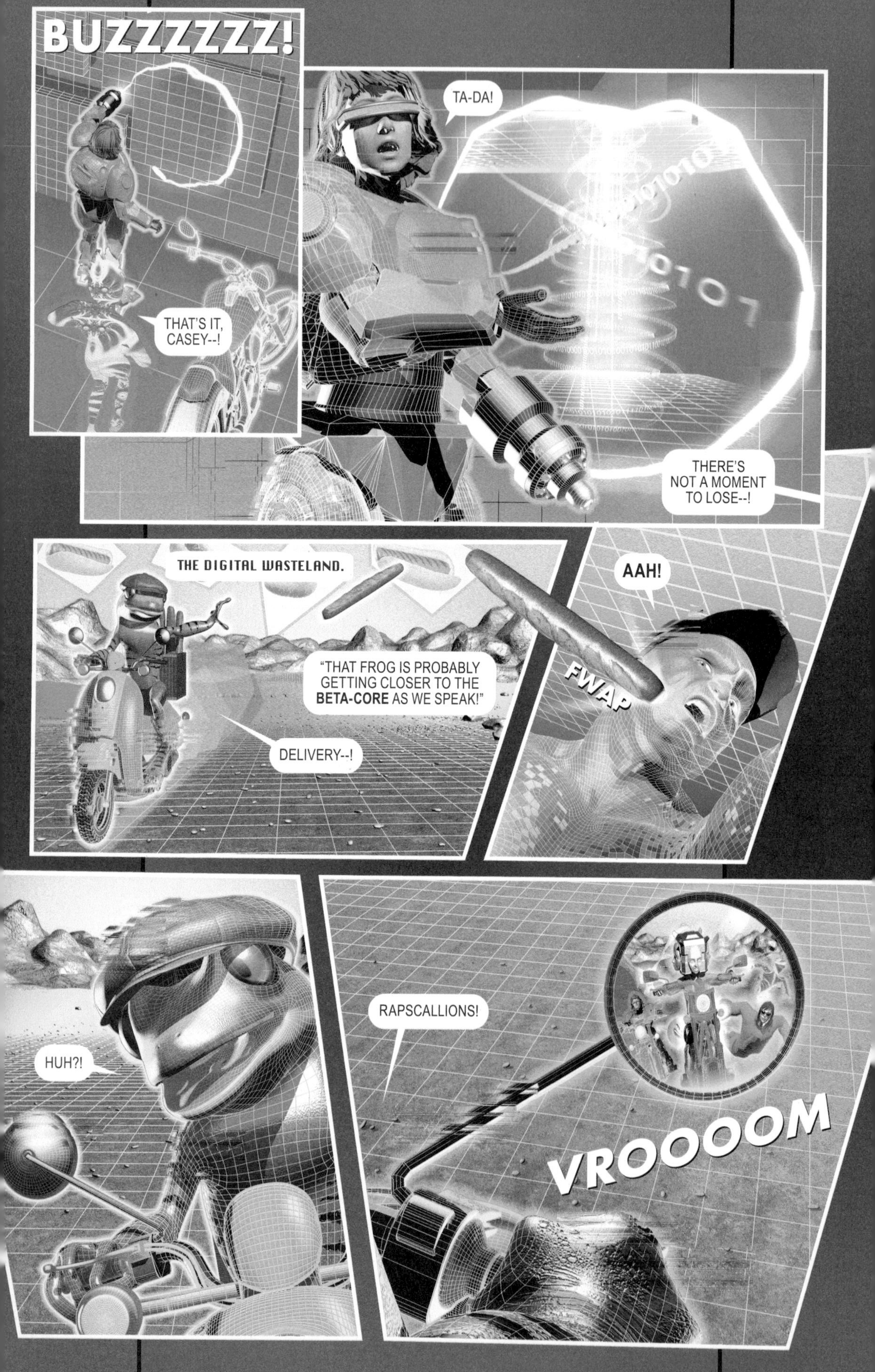
BUZZZZZZZ!
THAT'S IT, CASEY--!
TA-DA!
THERE'S NOT A MOMENT TO LOSE--!
THE DIGITAL WASTELAND.
"THAT FROG IS PROBABLY GETTING CLOSER TO THE **BETA-CORE** AS WE SPEAK!"
DELIVERY--!
AAH!
FWAP
HUH?!
RAPSCALLIONS!
VROOOOM

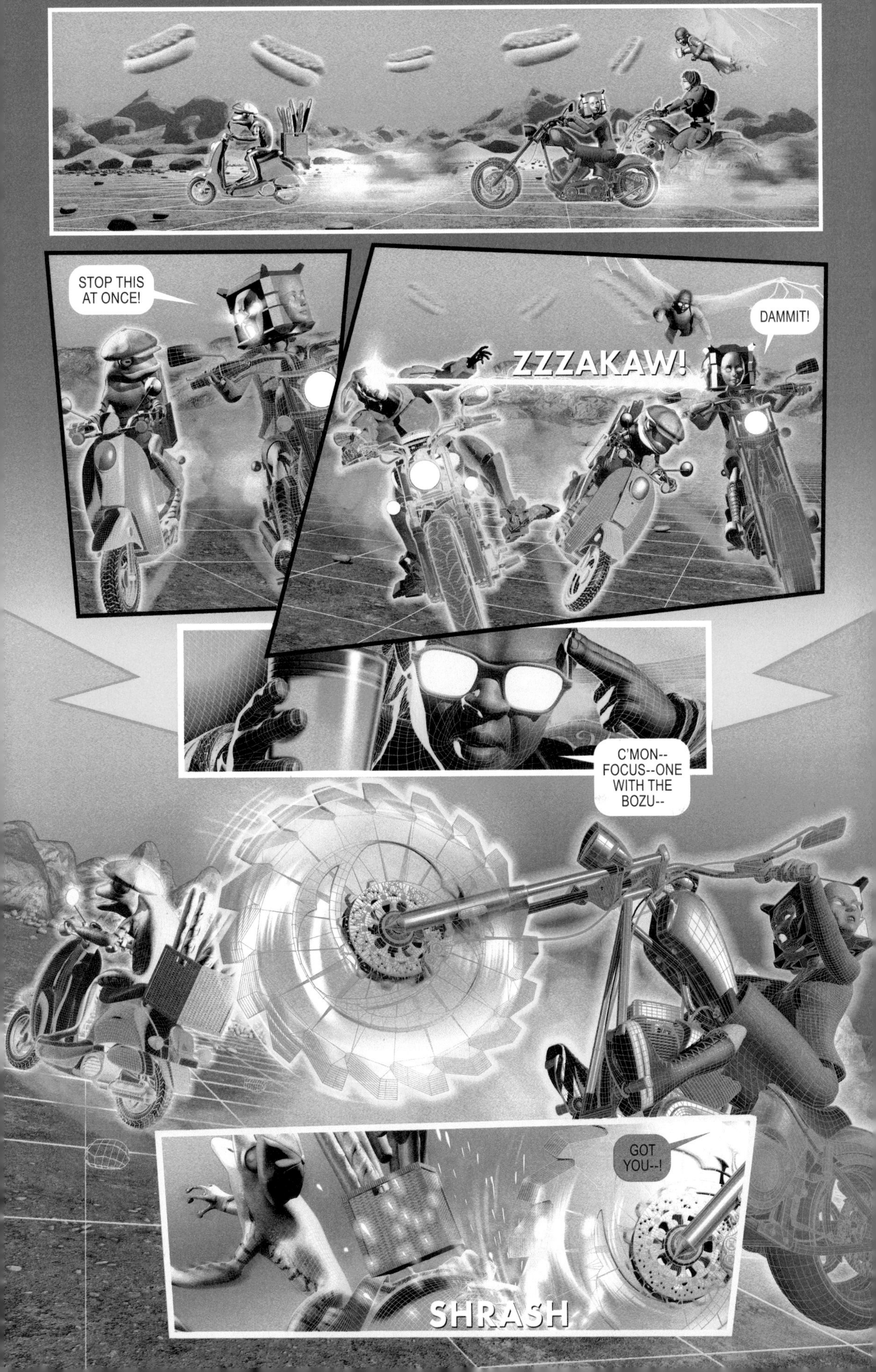
STOP THIS AT ONCE!
ZZZAKAW!
DAMMIT!
C'MON-- FOCUS--ONE WITH THE BOZU--
GOT YOU--!
SHRASH

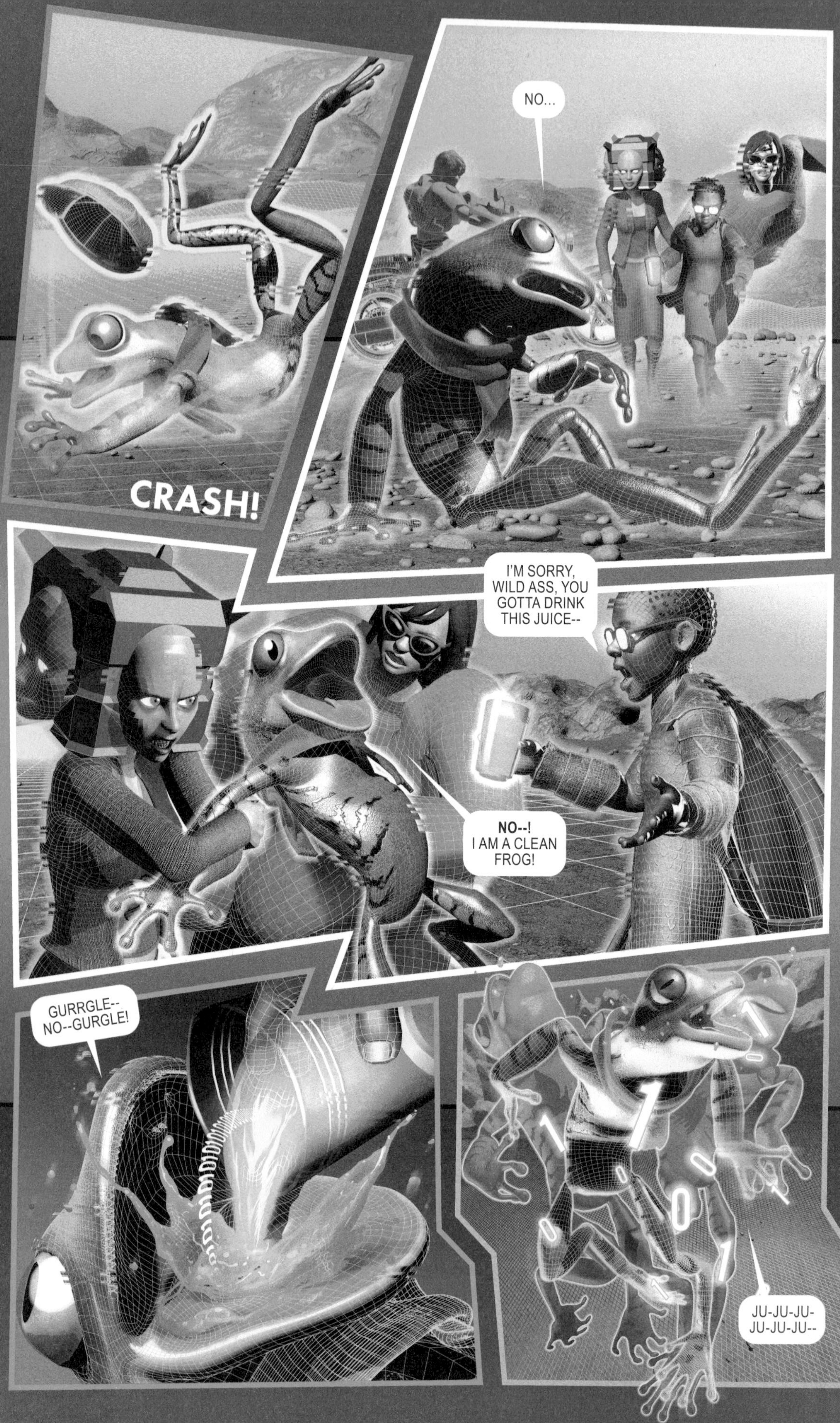
CRASH!
NO...
I'M SORRY, WILD ASS, YOU GOTTA DRINK THIS JUICE--
NO--! I AM A CLEAN FROG!
GURRGLE-- NO--GURGLE!
JU-JU-JU- JU-JU-JU--

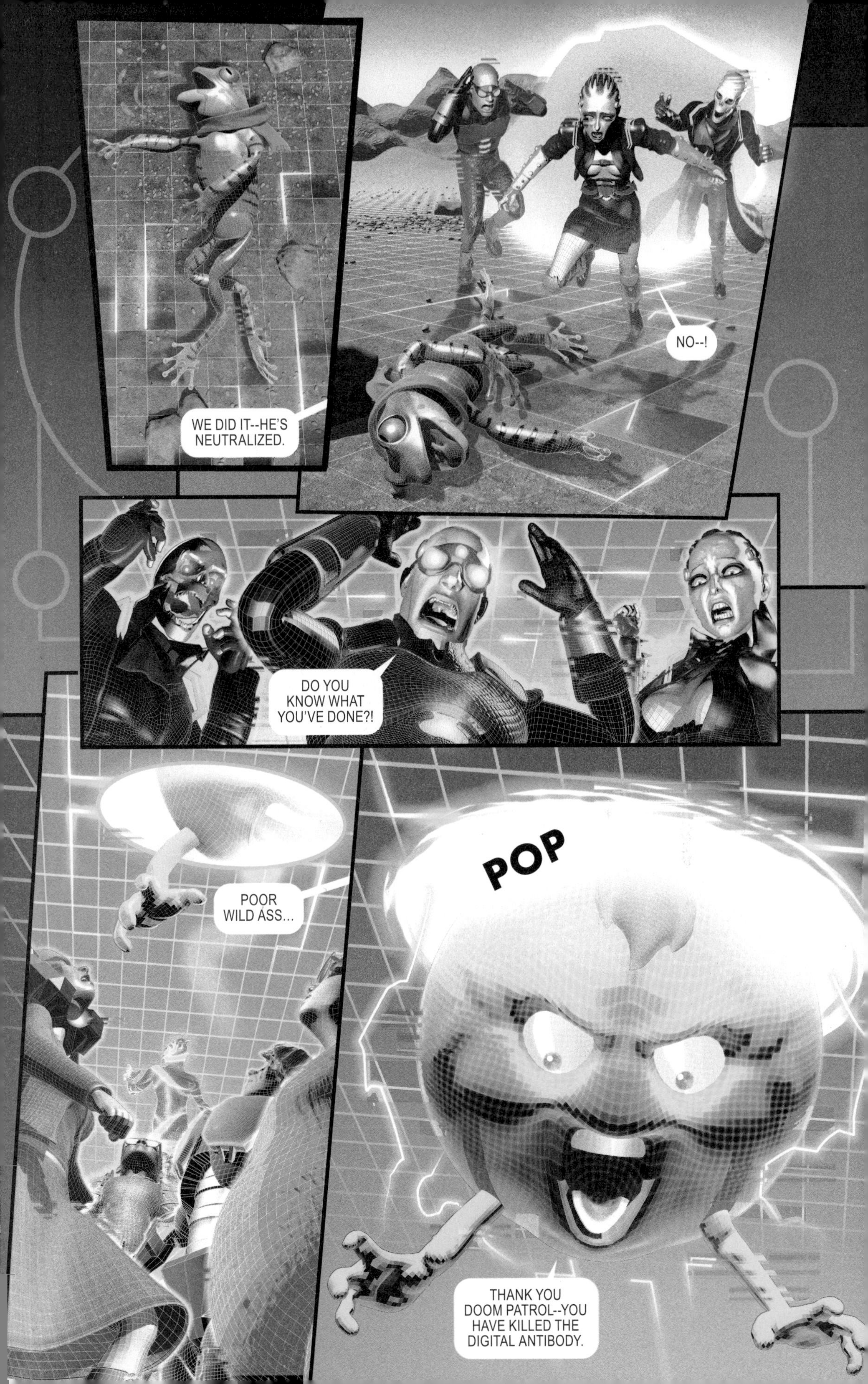
WE DID IT--HE'S NEUTRALIZED.
NO--!
DO YOU KNOW WHAT YOU'VE DONE?!
POOR WILD ASS...
POP
THANK YOU DOOM PATROL--YOU HAVE KILLED THE DIGITAL ANTIBODY.

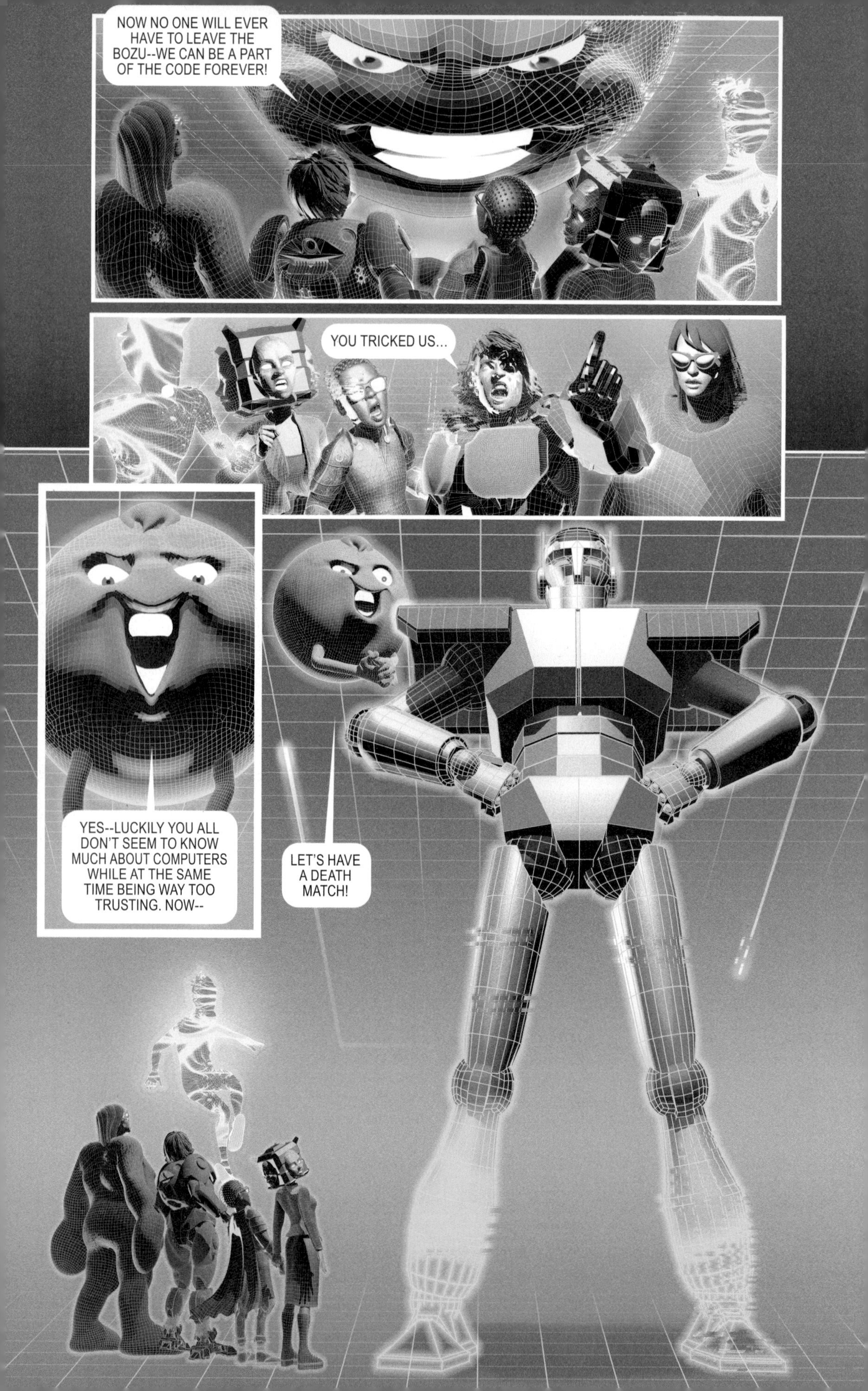
NOW NO ONE WILL EVER HAVE TO LEAVE THE BOZU--WE CAN BE A PART OF THE CODE FOREVER!
YOU TRICKED US...
YES--LUCKILY YOU ALL DON'T SEEM TO KNOW MUCH ABOUT COMPUTERS WHILE AT THE SAME TIME BEING WAY TOO TRUSTING. NOW--
LET'S HAVE A DEATH MATCH!

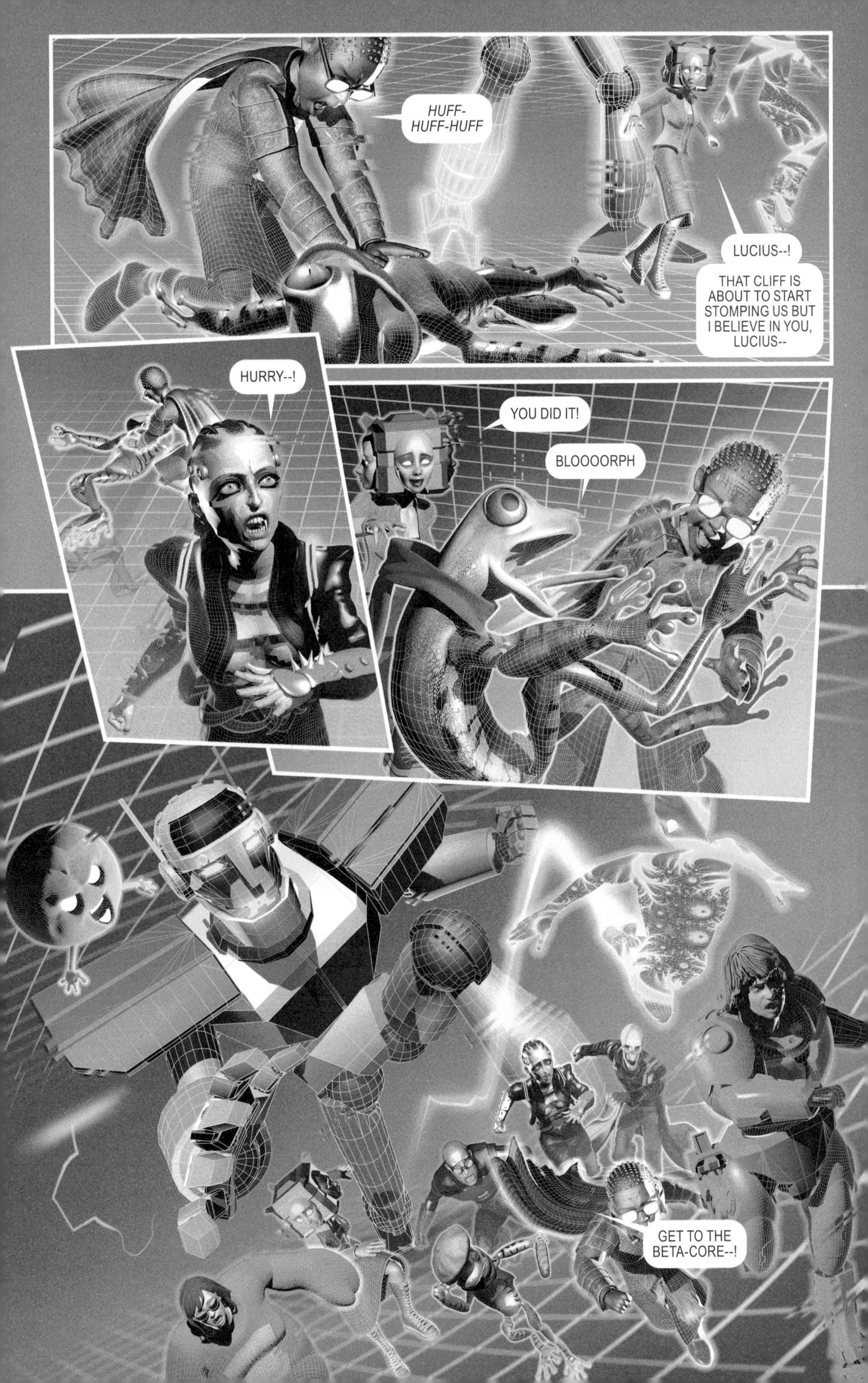
HUFF-HUFF-HUFF
LUCIUS--!
THAT CLIFF IS ABOUT TO START STOMPING US BUT I BELIEVE IN YOU, LUCIUS--
HURRY--!
YOU DID IT!
BLOOOORPH
GET TO THE BETA-CORE--!

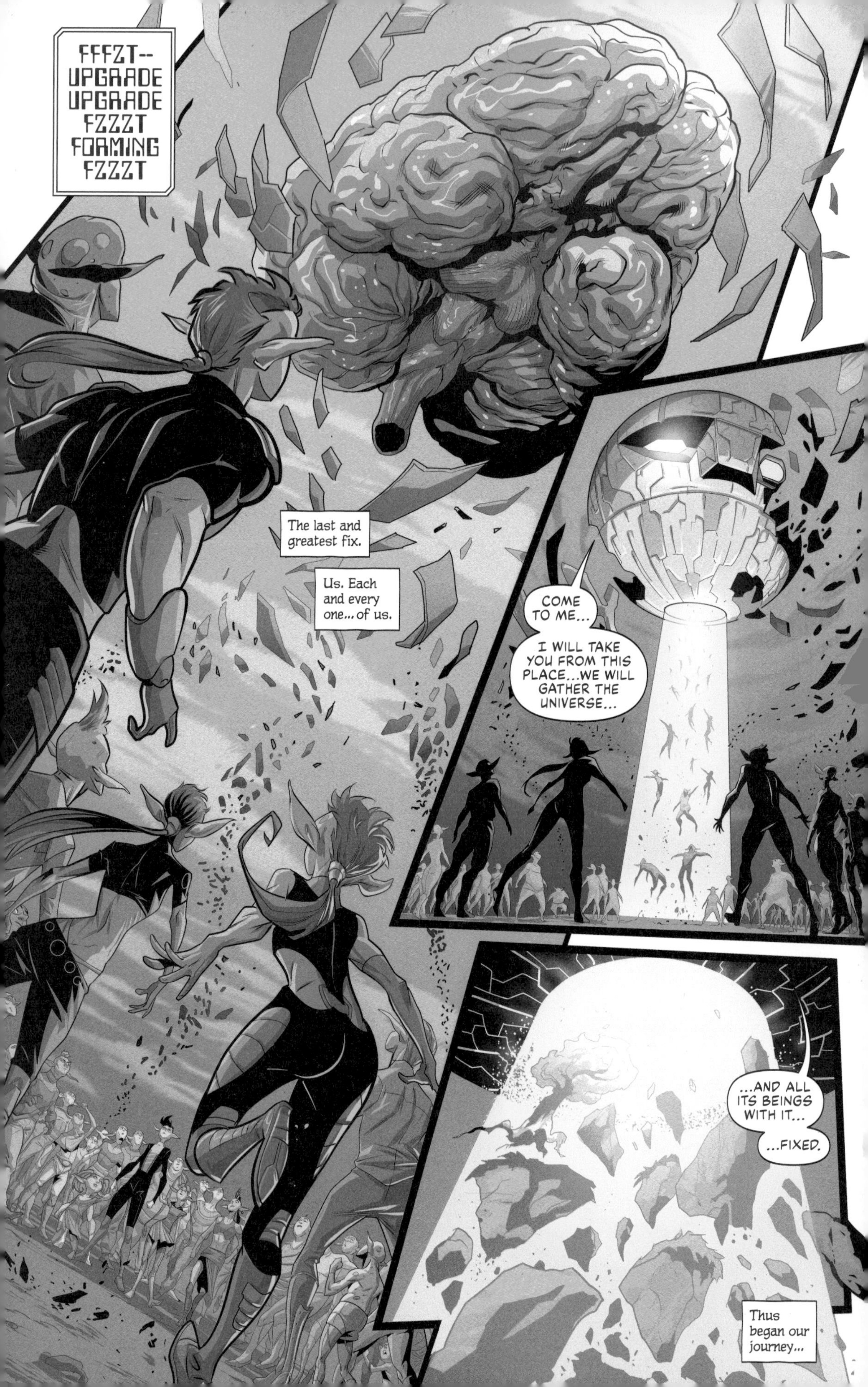
FFFZT--
UPGRADE
UPGRADE
FZZZT
FORMING
FZZZT
The last and greatest fix.
Us. Each and every one... of us.
COME TO ME...
I WILL TAKE YOU FROM THIS PLACE...WE WILL GATHER THE UNIVERSE...
...AND ALL ITS BEINGS WITH IT...
...FIXED.
Thus began our journey...

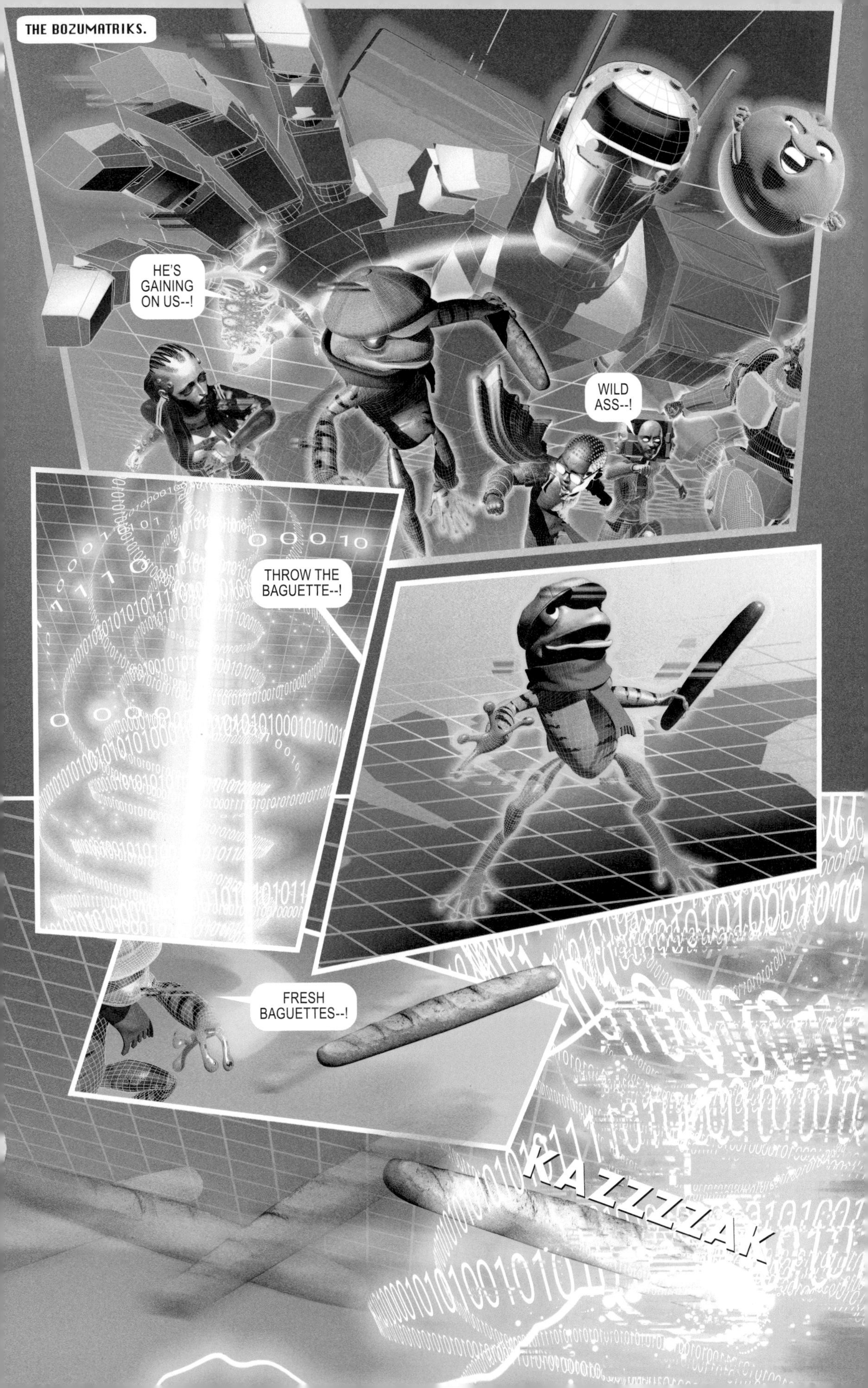
THE BOZUMATRIKS.
HE'S GAINING ON US--!
WILD ASS--!
THROW THE BAGUETTE--!
FRESH BAGUETTES--!
KAZZZZAK

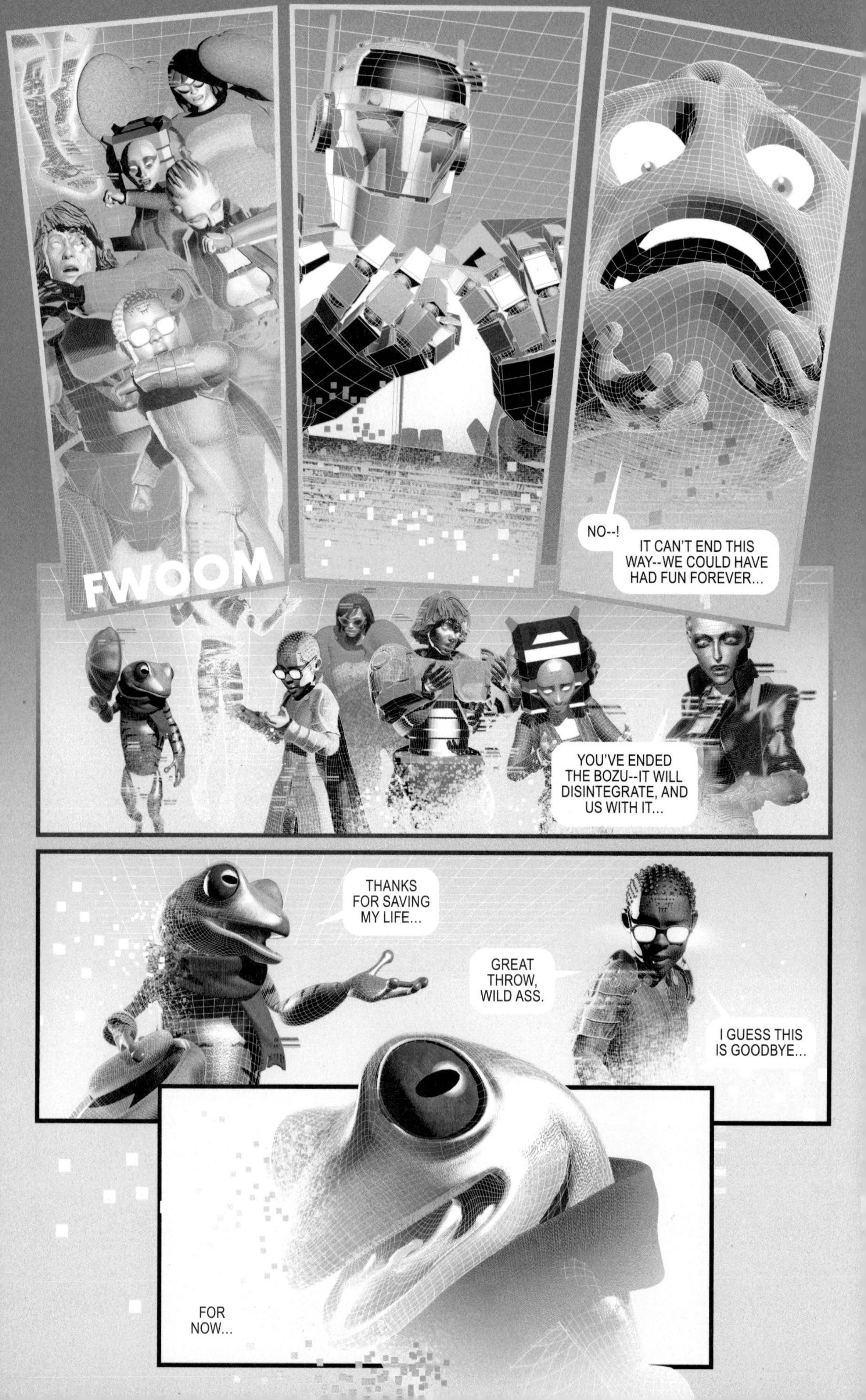
FWOOM
NO--!
IT CAN'T END THIS WAY--WE COULD HAVE HAD FUN FOREVER...
YOU'VE ENDED THE BOZU--IT WILL DISINTEGRATE, AND US WITH IT...
THANKS FOR SAVING MY LIFE...
GREAT THROW, WILD ASS.
I GUESS THIS IS GOODBYE...
FOR NOW...

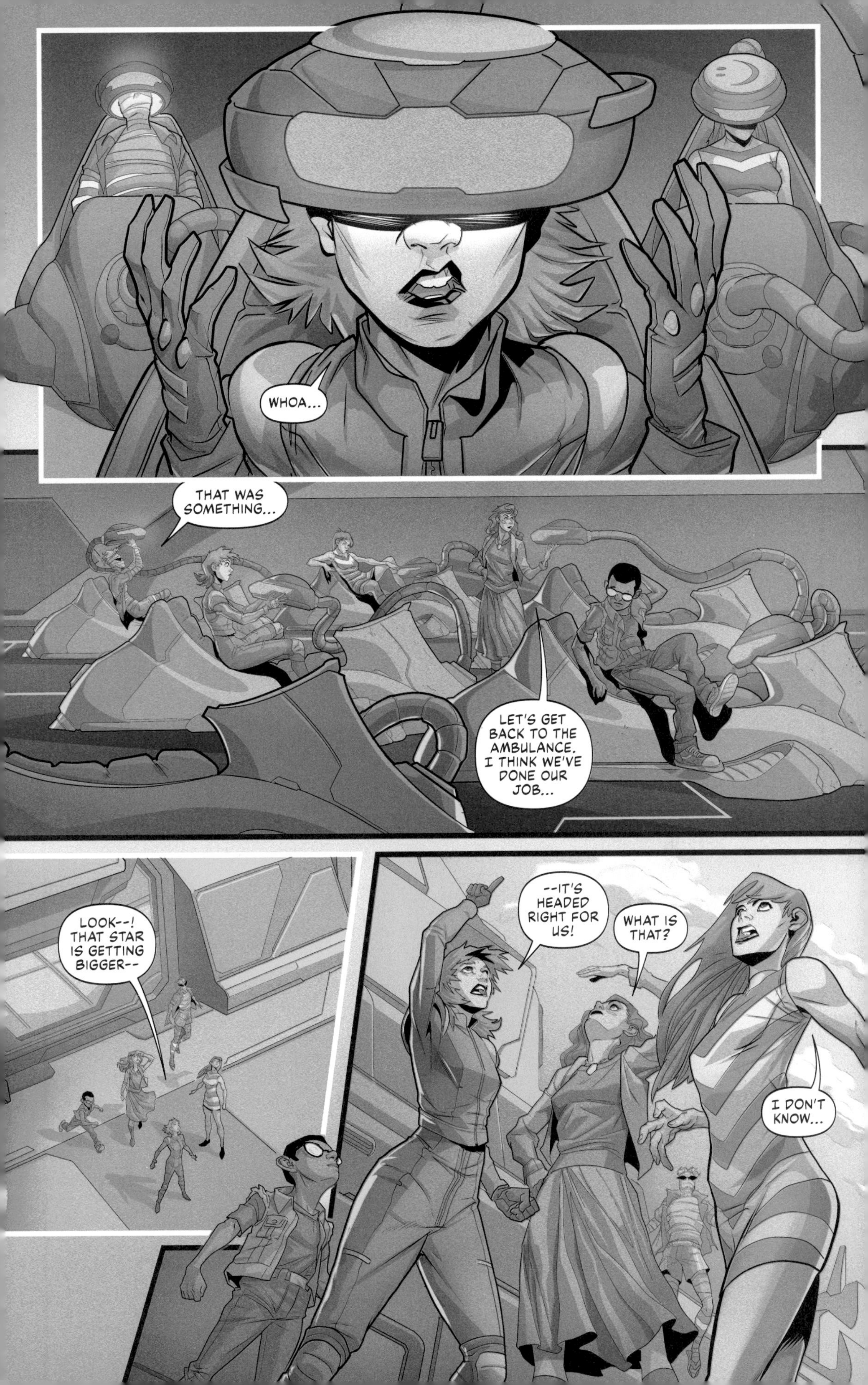
WHOA...
THAT WAS SOMETHING...
LET'S GET BACK TO THE AMBULANCE. I THINK WE'VE DONE OUR JOB...
LOOK--! THAT STAR IS GETTING BIGGER--
--IT'S HEADED RIGHT FOR US!
WHAT IS THAT?
I DON'T KNOW...

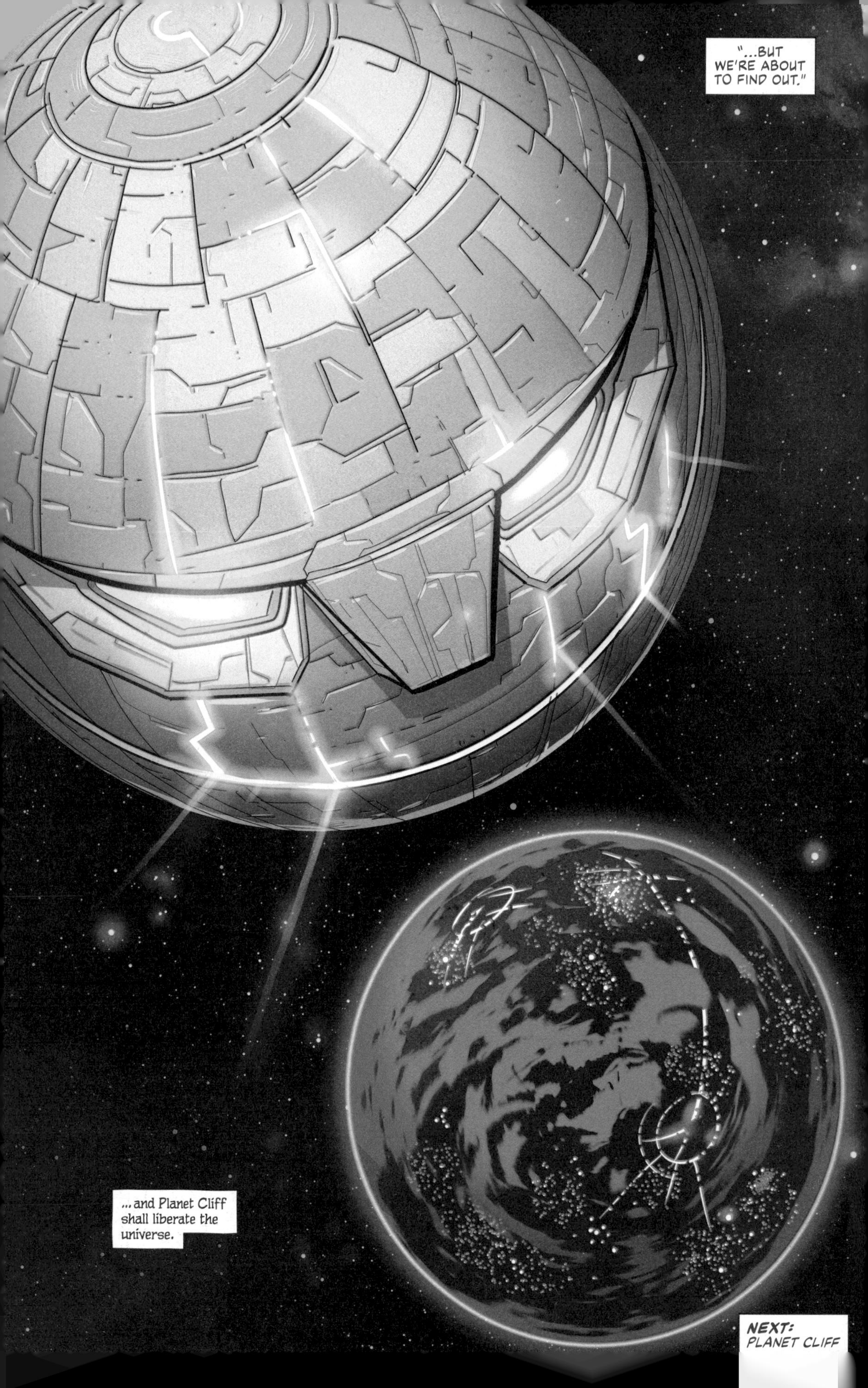
"...BUT WE'RE ABOUT TO FIND OUT."
...and Planet Cliff shall liberate the universe.
NEXT: PLANET CLIFF

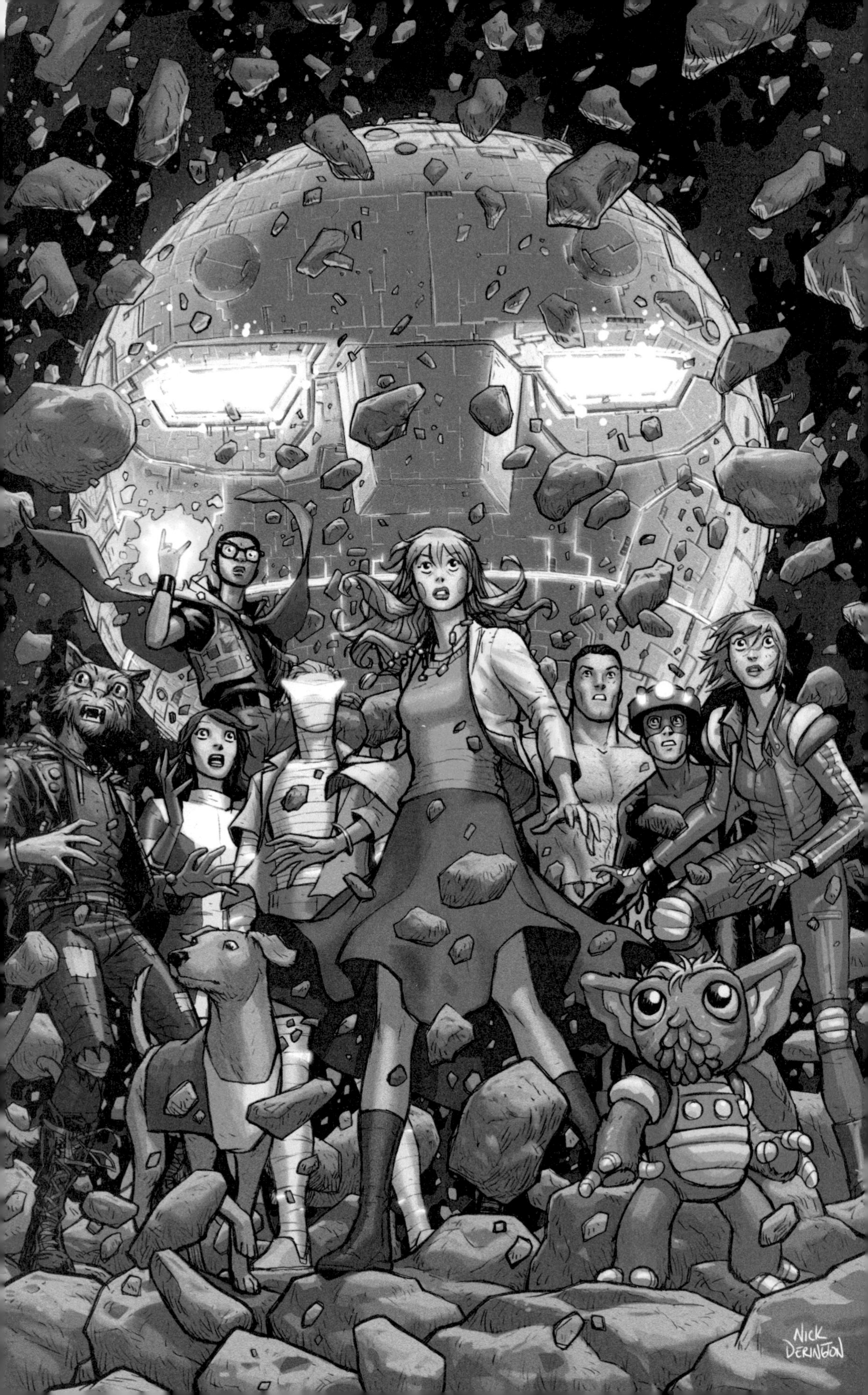
NICK DERINGTON

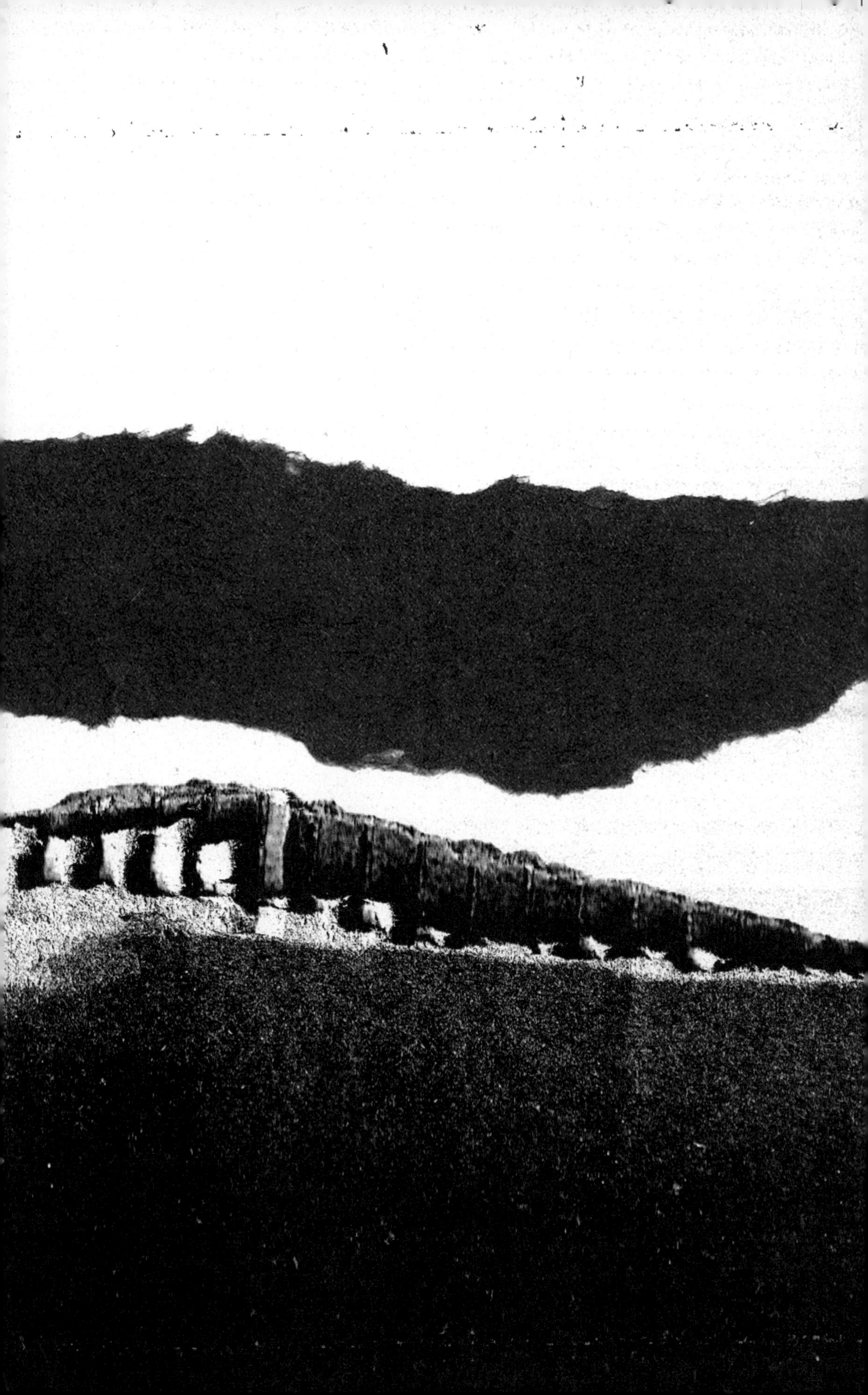

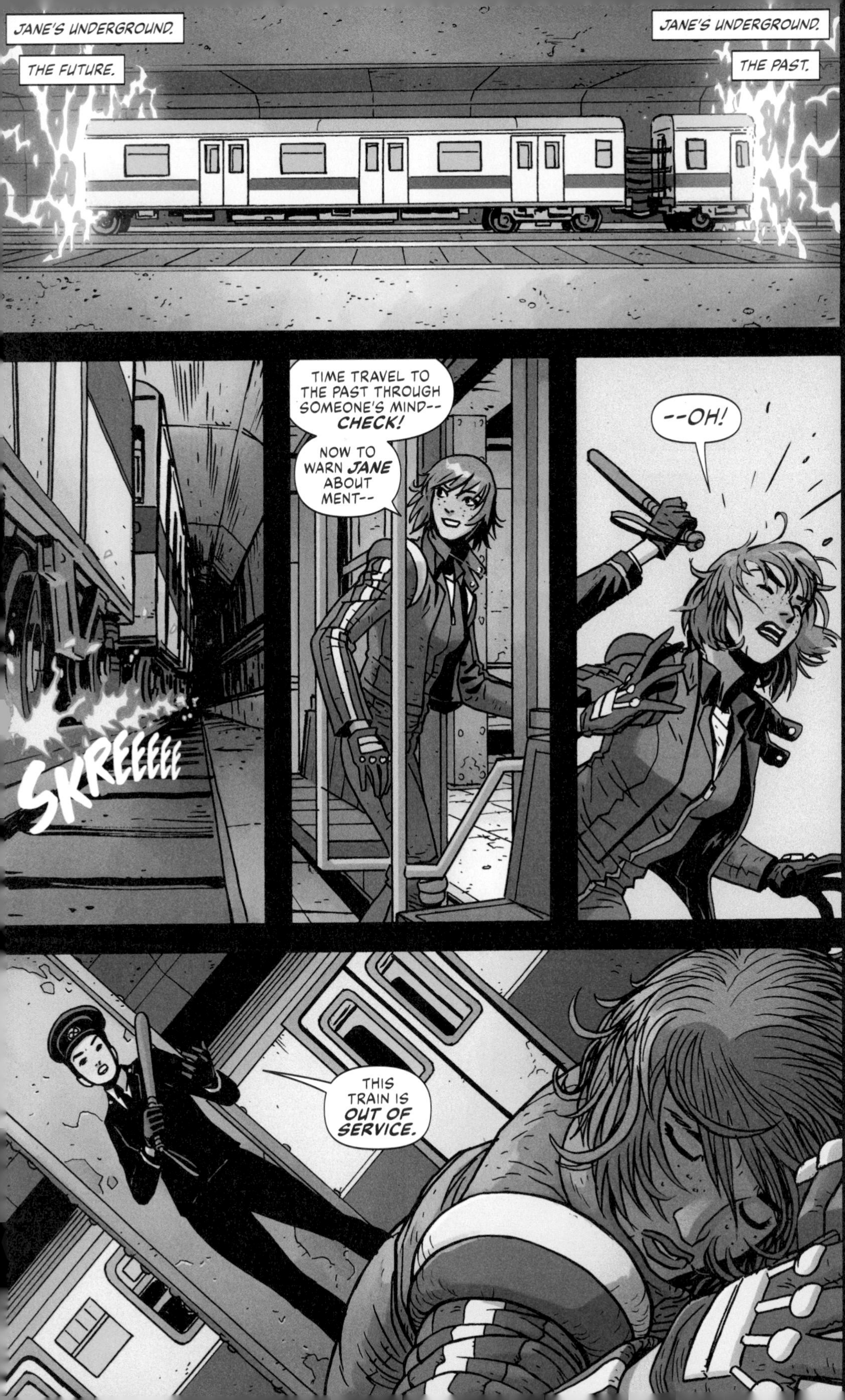
JANE'S UNDERGROUND.
THE FUTURE.
JANE'S UNDERGROUND.
THE PAST.
SKREEEEE
TIME TRAVEL TO THE PAST THROUGH SOMEONE'S MIND-- CHECK!
NOW TO WARN JANE ABOUT MENT--
--OH!
THIS TRAIN IS OUT OF SERVICE.

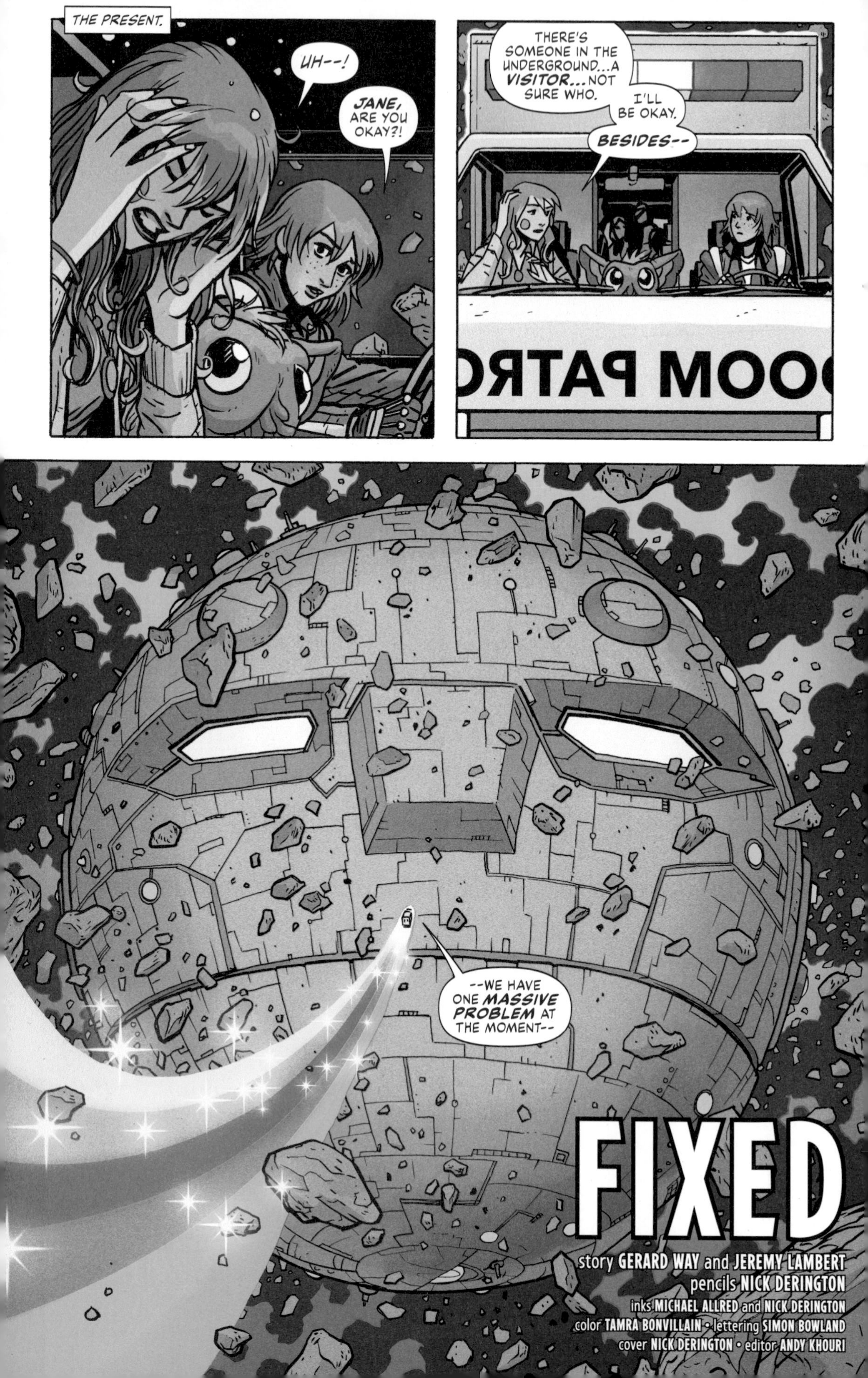
THE PRESENT.
UH--!
JANE, ARE YOU OKAY?!
THERE'S SOMEONE IN THE UNDERGROUND...A VISITOR...NOT SURE WHO.
I'LL BE OKAY.
BESIDES--
DOOM PATRO
--WE HAVE ONE MASSIVE PROBLEM AT THE MOMENT--
FIXED
story GERARD WAY and JEREMY LAMBERT
pencils NICK DERINGTON
inks MICHAEL ALLRED and NICK DERINGTON
color TAMRA BONVILLAIN • lettering SIMON BOWLAND
cover NICK DERINGTON • editor ANDY KHOURI

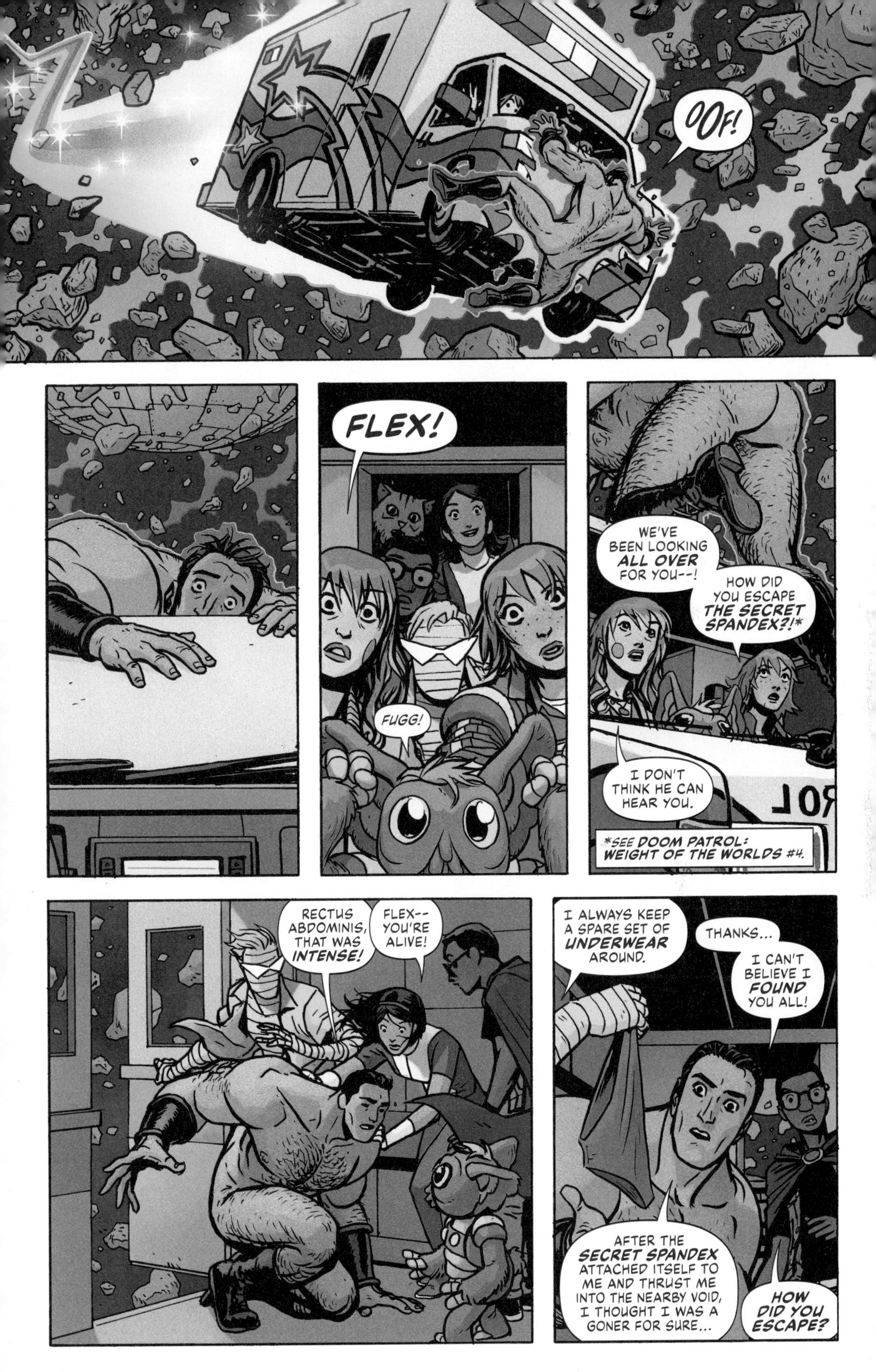
OOF!
FLEX!
FUGG!
WE'VE BEEN LOOKING ALL OVER FOR YOU--!
HOW DID YOU ESCAPE THE SECRET SPANDEX?!*
I DON'T THINK HE CAN HEAR YOU.
*SEE DOOM PATROL: WEIGHT OF THE WORLDS #4.
RECTUS ABDOMINIS, THAT WAS INTENSE!
FLEX-- YOU'RE ALIVE!
I ALWAYS KEEP A SPARE SET OF UNDERWEAR AROUND.
THANKS...
I CAN'T BELIEVE I FOUND YOU ALL!
AFTER THE SECRET SPANDEX ATTACHED ITSELF TO ME AND THRUST ME INTO THE NEARBY VOID, I THOUGHT I WAS A GONER FOR SURE...
HOW DID YOU ESCAPE?

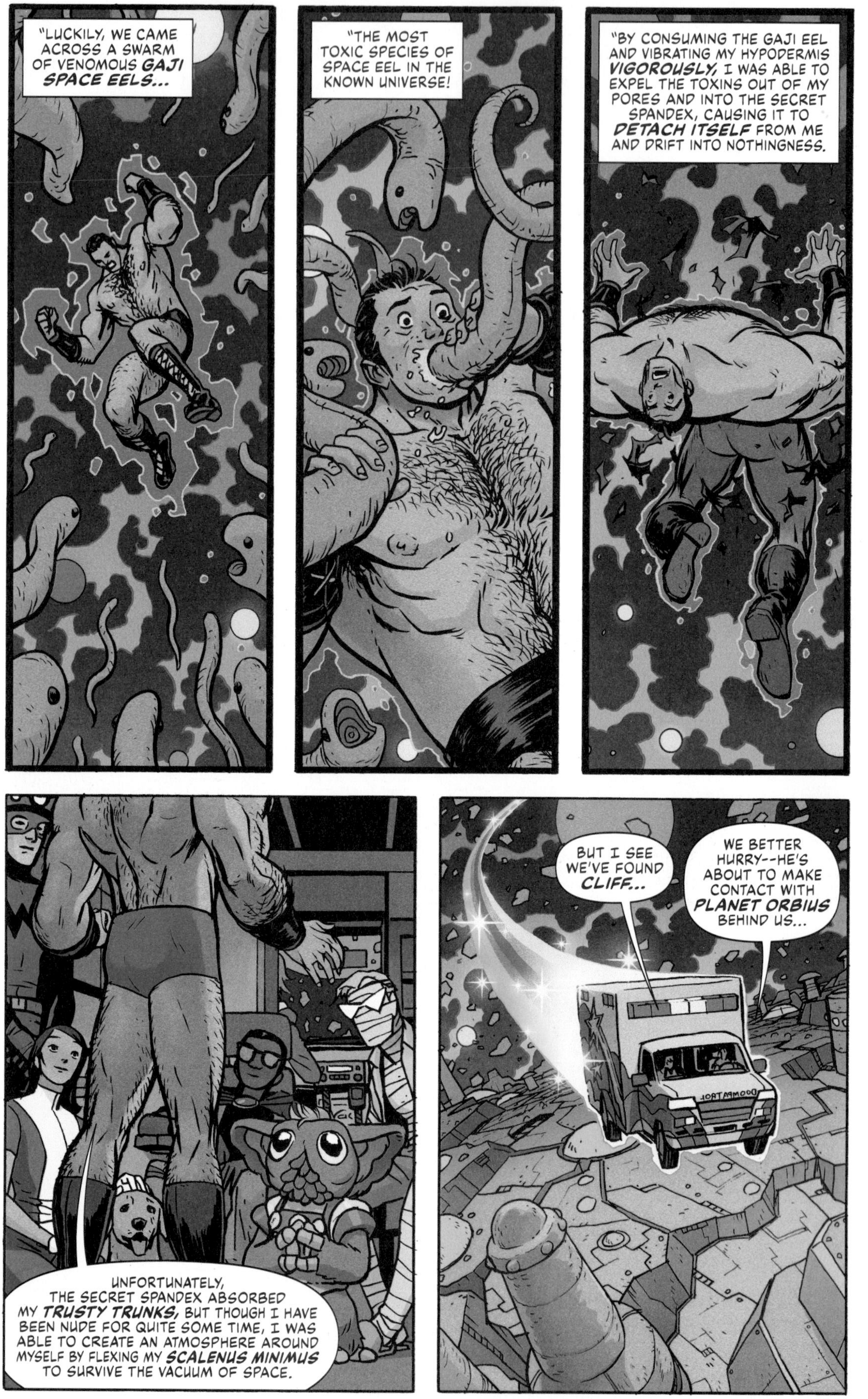
"LUCKILY, WE CAME ACROSS A SWARM OF VENOMOUS GAJI SPACE EELS...
"THE MOST TOXIC SPECIES OF SPACE EEL IN THE KNOWN UNIVERSE!
"BY CONSUMING THE GAJI EEL AND VIBRATING MY HYPODERMIS VIGOROUSLY, I WAS ABLE TO EXPEL THE TOXINS OUT OF MY PORES AND INTO THE SECRET SPANDEX, CAUSING IT TO DETACH ITSELF FROM ME AND DRIFT INTO NOTHINGNESS.
UNFORTUNATELY, THE SECRET SPANDEX ABSORBED MY TRUSTY TRUNKS, BUT THOUGH I HAVE BEEN NUDE FOR QUITE SOME TIME, I WAS ABLE TO CREATE AN ATMOSPHERE AROUND MYSELF BY FLEXING MY SCALENUS MINIMUS TO SURVIVE THE VACUUM OF SPACE.
BUT I SEE WE'VE FOUND CLIFF...
WE BETTER HURRY--HE'S ABOUT TO MAKE CONTACT WITH PLANET ORBIUS BEHIND US...
DOOMPATROL

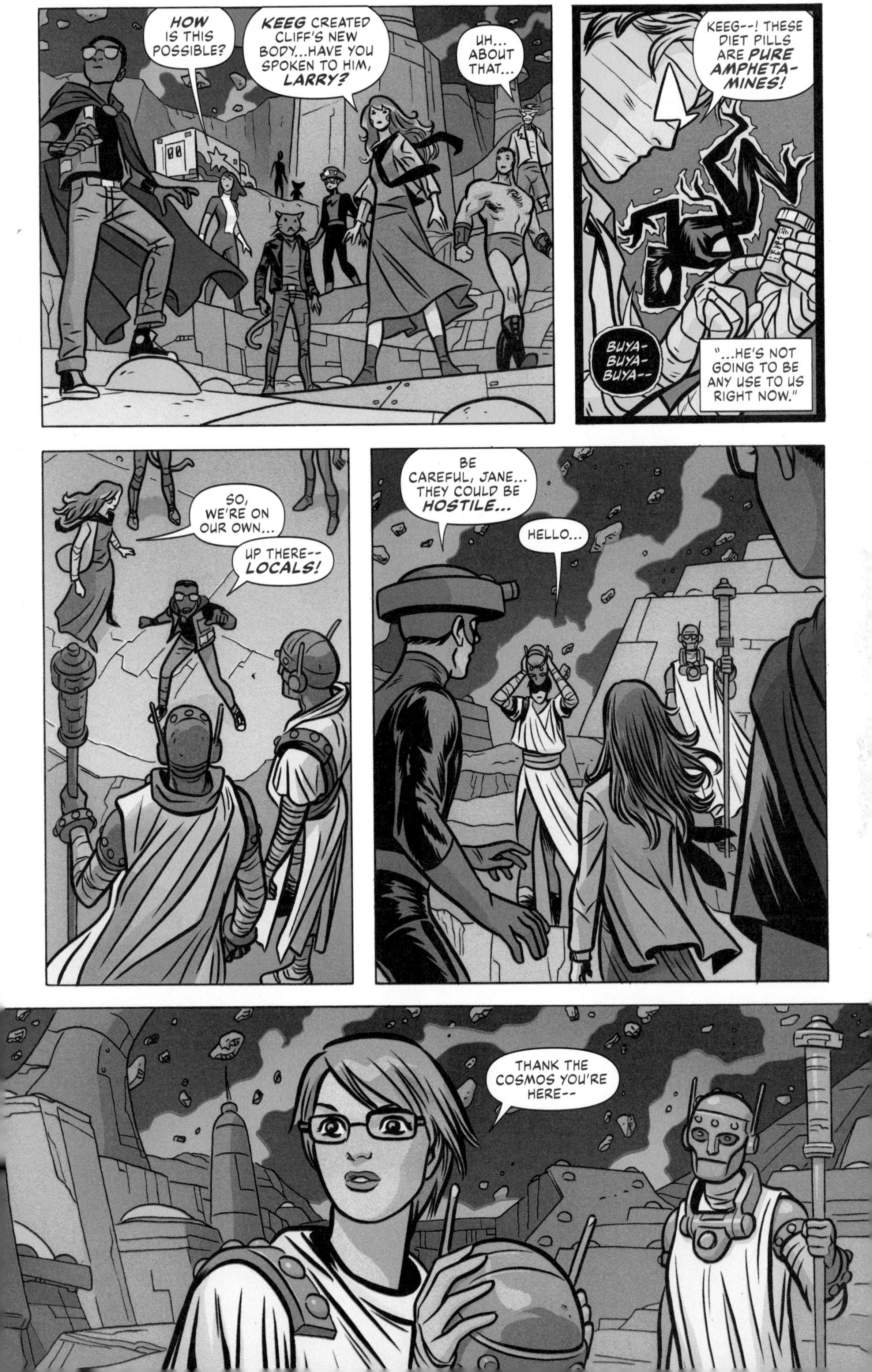
HOW IS THIS POSSIBLE?
KEEG CREATED CLIFF'S NEW BODY...HAVE YOU SPOKEN TO HIM, LARRY?
UH... ABOUT THAT...
KEEG--! THESE DIET PILLS ARE PURE AMPHETA-MINES!
BUYA-BUYA-BUYA--
"...HE'S NOT GOING TO BE ANY USE TO US RIGHT NOW."
SO, WE'RE ON OUR OWN...
UP THERE--LOCALS!
BE CAREFUL, JANE... THEY COULD BE HOSTILE...
HELLO...
THANK THE COSMOS YOU'RE HERE--

HUMAN!

I AM *ALISE*, AND MY COMPANION HERE IS MY GENEROUS FRIEND.

HEY...

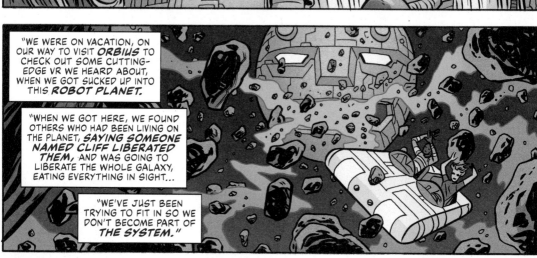

"WE WERE ON VACATION, ON OUR WAY TO VISIT *ORBIUS* TO CHECK OUT SOME CUTTING-EDGE VR WE HEARD ABOUT, WHEN WE GOT SUCKED UP INTO THIS *ROBOT PLANET.*

"WHEN WE GOT HERE, WE FOUND OTHERS WHO HAD BEEN LIVING ON THE PLANET, *SAYING SOMEONE NAMED CLIFF LIBERATED THEM,* AND WAS GOING TO LIBERATE THE WHOLE GALAXY, EATING EVERYTHING IN SIGHT...

"WE'VE JUST BEEN TRYING TO FIT IN SO WE DON'T BECOME PART OF *THE SYSTEM.*"

THE SYSTEM--?

CLIFF--! HE'S STARTED *EATING* PLANET ORBIUS!

PLANET ORBIUS.

HELP!

IT CONSUMES US!

I'M TELLING YOU, JANE--MY *HELMET* CAN FIX THIS, IF I COULD ONLY REMEMBER HOW I DID IT THE LAST TIME...*

CAN YOU USE YOUR HELMET TO FIND CLIFF'S *BRAIN?* PROBABLY AT SOME CORE OR CENTER OF THIS PLACE...

PROBABLY, BUT SURELY WE CAN PUT MY HELMET TO BETTER USE THAN THAT--

THAT SOUND--! *THE SYSTEM* COMES FOR US!

*SEE *WOTW* #3. MORE TIME TRAVEL STUFF.

YES, YOU HAVE A NICE, BIG, SHINY HELMET, MENTO-- *PLEASE FIND CLIFF'S BRAIN WITH IT--*

JANE!

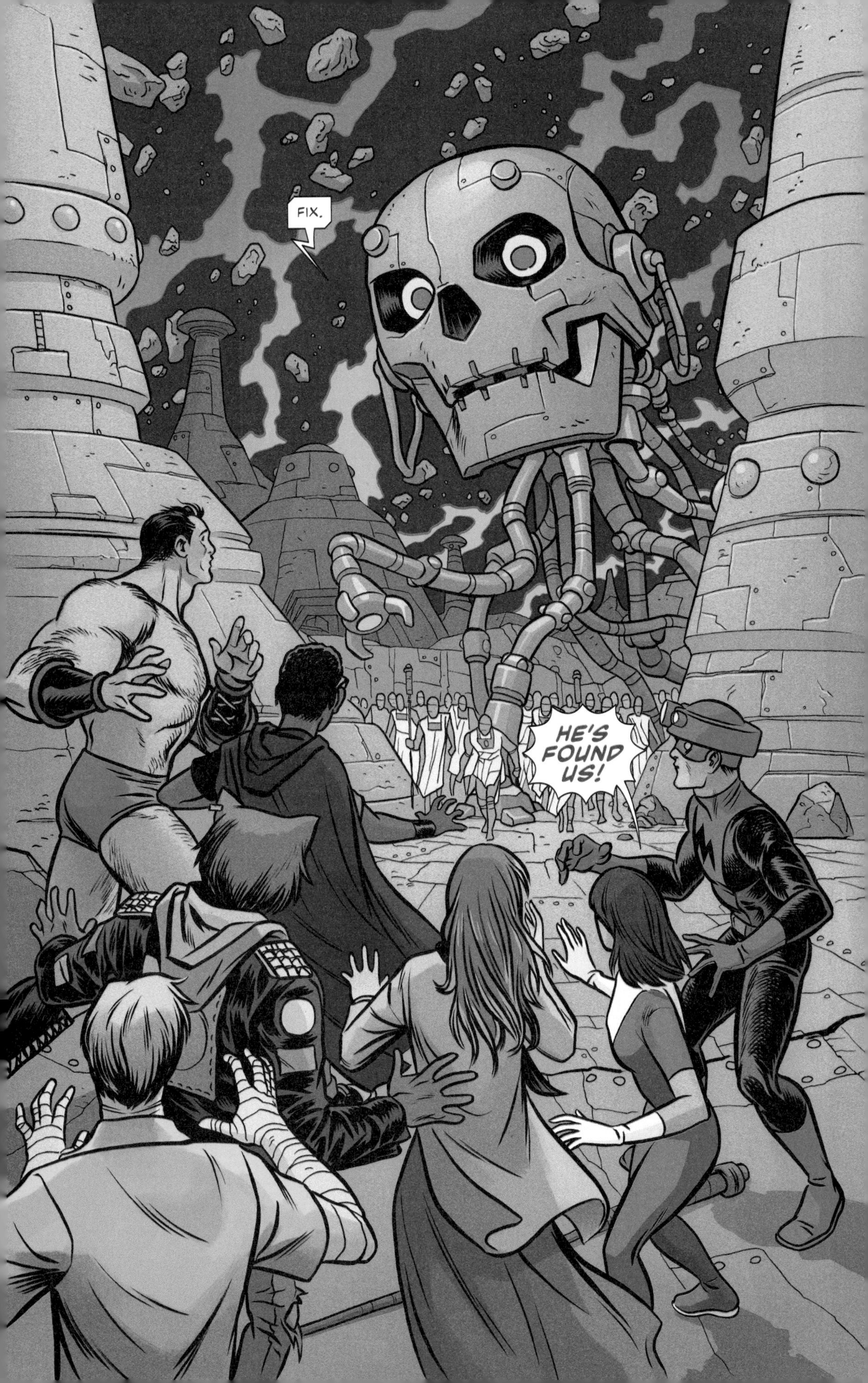
FIX.
HE'S FOUND US!

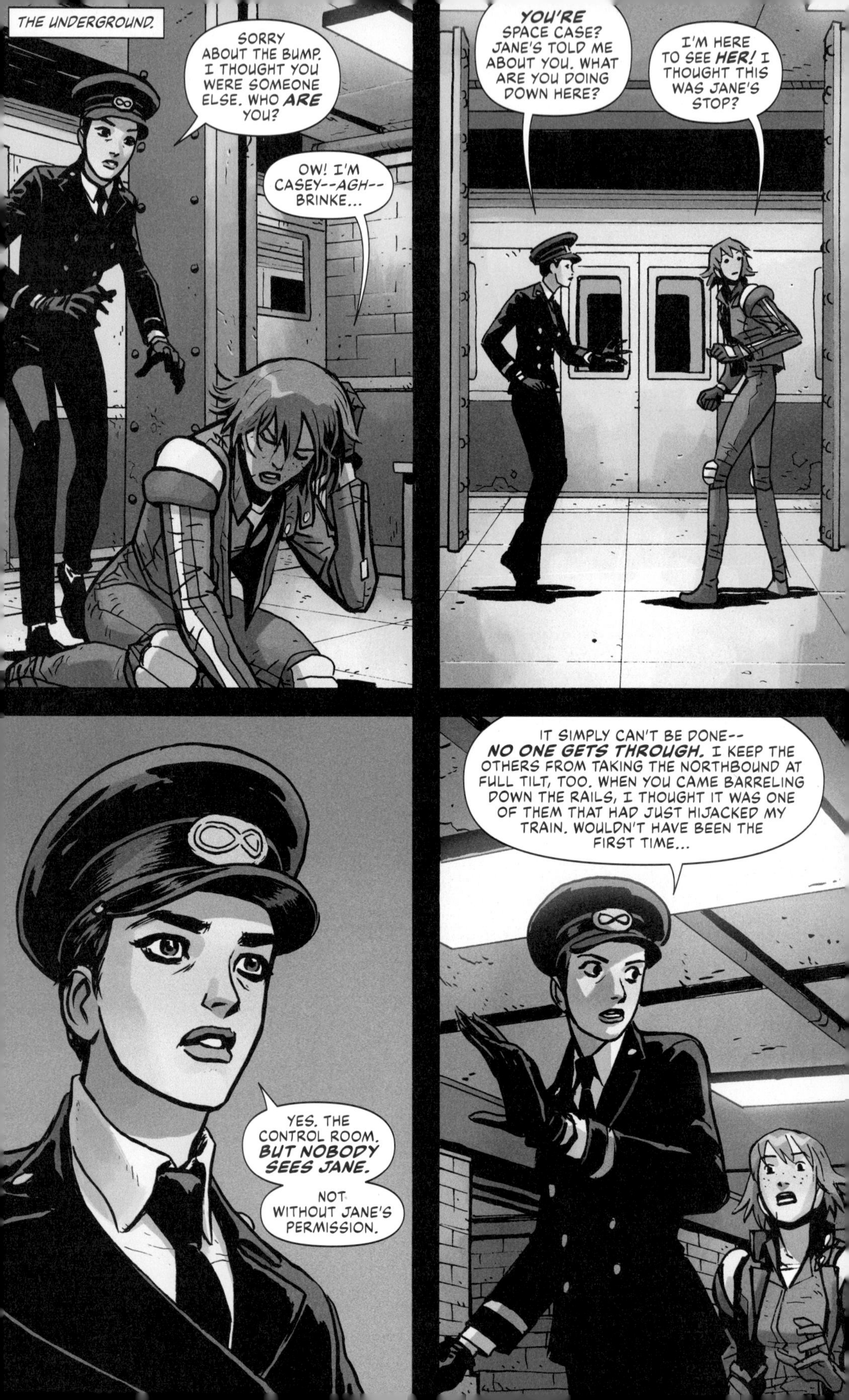
THE UNDERGROUND.
SORRY ABOUT THE BUMP. I THOUGHT YOU WERE SOMEONE ELSE. WHO ARE YOU?
OW! I'M CASEY--AGH--BRINKE...
YOU'RE SPACE CASE? JANE'S TOLD ME ABOUT YOU. WHAT ARE YOU DOING DOWN HERE?
I'M HERE TO SEE HER! I THOUGHT THIS WAS JANE'S STOP?
YES. THE CONTROL ROOM. BUT NOBODY SEES JANE.
NOT WITHOUT JANE'S PERMISSION.
IT SIMPLY CAN'T BE DONE-- NO ONE GETS THROUGH. I KEEP THE OTHERS FROM TAKING THE NORTHBOUND AT FULL TILT, TOO. WHEN YOU CAME BARRELING DOWN THE RAILS, I THOUGHT IT WAS ONE OF THEM THAT HAD JUST HIJACKED MY TRAIN. WOULDN'T HAVE BEEN THE FIRST TIME...

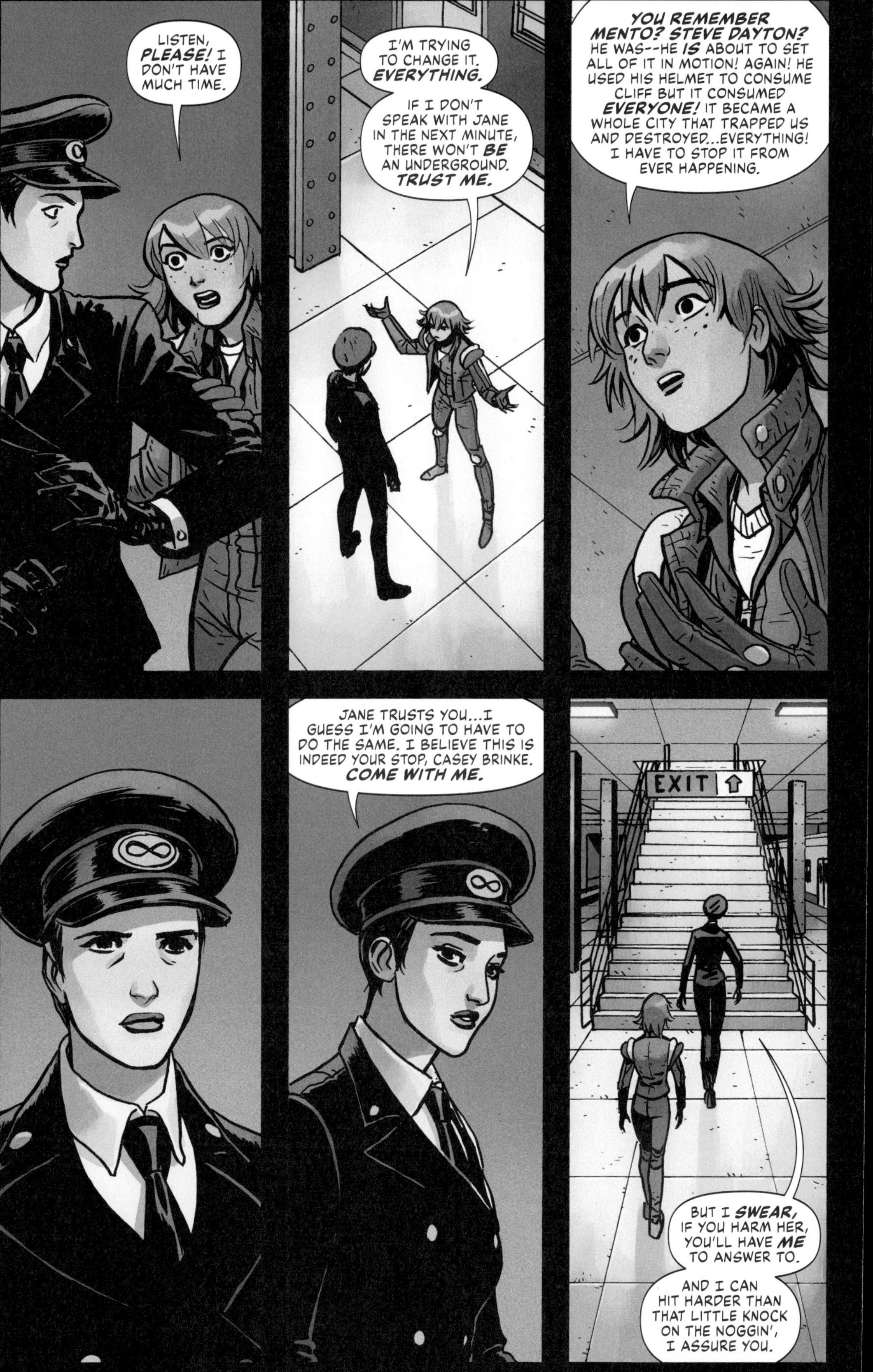
LISTEN, PLEASE! I DON'T HAVE MUCH TIME.
I'M TRYING TO CHANGE IT. EVERYTHING.
IF I DON'T SPEAK WITH JANE IN THE NEXT MINUTE, THERE WON'T BE AN UNDERGROUND. TRUST ME.
YOU REMEMBER MENTO? STEVE DAYTON? HE WAS--HE IS ABOUT TO SET ALL OF IT IN MOTION! AGAIN! HE USED HIS HELMET TO CONSUME CLIFF BUT IT CONSUMED EVERYONE! IT BECAME A WHOLE CITY THAT TRAPPED US AND DESTROYED...EVERYTHING! I HAVE TO STOP IT FROM EVER HAPPENING.
JANE TRUSTS YOU...I GUESS I'M GOING TO HAVE TO DO THE SAME. I BELIEVE THIS IS INDEED YOUR STOP, CASEY BRINKE. COME WITH ME.
EXIT
BUT I SWEAR, IF YOU HARM HER, YOU'LL HAVE ME TO ANSWER TO.
AND I CAN HIT HARDER THAN THAT LITTLE KNOCK ON THE NOGGIN', I ASSURE YOU.

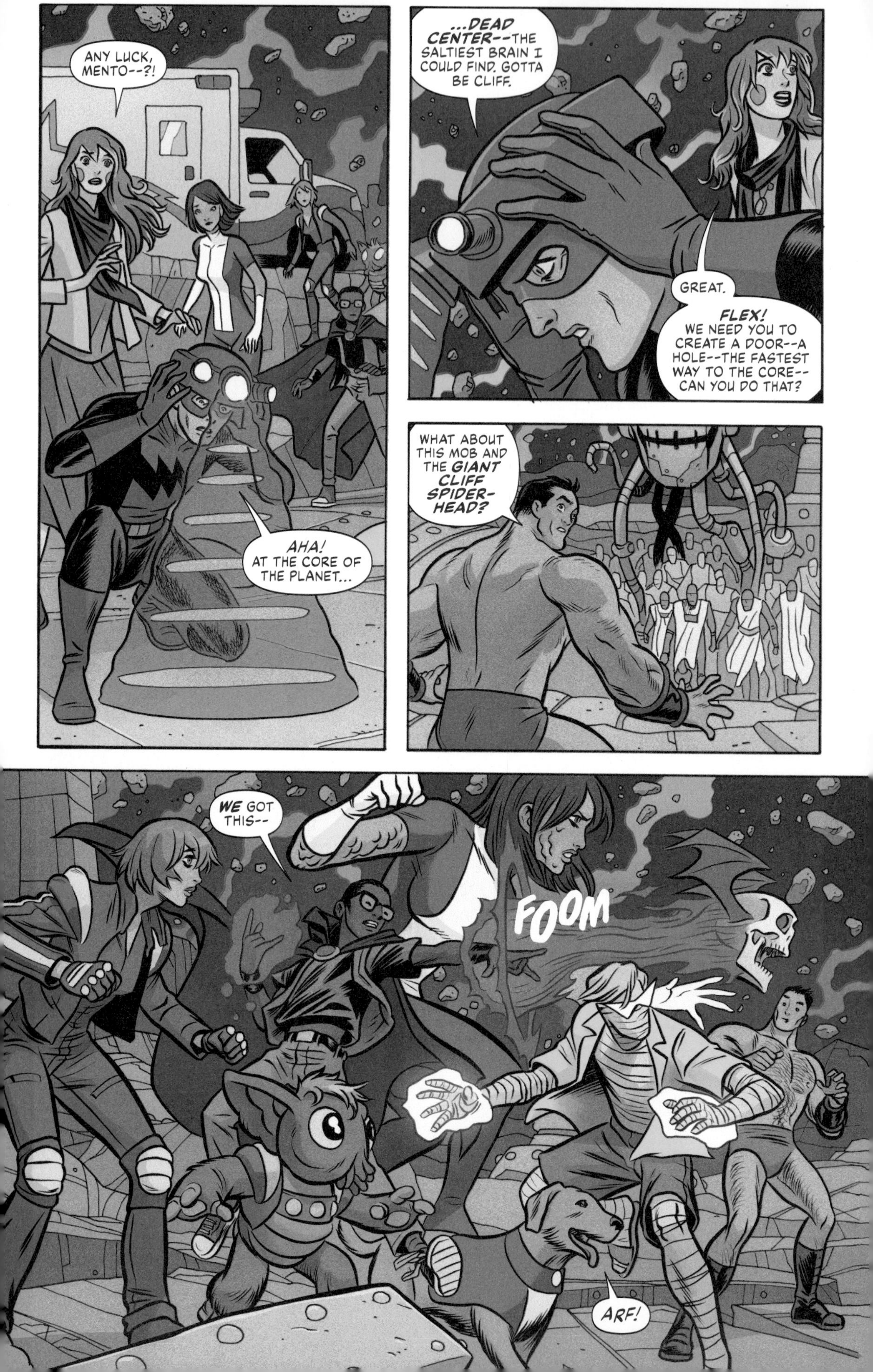
ANY LUCK, MENTO--?!
AHA! AT THE CORE OF THE PLANET...
...DEAD CENTER--THE SALTIEST BRAIN I COULD FIND. GOTTA BE CLIFF.
GREAT.
FLEX! WE NEED YOU TO CREATE A DOOR--A HOLE--THE FASTEST WAY TO THE CORE--CAN YOU DO THAT?
WHAT ABOUT THIS MOB AND THE GIANT CLIFF SPIDER-HEAD?
WE GOT THIS--
FOOM
ARF!

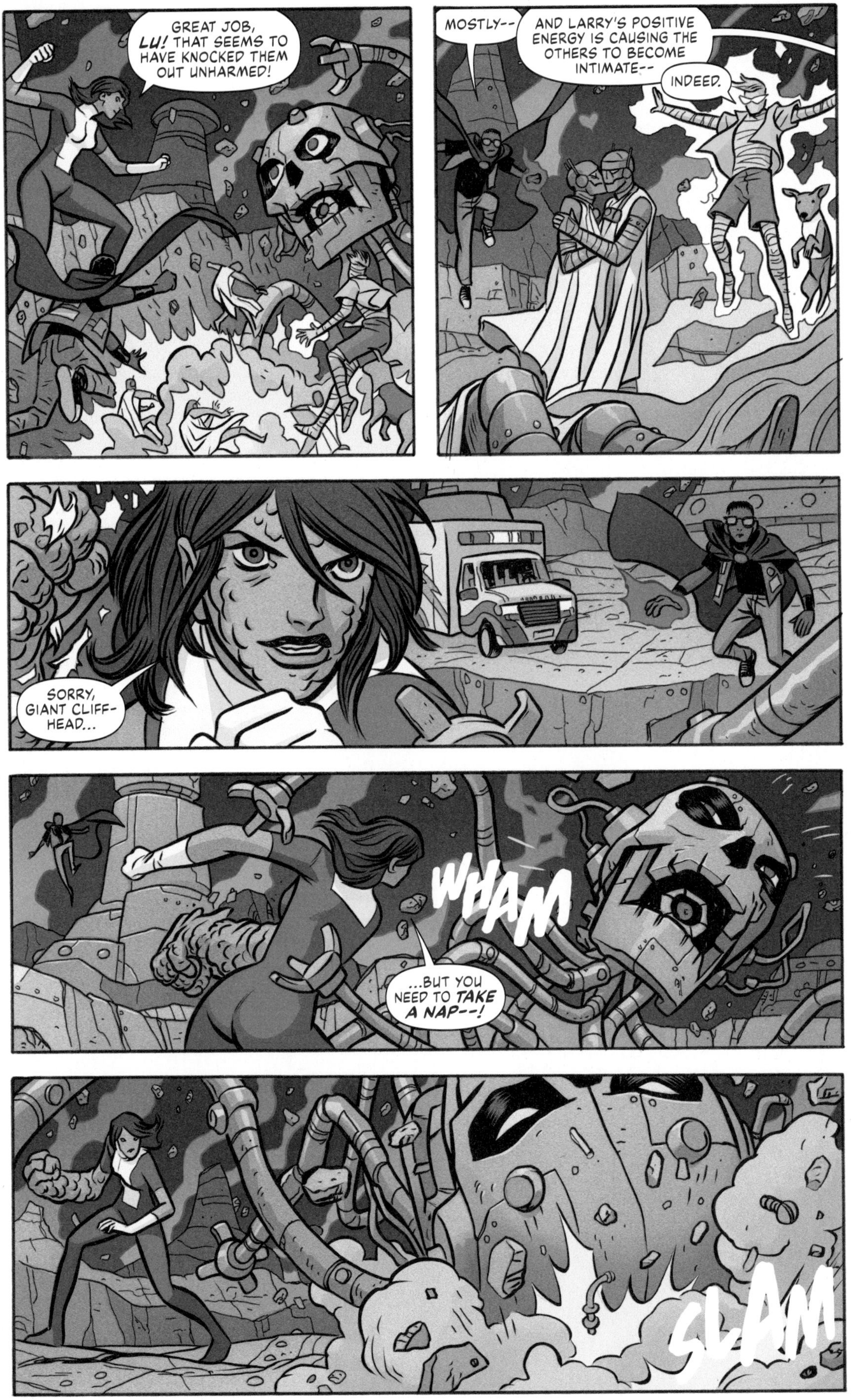

GREAT JOB, LU! THAT SEEMS TO HAVE KNOCKED THEM OUT UNHARMED!
MOSTLY--
AND LARRY'S POSITIVE ENERGY IS CAUSING THE OTHERS TO BECOME INTIMATE--
INDEED.
SORRY, GIANT CLIFF-HEAD...
WHAM
...BUT YOU NEED TO TAKE A NAP--!
SLAM

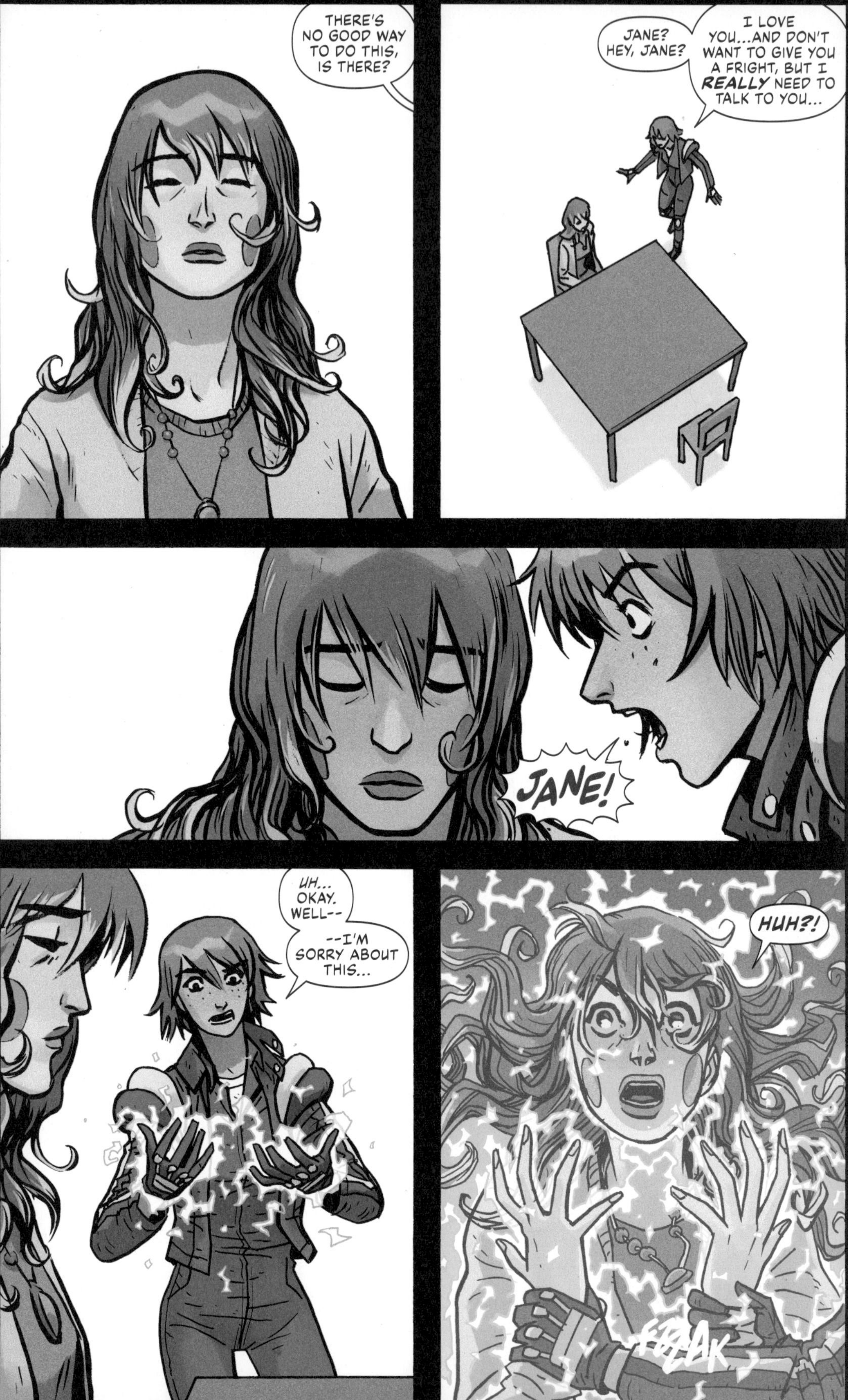
THERE'S NO GOOD WAY TO DO THIS, IS THERE?
JANE? HEY, JANE?
I LOVE YOU...AND DON'T WANT TO GIVE YOU A FRIGHT, BUT I REALLY NEED TO TALK TO YOU...
JANE!
UH... OKAY. WELL--
--I'M SORRY ABOUT THIS...
HUH?!

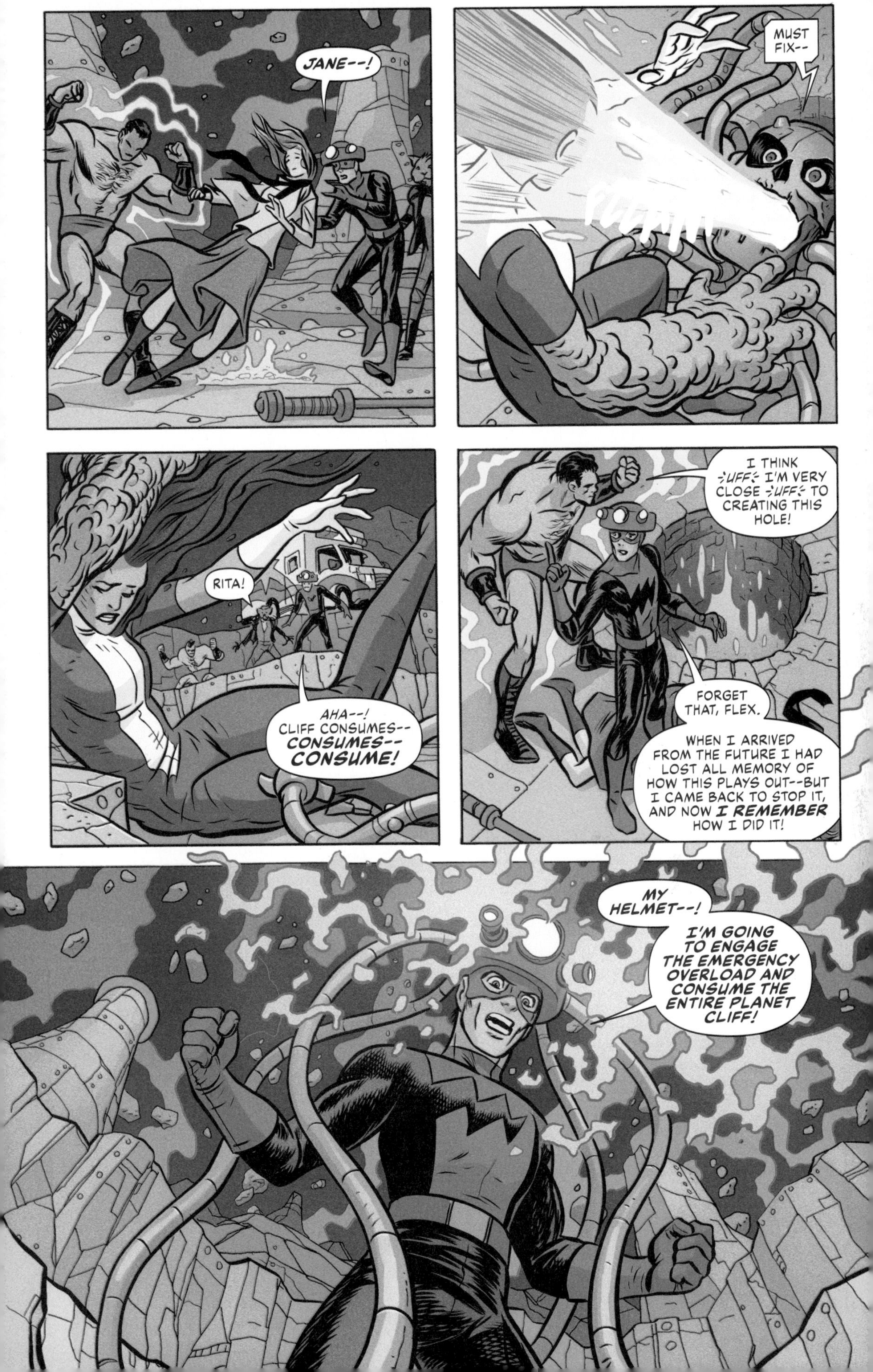
JANE--!
MUST FIX--
RITA!
AHA--! CLIFF CONSUMES-- CONSUMES-- CONSUME!
I THINK -UFF- I'M VERY CLOSE -UFF- TO CREATING THIS HOLE!
FORGET THAT, FLEX.
WHEN I ARRIVED FROM THE FUTURE I HAD LOST ALL MEMORY OF HOW THIS PLAYS OUT--BUT I CAME BACK TO STOP IT, AND NOW I REMEMBER HOW I DID IT!
MY HELMET--!
I'M GOING TO ENGAGE THE EMERGENCY OVERLOAD AND CONSUME THE ENTIRE PLANET CLIFF!

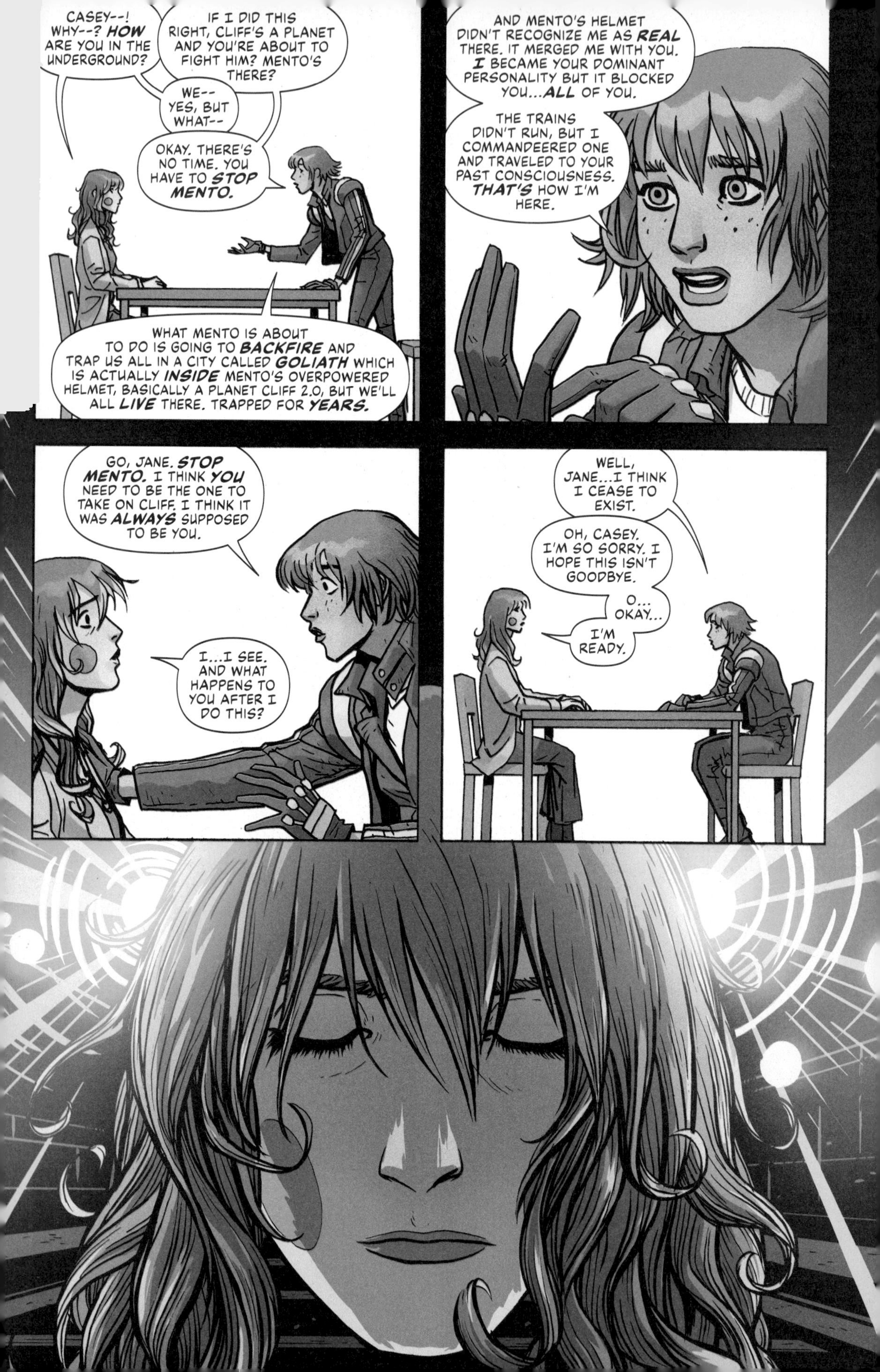
CASEY--! WHY--? HOW ARE YOU IN THE UNDERGROUND?
IF I DID THIS RIGHT, CLIFF'S A PLANET AND YOU'RE ABOUT TO FIGHT HIM? MENTO'S THERE?
WE-- YES, BUT WHAT--
OKAY. THERE'S NO TIME. YOU HAVE TO STOP MENTO.
WHAT MENTO IS ABOUT TO DO IS GOING TO BACKFIRE AND TRAP US ALL IN A CITY CALLED GOLIATH WHICH IS ACTUALLY INSIDE MENTO'S OVERPOWERED HELMET, BASICALLY A PLANET CLIFF 2.0, BUT WE'LL ALL LIVE THERE. TRAPPED FOR YEARS.
AND MENTO'S HELMET DIDN'T RECOGNIZE ME AS REAL THERE. IT MERGED ME WITH YOU. I BECAME YOUR DOMINANT PERSONALITY BUT IT BLOCKED YOU...ALL OF YOU.
THE TRAINS DIDN'T RUN, BUT I COMMANDEERED ONE AND TRAVELED TO YOUR PAST CONSCIOUSNESS. THAT'S HOW I'M HERE.
GO, JANE. STOP MENTO. I THINK YOU NEED TO BE THE ONE TO TAKE ON CLIFF. I THINK IT WAS ALWAYS SUPPOSED TO BE YOU.
I...I SEE. AND WHAT HAPPENS TO YOU AFTER I DO THIS?
WELL, JANE...I THINK I CEASE TO EXIST.
OH, CASEY. I'M SO SORRY. I HOPE THIS ISN'T GOODBYE.
O... OKAY...
I'M READY.

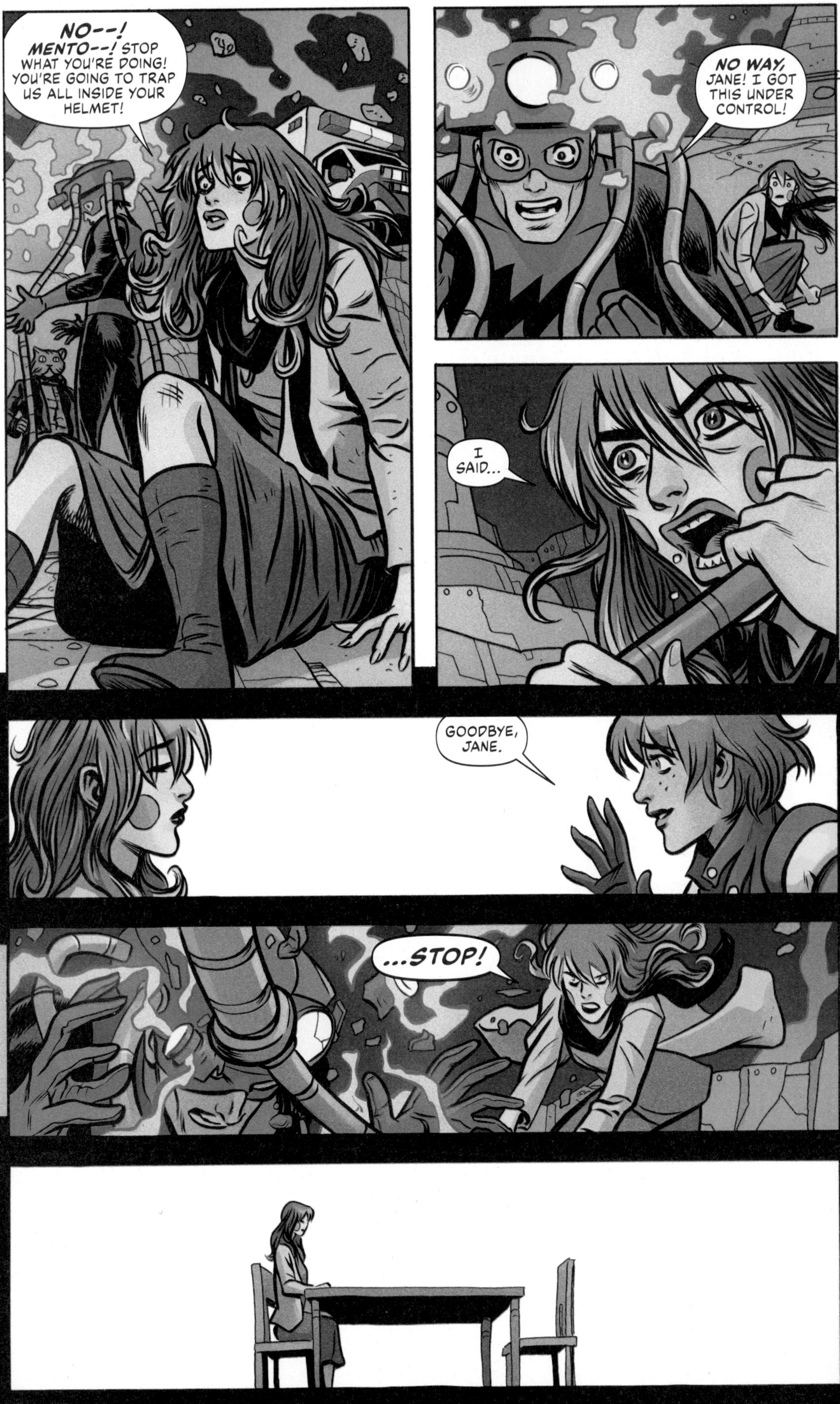
NO--! MENTO--! STOP WHAT YOU'RE DOING! YOU'RE GOING TO TRAP US ALL INSIDE YOUR HELMET!
NO WAY, JANE! I GOT THIS UNDER CONTROL!
I SAID...
GOODBYE, JANE.
...STOP!

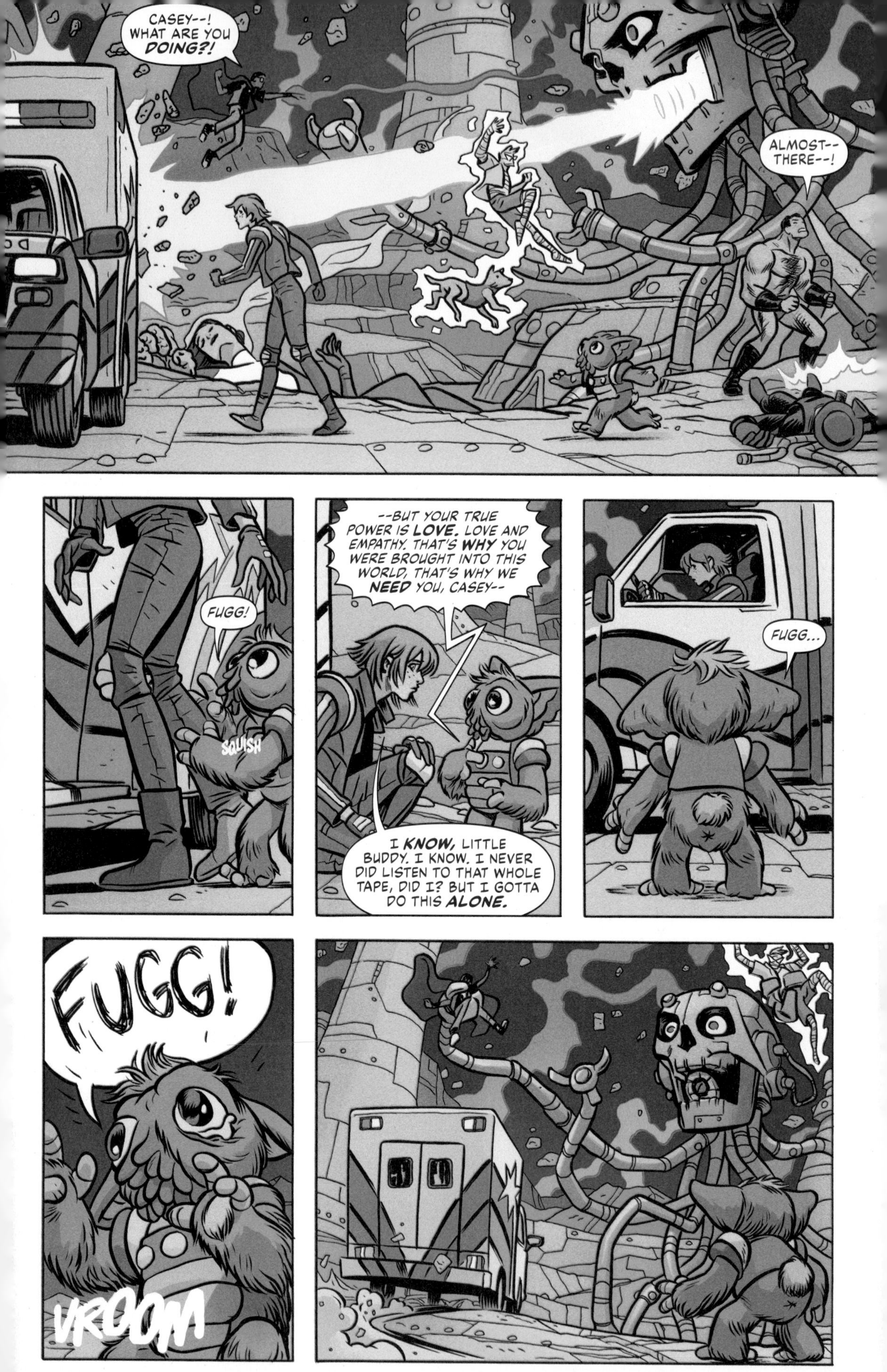
CASEY--! WHAT ARE YOU DOING?!
ALMOST-- THERE--!
FUGG!
SQUISH
--BUT YOUR TRUE POWER IS LOVE. LOVE AND EMPATHY. THAT'S WHY YOU WERE BROUGHT INTO THIS WORLD, THAT'S WHY WE NEED YOU, CASEY--
I KNOW, LITTLE BUDDY. I KNOW. I NEVER DID LISTEN TO THAT WHOLE TAPE, DID I? BUT I GOTTA DO THIS ALONE.
FUGG...
FUGG!
VROOM

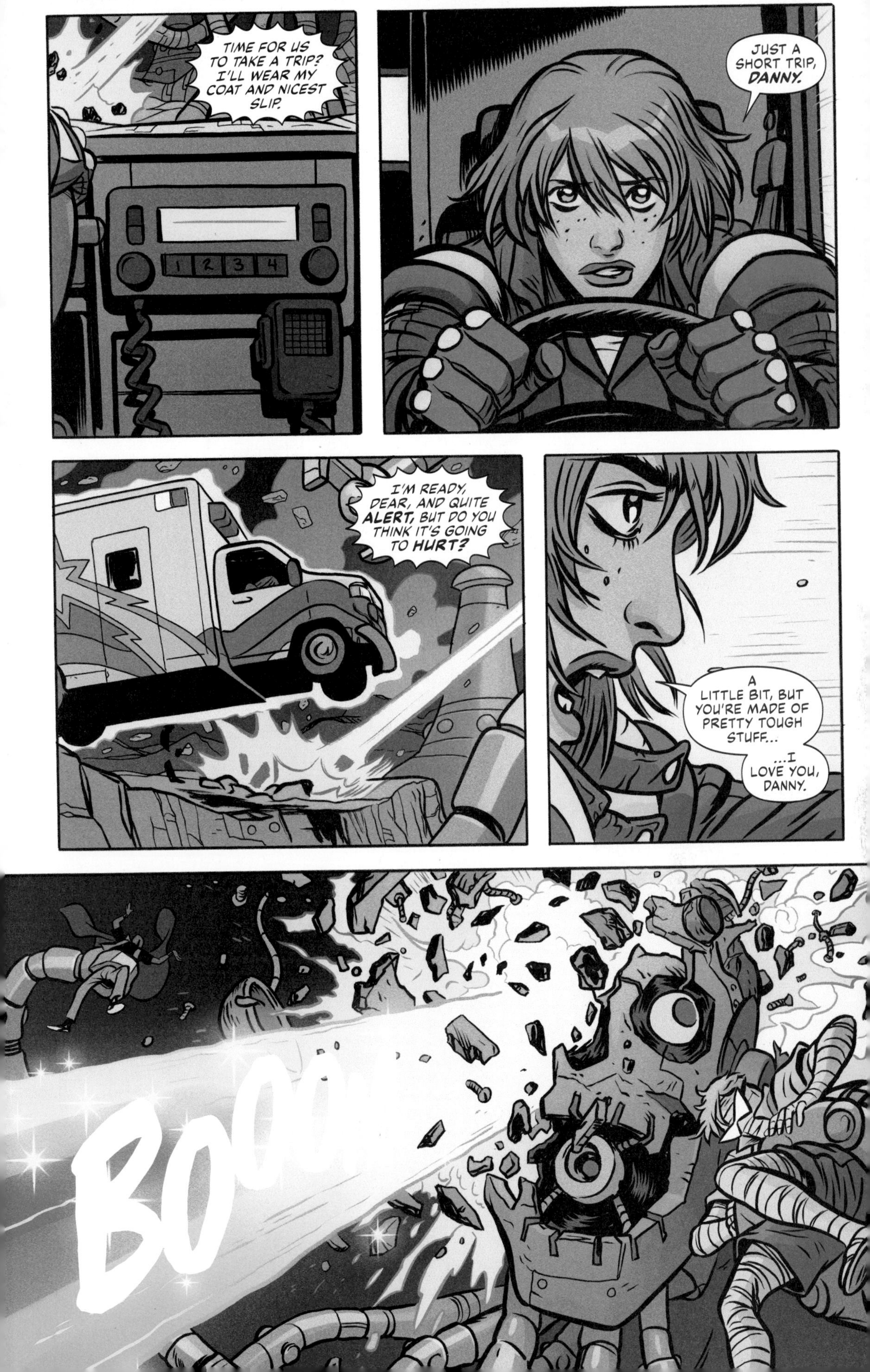
TIME FOR US TO TAKE A TRIP? I'LL WEAR MY COAT AND NICEST SLIP.
JUST A SHORT TRIP, DANNY.
I'M READY, DEAR, AND QUITE ALERT, BUT DO YOU THINK IT'S GOING TO HURT?
A LITTLE BIT, BUT YOU'RE MADE OF PRETTY TOUGH STUFF...
...I LOVE YOU, DANNY.
BOO

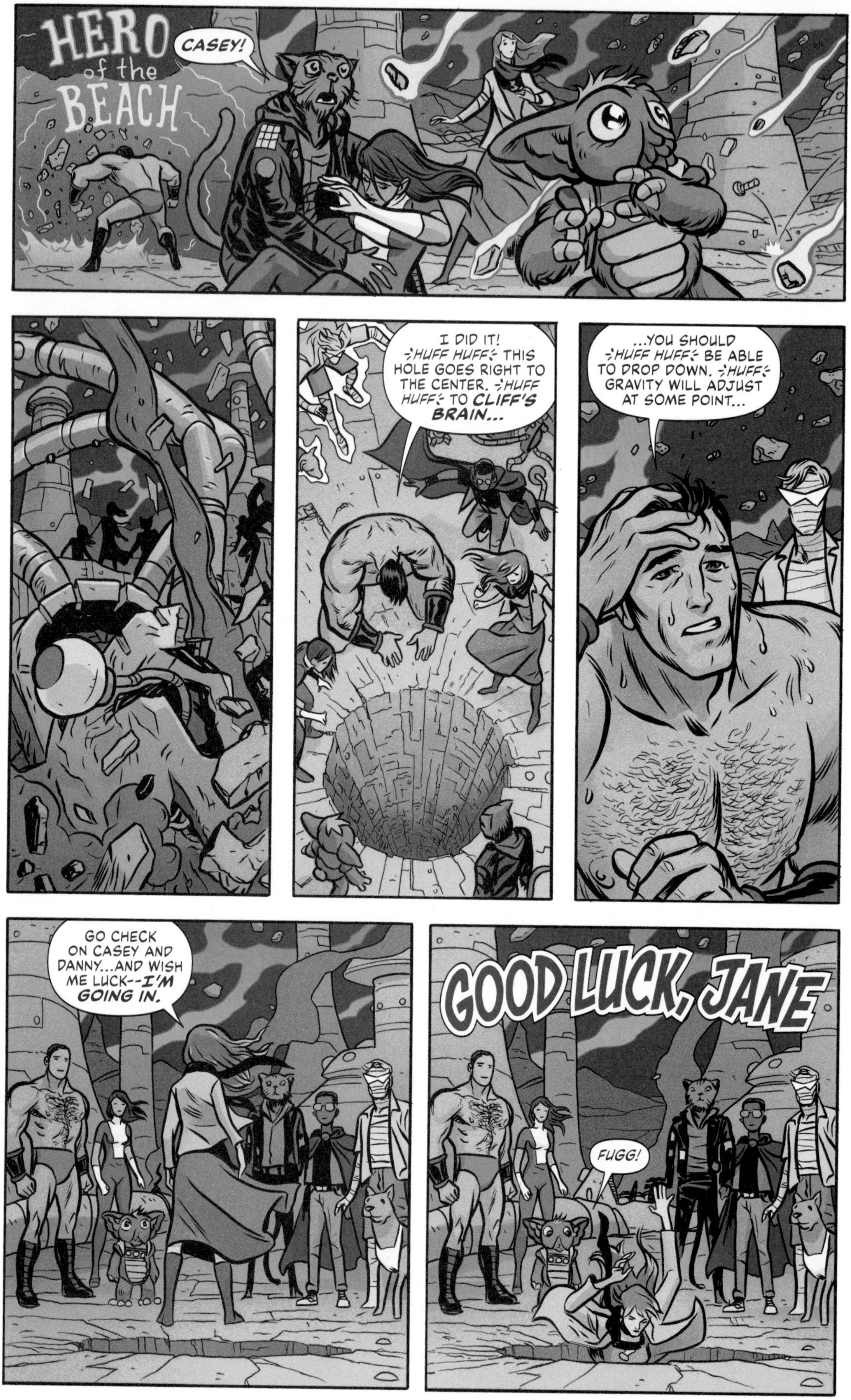
HERO of the BEACH
CASEY!
I DID IT! -HUFF HUFF- THIS HOLE GOES RIGHT TO THE CENTER. -HUFF HUFF- TO CLIFF'S BRAIN...
...YOU SHOULD -HUFF HUFF- BE ABLE TO DROP DOWN. -HUFF- GRAVITY WILL ADJUST AT SOME POINT...
GO CHECK ON CASEY AND DANNY...AND WISH ME LUCK--I'M GOING IN.
GOOD LUCK, JANE
FUGG!

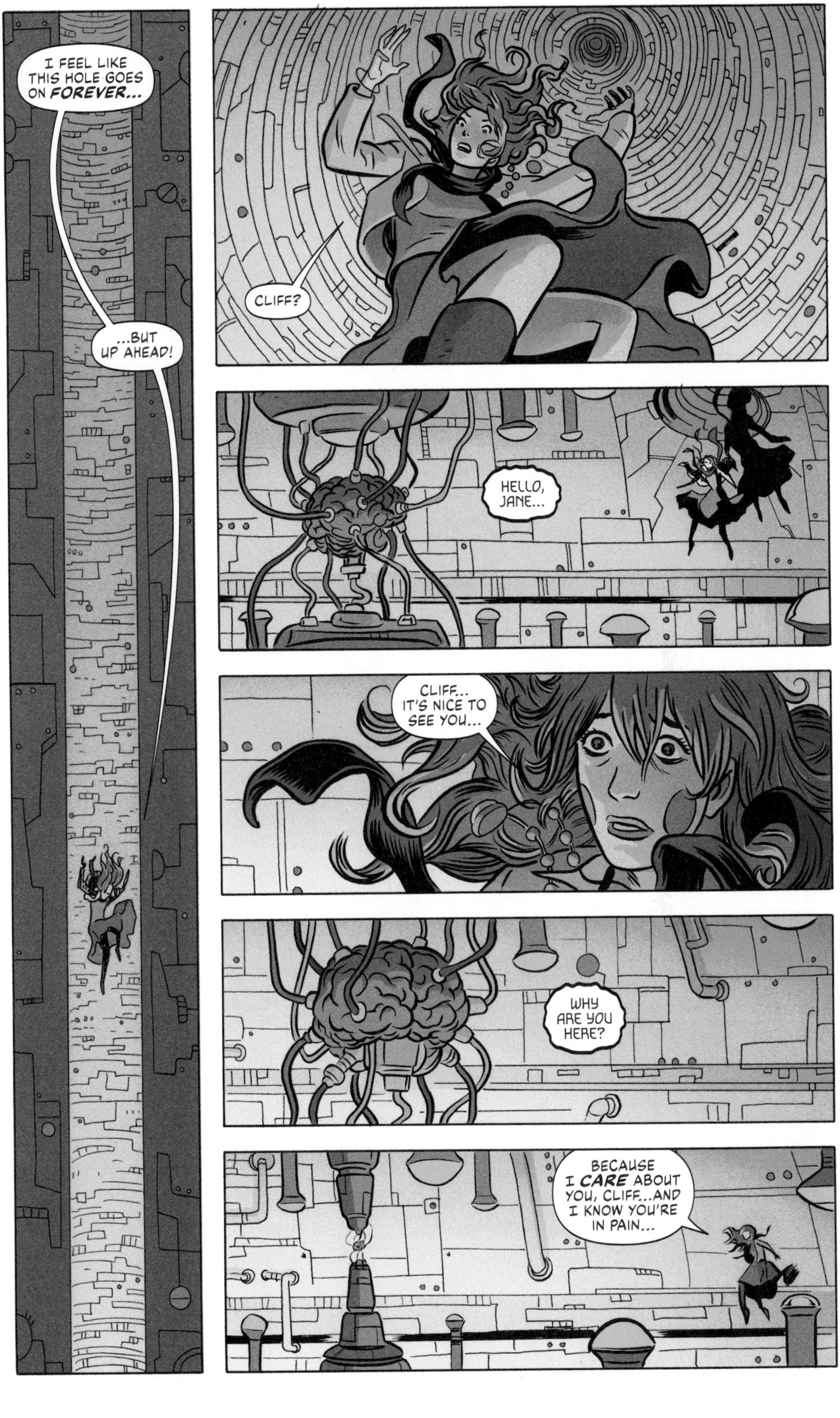
I FEEL LIKE THIS HOLE GOES ON FOREVER...
...BUT UP AHEAD!
CLIFF?
HELLO, JANE...
CLIFF... IT'S NICE TO SEE YOU...
WHY ARE YOU HERE?
BECAUSE I CARE ABOUT YOU, CLIFF...AND I KNOW YOU'RE IN PAIN...

YOU'VE BUILT THIS ARMOR AROUND YOURSELF, A *PLANET'S* WORTH, AND I THINK IT'S TIME YOU STEPPED AWAY FROM IT ALL.

WHAT'S THE POINT? I'LL JUST GET *HURT* AGAIN, ALWAYS DO...

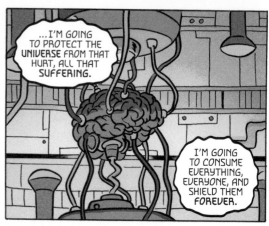

...I'M GOING TO PROTECT THE *UNIVERSE* FROM THAT HURT, ALL THAT SUFFERING.

I'M GOING TO CONSUME EVERYTHING, EVERYONE, AND SHIELD THEM *FOREVER*.

THAT'S...VERY *NOBLE* OF YOU, CLIFF. BUT YOU'LL NEVER TAKE IT ALL AWAY. WE'RE HUMANS, ALIENS, BEINGS WITH FEELINGS... WE CAN *ALL* BE HURT.

EVERY REJECTION THAT MAKES A BROKEN HEART. EVERY WORD SAID IN ANGER. EVERY MISTAKE OR SELFISH ACTION. EVERYONE THAT LEAVES...THEY ALL *CAUSE PAIN.* SO WE LIVE WITH THAT...

...BUT WE DON'T NEED TO KEEP IT. WE CAN *LET IT GO.*

IS THAT WHAT YOU THINK I NEED? TO LET IT GO?

NO... ...RIGHT NOW I THINK YOU NEED TO BE *HELD*.

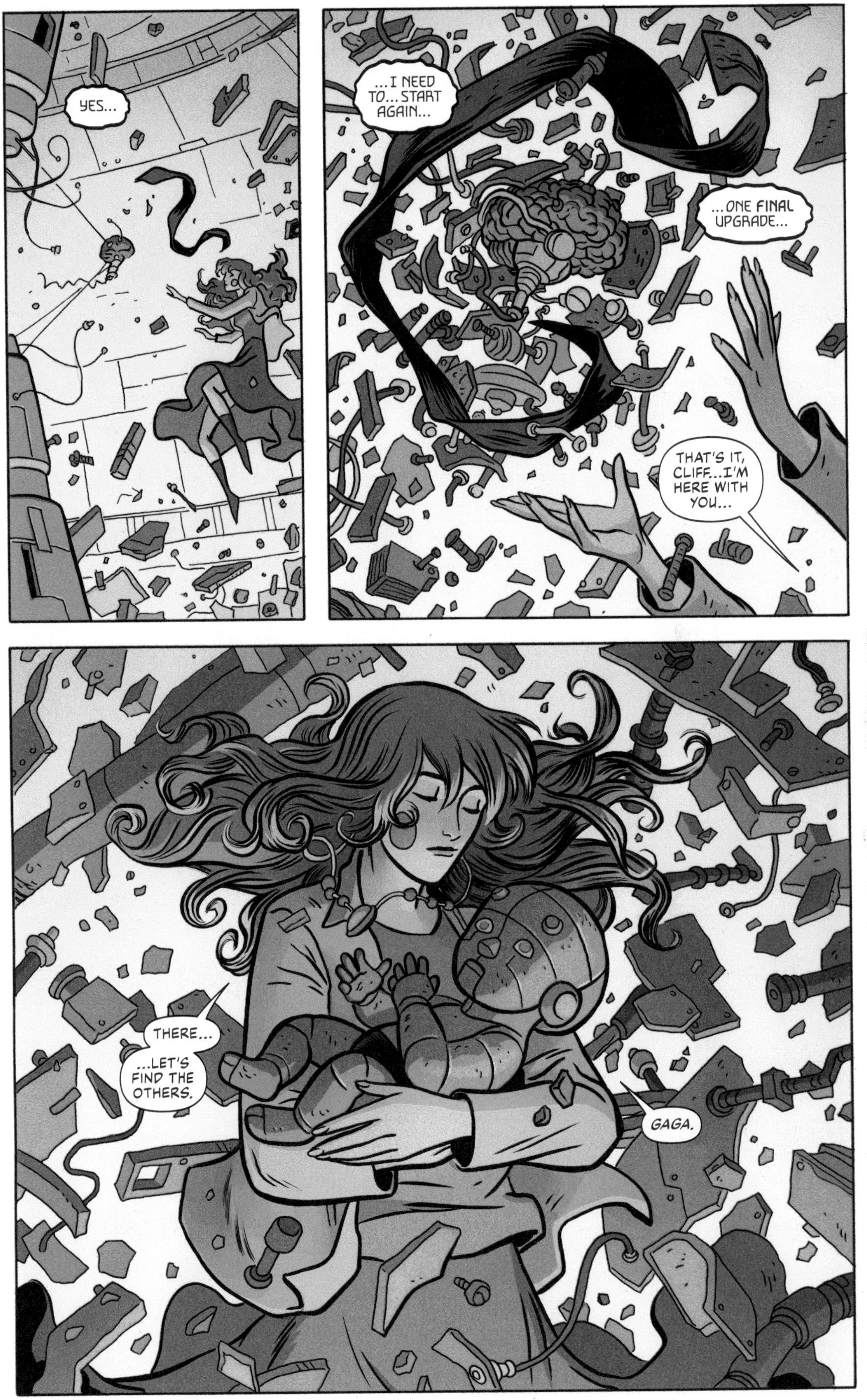
YES...
...I NEED TO...START AGAIN...
...ONE FINAL UPGRADE...
THAT'S IT, CLIFF...I'M HERE WITH YOU...
THERE...
...LET'S FIND THE OTHERS.
GAGA.

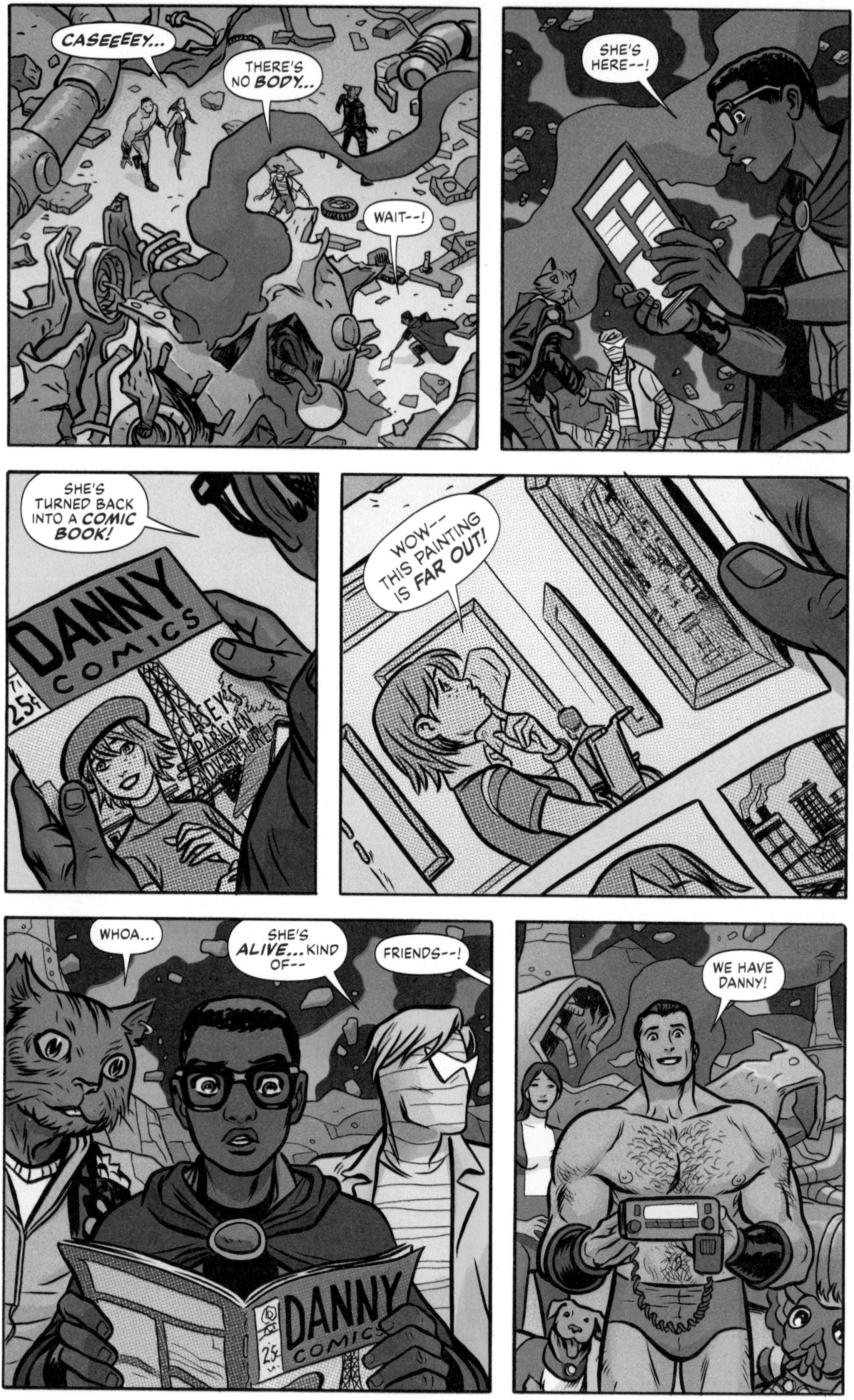
CASEEEEY...
THERE'S NO BODY...
WAIT--!
SHE'S HERE--!
SHE'S TURNED BACK INTO A COMIC BOOK!
DANNY COMICS
25¢
CASEY'S PARISIAN ADVENTURE!
WOW-- THIS PAINTING IS FAR OUT!
WHOA...
SHE'S ALIVE... KIND OF--
FRIENDS--!
WE HAVE DANNY!

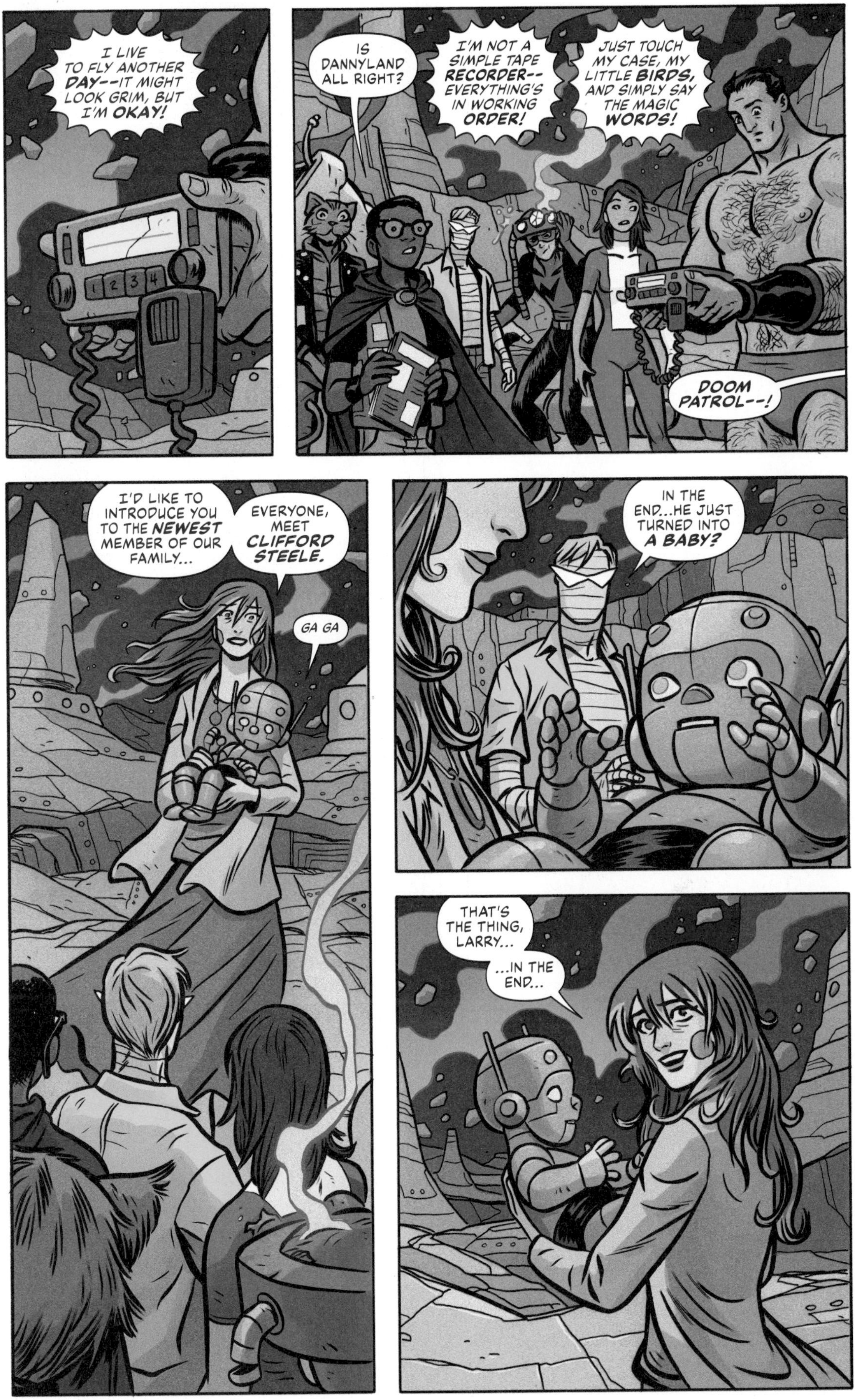
I LIVE TO FLY ANOTHER DAY--IT MIGHT LOOK GRIM, BUT I'M OKAY!
IS DANNYLAND ALL RIGHT?
I'M NOT A SIMPLE TAPE RECORDER--EVERYTHING'S IN WORKING ORDER!
JUST TOUCH MY CASE, MY LITTLE BIRDS, AND SIMPLY SAY THE MAGIC WORDS!
DOOM PATROL--!
I'D LIKE TO INTRODUCE YOU TO THE NEWEST MEMBER OF OUR FAMILY...
EVERYONE, MEET CLIFFORD STEELE.
GA GA
IN THE END...HE JUST TURNED INTO A BABY?
THAT'S THE THING, LARRY...
...IN THE END...

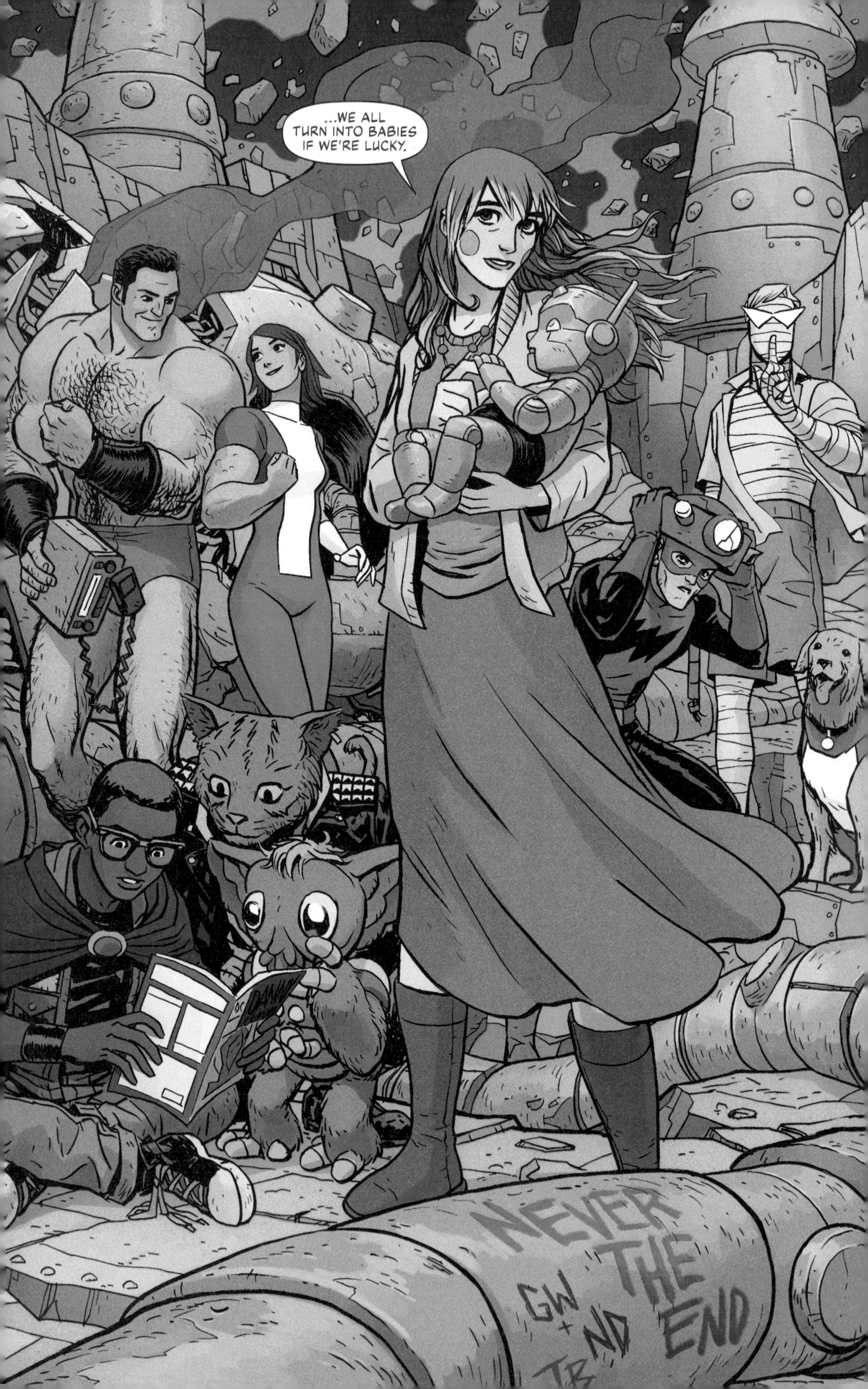
...WE ALL TURN INTO BABIES IF WE'RE LUCKY.
NEVER THE END
GW + TB

VARIANT
COVER
GALLERY

Variant cover art for issue #1 by MITCH GERADS

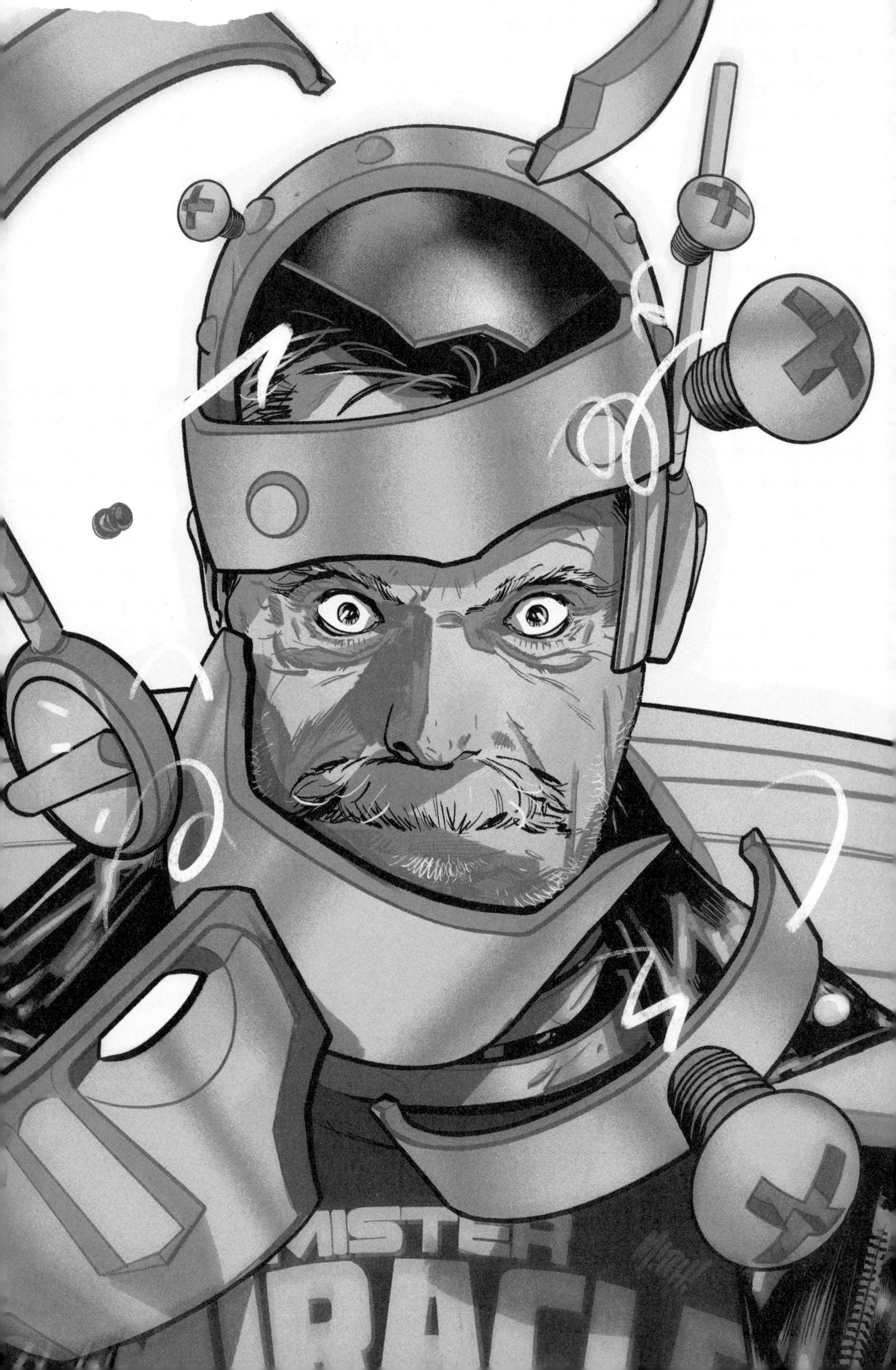
MISTER

Variant cover art for issue #2 by PAUL POPE

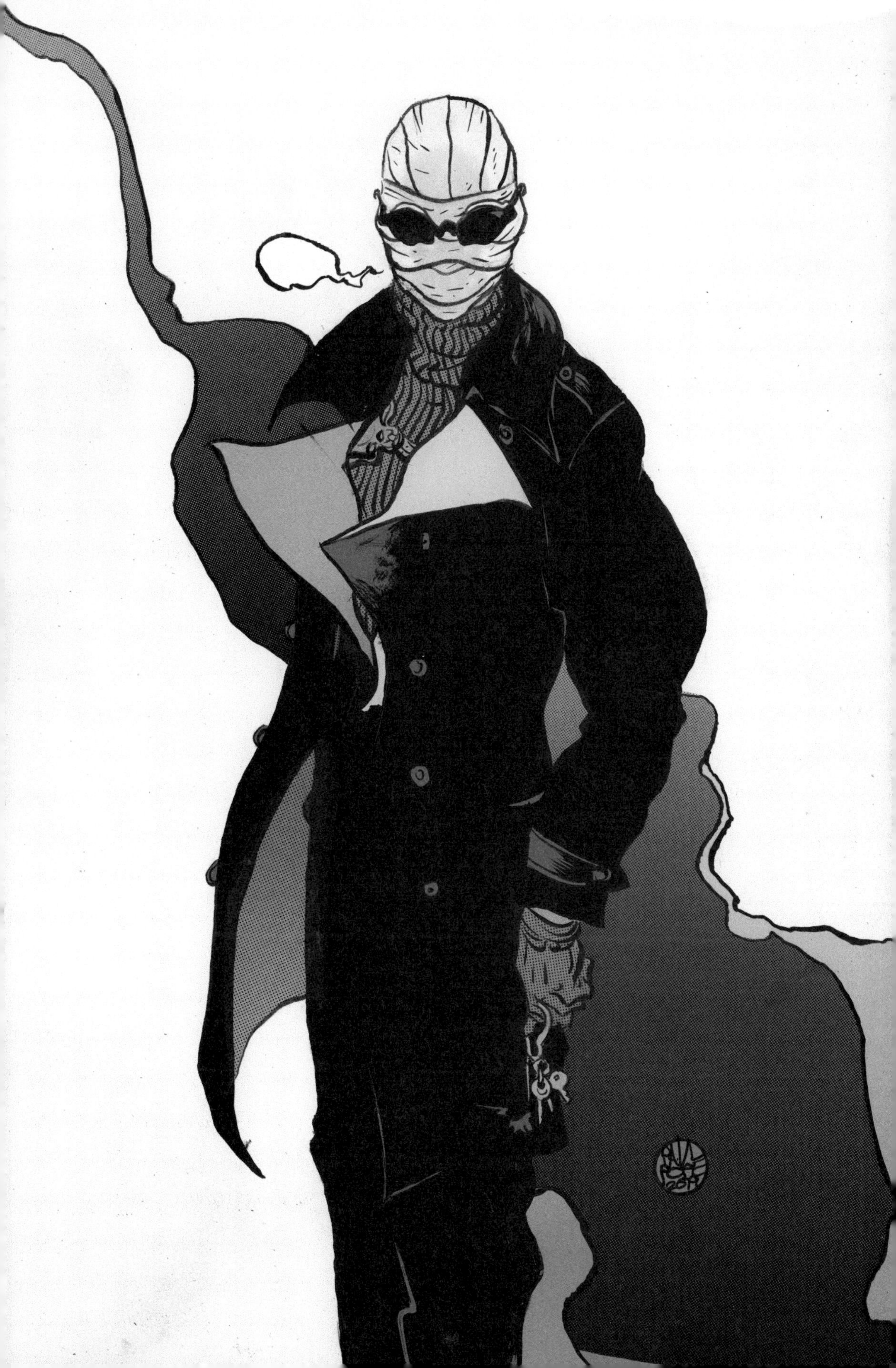

Variant cover art for issue #3 by JAY ANACLETO

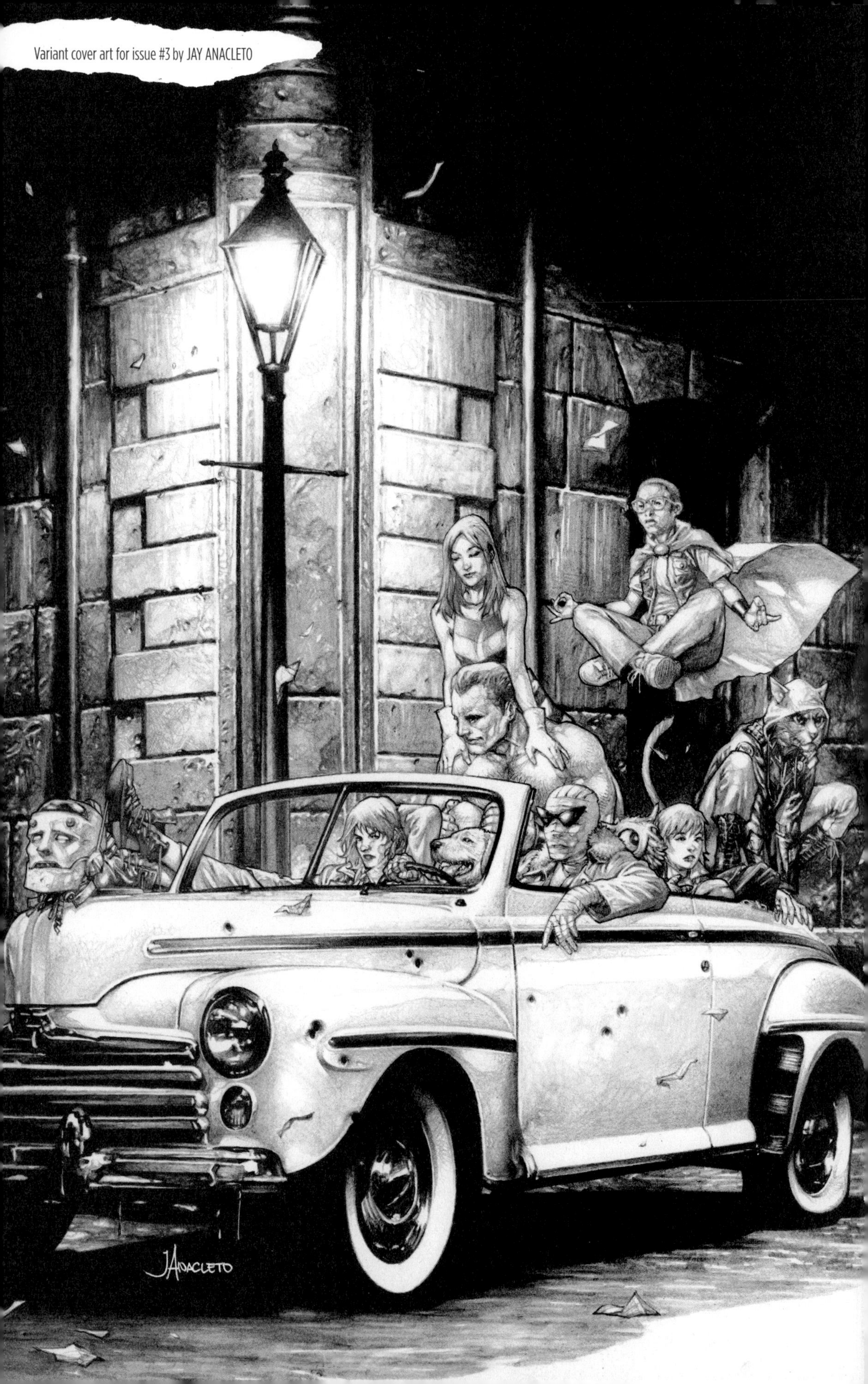
J ANACLETO

Unused cover art by BECKY CLOONAN

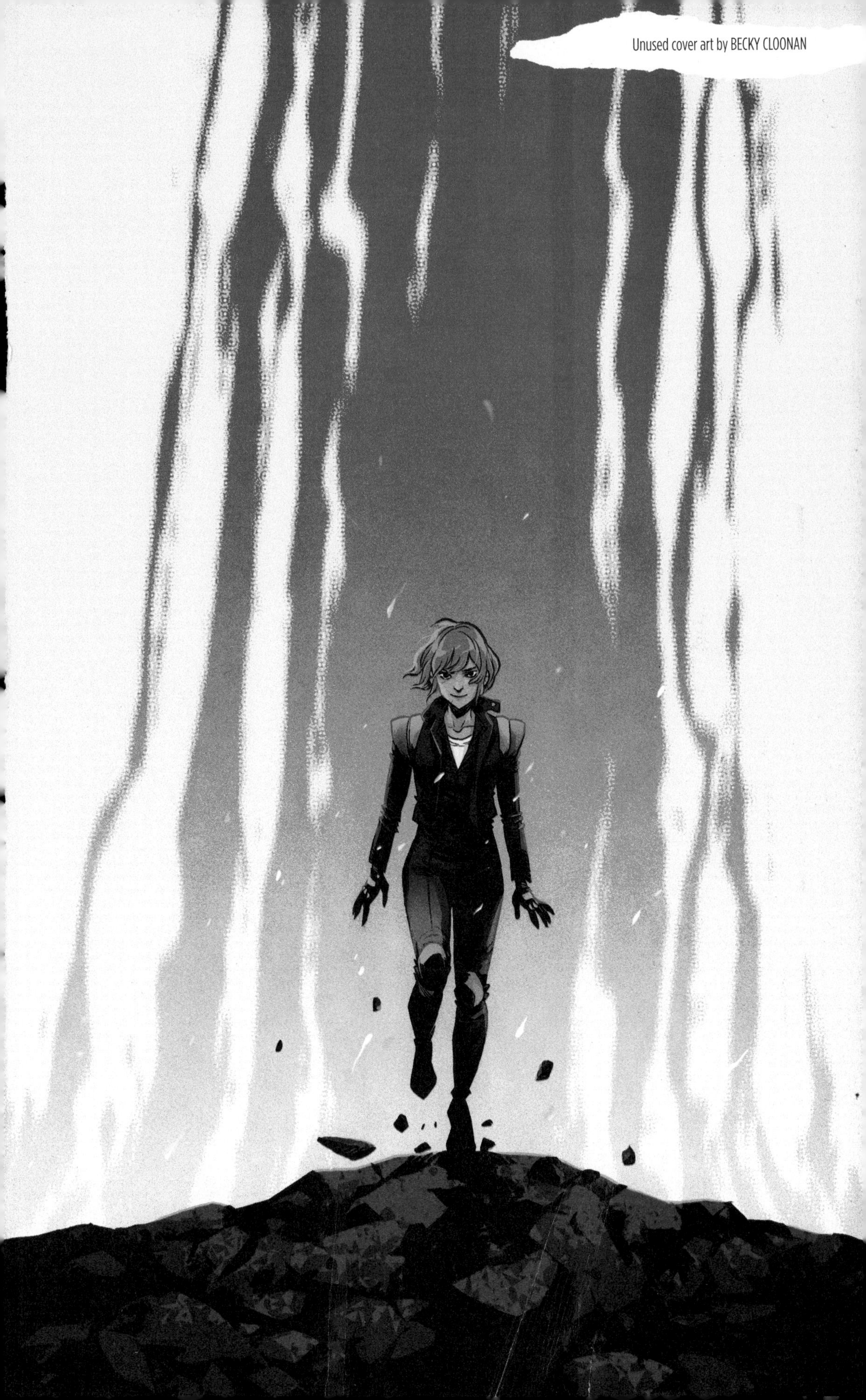

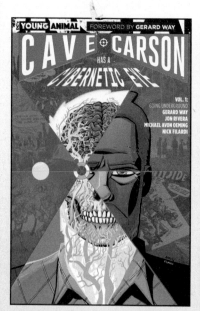